STUDIES IN SEGREGATION AND DESEGREGATION

*The material for this book is the result of the
International Geographical Union's discussion from the
Commission for 'Monitoring Cities of Tomorrow'*

Studies in Segregation and Desegregation

Edited by

IZHAK SCHNELL
Tel Aviv University

WIM OSTENDORF
University of Amsterdam

LONDON AND NEW YORK

First published 2002 by Ashgate Publishing

Reissued 2019 by Routledge
2 Park Square, Milton Park, Abingdon, Oxon, OX14 4RN
52 Vanderbilt Avenue, New York, NY 10017

Routledge is an imprint of the Taylor & Francis Group, an informa business

© Izhak Schnell and Wim Ostendorf 2002

All rights reserved. No part of this book may be reprinted or reproduced or utilised in any form or by any electronic, mechanical, or other means, now known or hereafter invented, including photocopying and recording, or in any information storage or retrieval system, without permission in writing from the publishers.

Notice:
Product or corporate names may be trademarks or registered trademarks, and are used only for identification and explanation without intent to infringe.

Publisher's Note
The publisher has gone to great lengths to ensure the quality of this reprint but points out that some imperfections in the original copies may be apparent.

Disclaimer
The publisher has made every effort to trace copyright holders and welcomes correspondence from those they have been unable to contact.

A Library of Congress record exists under LC control number:

ISBN 13: 978-1-138-72903-2 (hbk)
ISBN 13: 978-1-315-19011-2 (ebk)

Printed in the United Kingdom
by Henry Ling Limited

Contents

Preface	*vii*

1. Introduction	1

PART 1: AGENCY AND SEGREGATION

2. Itzhak Benenson and Itzhak Omer, *Measuring Individual Segregation in Space – A Formal Approach and Case Study*	11
3. Izhak Schnell, *Segregation in Everyday Life Spaces: A Conceptual Model*	39
4. Jean-Bernard Racine, *Migration, Places and Intercultural Relations in Cities*	67
5. Marina Marengo, *Interculturality: A Preferential Path in the Search for a New Urban Social Equilibrium?*	87

PART 2: SEGREGATION AND STATE POLICIES

6. Tineke Domburg-De Rooij and Sako Musterd, *Ethnic Segregation and the Welfare State*	107
7. Andreas Farwick, Britta Klagge and Wolfgang Taubmann, *Urban Poverty in Germany*	133
8. Wim Ostendorf, *Segregation and Urban Policies in the Netherlands*	159

PART 3: A COMPARATIVE PERSPECTIVE

9. Charles Small, *National Identity in a Transforming Quebec Society: Socio-Economic and Spatial Segregation in Montreal*	181

10. Ludger Basten and Lienhard Lötscher, *Segregation in the Ruhr* 221

11. André Horn, *New Perspectives on Urban Segregation and Desegregation in Post-Resolution South Africa* 247

12. Gu Chaolin and Christian Kesteloot, *Beijing's Socio-Spatial Structure in Transition* 285

Preface

The increasing interest in identity and ethnicity studies in social science has raised interest in the study of socio-spatial segregation. New paradigms and concepts that were introduced into scholarly debates on segregation on the one hand and new trends in different cities around the world, attracted a group of scholars from the Commission on 'Monitoring Cities of Tomorrow' to intensively discuss theoretical and practical aspects of segregation. This book is the result of two years' discussion on the issue that has yielded eleven chapters organised in three parts. The first part presents some original theoretical contributions to the study of segregation while the second part questions the relevancy of segregation studies for public policy and the third part describes new trends in cities that represent particularly interesting case studies.

We would like to thank those who have encouraged and supported us in bringing this volume for publication. We thank Professor Larry Bourne who was the first person to recognise the cumulative value of the work done by members of the commission as well as other members of the commission who took an active role in the discussions. We thank also Mrs Ora Kari for her language editorial work and Mrs Miriam Benenson for her editorial work.

1 Introduction

The study of segregation stimulates numerous discussions in the field of geography, and the increase in social heterogeneity, ethnicity and socio-cultural identities in globalised spaces has further intensified the discussion about segregation. Our concepts and methodologies were developed in four main stages reflecting trends in geography as a whole. Concepts adopted from urban ecological theory, in particular Parks' Durkheimian argument that 'social relations are so frequently and so inevitably correlated with spatial relations' (Park, 1926, in Peach, 1975, 1–30), became the cornerstone from which all else emerged. In the light of these ideas the city has been subdivided into a mosaic of homogeneous areas located in neutral, continuous and stable urban space (Shevky & Bell, 1955). Indices of segregation tend to compare degrees of unevenness among groups in discrete spatial units, which measure the distribution of social groups. These indices of dissimilarity may also be interpreted as the amount of effort needed for the relocation of a population in order to enable an even distribution of a group (Morgan, 1983; Boal, 1987; Morrill, 1991; Waldorf, 1993; Wong, 1998). All these indices measure the residential distribution of groups and reflect the ecological assumption concerning simple relations between the spatial and the social. This conclusion has been tested in a large number of empirical studies throughout the world using a logical positivist methodology (Peach, 1975; Massey & Denton, 1993).

Beginning in the late sixties and continuing mainly through the seventies, three phases of paradigmatic changes in explaining segregation have been recorded. The first phase was an attempt of behavioural geographers to explain the connections between the social and the spatial. Scholars like Wolpert (1964) and Pred (1967) called for the study of the location decisions of individuals in real life situations using bounded rational models. Morrill (1965) showed that the combined effect of many individual decisions motivated by personal preferences and limited by a set of constraints might often be described as a random process of spatial diffusion. During the seventies humanist and structuralist paradigms were adopted for the explanation of segregation. While humanists tried to unravel life experiences in the ghetto including those that might shape

2   *Studies in Segregation and Desegregation*

political actions (Cohen, 1980), structuralists attempted to explain spatial segregated forms in terms of political, economic and ideological structures and to expose the mechanisms that create segregation.

In the nineties new elements were brought into the discussion on segregation through the works of Sibley (1995), who introduced into the discussion the formation of social identity and sense of territoriality through the practices of daily life. Further discussion has been devoted to the impact of globalisation on segregation (Jackson, 1994) and to the associations among segregation, poverty and policy. These issues are at the core of the following volume.

The first part investigates some innovative ideas concerning the study of segregation in cities that undergo globalisation. The second part raises questions concerning the associations among segregation, poverty and policies, and the third part highlights patterns of segregation and desegregation in three countries – South Africa, China and Canada – each of them representing different aspects of multi-culturality and transformation.

Benenson and Omer, Schnell, Racine and Marengo suggest that segregation be treated as human behavior that should be analysed in terms of individual or household decision-making. All these researchers stress the biases caused by relying on aggregate data in a priori defined spatial units and prescribe re-aggregating households with similar behaviour toward segregation in such a way that segregated social areas will be the result of the analysis instead of pre-determined by the analysis. Benenson and Omer believe that their methodology may aid in the measurement of a social area's socio-spatial homogeneity vs. heterogeneity, thus challenging the assumptions of the Chicago school concerning homogeneous social areas. In addition they suggest measuring segregation relative to a hierarchy of territorial circles around the homes of the householders. They present evidence to show that only a few core Arab areas are highly segregated while most Arabs in Jaffa are distributed around these core areas in ethnically mixed spaces.

Schnell takes the argument even further arguing that some areas in post-modern cities may be highly heterogeneous with individuals maintaining socio-cultural lifeworlds highly isolated from their neighbours. At the same time individuals may maintain intensive social networks with meaningful others who live in more distanced spaces from their homes. Therefore, Schnell suggests analysing individual segregation in respect to their actual everyday life spaces instead of their residential neighbours. He suggests calculating both the probability of encountering either group of

Introduction 3

insiders or outsiders in the territorial bases where they live their daily lives and the proportion of actual meaningful networks with either insiders or outsiders. In the same way Racine and Marengo start their investigations with individuals regarding their practices in everyday life spaces. Racine sets a theoretical foundation for the introduction of socio-spatial layers of interstices in post-modern cities, in which agents may restructure their identities. Marengo asks weather immigration to urban centres may constitute culture of mixedness in which different social groups integrate on the level of urban daily life spaces. Such mixture is supposed to take place in hybrid centres of multiculturalism. Marengo uses an ethnographic methodology in order to investigate the ways in which these places are constituted and developing. As she puts it her approach opens new directions for the study of multi-culturalism in cities, more than leading for particular conclusions.

The four articles argue more or less explicitly that segregation should be understood not only in terms of the residential space of agents but also in terms of their everyday life circulation space. Benenson and Omer justify their hierarchical model on this ground, but they assume that each spatial circle in the hierarchy plays a predefined role in everyday human life. Racine and Marengo study socio-spatial segregation vs. integration in the specific places in which multi- and trans-culturalism are practised. Schnell tries to develop a systematic model which measures isolation vs. exposure in the everyday life activity spaces of agents. In their work they adopt Giddens's basic proposition and argue that everyday life spaces are the arena in which identity and social strategies of segregation are structured. Unlike the behavioural models in which agents were assumed to make autonomous location decisions under constrained circumstances, the articles in this part of the book conceive agency and structure as dialectically associated.

The second part of the book includes three papers that debate the association between segregation, poverty and policies in European cities. It is important to emphasise that the general approach to segregation by policymakers is based on residential space and not on the everyday life circulation space of agents. This is in contrast to the general approach taken by the articles in the first part of the book. Moreover, residential segregation, especially with respect to poverty or ethnicity, is generally considered to be detrimental because it presumably makes the situation of poverty worse and, therefore, should be prevented with the help of policy measures. This view is based on the fear that the American black ghetto, which has often functioned as a 'social prison', is coming or might come to

4   *Studies in Segregation and Desegregation*

European cities, resulting in ghettos that have extended negative effects for the residents involved. As a reaction to this fear, policies aimed at preventing segregation by dispersing certain population categories or by promoting the mixing of populations within neighbourhoods have become widespread.

However, such an approach can be criticised on several grounds, elaborated in the different contributions in this second part of the book. In the first place, the assumed negative impact of segregation based on the American experience has not been adequately analysed in connection with European cities. As has been suggested above, social networks are no longer confined to residential neighbourhoods. As a consequence, the residential neighbourhood is not congruent with the area where everyday life takes place. Therefore, the impact of segregation on everyday life might be more important than the impact of residential segregation. Secondly, even if such a negative impact of residential segregation can be established, it is important to consider which approach can be more successful: an indirect approach of mixing neighbourhoods or a direct approach of improving the position of the poor residents involved. Thirdly, the role of the state has to be considered. The welfare state of the USA is different from its counterparts in Western Europe and elsewhere, and it is important to take these differences into account before translating the American situation to other places.

Another flaw of policy measures aimed at preventing residential segregation is the lack of attention to the people who are directly involved: the residents, their characteristics and opinions. As has been studied by the Chicago school and as has been found by many other researchers, resident groups may be more interested in homogeneous than in mixed neighbourhoods. In such situations, values and opinions with respect to the residential environment and with respect to daily life tend to be more homogeneous and are more easily understood. Residents consider their residential environment important but not as a chance to meet and integrate with people having a different life style. Rather residents aim at controlling the social composition of their residential environment in order to create a situation of easy social relations. Policy measures aimed at integrating neighbourhoods generally do not consider and anticipate these kinds of opinions.

Policy measures aimed at desegregation are generally based on the implicit assumption that segregation not only has an impact of its own but that the total sum of this impact is negative. This is not automatically true. If segregation has an impact, this impact is negative in neighbourhoods

Introduction 5

with many disadvantaged people but positive in neighbourhoods without such people. Policies that are successful in mixing this population not only prevent a negative impact but any positive one as well. In other words, policy measures that are successful in mixing populations do not automatically have positive results. Furthermore, desegregation in itself does not necessarily have positive effects on reducing poverty and deprivation.

The papers in this second part concentrate on these issues. Domburg-de Rooij and Musterd concentrate on the role of the welfare state and come to the conclusion that the impact of the state is considerable, making it unlikely that ideas and experiences of the USA with respect to segregation will be applied in welfare regimes. Universal welfare states with a strong redistribution that prevent sharp divisions between the working class and middle class generally show low degrees of segregation, while residual welfare states such as the USA and Great Britain show much sharper patterns of segregation. Taubmann investigates the city of Bremen to determine if the social composition of the residential environment has an impact of its own. He comes to the conclusion, that this indeed is the case. Ostendorf comes to a similar conclusion for the situation in Amsterdam but also tries to analyse the total effect of mixing the population of neighbourhoods to see if it can be expected to be more positive than negative. He concludes that this is not the case. This finding challenges desegregation policies such as those of The Netherlands. Instead, a policy that approaches the residents themselves is to be considered.

The third part of the book presents four case studies, each of them adding an interesting lesson to our understanding of segregation and desegregation patterns. All the papers with the exception of Small's analysis of Montreal discuss changes in patterns of segregation and desegregation in the context of deeper structural changes in the political economy. Basten and Lötscher show how the industrialisation of the Ruhr area created complex forms of segregation. They argue that patterns of immigration to the mining centres of the area and the decisions of the mine companies to attract workers by renting company houses for them created a three-fold pattern of segregation. The first one is based on a class division between the working class in the company houses and the middle class in the inner towns. The working class neighbourhoods were further subdivided according to the number of years the immigrants had lived in the city. In particular, segregation between the veteran German workers and the Polish workers who had arrived later from Eastern Prussia is stressed. Ethnic segregation was further structured by racist prejudices

6 Studies in Segregation and Desegregation

against the Polish workers. During the 1920s the third generation of Polish workers who had assimilated into the society changed their citizenship, and the miners' houses were privatised. As a response, the Polish community spatially desegregated. With the transformation of the area in the second half of the twentieth century, waves of foreigners - mainly Turks - and suburbanisation created a new pattern of segregation in the Ruhr area with foreigners concentrated in the inner city and Germans located in the suburbs.

Horn offers a comprehensive analysis of patterns of desegregation in post-apartheid South Africa. Beyond the extremely interesting summary of relevant knowledge, he reaches several conclusions of more general importance. First, the transformation of a legal system does not necessarily change patterns of segregation. Second, there is a need to identify passive situations in which already structured patterns of segregation continue to persist due to the weakness of active forces of change which do not have the power to desegregate different populations. Third, desegregation is not necessarily associated with social integration; Schnell and Racine present models which show existing segregation in socio-spatial networks even when residential areas are mixed. Of four major processes - gentrification, filling of relatively sparsely populated areas, population mixing by densification and spontaneous desegregation - only the last two strategies have contributed to desegregation in South Africa, and only the last one may contribute to social integration.

Gu Chaolin's and Kesteloot's paper describes a current process of increased tendency toward segregation in the new era of China's integration into the world capitalist system. The biggest change in Beijing during the last decade has been a transition from the existing situation of social 'equality' to polarisation both in individual communities and in society as a whole. As a result, social variations and conflicting interests are growing, and new social groups are emerging. A new class at the lower end of the social ladder, made up largely of rural migrants has started to characterise Chinese cities. This so-called floating population is seen in new slums, under bridges and along highways forming new patterns of segregation.

The last paper by Small sheds a new light on Canadian cities with Montreal as an example. Montreal demonstrates the importance of issues such as national identity, socio-cultural policies, immigration and the conceptual discourse concerning 'race', 'ethnicity' and 'racism'. All directly influence social and spatial dissimilarity. The structuration of ethnic relations is presented in the context of industrialisation and

Introduction 7

immigration. Montreal's unique history has led to the formation of one of the most heterogeneous communities in North America with a much more open society than any in the USA. As in the case of South Africa, the analysis reveals inadequacies in current models of segregation. Small shows that the image of segregation is much higher than the measurement of segregation. Furthermore, there is no correlation between the degree of segregation and socio-economic status. In Montreal Jews are far more segregated than Blacks despite the fact that Blacks are much more exposed to racist attitudes.

Izhak Schnell   Wim Ostendorf

References

Boal, F.W. (1987), 'Segregation', in C. Peach (ed), *Social Geography, Progress and Prospect*, Croom Helm, Beckenham, New York.
Jackson, P. (1994), *Construction of Place, Race and Nation*, University of Minnesota Press, Minneapolis.
Jackson, P. & Smith, S. (1984), *Exploring Social Geography*, George Allen & Unwin, Sydney.
Massey, D. & Denton, N. (1988), 'The Dimensions of Residential Segregation', *Social Forces*, vol. 76, pp. 231-315.
Morgan, B.S. (1983), 'A Distance-Decay Interaction Index to Measure Residential Segregation', *Area*, vol. 12, pp. 211-216.
Morrill, R.L. (1965), 'The Negro Ghetto: Problems and Alternatives', *Geographical Review*, vol. 55, pp. 339-361.
Morrill, R.L. (1991), 'On the Measure of Geographical Segregation', *Geography Research Forum*, vol. 11, pp. 25-36.
Park, R.E., Burgess, E. & McKenzie, D.R. (1925), *The City*, University of Chicago Press, Chicago.
Peach, C. (1975), 'Introduction: The Spatial Analysis of Ethnicity and Class', in C. Peach (ed) *Urban Social Segregation*, Longman, London.
Pred, A. (1967), 'Behavior and Location', *Lund Studies in Geography Series B*, vol. 27, Gleerup, Lund.
Shevky, E. & Bell, W. (1955), *Social Area Analysis*, Stanford, California.
Sibley, D. (1995), *Geographies of Exclusion*, Routledge, London.
Waldorf, B.S. (1993), 'Segregation in Urban Space: A New Measurement Approach', *Urban Studies*, vol. 30(7), pp. 1170-1192.
Wolpert, J. (1966), 'Migration as an Adjustment to Environmental Stress', *Journal of Social Issues*, vol. 22(4), pp. 92-102.
Wong, D.W. (1998), 'Measuring Multiethnic Spatial Segregation', *Urban Geography*, vol. 19(1), pp. 77-87.

Part 1:
Agency and Segregation

2 Measuring Individual Segregation in Space – A Formal Approach and Case Study

ITZHAK BENENSON AND ITZHAK OMER

Introduction

The aim of measuring segregation is to examine spatial distributions of the populace according to a variety of features. With some exceptions (Waldorf, 1993; Schnell & Benjamini, 1999), the segregation phenomenon is described and measured for population *groups*. The most popular is the measurement of the clustering of the groups members, the exposure of members of one population group to another or dissimilarity in their spatial distributions (Peach, 1975; Massey & Denton, 1986). All the measures or *segregation indices* utilise aggregate data namely, numbers or fractions of groups over predetermined (usually administrative) partitions of the studied area. The resulting single number represents the state of an entire area. It is, therefore, *the global measure of segregation* that represents, for example, the exposure of an average member of one group to the members of another group. As such, global segregation indices reveal the central tendency of the phenomenon with respect to given spatial partitions but ignore the inherent spatial variation implied by the local conditions of individuals.

The group approach has a number of serious disadvantages, which were understood more than two decades ago. The most important is the dependence of the result on the scale of the partitions selected to represent the phenomenon (Lee, 1978; Peach, 1979). To overcome this and other problems, an access to geo-referenced personal data is needed (Boal, 1987). These data have always been scarce, but the situation has dramatically changed in recent years. Beginning in 1995, the population censuses in several European countries as well as Israel have been based on exact

12 *Studies in Segregation and Desegregation*

geo-referencing of the householders and households (ICBS, 2000). These detailed spatial data allow the development of *individual-based local measures of segregation* at the resolution of houses, streets, neighbourhoods and other residential divisions.

The fundamental purpose of the individual-based approach is to specify the *segregation situation of a single person relative to neighbours*, that is, to estimate the similarity, exposure or isolation of an individual relative to his/her neighbours in a house or within a neighbourhood. These relationships depend, first, on a person's location and socio-cultural identity and, second, on the identities of neighbours and the spatial structure of the neighbourhood. Consequently, the segregation situation over the area is expressed as a *spatial distribution*, not as a single number. An individual-based approach does not invalidate the global approach; on the contrary, it extends and complements the global one. Moreover, based on the homogeneity or heterogeneity of the distributions of the local indices, we can define new spatial partitions, which optimally represent the segregation phenomenon.

The aim of this paper is to suggest a conceptual and formal framework for implementation of the individual-based approach to segregation measurement and to apply it to data from the 1995 Israeli population census. Conceptually, our approach follows the humanistic-phenomenological stream in human geography (Relph, 1976; Tuan, 1977; Sack, 1980), with its stress on personal experience and relationships. Formally, we follow the approach of L. Anselin (1995) who proposed to proceed to local indices of segregation by expanding a global index into its local components. In what follows we first develop a framework for measuring urban residential segregation from the individual-based perspective. Second, we apply the developed approach to the study of Jewish-Arab residential segregation in the Tel-Aviv-Yaffo residential area.

Segregation as an Individual Phenomenon

The transition to an individual-based approach in measuring segregation is necessary, both conceptually and methodologically. From the methodological point of view, no matter which index is employed the aggregated data concerning the *a priori* given subdivision of space into a relatively low number of aggregating units introduces an uncontrolled bias into our understanding of segregation phenomena (Lee, 1978; Peach, 1979). Studies of the relation between the size and form of the census track and the value of segregation statistics demonstrate that the estimates do not remain constant when scale is changed. For example, the segregation indices for smaller units (and, thus, more areas) are usually higher than for larger ones (Boal, 1987). This phenomenon is clearly demonstrated by comparative studies of the residential segregation of population groups of different origins (Ireland, Britain Africa, Malta, Cyprus, etc.) in London and Birmingham (Woods, 1976), or of racial segregation in England and the United State (Jones & McEvoy, 1978). To avoid scale-dependency, the study of segregation phenomena should be performed with a common scale throughout (Boal, 1987; Lambert & Lambert, 1982). It can not be done when aggregated data only are available but becomes fairly feasible when individual data are at hand.

Conceptually, the traditional aggregate approach to segregation is part of the positivist stream in geography. As such, it has a tendency to ignore somewhat the variance and variety of the individual properties and relationships that provide the basis of the humanistic approach (Jackson & Smith, 1984). An individual-based approach to segregation measurement can be considered as a formal and quantitative expression of the humanistic perspective on the urban social environment. At the same time, the positivistic approach to hypothesis formulation and testing (Peach, 1975) remains valid. As a result, measurements at both individual and higher levels of aggregation could build a bridge between the positivist and humanistic stance toward segregation phenomena and, thereby, reduce the conceptual tension between them.

The individual and, thus, micro-scale segregation measurement is free from the constraints of predetermined spatial division and variation disregard. Alternatively, the size and form of a homogeneous or heterogeneous neighbourhood can be investigated as characteristics of the phenomenon. That is, segregation measurement not only uses spatial units but also creates them.

The Concept of Spatial Hierarchy

According to the humanistic-phenomenological approach, a human being can belong to and exist in several spatial aggregates concurrently. Transitions between them are also experienced. In order to define his/her ad hoc identity, an individual needs 'borders' or 'edges' of the place he/she perceives at any given moment (Tuan, 1977; Johnston, 1991). The spatial aggregates the person perceives are usually hierarchically organised, and

14 *Studies in Segregation and Desegregation*

the hierarchy of that individual's experience regarding the constructed environment can be defined by them (Relph, 1976; Ley, 1983). The emphasis on the spatial units belonging to specific levels of the spatial hierarchy and the shifting of this emphasis is viewed as a dialectic of insideness/outsideness (Relph, 1976). For example, the level of houses can serve as the basis of a person's hierarchy. The 'home area' of the individual (Lee, 1968), that is, the population of the closest neighbouring houses, can be considered as the next aggregate; neighbourhoods of increasing size could then be considered until the whole city is reached.

Taking residential relations as an example, we can consider racial segregation of a person *vis-à-vis* the other inhabitants in an apartment, in a house, in a group of neighbouring houses and so forth. A person and his/her family can exist simultaneously in strong segregation regarding the remaining residents of a house and in weak segregation regarding the population of the neighbouring houses. That person would, thus, exhibit different levels of segregation at different units of space/levels of resolution. As a result, an individual-based approach creates a common framework for the description of the multi-level spatial relations existing between individuals of different social groups.

To formalise the individual-based approach, we need to determine the representation of space and the measures of segregation that could be applied to describe individual-neighbourhood relationships. Location information on each object is a prerequisite for constructing the proposed hierarchical representation of the urban social residential space.

Hierarchical Representations of Urban Residential Space

Bottom-up approach A spatially located individual A is considered as belonging to the lowest level L_0 of the hierarchy D (Figure 2.1); the units of L_0 represent the locations of individuals. The units of the upper levels are defined by A's neighbours. For instance, the group at level L_1 can represent the inhabitants of the house in which A lives; the spatial unit delimiting this group can be a building. If the groups at L_1 are defined by houses, then level L_2 can be based on the population of the closest neighbouring houses, hence, a unit of this level is a set of houses which adjoins a house that A is located in. It is worth noting that A's house belongs to several units of level L_2, while it defines (is central to) one of these units only. Neighbourhoods of increasing dimensions can be considered as defining levels L_3, L_4, L_5, etc., until the highest possible level of the city as a whole, L_C, is reached. For each individual A, therefore, we consider the series of embedded spatial units $L_0^A, L_1^A, \ldots L_C^A$ as representing different levels of A's spatial hierarchy. It should be emphasised that the researcher sets the rules that define the neighbourhoods. In consequence, the levels of the constructed hierarchy reflect the researcher's interest in the relationships maintained between individuals and their neighbours within different neighbourhoods.

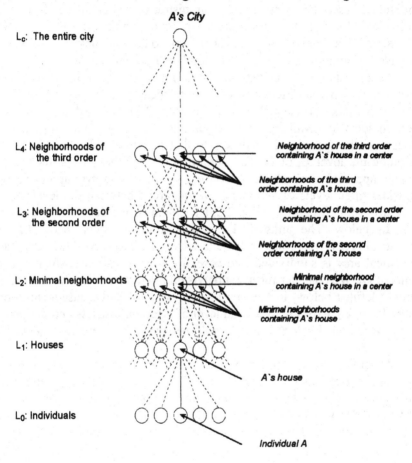

Figure 2.1 A hierarchical representation of urban residential space

No matter how the neighbourhoods are defined, sooner for individuals located closely together and later for those located far apart, we reach the level of hierarchy **D** where their neighbourhoods intersect. Beginning from this level, the intersection increases until we reach the neighbourhood L_C, which is common to all residents.

16 Studies in Segregation and Desegregation

Top-down approach Administrative divisions of the city can be used for determining hierarchy D as well. Usually, the city has up to five or six levels of administrative divisions: regions, electoral districts, zip zones, boroughs and so forth. Each unit of a higher level (e.g. city region) is subdivided into the units of a lower level (e.g. electoral districts). From the individual-based perspective, the administrative neighbourhoods of two individuals located at, say, different zip zones within the same electoral district do not intersect at a level of zip zones and below, while they completely coincide at a level of electoral districts and above.

As an example, let us take the Yaffo residential area, which we study below, and construct hierarchy D of its residential space according to the two approaches reviewed above (Figure 2.2). The data on Yaffo householders are available at the resolution of houses. Thus, we consider houses as the spatial units adjacent to that of households (level L_0), thus defining the level L_1 of D. The definition of the other levels depends on which approach we adopt. According to the top-down approach, we consider three levels of administrative hierarchy between the levels L_C of the 'city' of Yaffo and L_1 (Fig. 2.2, left column). We denoted them L_4, L_3 and L_2 below. The units of L_4, which is immediately below L_C, are statistical areas. According to Israel's urban administrative hierarchy, each statistical area is subdivided into several electoral districts, which are the units of L_3. We consider further subdivision of electoral districts into 'street cells' (defined below, in the 'Yaffo case' section) and, consequently, one more level, L_2, exists between the level of electoral districts and the one of separate houses. Each Yaffo household belongs to one unit only at each of the levels $L_0 - L_C$.

According to the bottom-up approach, we can define many levels between that of L_1 (houses) and that of L_C (the city). To define the level, L_2, adjacent to L_1, we consider the neighbourhoods of houses of the first order $U_1(H)$, which are composed of houses, perceived as immediate spatial proximates of H. As units of level L_3, we can consider the houses of $U_1(H)$ plus the houses next to H's neighbours, which, taken together, could be considered as H's neighbourhood of the second order - $U_2(H)$ and so forth (Fig. 2.2, right column). Each Yaffo household belongs to many spatial units at the level L_1 and the above levels.

Itzhak Benenson and Itzhak Omer 17

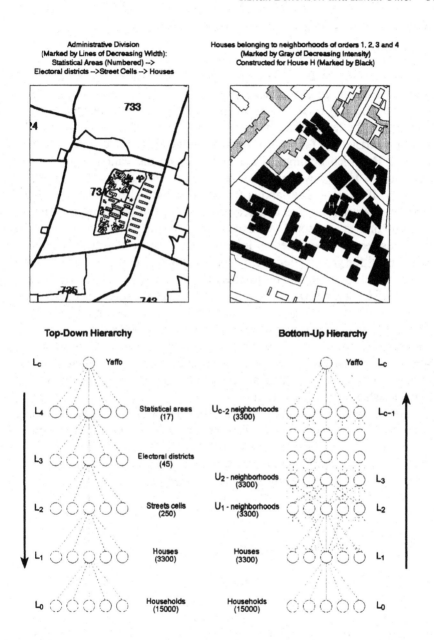

Figure 2.2 A hierarchical representation of residential space in Yaffo

18 *Studies in Segregation and Desegregation*

Measuring Segregation According to Spatial Hierarchy

The approach we have adopted to measuring segregation phenomena is based on hierarchy **D**, as described previously. The application of each specific *local segregation index* S_f, according to characteristic **f**, is defined by a pair (L_b, L_n) of D-levels, where L_b is the level below the level L_n. When L_b is the level representing separate individuals, for each individual **B**, characterised by f_B, we do the following: First, select neighbourhood **U(B)** of **B**, which belongs to L_N, and estimate the values of f_A for each individual **A** located within **U(B)**; second, calculate S_f based on f_B and the set of f_A. If L_b is a level above the level of individuals then we have to interpret characteristic **f** as characteristic of unit **B**. For example, 'religion', a dichotomous personal characteristic, having the possible values 'religious/secular', becomes an interval characteristic 'fraction of religious individuals' for groups, defined by spatial units. After an individual feature is interpreted for a group we estimate S_f based on f_B and the set of f_A for all units **A** of L_b belonging to **B**'s neighbourhood at L_n. It is worth noting that situations of conflicting results for L_b if chosen as the level of the individuals and L_b chosen as a higher level (say, of houses) are possible. If, for example, each house in a city has a population of 50% religious and 50% secular then each single individual is in a completely heterogeneous situation relative to any layer above, while the distribution of the houses' characteristics is absolutely uniform.

Below, we consider the level L_b to consist of either families or houses and always map the (spatial) distribution of local segregation index S_f according to characteristic **f**, over units **B** of L_b for the pairs (L_b, L_n) we choose to study. Eventually, the distribution of the local index S_f estimated for the pair (L_b, L_C) represents the state of segregation of individuals relative to the population of the whole city.

Local and Global Indices of Spatial Segregation

Global Indices of Spatial Segregation

As noted above, one can find a dozen analytically different global segregation indices used in geographic research beginning from the early 1950s (Geary, 1954; Duncan & Duncan, 1955). The indices can be roughly classified according to the phenomena they are meant to reveal. The latter are generally indicated in the index name – dissimilarity, exposure, clustering, compactness and so on (Massey & Denton, 1988). In parallel, the indices differ according to the number of population groups they relate to. The indices of spatial autocorrelation (used primarily for recognition of homogeneous spatial clusters) consider only the members of a single population group (Getis & Ord, 1996). Most other indices estimate the relationship between two groups (Wong, 1997), while some indices - Moran joint count statistics for multi-coloured maps (Goodchild, 1986) or Kendall phi (Kendall, 1970) - operate with an arbitrary number of population groups. Each global index represents the averaged state of an averaged representative of a given group with respect to this partition by means of a single number. It is obvious that global indices, by definition, ignore an inherent variation implied by specific individual's characteristics, location, structure of the neighbourhood and characteristics of the neighbours. As examples let us consider three popular global segregation indices which would be expanded into the series of local indices below.

- The Moran (1950) index **I** of spatial autocorrelation estimates a correlation between a characteristic at a given location and over the location's neighbourhood. The analytical expression for Moran **I** is as follows:

$$I = \Sigma_i(z_i - <z>)\Sigma_j w_{ij}(z_j - <z>)/(s^2\Sigma_i\Sigma_j w_{ij}) \quad (1)$$

where z_i, z_j are the values of the characteristic at locations i and j; $<z>$ denotes the mean of the variable z; the set of w_{ij} defines an *a priori* 'influence' of neighbouring locations j on location i; $s = \Sigma_i(z_i - <z>)/n$ denotes sampling variance and **n** is the number of observations.

- Lieberson's (1981) index **P** of 'exposure' of population group X to population group Y is defined as a probability for a randomly located member of group X to find a member of a group Y at the same location (X-member 'meets' Y-member at that location):

$$P = \Sigma_i(x_i / X)(y_i / t_i) \quad (2)$$

where x_i, y_i and t_i are the numbers of the members of X, y_i and the overall number of individuals at location i, and X is the number of X-members over the entire area. The multiplier x_i / X is an unconditional probability associate with prospect of finding a member of X at location i, while the term y_i / t_i is a conditional probability of a member of a group X, located at i, meeting a member of Y there.

20   *Studies in Segregation and Desegregation*

- The most popular index in segregation studies is an index of dissimilarity (Duncan & Duncan, 1955):

$$D = \Sigma_i |x_i / X - y_i / Y| \qquad (3)$$

where Y is the number of Y-members over the entire area, and the other variables remain the same as in (2).

Approaches to Measuring Local Spatial Relationships

The approaches to estimating local spatial segregation and the first local measures of segregation phenomena were suggested during the late 1980s (Getis & Ord, 1992), and their development and application in geography date from the last decade. The relationships between characteristics of individuals and their neighbours that we are interested in represent specific cases of dependencies between characteristics of observations located in close proximity to one another. These dependencies are studied by geostatistics (see Cressie, 1993, for review), and till now the geographical and geostatistical methodologies have developed almost independently. As a result of parallel developments, the measures of spatial relationship applied in geographical research share the title of 'spatial correlation/autocorrelation' with those applied in geostatistics but differ from them. The latter are much more developed and intensively investigated (Cressie, 1993). At the same time, the complexity of geographical phenomena (Gregory, 1985) limits the application of strict geostatistical methods, the latter requiring ergodicity (independence of history) and 'intrinsic behaviour' (expectation of the difference between observations depends only on distance between them) of the spatial process in study. In this paper we continue with a discussion of geographical measures of spatial relationships and delay the comparison of geographical and geostatistical measures for a future paper.

Local Indices of Spatial Segregation

Most of the attention in geographical literature is devoted to examining spatial clustering of population groups. Three local indices aimed at revealing the homogeneous or heterogeneous domains over the entire studied area are discussed below:

- Getis' G and G^* indices (Getis & Ord, 1992, 1996) are both based on moving averages of a characteristic over the neighbourhood.

- Local Moran index **I** (Anselin, 1995) estimates the correlation between the value of a characteristic at a given location and its mean value over the rest of the neighbourhood.
- Local Geary indices K_1 and K_2 (Getis & Ord, 1996; Anselin, 1995) estimate the variance of the characteristic within the neighbourhood.

We do not consider in this paper several other useful indices aimed at revealing spatial homogeneity, joint count statistics (Goodchild, 1986) and Kendall phi (Kendall, 1970), for instance.

The local Moran and Geary indices are obtained by expanding global index **I** of Moran (Moran, 1950) and **K** of Geary (Geary, 1954) into local components. We follow the same logic in 'localising' other segregation indices. The Getis' local indices correspond to a weighted average of a characteristic over the entire area.

Local Moran I To proceed from a global to a local version of the Moran index (1), L. Anselin (1995) isolates term I_i, defined by spatial unit i, and represents **I** as

$$I = \Sigma_i I_{i,U(i)} / (s^2 \Sigma_i \Sigma_j w_{ij}), \qquad (4)$$

where

$$I_{i,U(i)} = (z_i - <z>)\Sigma_{j \in U(i)} w_{ij}(z_j - <z>) \qquad (5)$$

According to our terminology, i denotes unit of a level L_b and $U(i)$ is a neighbourhood of i at upper level L_n. Each $I_{i,U(i)}$ can be considered a local index of autocorrelation between the characteristics of a unit i and characteristics of neighbours within $U(i)$. Below we set $w_{ij} = 1/(n_i - 1)$, where n_i is the number of L_b units within $U(i)$.

It follows from (5) that a positive and high value of $I_{i,U(i)}$ is obtained when both $z_i - <z>$ and weighted mean $\Sigma_{j \in U(i)} w_{ij}(z_j - <z>)$ over $U(i)$ are either high and positive or low and negative. As a result, high positive $I_{i,U(i)}$ identifies a homogeneous neighbourhood. A heterogeneous neighbourhood usually results in close to zero values of $I_{i,U(i)}$. The value of $I_{i,U(i)}$ is negative and significantly below zero when z_i and the weighted mean of z_j over $U(i)$ have different signs and both significantly differ out from zero.

Local K_1 and K_2 Two analytical versions of the Geary (Anselin, 1995) local index of spatial variance estimate the mean difference between the observations at close locations and are as follows:

22 Studies in Segregation and Desegregation

$$K_{1i,U(i)} = \sum_{j \in U(i)} w_{ij} |z_j - z_i| \qquad (6)$$

$$K_{2i,U(i)} = \sum_{j \in U(i)} w_{ij} (z_j - z_i)^2 \qquad (7)$$

where the terms have the same meaning as in (4) and (5).

The $K_{1i,U(i)}$ and $K_{2i,U(i)}$ are always positive, and the higher their value, the higher the heterogeneity of the neighbourhood. As above we select $w_{ij} = 1/(n_i - 1)$, using the local Geary index below. Both versions of the local Geary index are based on a global index of spatial variance (Geary, 1954; Goodchild, 1986):

$$K_1 = \sum_{ij} w_{ij} |z_j - z_i| / (s^2 \Sigma_i \Sigma_j w_{ij}), \ K_2 = \sum_{ij} w_{ij} (z_j - z_i)^2 / (s^2 \Sigma_i \Sigma_j w_{ij}) \qquad (8)$$

Getis' G, G* The indices of local autocorrelation proposed by P. Getis and K. Ord (Getis & Ord, 1992) are based on a comparison of the local average of a characteristic to its global average over the entire city; we use their latest version (Getis & Ord, 1996). The G-version ignores the characteristic of a unit and accounts for its neighbours only, while the G*-version accounts for the unit's characteristic as well:

$$G_{i,U(i)} = R_i(\sum_{j \in U(i), j \neq i} w_{ij} z_j - <z>_i) \qquad (9)$$

$$G^*_{i,U(i)} = R^*_i(\sum_{j \in U(i)} w_{ij} z_j - <z>) \qquad (10)$$

where $<z>_i = \sum_{j \neq i} z_j / (n - 1)$ and R_i and R^*_i are normalising coefficients. The global counterpart of Getis' indices is an average value of a characteristic over the entire city. As above we select $w_{ij} = 1/(n_i - 1)$ using the local Geary index below and do not account for normalising coefficients R_i or R^*_i.

It follows from (9) – (10) that positive and high values of $G_{i,U(i)}$ and $G^*_{i,U(i)}$ are obtained when the weighted means $\sum_{j \in U(i)} w_{ij} z_j$ or $\sum_{j \in U(i), j \neq i} w_{ij} z_j$ calculated over U(i), are essentially higher than the global mean. $G_{i,U(i)}$ and $G^*_{i,U(i)}$ are negative and relatively low when local weighted means fall below the global mean. As a result, either high positive or low negative $G_{i,U(i)}$ and $G^*_{i,U(i)}$ values identify relatively homogeneous neighbourhoods and make it possible to recognise whether the said characteristic, as found within this neighbourhood, is above or below the global average.

The localising of the global index into local components can be easily done regarding the other segregation indices used in geographic research. Let us illustrate this principle for the Lieberson exposure index and index of dissimilarity.

Lieberson exposure index Localising (2), we have to estimate an exposure of an X-member located at unit i to Y-members located within neighbourhood $U(i)$. The choice of the formula depends on the description of contacts of individuals. When an X-member has 'to visit the unit' in order to meet a Y-member located in it, then the exposure of the X-member to the Y-members within $U(i)$ is as following

$$P_{i,U(i)} = \Sigma_{j \in U(i)} w_{ij} (y_j / t_j) \qquad (11)$$

where w_{ij} ($\Sigma_{j \in U(i)} w_{ij} = 1$) is the probability of an X-member located at i to select a unit j.

When an X-member meets Y-members 'somewhere over $U(i)$', then the stage of unit selection is irrelevant and the exposure of X-member to the members of Y is simply

$$P_{i,U(i)} = \Sigma_{j \in U(i)} w_{ij} y_j / \Sigma_{j \in U(i)} w_{ij} t_j \qquad (12)$$

where w_{ij} is interpreted as a probability for an X-member located at i to meet an inhabitant of a unit j.

According to formulae (11) - (12) the local Lieberson exposure index is nothing more than a moving average of the fraction of Y-group members calculated at each i over $U(i)$. Moreover, for the case of (11), one can see that $P_{i,U(i)} = G^*_{i,U(i)} - <z>$.

To conclude, let us consider a simple numerical example of local Lieberson P. Let the city consist of a high number N of houses, and the house i_0 and each of n houses within i_0's neighbourhood $U(i_0)$ is occupied by one representative of X and one of Y, while for the other houses, the numbers of X- and Y-members are 99 versus 1. According to (2), the global value of P (that is the probability of an arbitrary X-member meeting a Y-member over the entire area) is slightly below $N \cdot (99 / (99 \cdot N)) \cdot (1 / 100) = 0.01$, due to a high number of houses with 99 X-members in them. Let all the neighbourhoods $U(i)$ be of similar size and form and let the weights w_{ij} in (11), (12) equal one for $j \in U(i)$ and zero for locations j outside of $U(i)$. The value of $P_{i_0,U(i_0)}$ for an X-member equals, thus, $\Sigma_{j \in U(i_0)} 1 / \Sigma_{j \in U(i_0)} 2 = 0.5$. The value of $P_{i,U(i)}$ for arbitrary location $i \# i_0$ within $U(i_0)$ decreases with an increase of distance between i_0 and i and reaches the value of 0.01 at distances of two radii of $U(i_0)$ and higher. The resulting global and local values of P straightforwardly correspond to the intuitive meaning of the Lieberson coefficient. A member of X located at i_0 has almost no chance (p ~ 0.01) of meeting a member of Y over the entire area,

24 Studies in Segregation and Desegregation

while his/her chance of meeting a Y-member within the neighbourhood equals 0.5 and decreases when his/her location is more distant from i_0.

As we did for the exposure index, we can localise any other standard index of spatial segregation. For an index of dissimilarity, for instance, the standard formula (3) is transformed into

$$D_{i,U(i)} = |x_i / X_{U(i)} - y_i / Y_{U(i)}| \qquad (13)$$

where $X_{U(i)} = \Sigma_{j \in U(i)} w_{ij} x_j$ and $Y_{U(i)} = \Sigma_{j \in U(i)} w_{ij} y_j$.

For a hypothetical example above, the global D is slightly below 0.98, while $D_{i0,U(i0)}$ equals zero (distributions of X- and Y-members are similar within $U(i_0)$), both corresponding to an intuitive understanding of a dissimilarity index.

The Problem of Statistical Inference for Local Segregation Indices

An approach to 'localisation' such as the one above is very simple. The problem of statistical inference for obtained indices is, in contrast, rather complex. Two approaches to statistical inference regarding local measures of segregation are considered in the literature. The theoretical approach is based on maximum likelihood estimates of index variance (Getis & Ord, 1996; Anselin, 1995) which are very imprecise until rather restrictive assumptions are fulfilled. The maximum likelihood approach results in indices varying within non-standardised intervals, and, thus, the comparison of the indices calculated for neighbourhoods of different size becomes problematic. The alternative is a *resampling* computational approach, based on Monte-Carlo simulations (Anselin, 1995). Resampling is better fitted to the poorly defined statistical situations we study and its relatively heavy calculations are of minor importance with state-of-the-art hardware. The logic of the resampling approach is as follows. First, consider the sample as an entire population. Second, randomly relocate the bearers of characteristics (say, individual householders) over space and estimate the parameters of the artificial spatial distribution thus obtained. Third, repeat the second step numerous times (usually 1000-10000 repetitions are made) and construct the distribution of index estimates at each location. To reveal the locations, where the indices are significantly high or low, one has to compare the actual value of an index to the percentiles of the distribution obtained at the third step. The limitations of the scope of this paper prevent further discussion of the problem of statistical inference. The problem will be discussed extensively in a subsequent paper.

Itzhak Benenson and Itzhak Omer 25

Case Study: Yaffo

What follows is an attempt to understand the possible results of the individual-based approach when geo-referenced personal data are available. In the following we study the ethnic residential distribution in the Yaffo region of Tel-Aviv, based on geo-referenced data, at the level of householders, taken from the 1995 population census.

Description of the Region

Yaffo is a region of Tel-Aviv (officially called Tel-Aviv-Yaffo) occupied by Arab and Jewish residents. Its area is about 7 km^2. The population in 1995 was about 39,000, of which the Jewish majority comprised about 70% and the Arab minority, the other 30%. Until the 1948 War of Independence, Yaffo was an independent Arab city of 70,000. After the War, only 3,000 of the original Arab inhabitants remained almost all concentrated within the small Adjami neighbourhood. Jewish immigrants came to populate the other parts of Yaffo (Portugali, 1991; Omer, 1996). During the period 1955-1995, the Arab population of Yaffo continuously grew and spread throughout the region, while the Jewish majority gradually left (Figure 2.3).

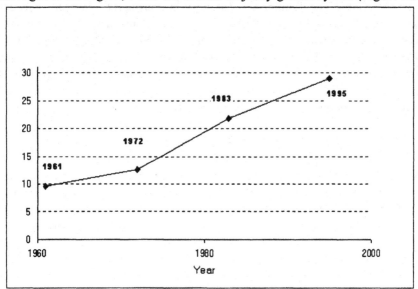

Figure 2.3 Arab population growth in Yaffo

Exact data are available for the period 1961-1995, when the size of the

26　*Studies in Segregation and Desegregation*

Arab population increased from 5,000 (8% of the population of Yaffo) to 12,000 (30%), while the Jewish population declined from 58,000 (92%) to 27,000 (70%).

The Population and Location Data

The main source of data for the study is the Israeli Census of Population and Housing for 1995 (ICSB, 2000). Unlike the previous census, the data from the 1995 census are geo-referenced at the level of householders. That is, one of the fields of the database record for the householder contains a unique identifier of the polygon representing the building he/she lives in. Buildings (represented by foundation polygons) are organised as a layer of a census GIS, constructed for the whole of Israel. In addition, census GIS contains layers of streets, statistical areas, electoral districts and open spaces (ICSB, 2000). The geo-referenced data on individuals and households are available for supervised study at ICBS. This paper is based only on the 'religion' of the householder, defined by six categories in the census questionnaire: 'Jewish', 'Moslem', 'Druze', 'Christian', 'Foreign worker' and 'Unknown'. For the purposes of the current study we have combined the categories of 'Moslem', 'Druze' and 'Christian' into one entitled 'Arab'. The 'Unknown' category is considered 'Jewish', because the majority of these householders are new immigrants whose Jewish affiliation has yet to be officially recognised. We use MapInfo (MI) GIS version 5.0 and Vertical Mapper (VM) version 1.5 as tools for the geographical analysis. The topological analysis is done by means of ArcCad GIS. The procedures for calculating local segregation indices are developed as MapBasic (MB) extensions of MI.

Construction of the Hierarchy of Spatial Units for Yaffo

In order to apply the local approach to measuring segregation we have to construct the hierarchical representation **D** of the urban space. The hierarchy can be defined either by ethnographic methods, which are based on intensive empirical studies (Lee et al., 1994) or by a formal procedure. Since our aim is to illustrate the use of local segregation indices, the formal approach is sufficient.

Top-down hierarchy $\mathbf{D_{t\text{-}d}}$, *based on administrative division* Urban population data in Israel are compiled according to administrative divisions, the latter being based on the street network. The standard census spatial unit is called the 'statistical area', and contains about 1000 households. Two more detailed partitions of an urban space can be considered. First is the level of electoral districts, which divide statistical areas into two-to-five sub-regions. Their digital map is also available from ICBS. To go into greater detail, we used the ArcCad topological analysis tools and constructed 'street cells' - minimal closed polygons formed by the street network. Each electoral district consists of three-to-seven street cells. The levels of separate houses and households complete the hierarchy. The D_{t-d} hierarchy of Yaffo space is shown on Figure 2.2.

Bottom-up hierarchy D_{b-u}, *based on houses' adjacency* For the bottom-up approach, the two lowest levels L_0 and L_1 are those of householders and separate buildings. We do not consider the level of single individuals regarding the spatial distribution of "religion" because mixed families are extremely rare. The most important step in constructing bottom-up hierarchy is the transition from the level of houses to the level of minimal neighbourhoods (neighbourhoods of the first order). Our purpose is to define these neighbourhoods in an intuitively acceptable manner that avoids computational complexities. We do so based on the coverage of the Voronoi polygons constructed around the centroids of populated buildings (Figure 2.4) by means of VM tools. We define two houses as adjacent if their Voronoi polygons have a common edge. Consequently, we define the neighbourhood of the first order of a house H as a set of houses $U_1(H)$, where each $G \in U_1(H)$ satisfies the following conditions:

1. G is adjacent to H;
2. The distance between centroids of G and H is less than a given threshold value (we set it equal to 100 m for the case of Yaffo);
3. G and H are on the same side of a street if it has two or more traffic lanes.

We translate these three conditions into an MB procedure that, based on the layers of houses, their Voronoi polygons and streets, constructs $U_1(H)$ for each house H (Figure 2.4). $U_1(H)$ constructed for each house H define, therefore, level L_2 of D_{b-u}.

The neighbourhoods of higher orders are defined recursively; namely, the neighbourhood $U_k(H)$ of the order k (k = 2, 3...) is defined as $U_{k-1}(H)$ plus the houses next to houses of $U_{k-1}(H)$ or, formally, as

$$U_{k+1}(H) = \{F \mid F \in U_1(G) \text{ AND } G \in U_k(H)\} \qquad (14)$$

28 *Studies in Segregation and Desegregation*

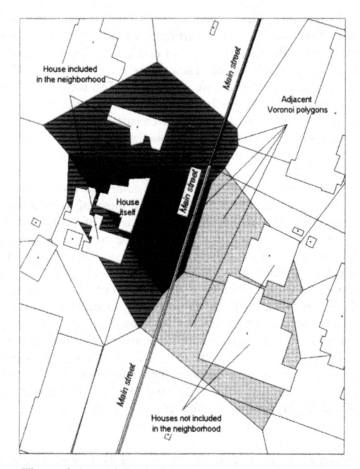

Figure 2.4 A neighbourhood according to order 1

Based on the table of the neighbours of the first order, the MB application constructs neighbourhoods of higher orders for each house **H**. As is noted above, the overlay between $U_k(H)$ and $U_k(G)$ of houses **H** and **G** increases as **k** increases.

Analysis of Arab-Jewish Residential Segregation

Segregation according to a top-down hierarchy Let us begin with the simplest maps of exposure (Lieberson $P_{i,U(i)}$) of a person in the Arab population constructed for families at level L_0 versus the other four levels of the administrative hierarchy D_{t-d} (Figure 2.5). We set the weights w_{ij} in

Itzhak Benenson and Itzhak Omer 29

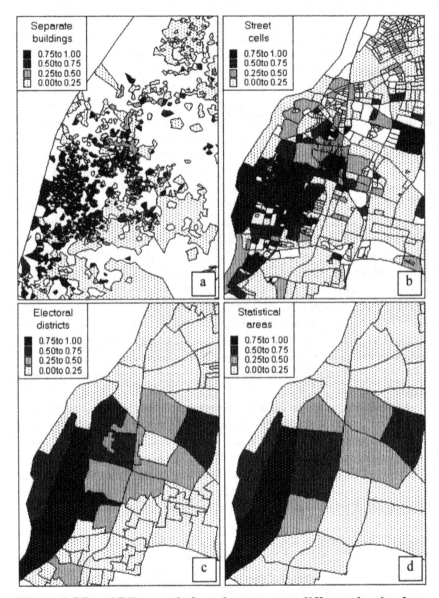

Figure 2.5 **Local Liberson index of exposure at different levels of the administrative hierarchy**

(11)–(12) all equal units divided by the number of neighbours, which makes the expressions (11) and (12) identical for $P_{i,U(i)}$. Moreover, for these specific weights the value of $P_{i,U(i)}$ for a pair of levels (L_b, L_n) is

30 Studies in Segregation and Desegregation

independent of the choice of L_b. In addition, let us recall, that the maps in Figure 2.5 represent distributions of $G^*_{i,U(i)}$ - see (10) - and, thus, the distribution of $G^*_{i,U(i)}$ is also independent of the choice of L_b.

The most important conclusion stemming from the visual comparison of indices distributions in Figure 2.5 is that the exposure of a person to the Arab population according to P and the heterogeneity of Arab population according to G^* vary over Yaffo. Following the D_{t-d} hierarchy, exposure of a person to the Arab population can be high within an electoral district and low within a statistical area, and the heterogeneity of the ethnic residential distribution according to electoral districts within a statistical area can be the same as over the whole of Yaffo (Figure 2.5c, d). The same is true when comparing heterogeneity at the level of street cells regarding the level of electoral districts. It is worth noting that some street cells at the lower levels of D_{t-d} do not contain dwellings at all. As a result, the fraction of Arab population becomes undefined for these cells as well as for the high number of unpopulated buildings in Yaffo (Figure 2.5a, b). Finally, the maps at the level of electoral districts and statistical areas 2.5c and d do not add much, if anything, to understanding residential segregation in Yaffo created by high-resolution maps 2.5a and 2.5b. We do not map other segregation indices for the D_{t-d} hierarchy because the results are very similar to those in Figure 2.5; namely, the maps constructed for higher levels do not change the impression regarding the segregation situation in Yaffo.

Let us construct distributions of segregation indices for the bottom-up hierarchy D_{b-u}. It is worth noting that according to the mean area of the house's Voronoi polygon, the mean size of the neighbourhoods of order 4 corresponds to the size of a street cell, and the size of the neighbourhoods of order 8 corresponds to an electoral district. In the following, to map the results of analysis, we always divide the interval of index variation into three classes, corresponding to high, low and intermediate values of an index.

Bottom-up hierarchy Here we compare spatial distributions of exposure $P_{i,Uk(i)}$ to Arab population and the indices $G^*_{i,Uk(i)}$, $I_{i,Uk(i)}$ and $K_{Ii,Uk(i)}$ constructed for the Arab population at the levels L_1 (families) and L_2 (houses) versus levels defined by the neighbourhoods of orders $k = 1, 2, 4$ and 8, that is versus L_3, L_4, L_6, L_{10}. The spatial distributions of these indices are presented in Figures 2.6–2.8. Prior to analysing each index separately, let us point out two important differences which stem from a comparison of Figure 2.5 and Figures 2.6–2.8. First, it is difficult to locate

Itzhak Benenson and Itzhak Omer 31

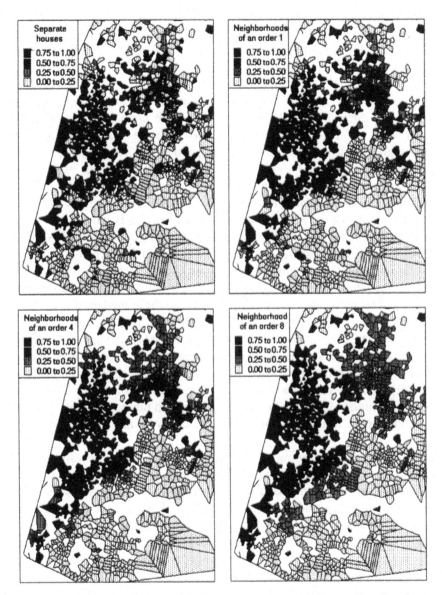

Figure 2.6 Local Liberson index of exposure at different levels of the hierarchy

the boundaries between relatively homogeneous areas in Figure 2.5, whereas in Figures 2.6–2.8 the locations of the boundaries remain constant. In the maps constructed for higher levels of the hierarchy the boundaries

32 Studies in Segregation and Desegregation

may 'disappear', but, nevertheless, they do not move in space. Second, the boundaries between homogeneous/heterogeneous domains in Figures 2.6–2.8 do not correspond to the boundaries between street cells, electoral districts or statistical areas.

Lieberson P and Getis G* We have noted above that the values of $G^*_{i,Uk(i)}$ and $P_{i,Uk(i)}$ differ in global fraction of the Arab population in Yaffo, the latter equal to 0.25. This is why we can consider the maps in Figure 2.6 as representing distributions of both $G^*_{i,Uk(i)}$ and $P_{i,Uk(i)}$. As above, we use the unit weights w_{ij} in (11) – (12), which implies that the values of $P_{i,U(i)}$ and $G^*_{i,Uk(i)}$ for a pair (L_b, L_n) do not depend on the choice of L_b.

The impression made by the areas of concentration of the Arab and Jewish population in Yaffo as mapped in Figure 2.6 is unambiguous. We can clearly distinguish domains of homogeneous populations of Arabs or Jews; these domains are characterised by values of $P_{i,Uk(i)}$ or $G^*_{i,Uk(i)}$ close to the maximum or the minimum for all **k**. The rest of the Yaffo area, where the values of $P_{i,Uk(i)}$ and $G^*_{i,Uk(i)}$ are far from the extremes for some or all **k**, cannot be uniquely classified because these moderate values may be obtained in two ways. First, they may result from relatively homogeneous $U_k(i)$, where the fractions of the Arab population in all the houses are similar and far from the extreme values. Second, they may be obtained for heterogeneous $U_k(i)$. The houses for which $P_{i,Uk(i)}$ and $G^*_{i,Uk(i)}$ are far from the extremes for all or some **k** comprise about 20% of all populated houses in Yaffo. In order to understand this segregation situation, we continue the analysis by means of local Geary K_1 and Moran **I** indices.

Local Geary K_1 According to (6), $K_{1i,Uk(i)}$ is low when the values of the characteristic are similar for all the houses within $U_k(i)$ (Figure 2.7). Thus, in addition to homogeneous areas of extreme fractions of Arabs and Jews disclosed by $P_{i,Uk(i)}$ and $G^*_{i,Uk(i)}$, low values of $K_{1i,Uk(i)}$ for units taken as houses, mark the domains where the ethnic make-up of the houses is similar, although it is far from the extremes of 1:0 or 0:1. At the same time, the values of $K_{1i,Uk(i)}$ over these domains for units representing families, cannot be low. That is, the individuals located within these areas are in highly heterogeneous situations relative to their neighbours in the house. On the map, K for a person implies two values at a unit.

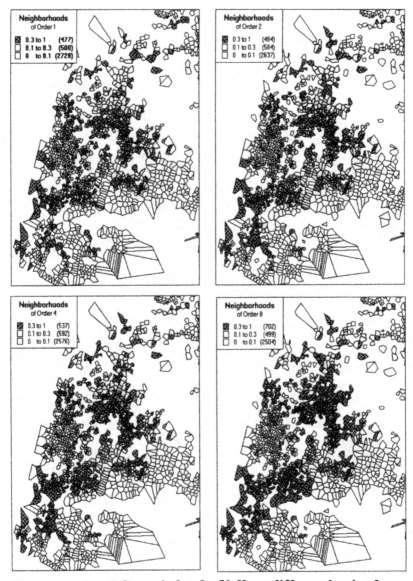

Figure 2.7 Local Geary index for Yaffo at different levels of the hierarchy

Local Moran I According to (5), high positive values of $I_{i,Uk(i)}$ (Figure 2.8) indicate clusters of houses of size $U_k(i)$, where the fraction of Arabs is far from the global mean. Consequently, $I_{i,Uk(i)}$ could be high over the areas where the values of $P_{i,Uk(i)}$ and $G^*_{i,Uk(i)}$ are either maximal or minimal

34 *Studies in Segregation and Desegregation*

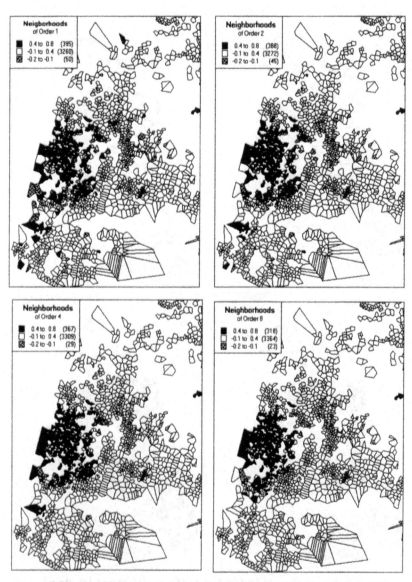

Figure 2.8 Local Moran I index for Yaffo at different levels of the hierarchy

(compare Figures 2.6 and 2.8). In the Yaffo case this relationship holds for domains of high fractions of Arabs only, where $P_{i,Uk(i)}$ and $G^*_{i,Uk(i)}$ are close to the maximum. For those domains containing mostly Jews ($P_{i,Uk(i)}$ and

$G^*_{i,Uk(i)}$ are close to the minimum), this does not hold, and $I_{i,Uk(i)}$ is close to zero due to a relatively low fraction of Arabs in Yaffo (18.8%). Therefore, $I_{i,Uk(i)}$ is insufficient as an indicator of heterogeneous or homogeneous Jewish areas in Yaffo, and its value is close to zero in both cases. The areas having intermediate values of $P_{i,Uk(i)}$ and $G^*_{i,Uk(i)}$ show mainly negative values of $I_{i,Uk(i)}$, which indicates a heterogeneous situation and confirms the results obtained by means of $K_{1i,Uk(i)}$. As a result, no new information is recognised by means of $I_{i,Uk(i)}$ for the case of Yaffo. Local Moran I is weaker than $P_{i,Uk(i)}$ and $G^*_{i,Uk(i)}$ in disclosing the homogeneous domains in Yaffo and is similar to $K_{1i,Uk(i)}$ in disclosing heterogeneous domains.

Combination of indices as a tool for determining personal segregation situations To this point, we have studied the ability of indices to indicate domains of homogeneous and heterogeneous ethnic structure. Let us consider the hypothetical member **A** of an Arab ethnic group located at house **I** and then describe 'the segregation situation of **A**' in terms of the values of $P_{i,Uk(i)}$ and $K_{1i,Uk(i)}$ for different k. We do not take $G^*_{i,Uk(i)}$ and $I_{i,Uk(i)}$ into consideration because the former is equivalent to $P_{i,Uk(i)}$ while the latter does not add significant information in the Yaffo case.

The simplest situation is that of individual **A** residing in a house **I**, which is located within a domain having the highest values of $P_{i,Uk(i)}$ (and, consequently close to zero $K_{1i,Uk(i)}$) for all k. In this case, **A** is located within an almost homogeneous Arab environment within the house, at the level of adjacent houses and above, up to the level of everyday local activity (a neighbourhood of order 8), with the latter containing local shops and religious and cultural centers. High values of $P_{i,Uk(i)}$ indicate that **A** is not exposed to any Jewish population until visiting distant locations. When **A** is located in the house, which is within an area of minimal $P_{i,Uk(i)}$ (and close to zero $K_{1i,Uk(i)}$) for all k, the situation is reversed. That is, **A** is found within a homogeneous Jewish environment within the house and at all levels of the urban hierarchy above the house.

The areas of either homogeneous Arab or Jewish population cover about 80% of Yaffo. Let us try to conceptualise the segregation situation if **A** is located in a house in the remaining 20% of Yaffo's territory. The basic properties of a person's segregation situation here are disclosed by $K_{1i,Uk(i)}$. A low $K_{1i,Uk(i)}$ for all k characterises a uniform situation, one where **A** perceives each house in the neighbourhood $U(i)$ as having equal and intermediate fractions of an Arab population. The non-uniform case is characterised by K_1 fluctuating with k. Concerning Yaffo, only non-uniform situations are observed; that is, $K_{1i,Uk(i)}$ varies with k for the

36 Studies in Segregation and Desegregation

majority of locations within the areas displaying intermediate values of $P_{i,Uk(i)}$. A's segregation status, if A is located in a house for which $K_{1i,Uk(i)}$ fluctuates, depends on the range of these fluctuations. If the range is high, then A perceives all the possible variations of the ethnic structure that can be observed in Yaffo within a radius of everyday local activity. For the intermediate range of fluctuations, A remains within heterogeneous but predominantly Arab (characterised by high values of $P_{i,Uk(i)}$) or Jewish (low values of $P_{i,Uk(i)}$) neighbourhoods.

Comparison of the Local and Global Measurements of Segregation

The global mean fraction of Arabs in Yaffo (corresponds to Getis G^*) equals 0.188. The Geary K_1 and Moran I global indices, calculated for houses in neighbourhoods of orders 1, 2, 4 and 8, equal $K_1 = 0.099$; 0.104; 0.112; 0.125 and $I = 0.096$; 0.094; 0.090; 0.085, respectively. Taken alone, these intermediate values demonstrate that ethnic residential distribution in Yaffo is not homogeneous, while its global heterogeneity is not high. To understand the pattern of residential distribution, a local analysis is necessary.

Conclusion

The purpose of this paper is to present the general individual-based approach and to apply it to a real-world situation. However, a number of important problems await further study. First, from the theoretical-statistical point of view, we have to understand the power of the 'geographical' indices we use, that is, their ability to identify segregated patches in the noisy environment. At the same time, we have to compare the results with those obtained by standard geo-statistical methods. An analysis of non-uniform artificially constructed distributions is the way to do so. Second, we have only analysed one relatively simple situation with two dominant homogeneous areas and a boundary region between them although the importance of the local indices increases with an increase in the variance in the area size. We are currently studying the distribution of the population of the entire city of Tel-Aviv by income, origin, age and educational levels according to this method. Third, we have not considered the reasons for the segregation phenomena we have observed. For example, there might be constraints of the constructed environment (architectural types and dwelling prices, for instance) and a tendency of similar householders to locate in close proximity. In the case of Yaffo, the correlation between the environmental factors, fraction of the Arab population and the architectural style of a building is relatively high (Omer, 1996) and can be considered an important factor contributing to the persistence of homogeneous Arab or Jewish areas in Yaffo.

Segregation estimates at different levels of the urban hierarchy can be applied in several ways. First, revealed homogeneous areas provide a basis for the appropriate division of an area for presenting census counts. A priori given census divisions mask the spatial distribution according to ethnic, cultural and other characteristics of a city's population (Figure 2.5). Alternatively, a division based on neighbourhoods emphasises them (Figures 2.6–2.8). Second, if we can explain segregation patterns by means of the properties of the constructed environment or by means of the direct interactions between individuals when choosing a residence, we can account for this relationship in the planning processes and generate, maintain or destroy spatial segregation between ethnic groups by physically restructuring the neighbourhoods.

To conclude, the proposed approach can decrease the conceptual tension between the positivist and humanistic streams in geography. While the aggregated approach contradicts the conceptual basis of the humanistic stream, an individual-based approach directly concentrates on the variation among individuals. The use of spatial hierarchy and segregation estimation can bridge the two streams.

References

Anselin, L. (1995), 'Local Indicators of Spatial Association – LISA', *Geographical Analysis*, vol. 27 (2), pp. 93-115.
Anselin, L., Getis A. (1992), 'Spatial Statistical Analysis and Geographic Information Systems', *The Annals of Regional Science*, vol. 26, pp.19-33.
Boal, F.W. (1987), 'Segregation', in M. Pasion (ed), *Social Geography: Progress and Prospect*, Croom Helm, Beckenham.
Cressie, N.A.C. (1993), *Statistics for Spatial Data*, Wiley & Sons, New York.
Duncan, O. & Duncan, B. (1955), 'A Methodological Analysis of Segregation Indices', *American Sociological Review*, vol. 20, pp. 210-217.
Geary, R.C. (1954), 'The Contiguity Ratio and Statistical Mapping', *Incorporated Statistician*, vol. 5, pp. 115-141.
Getis, A. & Ord, J.K. (1992), 'The Analysis of Spatial Association by Use of Distance Statistics', *Geographical Analysis*, vol. 24, pp. 189-206.
Getis, A. & Ord, J.K. (1996), 'Local Spatial Statistics: An Overview', in P. Longley & M. Batty (eds), *Spatial Analysis: Modeling in a GIS Environment*, Geoinformation International, Cambridge (UK), pp. 269-285.

38 Studies in Segregation and Desegregation

Goodchild, M. (1986), 'Spatial Autocorrelation', *CATMOG*, 47, GeoBooks, Norwich.

Gregory, D. (1985), 'Suspended Animation: The Stasis of Diffusion Theory', in D. Gregory & J. Urry (eds), *Social Relations and Spatial Structures*, Macmillan, London, pp. 296-336.

Israeli Central Bureau of Statistics (2000), 'Socio-Economic Characteristics of Population and Households in Localities and Statistical Areas', *Pub. No. 8 in the 1995 Census of Population and Housing Series*, State of Israel, Central Bureau of Statistics Publications, Jerusalem.

Jackson, P. & Smith, S.J. (1984), *Exploring Social Geography*, George Allen & Unwin, New York.

Johnston, R. J. (1991), 'People and Places in the Behavioral Environment', in: F.W. Boal & D.N. Livingstone (eds), *The Behavioral Environment*, Routledge, London.

Jones, T.P. & McEvoy, D. (1978), 'Race and Space in Cloud-Cuckoo Lane', *Area*, vol. 10, pp. 162-166.

Kendall, M.G. (1970), *Rank Correlation Methods*, 4th edition, Griffen, London.

Lambert, J. & Lambert, C. (1982), 'Race, Ethnicity and Urban Change', in A. Cochrane & L. McDowell (eds), *Urban Change and Conflict*, Open University Press.

Lee, B.A., Oropesa, R.S. & Kanan, J.W. (1994), 'Neighborhood Context and Residential Mobility', *Demography*, vol. 31(2).

Lee, T.R. (1968), 'Urban Neighborhood as a Social-Spatial Scheme', *Human Relations*, vol. 21, pp. 241-268.

Lee, T.R. (1978), 'Race, Space and Scale', *Area*, vol. 10, pp. 365-367.

Ley, D. (1983), *A Social Geography of the City*, Harper & Row, New York.

Lieberson, S. (1981), 'An Asymmetrical Approach to Segregation', in C. Peach, V. Robinson & S. Smith (eds), *Ethnic Segregation in Cities*, Croom Helm, London.

Massey, D. & Denton, N. (1988), 'The Dimensions of Residential Segregation', *Social Forces*, vol. 76, pp. 281-315.

Moran, P.A.P. (1950), 'Notes on Continuous Statistical Phenomena', *Biometrika*, vol. 37, pp. 17-23.

Omer, I. (1996), *Ethnic Residential Segregation as a Structuration Process*, Unpublished Ph.D Thesis, Tel-Aviv University, Tel-Aviv.

Peach, C., (1975), 'Introduction: The Spatial Analysis of Ethnicity and Class', in C. Peach (ed), *Urban Social Segregation*, Longman, London.

Peach, C. (1979), 'Race and Space', *Area*, vol. 11, pp. 82-89.

Portugali, J. (1991), 'An Arab Segregated Neighborhood in Tel-Aviv: The Case of Adjami', *Geography Research Forum*, vol. 11, pp. 37-50.

Relph, E. (1976), *Place and Placelessness*, Pion, London.

Sack, R.D. (1980), *Conceptions of Space in Social Thought: A Geographic Perspective*, Macmillan, London.

Schnell, I. & Benjamini, Y. (1999), 'Socio-Spatial Lifestyles and Segregation', www.cybergeo.presse.fr, April 1999.

Tuan, Y.F. (1977), *Space and Place: The Perspective of Experience*, University of Minnesota Press, Minneapolis.

Waldorf, B.S. (1993), 'Segregation in Urban Space: A New Measurement Approach', *Urban Studies*, vol. 30 (7), pp. 1151-1164.

Wong, D. (1997), 'Spatial Dependency of Segregation Indices', *Canadian Geographer*, vol. 41 (2).

Woods, I.R. (1976), 'Aspects in the Calculation of Segregation Indices: London and Birmingham, 1961 and 1971', *Tijdschrift voor Econ. en Soc. Geografie*, vol. 67 (3).

3 Segregation in Everyday Life Spaces: A Conceptual Model

IZHAK SCHNELL

Introduction

Until the nineties most of the literature on spatial segregation focussed on the discovery of spatial forms of segregated places in Cartesian space, while analysing the forces that shape these segregated forms separately based either on positivist, behavioural, or structural approaches (Jackson & Smith, 1984). In accordance, spatial segregation has been defined in terms of the uneven distribution of predefined social groups in space and as a state of isolation in both social interaction and residential space dimensions (Boal, 1978; 1987).

These approaches suffered from three main weaknesses. First, the spatial and social dimensions were not associated with each other by any common theoretical framework (Harvey, 1989). Instead, it was assumed that social distance and spatial and temporal distances were monotonically correlated. Greater social differences among social groups should result in stronger spatial segregation for longer periods of time.

Second, the literature on spatial segregation failed to specify the meanings of particular segregated distributions for inter-group factors such as isolation and marginalisation. For example, the possibility that two communities with equal dissimilarity indices of about I.D. = 90 may represent completely different situations of segregation was not considered. One may represent a highly isolated group, whose communication routes with other social groups in space is blocked, and this isolation is used as a means to marginalise or even delegitimise the group. The other may represent a group of people who choose to share a common neighbourhood but who maintain open routes of communication with other groups and display a willingness to accept outsiders who adopt their lifestyle or to allow their members to leave the neighbourhood.

Third, it was assumed that segregated territories are inevitably continuous units of space, characterised by self-evident ethnic, racial or other identities, shared by society at large. Furthermore, it was assumed

40 Studies in Segregation and Desegregation

that the life conditions of individuals are determined, to a large extent, by their compact communal surroundings within relatively closed boundaries. The goal of this paper is to develop a general conceptual framework for the analysis of socio-spatial segregation. I argue that segregation characterises the experiences of individuals in their daily life. In accordance, I suggest focussing on the analysis of the structures of interaction of agents with meaningful others in their everyday life spaces. The study begins with an analysis of the segregation of individuals in their homes as their daily life 'zero points' and in respect to their actual everyday life spaces. Two aspects of segregation may be raised. First is recording the social identity of potential and actual meaningful others in agents' everyday life spaces, leading to the aggregation of individual members of identified social groups who also share a similar sense of identity and orientation toward segregation. This may lead to test agents with a similar configuration of identities and orientation toward a segregation tendency to agglomerate into segregated regions. Thus, the boundaries of segregated regions become one of the results of the analysis, unlike current measurements, which predefine boundaries (Schnell & Benjamini, 1999). Second is investigating typical forms of groups for the restructuring of segregating practices as part of the synergetic constitution of territorial and social identities within shared everyday life spaces.

Basic Propositions

I suggest basing the proposed model of socio-spatial segregation on a new set of basic propositions: First, globalised spaces are treated as kaleidoscopes of a multitude of simultaneous events that occur in different spaces and places (Foucault, 1997), each of them interpreted differently by members of different social groups. This conception of space raises the importance of micro-spaces as the contexts of actions on the part of individuals and social groups as they live their daily life. Inspired by neo Kantian philosophers such as Casirer and existentialist ones such as Kierkegaard, geographers increasingly recommend treating space as a multi-layered phenomenon (Buttimer, 1981; Harvey, 1989; Lefever, 1991; Soja 1996; Castells, 1996).

The basic layer is the material one that constitutes the infrastructure of our technological and information society. This is a complex, open and self-organising spatial system in which matter, energy and people interact with their environments (Portugali, 1997).

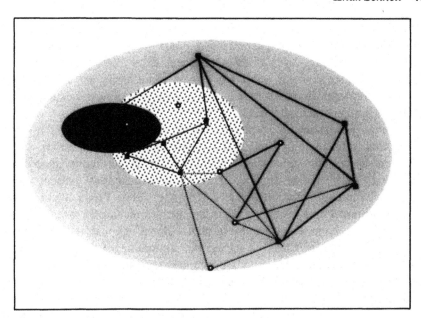

Figure 3.1 The form of a group cultural space

Legend

- ⬛ Formative territory
- ▦ The segregated group residential areas
- ■ The segregated group places
- ○ Others' places
- ········· A non-segregated socio-spatial network
- ——— A segregated socio-spatial network
- ▒ A group's spatial horizon of awareness

The second layer is the cultural one which is constituted as a communal text written and rewritten daily by members of the socio-cultural group. Cultural space may represent a lifeworld organised around several socio-spatial elements. The form of such a layer may crystallise around a 'formative territory' as the cradle of the group identity and a set of 'places' as the group centres of care, with some of these places located within the formative territory and some of them outside it.

The third element is a set of communication networks spread around the group's spatial horizons of collective awareness as the fourth element

42 *Studies in Segregation and Desegregation*

of cultural spaces (Figure 3.1). In heterogeneous societies, which are so common in this era of globalisation, each socio-cultural group may constitute a different layer of cultural space. These cultural layers, unlike traditional conceptions of relatively closed social areas, are characterised by relatively open horizons which may create large interstices among the different groups' cultural spaces.

Social groups are no longer treated as if they are contained by their immediate surroundings but as the beginning of an exploration of the different routes through which people arrive at particular places and transcend their diverse traffic of ideas and meanings without being necessarily contained by these places (Massey, 1984). This is a conception of discontinuous and relatively open territorial boundaries, which allow a merger between the local and the global. 'Glocal' (global + local) spaces become possible because of accessible communication infrastructures, social communication networks and intersections and a cultural ethos that together inform the search for local identities while maintaining openness and responsibility for the world at large (Castells, 1996).

Inter-group relations may not be managed from exclusive territorial bases, but from different spatio-cultural layers with large interstice territories and spaces (Piette, 1990; Racine & Megar, 1997). This brings into focus a new set of questions concerning the relations among social groups that project different meanings to the same spaces and locations. Competition over the assignment and control of meanings to spaces and locations may create a variety of possible situations:

- Mono-cultural domination over exclusive territories as it has been assumed in the Cartesian model of space and as it may be experienced by highly segregated groups.
- Pluri-cultural interstices in which different groups assign different meanings to particular locations regardless of alternative meanings assigned by other groups to the same locations.
- Multi-cultural interstices in which different groups assign different meanings to particular locations while at the same time appraising alternative meanings assigned by alternative groups to the same locations.
- Trans-cultural interstices which are shared by more than one group. Such places have the potential for inter-group co-operation, assimilation and acculturation.

Izhak Schnell 43

- Conflictual interstices in which different groups assign conflicting meanings to the same places, viewing alternative meanings as a threat to their identities.
- Empty interstices, which supply neutral spaces for all cultural groups with none of the groups transforming these spaces into meaningful territories and places.

In this respect, segregation may be defined as the struggle of a group to avoid the stress of interstices in their cultural spaces by two possible strategies. First is an attempt to dominate a mono-cultural territorial unit within relatively closed boundaries. Second is to create a network of intra-group communication networks within a boundless spatial horizon that is isolated from communication networks with intersticed spatial layers. Territorial division of space into bounded units, associated with the dichotomous categorisation of these territories as 'ours' against 'theirs', is deeply rooted in human experience as a way to increase the sense of meaningfulness, control, norms and, thus, the security and comfort of marginal groups (Relph, 1977). In today's globalised everyday life this process may become a matter of survival for marginal groups which may lose confidence in their ability to maintain their identities in more open and complex multi-layered spaces (Habermas, 1991). This complexity stems from three characteristics of globalised spaces: The mixture of different groups in shared spaces forming interstices with competing sets of meanings; the vast infiltration of global information into locales; and the fragmentation of everyday life activity orbiting into separate territorial units devoted to such things as dwelling, work, shopping and leisure. Sibley (1995) analyses the structuration of segregated territories as a purification process of space in search of ethnically authentic roots by the inclusion of similar others and the exclusion of different others. Such a strategy may be adopted by powerful groups in order to marginalise subordinate groups (Sack, 1983) but also as a marginal group's strategy for survival (Sibley, 1995, 1998). I propose to also consider the second type of strategies in which social groups isolate their socio-spatial layers from intersticed socio-spatial layers, which are associated with segregation.

Second, we adopt Giddens' proposition concerning the duality of agency and structure. Giddens looks at the simultaneous manner in which structures enable human agency and agency influences structure in a way that transcends the dualism of deterministic views of structure and voluntaristic views of agency (Giddens, 1984). According to the theory, the recursive interaction of agency and structure is played out through the

44 Studies in Segregation and Desegregation

media of time-space. Agents and structures participate in the regionalisation of time-space. Following Buttimer's interpretation of Vidal De La Blache's concept of 'Geners De Vie', everyday life spaces are defined in terms of networks of interactions starting from the zero point of the home and reaching out to people's horizons of involvement in their daily life (Buttimer, 1981). This orbit of everyday life activities is people's major arena for the constitution of their selves and their lifeworld (Buttimer 1977; Giddens, 1984). Thus, the structuration process may concern the simultaneous restructure of human and place identities.

Lifestyles may differ in the ways in which localised time-space organisations are ordered within more deeply sedimentary social systems. One such difference is the importance of face-to-face interactions in a group's time-space routines relative to the importance of distanced ones, with increasing salience assigned to distanced interactions and influences in open lifestyles. The association of social lifestyle with location in social space and in the construction of daily activity orbits is based on the assumption that any social project requires meeting with others and movement in space. Hence, social 'projects' and spatial 'paths' are dialectically associated as are human lifeworlds and their outer surroundings (Hagerstrand, 1975; Pred, 1989).

The theory of structuration implies that agents' everyday life spaces are the basic arenas in which segregation may be practised as one possible set of socio-spatial strategies that social groups adopt. Segregation may be defined, in this context, as a set of strategies directed toward distancing social groups from the rest of society within either closed territorial boundaries and/or sets of intra-group networks within an isolated spatial layer. At the other pole of this set of strategies, social groups may practice openness to the world beyond local boundaries and intra-ethnic networks.

Third, the formation of identities and sense of territoriality is an essential aspect of the socio-spatial struggles of inter-groups and their use of segregation strategies as part of them. An analysis of the structuration of the sense of self and collective identities as well as of the sense of 'others' reveals that these concepts develop in a communicative interplay between individuals and reference groups on the level of contents as well as of social relations. Individuals are required to develop complex configurations of their personal and collective identities as well as the identities of others with some of them representing human individuality as indivisible, distinctive and unique senses of selves, while others represent shared identities with other members of a group. The debate between modernist and postmodernist philosophers exposes a range of possible forms of constituting identities along a continuum that may assign privileged status either to the 'other' or to the 'self'.

At the one pole human beings may adopt a postmodernist attitude by assigning an ontological privilege to the 'other' (Derida, 1986, 1987; Levinas, 1971, 1988). Derida and Levinas claim that the 'other' is always different from anybody's sense of the 'other' even when encountered with deep empathy. They conclude their arguments with a moral demand to accept the others' 'otherness' without exception. This sense of otherness, however, is not necessarily an estranging experience, since through empathic inclination one may display traces of the 'other'. Both Derida and Levinas, call for social relations that may balance between peoples' openness to accepting the others' personal and collective identities as unique and privileged entities and empathy toward the other's appearances which are based on the recognition that some similarities among individuals and groups may be perceived. Since in globalised everyday life individuals may be exposed to a multitude of reference groups and be able to enter into encounters with each of them via telecomunication systems as well as to easily withdraw from them, they may tend to develop low commitments to any of them (Bauman, 1995). According to post-modern ethics a person or a group may develop a cohesive sense of identity, which is based more on a sense of internal continuity and unity than on sameness or negation of other reference groups (Noy, 1982, 1995). In the same way, others may be perceived as unique and autonomous entities worthy of empathy instead of being reduced to their generalised images as either similar or different others. As a consequence individuals may form complex configurations of identities in respect to different reference groups, allowing for each fragment to move into the centres of their identity fields according to circumstances (Lewin, 1951).

At the other pole, individuals may adopt modernistic social psychological attitudes and treat others as the background for the constitution of people's personal and collective identities (Mead, 1934; Tajfel, 1981). Sameness with particular reference groups and sometimes negation of some others may become major driving forces in the constitution of identities. Urban lifestyles frequently are perceived to represent such forms of identity formation. Individuals choose to constitute primary relations with similar reference groups while treating the rest as strangers (Fischer, 1985; Lofland, 1973). Buber (1967) used to believe in the human possibility of achieving a true understanding of some others by entering into intimate relations with them. But the most extreme situation may be defined as the **segregated form of identity formation**. In such

46 Studies in Segregation and Desegregation

cases others are reduced into similar members of 'my' group and incompatible members of negated groups, with both reference groups playing a dominant role in the formation of segregated identities. In these cases others are generalised allowing for the segregated collective identity to dominate individual configurations of identities.

According to the fourth proposition, we have argued that social practices are always situated in space as active participants in the formation of segregated identities. Therefore, I consider territoriality to be the basic concept that unifies social groups with particular spaces in one conceptual framework. Territoriality relates to the constitution of meaningful bounded fields in the everyday life spaces of individuals and groups as part of the human-space dialectic. In the dialectic human beings develop attachments to their territories, gain some type of autonomy and control over their territories and mutually constitute their own and their territories' identity (Brown, 1987; Schnell, 1995; 1997). This human-space dialectical structuration of attachment, control and identity may be experienced in different scales and contexts: personal autonomy (Sommer, 1969), intimate group autonomy (Altman, 1975), and national self-determination (Anderson, 1986; Chisholm and Smith, 1990). Segregating practices may be defined as a set of territorial strategies that social groups use in order to increase inter-group distances – dominating territorial fields, closing inter-group boundaries and channelling socio-spatial interactions into intra-group networks.

When social groups compete at constituting territorial identities in shared spaces, power relations may become essential. Segregating practices may strive to marginalise or even delegitimise the other group's territorial interpretative frames and institutionalise its own in order to avoid ambiguities of interstitial spaces. Social groups which are not socialised to the complexity of pluri-cultural lifestyles in multi-layered spaces, and/or whose identities may be threatened within the framework of open multi-layered spaces, by internal or external forces may more likely adopt one of the two suggested territorial strategies.

The current model is based on the argument that segregation as a socio-spatial strategy, may be structured and restructured both in everyday life spaces and in socially structured sets of daily practices. In the spatial context segregation is measured as agents weighed probabilities to encounter members of alternative groups in performing major social projects within major everyday life spaces. In the social context segregation is interpreted as agents' use of socially structured segregating practices. Such practices tend to conform to a basic structure, which increases distances among members of different groups in a variety of forms (Figure 3.2). The next section of the paper will develop the socio-spatial segregation index in agents' everyday life space, followed by an additional section, which investigates the structure of segregating practices.

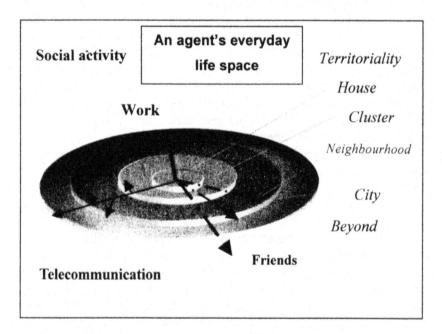

Figure 3.2 An agent's everyday life space

Segregation in Everyday Life Space

The first part of the model focusses on agents' isolation or exposure to inter-group face-to-face and distanced interactions using a mathematical index proposed by Schnell and Benjamini (1999). It is studied from the agents' locales both in their interaction and territorial contexts and in respect to their everyday life spaces. The key question in the interactive context concerns the meaningful others in the performance of major everyday life practices. The key question in the territorial context concerns the meaningful territorial bases upon which daily actions are practiced (Figure 3.2). The identity of meaningful others in agents' interactions may represent one's actual isolation or exposure, while the composition of the population in the aforementioned territories may represent people's

48 *Studies in Segregation and Desegregation*

probability to encounter others, either from their group or from alternative groups.

The justification for distinguishing between the interactive and the territorial contexts also receives certain empirical support in studies on the relocation of the poor in the city. Buttimer (1981) showed that the relocated in Glasgow failed to reconstitute a satisfying daily activity orbit around their new homes despite the fact that they were relocated close to their former neighbours. Fried (1963) showed how the relocation of the West Enders in Boston caused alienation and pathology among Italians as a response to the disruption of spatial identity regardless of group identity. In Germany there is even more direct evidence that desegregated migrant workers in residential space are not necessarily more likely to make inter-group contacts (Alpheis, 1990; Nauck, 1988).

Everyday life activities are frequently divided into several spheres of practices, with most literature distinguishing among work, social contacts, shopping, personal arrangements and leisure activities. The most significant distinction in capitalist societies is the socio-spatial separation between home and work with increasing attention devoted to leisure activities with friends. We add to these two spheres of direct encounters with meaningful others in the work and friends spheres, the realm of telecommunication, which through cheap international telephone systems, internet and other telecommunication systems has drawn a fraction of global horizons into agents' everyday reach. In each of these three spheres of daily activities we investigate the social composition of agents' meaningful others whether they belong to the same social group or to alternative ones.

Territorial bases are hierarchical in character with four qualitatively concentric scales (Saarinen, 1976; Rowles, 1981). The most intimate scale is of personal space which surrounds individuals like bubbles (Hall, 1966; Sommer, 1969) but which we consider to be irrelevant to our study. In the second scale the zero point of an agent's sense of territoriality is located at the home as the representation of the agent's identity and as the focus of everyday activities (Cooper, 1975). At the same time, home territories are perceived to be essential for the formation of autonomous identities (Bachelard, 1969; Altman, 1975). The range of daily activities is the third territorial sphere in which agents reach out of their homes to fulfil their daily necessities such as work, shopping and leisure. This scale is frequently sub-divided into three different sub-scales. The most intimate one is of clusters of neighbouring homes along a common street in which people are recognised and social interactions with neighbours tend to take place (a cluster). The intermediate one is the neighbourhood as a territorial setting which represents agents' social identity and lifestyle. The third and widest scale is the neighbourhood unit, which supplies its residents with daily services. Recent research, conducted in Tel Aviv, has confirmed the relevance of the two more intimate characteristics of neighbourhoods as centres of social interactions, and as representing groups' identities. However, they were only indeterminate evidence of the relevance of the neighbourhood as a centre of daily services (Schnell & Goldhaber, 1999). The highest scale is that of far more extensive spatial units such as city and states, with which agents become acquainted through mass communication and socialisation.

Geographers have identified several models that describe different ways of using everyday life spaces as part of a wider social lifestyle. Buttimer (1981) distinguished between localist and urbanite lifestyles. Localists are characterised by their concentric and narrow orbits of daily activity patterns, which are also associated with strong attachment to their home vicinity. Urbanites are characterised by their high mobility in the metropolitan area and by the fragmentation of their activity orbits into separate socio-spatial contexts. Hall (1984) characterised a suburban lifestyle as a dual space of home and community in the homogeneous suburb on the one hand, and work, shopping, services and social activities performed in the wide metropolitan reaches, on the other hand. The new middle class has introduced a new post-modern lifestyle, characterised by condensed time-space practices, which extend over long hours within the dense and heterogeneous inner city milieux (Rose, 1984; Short, 1989; Schnell, 1996). In addition, studies on the activity of ghetto members' activity patterns portray dense and short distance movements with intensive intra-ethnic networks, which are restricted to the boundaries of the ethnic enclave (Boal 1987; Waldinger, 1993). I argue that a reliable index must take into consideration the segregation of agents in respect to the different territories in which they conduct their everyday life. This means that close neighbours may experience different degrees of segregation depending on their styles of participation in everyday life spaces (Schnell & Benjamini, 1999).

In measuring the rate of isolation of agents from or exposure to members of other groups, I represent the agent interactive dimension by the group identities of meaningful others in the three major spheres of daily activities: work, friends and telecommunication. I represent the territorial dimension by the probability that agents will be exposed to members of other groups in the four major hierarchically ordered territorial bases: close

50 Studies in Segregation and Desegregation

vicinity, neighbourhood, city and the rest of the world (Figure 3.2). The equation for segregation suggested by Schnell and Benjamini (1999) defines an initial rate for a person's segregation and a weighing method. In order to enable the weighing on a meaningful scale, the initial rate which is originally measured by a proportion p is re-expressed into the logistic scale: $s(p)=log(p/(1-p))$. Averaging segregations at different activity spheres and territorial bases is done in much the same way as explanatory variables explain the probability of an outcome in a logistic regression. As p varies between 0 and 1, $s(p)$ varies monotonically over the entire unbounded range. At $p=1/2$, $s(p)=0$, and it is further anti-symmetric for this value: $s(p) = - s(1-p)$.

The index of segregation at each of the lowest levels is the logistically transformed number of the group's members n_i, out of the number of alternative group members N_i in the relevant territorial bases or activity spheres. Thus for example, for the House territory with $n_i(H)$ and $N_i(H)$ defined as above, the logistically transformed segregation is

$$\log \left(\frac{n(H)_i / N(H)_i}{1 - n(H)_i / N(H)_i} \right) = \log \left(\frac{n(H)_i}{N(H)_i - n(H)_i} \right)$$

In practice a third value is added to each of the counts. Statistically, this sets the transformed values, at approximately their expected values for a sample from the logistic distribution. Technically, this also enables the use of the logistic transformation when $n_i = N_i$ or when $n_i = 0$, (Tukey 1977). Therefore, the index for the segregation of the vicinity, for example, is defined as

$$SP(H)_i = \log \left(\frac{n(H)_i + \frac{1}{3}}{N(H)_i - n(H)_i + \frac{1}{3}} \right)$$

The proposed index for socio-spatial segregation is calculated as the average value of the segregation in the interactive and the territorial dimensions, each of the two, in turn, being the average of three activity spheres and four territorial bases. Below, the specific formulation, which includes the seven aforementioned interactive spheres and territorial bases, is given. This formulation is suggested as a standard structure in order to make the index friendlier for comparative studies. Nevertheless, the index is open to the consideration of alternative social or spatial categories if they are relevant for the analysis of the constitution of everyday life practices of particular groups.

The weighing process is essential to the characterisation of the overall segregation assessment and may involve two sets of weights: time related weights and salience related weights. One set of time weights measures the proportion of time the agent spends in each territorial base for the spatial segregation index. A second set of time weights measures the proportion of time the agent spends in each daily activity for the social segregation index. Similarly, two other sets of weights express the relative salience that agents assign to each of these spatial and social settings. The information leading to the weights can be based on actual observations, on registered self-reporting (diaries) or on the respondents' answers to a questionnaire.

If $T_i(r)$ is the time spent at home territory r, and $V_i(r)$ is its perceived salience, we form their product $W^*_i(r) = T_i(r) \, V_i(r)$, and normalise it by the sum of these weights over all territorial bases,

$$W_i(r) = W^*_i(r) \Big/ \sum_{4\,territories} W^*_i$$

to acquire a set of weights that equal 1. Then, we define

$$SP_i = \sum_{4\,territories} W_i(r) S_i(r)$$

Similarly, if $T_i(a)$ is the time spent at activity a, and $V_i(a)$ is its perceived salience, we form their product $W^*_i(a) = T_i(a) \, V_i(a)$, and normalise it by the sum of these weights over all activity spheres,

$$W_i(a) = W^*_i(a) \Big/ \sum_{3\,actions} W^*_i$$

to obtain a set of weights whose sum is 1. Then, we define

$$SO_i = \sum_{3\,actions} W_i(a) S_i(a)$$

To obtain the overall socio-spatial segregation index, we combine SP_i and SO_i using two fixed weights $W(SP)$ and $W(SO)$ whose sum is 1, to obtain the weighed average.

$$SPS_i = [W(SP) \, SP_i + W(SO) \, SO_i]$$

52 Studies in Segregation and Desegregation

In conclusion, socio-spatial segregation is calculated as an agent's weighed average rate of isolation expressed on a logistic scale in a set of interactive and territorial contexts within everyday life spaces. The individual weights reflect the relative weight of each of these interactive and territorial dimensions of the agent's everyday life, both in terms of time spent and in their perceived importance.

The **SPS** index of segregation enjoys the same properties as the initial segregation indices it averages. It varies over the entire range of numbers, positive values indicating high degrees of socio-spatial isolation of the individual from members of alternative groups and negative values indicating high degrees of exposure to members of other groups. Values close to *0*, (e.g. *-1< **SPS** < +1*) express an inter-group mixture of about equal probability for socio-spatial interactions with members of the same group or of other groups. It may add some helpful insight to recall that the re-expression $e^{SPS}/(1 + e^{SPS})$ takes the value of the combined **SPS** back into the probability range of *0* to *1*.

It is important to emphasise that the proposed segregation index $\textbf{SPS}_i$ is evaluated for individuals residing at their site. A different question is how to study the spatial pattern of those who live in segregation. The most common solution would be to create an isoline map based on the triangulation of the values of the segregation rates of agents. Schnell, Benjamini and Ben-Adiva (1999) have made use of this method, but several other common mapping solutions may be implemented as well. Nonetheless, there may be some difficulties from the fact that two agents residing in the same place, while sharing the same territorial related basic initial segregation values, may end up with different $\textbf{SPS}_i$, either because of different weights or because of different social segregation levels $\textbf{SO}_i$. A second cause of difficulty is those sites with no agents from the studied group. Using computerised mapping methods such as homopletic maps or response surface analysis may solve the first problem. A remedy for the second problem is to use only the spatial component in the definition, i.e. setting $\textbf{SPS}_i = \textbf{SP}_i$. At this point it is worthwhile mentioning that adding one third to the initial proportion of the group members relative to others enables the calculation of the spatial indices even in places where no individual from the investigated group resides. Furthermore, in such a case, if one house has 10 individuals and the other has 40, the **SP** at the location of the first house will be higher then at the other, correctly reflecting the spatial segregation that individuals from the investigated group have if they join either house. I turn now to the investigation of the structure of segregating practices that may be institutionalised in segregated situations.

Izhak Schnell 53

The Structure of Segregating Practices

The quantitative analysis of potential and actual encounters with members of other groups in everyday life must be supplemented by a qualitative analysis of the structure of segregating encounters in everyday community practices. Segregation is defined in this respect as agents' structuration of separatist practices among social groups. Each segregating practice may be characterised by a typical structure. The two following examples are chosen from several hundreds of interviews and quotations from the Israeli Palestinian experiences in Jaffa and the Jewish ultra-orthodox. They may demonstrate the basic structure of any segregating practice.

The first example occurred on June 29, 1997. A group of ultra-orthodox Jews demonstrated in Jerusalem. They threw stones at passing cars on Bar Ilan Boulevard - a main route that crosses an area which ultra-orthodox residents have recently dominated. In addition, they threw stones and glass bottles at the police. A taxi driver was wounded and several police cars were destroyed (Yediot Achronot, 1997).

In the second example an Arab from Jaffa described his feelings about where he lived:

> We never were able to realise what our future in this place is. Would we continue to live here or not? We felt as if our lives here were temporary and the government housing companies would decide to destroy the neighbourhood and we would be forced to leave the place either by requisition or with low compensations.

The most fundamental characteristic of these segregating practices is a basic structure, which distinguishes between agents who directs action toward other agents in order to distance particular agents (Figure 3.3). The

Agent(s) direct action to **Other(s)** in order to distance	**Subjects of action**

Figure 3.3 The basic structure of a segregating practice

subjects of the act of distancing may be from a segregated group, from a negating group or a third side in inter-group relations. In the case of the ultra-orthodox, the agents were members of a segregated group who directed actions toward outsiders in order to distance them from the group

54 Studies in Segregation and Desegregation

territory. In the second case of the Palestinian from Jaffa, the Ministry of housing (outsiders) is perceived to be the potential agent who may direct action toward the Arab community (insiders) in order to exclude them (insiders) from the neighbourhood.

These examples show that segregating practices may be defined as the attempt of agents to increase social and spatial distance among individuals and social groups. This may be achieved by delineating inter-personal or inter-group boundaries and closing these boundaries. In this context I do not use the concept of exclusion because exclusion and inclusion are dichotomous while segregating practices should be understood along a continuum between exclusion and inclusion. Accordingly, social groups may either act in order to increase inter-group distances to some degree - segregating themselves or other groups - or to decrease distances, so promoting trans-cultural and multi-cultural spaces characterised by either socio-spatial integration or at least mutual tolerance.

In each of the segregating practices an identification system may be recognised. In the two examples reality is perceived as comprised of relations between two worlds: the segregated group - either ultra-orthodox or Israeli Palestinians - against Zionists. Individuals emphasise their collective identity as members of an ethnic, racial or class group, identifying themselves against generalised others who lose in their eyes their identities as individuals.

Three complementary aspects typify the identification system that characterises segregating social practices (De-Rivera, 1977; Schnell, 1994, 1997). First, individuals and groups may constitute a generalised sense of 'us' against a generalised sense of 'others'. This basic process of 'identification of collective identities which distinguishes between 'them' and 'us' creates inter-group boundaries and increases socio-spatial distance (Hoggett, 1992; Sibley, 1995; Schnell, 1997). Moreover, segregating practices tend to depress the constitution of segmented identities which denote complex configuration of sub-identities including personal ones. Instead, segregating practices restructure inclusive collective identities, which undermine the salience of alternative sub-identities, particularly individual ones. Inter-group boundaries are fixed and strengthened in the structuration of 'our' group against the others.

Secondly, individuals and groups may develop a strong sense of 'identification with' the group and a strong sense of 'estrangement' from the others. The process of getting closer to others from the group and increasing the distance from others outside the group may be associated with feelings such as security and warmth, while distancing from others outside the group may be associated with feelings such as fear, insecurity and even alienation (De-Rivera, 1977; Relph, 1977). Attempts to close boundaries between 'our' group and others seem to be a sensible response to the feelings of insecurity and fears in segregating practices (Gilman, 1985). Such practices may become oppressive to individuals both from the group and the other group. Individuals from the group may be required to identify with the group to a degree that undermines their individuality and emphasises sameness to the group's elite and opposition to members of other groups. At the same time, members of other groups may be reduced to strangers and stereotypes. In most cases the stereotypes represent the negation of the group's identity and supply the justification for their attempts to distance the two groups from each other.

Thirdly, segregating practices tend to identify members of the group as superior to the others outside the group who are perceived as inferiors. This is a sensible response to emotions such as a sense of belonging, warmth, security and sympathy to members of the group and fears, insecurities and strangeness toward the others. In such cases segregating practices may easily lead to de-personalisation, pseudo-rationalisation of deprivation and in extreme cases even de-legitimisation and de-humanisation of the others (Tajfel, 1981).

In summation, segregating practices may be experienced along a continuum starting from the restructure both of selves' and others' identities in such a way that collective identities of 'us' against 'them' dominate the field of identities, marginalising personal and collective segmented identities. In stronger segregating practices, a strong sense of identification with the group may be supplemented with a strong sense of estrangement and even alienation from members of other groups. In the most extreme cases of segregation, strangers may be stereotyped, undermining or even de-legitimising their collective identity. In this sense, the ultra-orthodox Jews threw stones in the first example on generalised and objectified non-believers and not on individual human beings. In the case of the Palestinians from Jaffa, the Arab speaker questions whether the government establishment recognises the legitimacy of his community. Both examples demonstrate the tendency of segregated people to perceive the world around them in dichotomous terms – the segregated group against the others. The segregated group's collective identity becomes a highly salient aspect of their overall configuration of identities, encountered regularly in central aspects of their daily life. They show a strong tendency to identify themselves with their own group and to de-legitimise the other (Zionist, in these cases) identity.

56 *Studies in Segregation and Desegregation*

The proposed structure enables identification of the agent's social belonging and thus the ability to distinguish between segregating practices that are initiated by members of the segregated group and those which are initiated by members of the rest of society. Thus, we suggest a more effective methodology that may distinguish between voluntary and forced segregating practices. The methodology reveals that in particular cases of both voluntary and forced segregation, segregating practices may be identified and characterised. In contrast to segregating practices, social groups may adopt practices that are oriented toward getting closer to or including 'others'. This strategy of either integration into a community or multi or trans-cultural dialogue should be the focus of a separate study.

The identification process adds some complexity to the basic structure of segregating practices since each of the three elements of the structure may be classified either as members of the segregated group or members of a competing group. This leads to distinctions among eight different types of segregating practices (Table 3.1). The eight possible strategies for actions present four narratives, each of which may be initiated either by members of the segregated group or by members of competing groups.

Table 3.1 The range of possible segregating practices

No.	Agent	Direct action Toward	Concerning Subjects	Segregating narrative
1	Insiders	Insiders	Insiders	Group's self isolation
2	Insiders	Insiders	Outsiders	Group marginalises others
3	Insiders	Outsiders	Insiders	Group restricts encounters
4	Insiders	Outsiders	Outsider	Conflict by insiders
5	Outsiders	Insiders	Insiders	Conflict by outsiders
6	Outsiders	Insiders	Outsiders	Others restrict encounters
7	Outsiders	Outsiders	Insiders	Others marginalise group
8	Outsiders	Outsiders	Outsiders	Others isolate group

The first strategy in which the actions of agents are directed toward distancing members of their own group may lead to self-isolation of the segregated group from the rest of society. When agents direct actions toward members of their own group concerning the distancing of members of the other groups, they marginalise the other group. In the third strategy in which agents direct their actions toward members of the other group

Izhak Schnell 57

concerning the distancing of these others, a conflictive situation develops between the segregated group and the rest of society. The offensive side in the conflict is dependent on the initiator of the actions. The last strategy, in which agents direct actions toward members of other groups concerning the distancing of themselves from the others leads to restricted encounters in which the agents use one or more of the strategies to undermine the value or the relevancy of the others.

The Territorial Context of Segregating Practices

The strong need of the ultra-orthodox to avoid any interstice spaces of ambiguity may be demonstrated in Kiva's experience as the writer Bar-Yosef (1985) articulates:

> He was afraid of the experience and scared to confront secular worldviews. God fearing people ought to remain rooted in the home of God and to flourish in places of worship. They are not expected to mix with marginal and faulty others who may expose them to heretical and contaminating ideas. To close us in the home of God is a safer route. Any attempt to search for new routes may be too risky, like a person entering a forest full of snakes, scorpions and beasts of pray.

Arab adolescents from Jaffa present more moderate worldviews in which ethnic boundaries are more fluid. They describe their fear of leaving their enclave and entering leisure centres on weekend nights without the company of a whole group and without hiding their original identity. Despite their fears, they allow for some spatial interstices although these interstices reinforce their subordinate status outside their formative territory.

Formative territories in the experience of the Palestinians are the Arab traditional neighbourhoods in which the Palestinian history is embedded. These neighbourhoods became cores of sentiments for Arab dwellers (Ben-Arzi, 1973) and reminders of the golden age of a Palestinian majority in the Jewish renewed hill of ancient Jaffa, as in the country as a whole. The core of this formative territory may be the mosque, as one secular young woman expressed so effectively:

> Everyday when I return home from the Jewish areas and I confront the Arab traditional houses, I hear the Arab language in the streets, and above all, I hear the muezzin, and I feel the relief of returning home. The

58 *Studies in Segregation and Desegregation*

muezzin call to the believers sounds to me like a well known mantra that reminds me that life in this area is run by Arab norms (Interview).

Formative territories in the experience of the ultra-orthodox may be divided into front and back ones. Front places are synagogues and religious schools that are both cores of religious and communal life and places from which the congregation is controlled and organised. The ultra-orthodox control system tends to value collective identities over personal ones. Kiva's desperate attempt to fight the rise of self-awareness by devoting himself to the demanding routines of religious practices may demonstrate it:

> He devoted himself to studying the Bible. He committed himself to going over all the interpretations again and to reviewing Psalms daily. Every morning he went to wash in the water hole. He stayed long for morning and evening prayers in a way that made him busy all day long. He closed his ears to any defunct chat. He committed himself to returning to his youth school in Jerusalem and to joining the self-assured community of scholars (Bar Yosef, 1985, 43-44).

In this example Kiva uses the strict demands put on a religious person in order to frame himself within the social norms and not allow himself free time for hesitation. He looks for communal support in his well-known school (*shule*). By committing himself to the *shule* lifestyle Kiva tries to depress any feelings that might lead him to reconstitute his identity autonomously and to fuse into the collective identity. This is not just a voluntary commitment to the *shule* as a formative territory but a response to a strict social control mechanism:

> Obedience is learnt from early childhood... This is the essence of the educational system. Complete obedience to parents, rabbis, to the wise men of their generations, to the Bible and to God's words (Bar Yosef, 1985, 244).

When he felt the need to refresh himself in a secular milieu, he was not able to overcome the control mechanisms:

> How would he leave his home without a convincing excuse?... For two weeks he searched for any excuse but could not find any. His everyday life was so organised, fixed and thin that any action out of the routine required explanations and wonder (Bar Yosef, 1985, 182).

Izhak Schnell 59

Distinction between back zones and front zones in ultra-orthodox territories may be associated mainly with gender. Synagogues, *shules* and religious public buildings, which are front zones, are dominated by men, while back zones are the spaces dominated by women and associated with family life and child rearing. Gender separation receives its impetus from the synagogue in which women are isolated into a peripheral section. In terms of chronology, it starts in kindergarten and extends to all life's circles, excluding private life at home. At the age of twelve girls are forced to join the women's section in the synagogue.

> Tamar described her feelings of insult as if she had been thrown out of the Garden of Eden without knowing what wrong she had done (Rotem, 1992, 165).

Women are considered the princesses of home spaces. These spaces are enlarged to include the domains of children as well as limited and well-controlled work environments. Women view their roles as child rearing, supporting husbands to enable them to study and managing their homes. In return they gain safe surroundings:

> Women search for protection. That is why ultra-orthodox women look for well-structured and tightly disciplined lifestyles which supply them with protection. If she really had wanted to cross boundaries.... In the general society she would have felt lost. All her urges and fears would have erupted (Rotem, 1992, 16).

Gita continued to describe:

> how she avoided buses and when she was once forced to use a bus she was shocked by the enormous pictures on the walls. Since then she has put all her efforts into distancing her children from a world full of cheap infernal stimuli (Rotem, 1992, 40).

These examples show how social groups may constitute mono-cultural worlds, which discriminate between intra- and inter-group forms of interaction. Intra-group interactions follow the narrative of bringing agents closer to each other, promoting group solidarity and distancing others. Segregating strategies may also discriminate between back and front spaces. Particularly sensitive segments of segregated groups may be protected from exposure to the outer world in back spaces. At the same time segregated groups may represent themselves to their own members as

60 *Studies in Segregation and Desegregation*

well as to others in front spaces, thus allowing some degree of exposure to the outer world.

The last question to be addressed is how segregated spaces constitute meaningful territories? The examples above imply the possibility of social groups having territorial awareness at different dimensions of spatial experience. Some of them even suggest the possibility of integrating more than one of these dimensions in one segregating practice. Generally, I identify four spatial dimensions in which the ultra-orthodox constitute their segregated territory.

First, a perceptual and mythical space is socially constituted in ultra-orthodox practices, as it is articulated in one of our first quotations. Kiva negates a topophilic bounded field of the ultra-orthodox milieu with a topophobic space of the non ultra-orthodox milieu. This territorial delineation of a highly closed bounded field, embedded with attachment and legitimised status vs. detachment and illegitimatised status devoted to outer spaces, takes place in Kiva's and the ultra-orthodoxy's mythical conceptions of the world. Kiva's mythical conception of territoriality affects his corporeal behaviour in social space. He avoids living and working outside his topophilic territorial base.

Secondly, social space is structured and restructured in a way that ensures that boundaries are closed and allow only inter-group interactions and territorial domination. The ultra-orthodox practice such strategies in various contexts. For example, since the early stages of Zionism, the ultra-orthodox have stressed the importance of settling their people in locations which will only expose them to an ultra-orthodox milieu and isolate them from non-believers:

> Try as much as you can to buy land in the vicinity of Jerusalem, the holy city. In this manner, the holiness of Jerusalem and the teaching of their wisdom will effect you in your settlements. Your children will be educated according to the Bible. You will be able to send them to religious schools in Jerusalem. This is not the case in the Galilee and in Jaffa. In these places unfortunately bad winds are already blowing, winds that uproot the Bible and those observing it because these settlements were founded by the free people (Zonenfeld in Shilhav, 1987).

The Rabbi of Satmer concludes:

> In our times, when darkness covers the land, no human being is allowed to live in a town that is not surrounded by a wall of holiness, to defend

Izhak Schnell 61

the few ultra-orthodox Jews who remain loyal to God and to his Bible (Shilhav, 1987).

This means that Kiva's need to continue his life in territorial formative cores even when the purpose is to distribute the knowledge and the love for the Bible is founded on a well-structured set of practices.

Thirdly, a material space is constituted by constructing Jewish buildings. Rabbi Roter articulated it clearly when he argued that two factors define a good milieu: Jewish *shules* (synagogues with religious schools) and righteous people. These factors are so crucial in determining territoriality that even the land of Poland, in which there were many *shules* and righteous people, was considered to be as holy as the Holy Land.

Fourth, a cosmic conception of space is adhered to as the ultra-orthodox seek to achieve domination over residential areas whose boundaries they seek to control. But the world of our everyday life is not just a neutral context of Jewish life. The land of Israel has a unique status as a holy territory. Only in the land of Israel can all the commandments be observed. But this cosmic holiness is a potentiality which can only be actualised if Judaism is also practiced in material, social and mythic spaces as well.

The discussion suggests that segregation may be understood as a set of social and territorial strategies used by individuals and social groups in their everyday life rather than a spatial form constituted by social macro forces. Such a model exposes four different components of any segregating practice as it emerges from the ultra-orthodox case, some examples from the Israeli Palestinian community and the expansion of these cases to a more comprehensive conceptual framework. In each component a set of alternatives has been identified (Table 3.2).

Table 3.2 The structure of segregating practices

Initiator	Narrative	Distancing strategy	Spatial dimension
Insider	Isolation	Identification of	Mythic
Outsider	Conflict	Identification with	Social
	Restriction	Identification as	Material
	Marginalisation		Cosmic

According to the model the different combinations of these options define the range of possible segregating practices which may be practiced

62 Studies in Segregation and Desegregation

in any case of spatial segregation. The model is comprised of four components, and each of them may be articulated in two to four different alternative forms. The first component identifies whether the initiator of a segregating practice is an insider or an outsider. The second component typifies the narrative of the distancing action. The third component characterises the forms of identification involved in the segregating practices, and the fourth component describes the spatial dimensions upon which the structuration process acts. I argue that one of the earliest tasks in any investigation should be to identify the range of practices, to identify those practices that are deeply structured in society and to analyse their influences on the group's life chances and its openness to the world.

Conclusion

The structuration of segregating practices takes place in everyday life spaces as a means of constituting a group identity. It is argued that social groups may choose to segregate themselves in order to escape to mono-cultural spaces in which their identities may be secured. They may do it by constituting for themselves a mono-cultural territorial base and/or mono-cultural interaction networks. Segregating social groups tend to constitute a collective identity, which may dominate personal identities within the group and negate the identities of alternative groups. Once segregated spaces are highly identified in ethnic or other relevant terms, the group identity as well as the negation of other identities may be regarded as key factors in the socio-spatial structuration of segregating practices. At the same time segregating practices may reinforce the structuration of the group identity as separated and superior to alternative ones.

Segregation is measured here in three aspects. First is the probability for mono-cultural interactions in the everyday life spaces of agents based on the distribution of the relevant populations in space. Second is the frequency of actual choices of mono-cultural interactions in everyday life spaces. Third is the identification of segregating practices and the analysis of their structures (Figure 3.4).

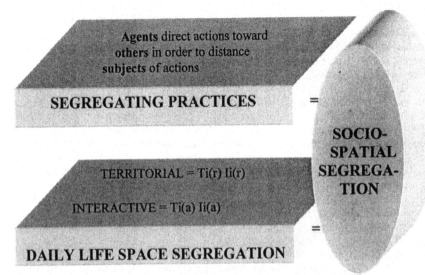

Figure 3.4 A general model of segregation in everyday life space

References

Alpheis, H. (1990), 'Erschwert die ethische Konzentration die Eingliederung?', in H. Esser, & J. Friedrichs (Hrsg), Generation und Identitet, Opladen,Westdeutscher Verlag, pp. 147-184.

Altman, I. (1975), *The Environment and Social Behavior: Privacy, Personal Space and Crowding*, Brooks/Cole, Monterey, California.

Anderson, J. (1986), 'Nationalism and Geography', in J. Anderson (ed), *The Rise of the Modern State*, Wheatsheaf, Brighton, U.K.

Bachelard, G. (1969), *The Poetics of Space*, Beacon Press, Boston.

Bar-Yosef, Y. (1985), *A Heretic Despite Himself*, Keter, Jerusalem, Israel.

Bauman, Z. (1995), 'Making and Unmaking of Strangers', *Thesis Eleven*, vol. 43, pp. 1-16.

Ben Arzi, Y. (1979), 'Arab Internal Migration in Haifa and the Formation of a Residential Pattern', *Horizons in Geography*, vol. 3, pp. 27-38.

Boal, F. W. (1978), 'Ethnic Residential Segregation', in D. T. Herbert & R.J. Johnston (eds) *Social Areas in Cities*, John Wiley & Sons, N. Y. pp. 57-96.

Boal, F. W. (1987), 'Segregation', in C. Peach (ed), *Social Geography, Progress and Prospect*, Croom Helm, Beckenham, New York.

Brown, B.B. (1987), 'Territoriality', in D. Stokols & I. Altman (eds), *Handbook of Environmental Psychology*, John Wiley, New York.

Buber, M. (1967), *The Philosophy of Martin Buber* in P.A. Schilpp & M. Friedman (eds), La Salle, Open Court.

Buttimer, A. (1976), 'Grasping the Dynamism of the Life World', *Annals of the Association of the American Geographers*, vol. 66, pp. 277-292.

Buttimer, A. (1981), 'Social Space and the Planning of Residential Areas', in A. Buttimer & D. Seamon (eds), *The Experience of Space and Place*, St. Martin's Press, New York.

64 Studies in Segregation and Desegregation

Castells, M. (1996), *The Information Age - Economy, Society and Culture: Volume I - The Rise of the Network Society*, Blackwell, London.

Chisholm, M., Smith, D. (1990), *Shared Space: Divided Space*, Unwin Hyman, London.

Cooper, C. (1975), *Easter Hill Village*, Free Press, New York.

Derida, J. (1986), *Alterite*, Osiris, Paris.

Derida, J. (1987), *Deconstruction and Criticism*, Continuum, New York.

De-Rivera, J. (1977), *A Structural Theory of the Emotion*, International Universities Press, New York.

Fischer (1985), *The Urban Experience*, Harcourt Brace Jovanovich, New York.

Foucault, M. (1997), 'Of Other Spaces', *Politics-Poetics Documenta X - the Book, Cantz*, pp. 262-272.

Fried, M. (1963), 'Grieving for a Lost Home', in L.J. Duhl, *The Urban Condition*, Simon & Schster, New York.

Giddens, A. (1984), *The Constitution of Society: Outline of the Theory of Structuration*, Polity Press, Cambridge.

Gilman, S. (1985), *Difference and Pathology: Stereotypes of Sexuality, Race and Madness*, Cornell University Press, Itharca, New York.

Habermas, J. (1991), *Society and Identity*, Poalim Press, Tel Aviv.

Hagerstrand, T. (1975), 'Space, Time and Human Conditions' in A. Karlqvist, Lundqvist & L. Snickars (eds), *Dynamic Allocation of Urban Space*, Saxon House, Farnborough.

Hall, E. T. (1966), *The Hidden Dimension*, Doubleday and Company,New York.

Harvey, D. (1989), *The Urban Experience*, Johns Hopkins University Press, Baltimore.

Hoggett, K. (1992), 'A Place for Experience: A Psychoanalytic Perspective on Boundary, Identity and Culture', *Society and Place D.*, vol. 10, pp. 345-356.

Jackson (1994), *Construction of Place, Race and Nation*, University of Minnesota Press, Minneapolis.

Jackson, P. & Smith, S. (1984), *Exploring Social Geography*, Allen and Unwin, London.

Lefebver, H. (1991), *The Production of Space*, Blackwell, Oxford & Cambridge.

Levinas, E. (1981), *Otherwise than Being or Beyond Ethics*, Martinus Nijhoff, The Hague.

Levinas, E. (1988), *Auterment quetre ou au-dela de l'essence*, Martinus Nijhoff, The Hague.

Lewin, K. (1951), *Field Theory in Social Science*, Harper, New York.

Liberson, S. (1981), 'An Asymmetrical Approach to Segregation', in C. Peach, V. Robinson, & S. Smith (eds), *Ethnic Segregation in Cities*, Croom Helm, New York, pp. 61-82.

Lofland, L. (1973), *A World of Strangers*, Basic Books, New York.

Massey, D. (1984) *Spatial Divisions of Labour: Social Structures and the Geography of Production*, Macmillan, London.

Mead, G. H. (1934), *Mind, Self and Society*, University of Chicago Press, Chicago.

Morgan, B. S. (1983), 'A Distance-Decay Interaction Index to Measure Residential Segregation', *Area*, vol. 12, pp. 211-216.

Morrill, R. L. (1991), 'On the Measure of Geographical Segregation', *Geography Research Forum*, vol, 11, pp. 25-36.

Nauck, B. (1988), 'Sozial-okologischer Kontext und auserfamiliare Beziehungen. Ein interkultureller und interkontextueller Vergleich am Beispiel von deutschen und Turkischen Familien', in 'Kolner Zeitschrift fur Soziologie und Sozialpsychologie', *Sonderheft* vol. 29, pp. 310-327.

Noy, P. A. (1982), 'Revision of the Psychoanalytic Theory of Affect', *Annual Psychanal.*, vol. 10, pp. 139-178.

Izhak Schnell 65

Noy, P. A. (1995), 'What Is the Self in the Psychology of the Self', *Sichot*, vol. 9 (3), pp.180-190.

Piette, A. (1990), 'Lécole de Chicago et la ville cosmopolite d'aujourd'hui: Lectures et relectures critiques' in A. Bastener & F. Dassetto (eds), *Imaginations et nouveaux pluralismes, une confrontation de société*, Editions Universitaires, De Boeck, Bruxelles.

Portugali, J. (1997), 'Self-Organizing Cities', *Futures*, vol. 29 (4/5), pp. 353-380.

Pred, A. (1989), 'Of Paths and Projects: Individual Behavior and Its Social Context', in K. R. Cox, & G. Golledge (eds), *Behavioral Problems in Geography Revisited*, Methuen, New York.

Racine, J. B. & Mager, C. (1997), *The Foreigner and the City*, Institute Géographie (Unpublished Paper).

Relph, E. (1977), *Place and Placelessness*, Pion Limited, London.

Rose, D. (1984), 'Rethinking Gentrification beyond Uneven Development in Marxist Urban Theory', *Society and Space*, vol. 2, pp. 47-74.

Rotem, Y. (1992), *Distant Sister*, Steimatzki, Tel-Aviv.

Rowles, G. D. (1981), 'Toward Geography of Growing Old', in A. Buttimer & D. Seamon (eds), *The Experience of Space and Place*, St. Martin Press, New York.

Saarinen, T. F. (1976), *Environmental Planning*, Miflin Co., Boston.

Sack, R. (1986), *Human Territoriality*, Cambridge University Press, Cambridge.

Schnell, I. (1994), *Perceptions of Israeli Arabs: Territoriality and Identity*, Avebury, Aldershot.

Schnell, I. (1997), 'Nature and Environment in the Socialist-Zionist Perceptions: Sense of Desolation', *Ecumene*, vol. 4 (1), pp. 69-85.

Schnell, I. (1999), *Migrant Workers in Tel Aviv*, Floersheimer Institute for Policy Studies, Jerusalem (Hebrew).

Schnell, I. & Benjamini, Y. (1999), 'Socio-Spatial Lifestyles and Segregation', *Cybergeo*.

Schnell, I., Benjamini, Y. & Ben-Adiva, A. (1999), 'An Alternative Measurement for Segregation: Migrant Workers in Tel Aviv', paper presented in Sinaia, Romania at the conference of the Commission of Urban Development and Urban Life.

Schnell, I. & Goldhaber, R. (1999), 'The Social Construction of Neighbourhoods in Tel Aviv', *Horizons in Geography* (Hebrew).

Shilhav, Y. (1987), 'Religious Impact on Cultural Space: Ultra-Orthodoxy in Jerusalem', *City and Region*, vol. 19-20, pp. 28-51.

Short, J.R. (1989), 'Yuppies, Yuffies, and the New Urban Order', *Trans. Br. Geogr.* Vol. 14, pp. 173-188.

Sibley, D. (1995), *Geographies of Exclusion*, Routledge, London.

Sibley, D. (1998), 'The Problematic Nature of Exclusion', *Geoforum* vol. 29 (3), pp. 119-123.

Soja, W. E. (1996), *Thirdspace: Journeys to Los Angeles and Other Imagined Places*, Blackwell, Oxford.

Sommer, R. (1969), *Personal Space*, Prentice-Hall, Englewood Cliffs, New Jersey.

Tajfel, H. (1982), *Social Identity and Intergroup Relations*, Cambridge University Press, Cambridge.

Tukey, J. W. (1977), *Exploratory Data Analysis*, Addison-Wesley, Massachusetts.

Waldinger, R. (1993), 'The Ethnic Enclave Debate Revisited', *Events and Debates*, pp. 444-452.

4 Migration, Places and Intercultural Relations in Cities

JEAN-BERNARD RACINE

As J.W. Berry and J.A. Laponce (1994) have pointed out, ethnicity, far from losing ground as was believed twenty years ago, runs the risk of becoming in the twenty-first century what social classes represented in the twentieth century: a major source of social tension and political conflict as well as an outstanding source of creativity and diversification, giving rise to enormous academic research, explanation and theory. However problematic the connotations associated with these concepts may be, *pluri-ethnicity* and *multiculturalism* form essential dimensions of the 'research scene' and discussions within the social sciences, whether the research is fundamental reflection or action oriented. This research leads one to question the significance of coexisting within both belonging and difference (Bastenier & Dassetto, 1990; Brun & Rhein, 1994; Haug, 1995). The distance to be covered is today considered crucial in order to pass from co-presence to interaction. The defence of an identity does not need to be inscribed in 'an absolute cultural relativism which necessarily leads to segregation and the ghetto' or to become an 'obsession combined with the refusal of all difference' (Touraine, 1996). Of course, C. Raffestin (1993) would say, 'the frontier is fundamentally a regulating mechanism which guarantees existence against the dangers of chaos'. The fact remains that if 'the defence of minorities and their rights can appear at first glance as a manifestation of multiculturalism', 'it often leads in the opposite direction, in that of hermetically closed communities and as such hostile to the coexistence with different cultures'.

Furthermore, it must be pointed out that today ethnicity is no longer considered a timeless, unchanging set of 'cultural traits' (beliefs, values, symbols, rites, codes of conduct and courtesy, language, dress and culinary habits, etc.) handed down from generation to generation within the history of the group; it is the result of the actions and reactions between the group and other groups, which are part of a perpetually evolving social organisation (Poutignat & Streiff-Fenart, 1995). Furthermore, it is the study of these inter-ethnic interactions which, in sociology as well as in

68 *Studies in Segregation and Desegregation*

geography, actually renews the set of problems and the methods of social and cultural geography. By examining the urban fabric and the social transactions that take place, these studies strive to discover how ethno-cultural groups succeed in maintaining the boundaries which differentiate them from other groups and allow them to live in a 'distance-proximity' system particular to inter-ethnic coexistence. This is much desired by someone like J. Remy (1990) or this author (Racine, 1998).

Across the evident selection of migratory flows within urban national systems, urban and demographic geography often currently refer to the question of minorities and, in particular, to that of the foreigner. The new element that identifies foreigners – an ancestral, almost consubstantial, attribute of the city – as a new category of urban actors presently in the limelight, arises out of the period of crisis which began in the seventies. In this period of crisis, social antagonisms are not expressed within industries or firms but between those who are inside and those who are outside and unemployed. In order to guarantee the solidarity of the group, it is necessary to find a scapegoat. We have always known that this is easy; the foreigner becomes the source of all evil. Nationalism and xenophobia seem to have taken over the reins from class conflicts arising from employment issues. It is necessary to distinguish between groups of foreigners since hierarchies appear quickly between different categories of foreigners, and these categories are mobile.

The city is always first a meeting place and mosaic (Grafmeyer, 1994) before it is an institution, personality, culture or even spectacle and piece of art. The presence of the foreigner in the city intersects with the fundamental principle of heterogeneity, one of the great structural invariants that we associate, along with centrality, centration, verticalisation, mechanisation, mediation, and power, with the idea of the city (Raffestin, 1979). At the heart of these issues, however, one question remains fundamental: the place made for the foreigner in urban space. In other words, the question of segregation or integration, with their extreme cases of marginalisation or exclusion on the one hand and assimilation on the other is major. The place to be made for foreigners in the city and the help to be given in view of their integration are at the heart of urban problems today and lead all types of experts to ask, among many questions, whether urban policies of mixing are necessarily the solution. Can we and should we envision the dynamics of relationships to the other in urban space in other ways? Is a cosmopolitan city viable? Will we be able to 'live together, equal and different' (Touraine, 1997)?

Let us take the centre of our cities. They are always full, wrote Roland Barthes (1993). It is in the centre that the values of civilisation are assembled and condensed: spirituality (churches), money (banks), words (plazas, cafés, promenades).... In other words, the centre has, because of its geographic position at the intersection of all paths, the vocation of assembling services and facilities. However, the centre is above all the place where the common values of the city are represented. We must ask ourselves what the centre of our cities offers today. Certainly it generally remains a great stage in the urban theatre. Nonetheless, if the play is written by a minority, it will be ignored by all those who do not identify with it.

Restoring substance to the city means dissipating the misunderstandings. It implies pointing out the barriers that have insidiously replaced the octrois and the ramparts in order to destroy them. It means doing what is necessary so that the inhabitants of the city may not only live together and meet each other but also, above all, recognise each other in their shared space (André, 1994).

From the 'Pluri' to the 'Inter': An Aim to Be Defined

It is always fitting to define a conceptual vocabulary which is essential for any type of serious study on interaction and which goes beyond a concept of segregation. That may be a temporary starting point, but this research distances itself as much as possible and questions it all along.

Pluri, multi, trans, inter. By analogy it could be said that that which allows one to think of interculturality is the same as that which should ideally characterise the interdisciplinary practices that geographers are proud of considering the stimulating elements within the social sciences. There is a world of difference between the superimposition of cultures and disciplines (the *pluri* and the *multi*) and the discovery of common axioms (condition for the *trans*) and the authentic interaction proper to interdisciplinary research. Authentic interaction simultaneously implies, beyond the simple communication of ideas, the integration of directive principles, of epistemology, methodology, approaches or the organisational elements of a community or of research.

It may also be noted that in societies where the immigrant is a stable reality rather than a temporary presence, in other words, an integral part of the host society, it is not possible to think of migration policies, particularly policies of integration, without also thinking of the exchanges that exist

70 *Studies in Segregation and Desegregation*

between the various cultures in interaction within a society. But these exchanges are not, *per se*, assimilative or multiculturalist practices. V. de Rudder and I. Taboada-Leonetti (1982) discussed the subject some time ago, saying that it 'seemed necessary to study social practices with regards to space, as often conflictual but dynamic cultural elaborations, and to give special prominence to the interactive aspect of the collective practices of urban space'. Taking into account the different types of terminology dealing either with a strategic choice or a choice in subject matter, they consider interculturality a fundamental 'introduction of persons belonging to different cultures' and formulate the explicit hypothesis that this co-presence 'activates in each one a quantity of references unknown to the other participants' (Carré, 1994). E. M. Lipiansky (1992) further defines interculturality as an 'interactive field where one questions the relationships that are created between culturally identifiable subjects (individuals or groups)'.

More than a half a century after the pioneering works of the Chicago School, these discussions are still relevant. The foreigner carries with him an 'elsewhere', the richness of which enchants or disturbs us, and he imposes on our cities the reality of 'difference' based on an 'otherness' of varying degree. This 'otherness' conditions the life of those who are different. As to the ugly word 'segregation', we obviously are discussing a larger phenomenon than merely that of the foreigner. Cities are experiencing the repercussions of sociological, economic and demographic mutations which, when combined, may provoke a real tearing of the urban fabric and engender further segregation. If spatial segregation is a fact for the poor, it results from both the mechanisms of the market economy and the desire of people who are able to choose their living environment. This is why everyone today acknowledges, in the name of the 'right to the city', the necessity to fight against spatial marginalisation and to maintain the unity of the area.

The Paradigm of the Cosmopolitan City

If the question of the foreigner and the relation to the 'other' in space remains central and becomes even more important, we may inscribe this phenomenon within the larger question of the future of the cosmopolitan city, the latter finally becoming, what some have qualified as the new urban paradigm or 'utopia' (Latouche, 1998). Thus, the cosmopolitan city – of which Toronto, considered the most ethnically diverse city in the world by

Jean-Bernard Racine 71

the UN, is the closest incarnation – appears as a privileged space gathering together several identity-based groups (nations, ethnic groups, religions) where each community maintains a distinct, autonomous, relatively permanent existence enriched by outside influences; where each group is recognised and manifests itself through particular institutions, events and spaces; where plurality is sought and encouraged by the groups themselves and by the political authorities; where each community maintains a certain distance in relation to the other communities yet encourages exchange and mutual tolerance; where public spaces exist and where the various communities meet and even confront each other.

If we follow D. Latouche's comments, this all comes about as if, when the first generation of American urban planners, in order to revive their rational idealism, were imagining new tools, such as zoning, or encouraging withdrawal and the transformation of cities into assorted suburban islands and edge cities, other urban visionaries were suggesting that crowding, insecurity and anonymity, the apparently unavoidable urban ills, were perhaps in fact the foundations of a new civilisation. In other words, perhaps, the future involved taking the city as it was and merging it with a utopia of *metropolism*, along the thinking of the Chicago School who saw many good qualities amongst what others considered a dangerous, unhealthy, uncontrollable urban muddle. In this muddle, the metropolis comes to the fore. The recent craze for cosmopolitanism is none other than its latest incarnation, less based on the logic of domination as is *metropolism* and more on the city as a source of life, liberty and creativity, as space to be developed.

At this time when all are seeking their place in the city, it is appropriate to ask what forms the city might take on and what social practices and levels of integration would arise from a converging and crystallising of foreign populations with the host population. Each of us knows, however, that this presupposition of the contribution of heterogeneity to a homogenous society, unfortunately the basis of different models and concepts proposed by researchers in the social sciences, does not correspond with reality. D. Latouche attacks the failures of cosmopolitanism in America and the enduring domination of the private. He deplores the absence of an urban project, the preference for homogeneity, the chain reactions of immigration, the ravages of enclavism and the difficulties of large coalitions. 'How do you construct an elsewhere that is also somewhere?' Clearly, assimilation is no longer defined as it once was. The same is true for integration, which we understand only refers to a ground level when it is limited to socio-professional insertion or

72 *Studies in Segregation and Desegregation*

educational structures. However, these dimensions have their importance as it is clear that institutions such as the workplace and school drive the cultural norms of the society.

The Discontinuity of Migrant Space: Questioning the Effects of Urban Policies of Mixing

It has always been thought that residential segregation has an effect on other aspects of ethnic assimilation, that whether voluntary or not, segregation limits the possibility of choice and slows the exchange of knowledge and experience. This has almost been gospel for urban planners and geographers and has led them to absolutely value the principle of urban mixing. In the 1970s authorities involved in local planning supported strategies which aimed at the dissolution and dispersion of residential concentrations. Recent research, particularly in Germany (Alpheis, 1993), calls for more caution. This work shows that other partners and other factors may intervene, such as the effects of renovation in city centres, the fact that the possibility of contact does not necessarily guarantee actual inter-ethnic contact and the knowledge that young immigrants are not automatically limited to intra-ethnic contacts when their compatriots are proportionally numerous. We are uncovering fallacious correlations linked to an overly systematic utilisation of aggregated data that leave out individual behaviours and possibilities which are highly differentiated in terms of social mobility. Studies of the factors contributing to the success – or failure – of integration have also pointed out another major conclusion: the importance of the forms of participation of individuals within a multitude of networks that define the intensity of social links (Tarrius, Marotel & Peraldi, 1988 and 1994). It is necessary to point out that in the study of ethnic assimilation, ethnic concentration or residential segregation are usually perceived as dependent structural variables, and perhaps it is forgotten that other characteristics of the social environment, such as the degree of cosmopolitanism or the degree of discrimination against minorities, may also play a role. These latter factors are rarely studied in depth. It is also important to take note of the studies which have moved from the analysis of spatial units to the analysis of networks and are beginning to establish that ethnic segmentation may be a very stable form of integration without assimilation and that the number, proportion, density, and degree of concentration of immigrants in the city do not seem to play the key role that others attribute to them in theory. This suggests that the chain of contextual mechanisms thought to facilitate a greater dispersion of foreigners over residential zones does not necessarily come into play. The idea that interethnic contacts are a central element in the process of assimilation is not necessarily confirmed.

As I. Schnell (1999) recently put it, 'most segregation measurements are based on the dissimilarity index, which in practice measures social groups' degree of uneven distribution in residential space. More sophisticated indexes improve the measurement by calculating the effort needed in order to return to an even distribution'. He proposes 'to develop an index that measures the degree of isolation and exclusion that social groups may experience in living their daily life. Segregation should represent not only a person's location in respect to the identities of his/her neighbours in residential space, but also in respect to the structure of his/her daily activity spaces. Thus, everyday life spaces are treated as major arenas for the structuration of society and human agency with segregation defined as a territorial strategy that social groups may adopt in order to isolate themselves or others from the rest of society. Our proposed index measures degrees of isolation of individual members of a social group from or exposure to other groups' populations at their sites, as a continuous function in space and in respect to the actors' actual everyday life spaces'.

But we must specify that a complementary hypothesis on which new developments in research are based highlights the fact that it is the participation of individuals in a multitude of networks that defines the intensity and the form of social ties. In that respect, the existence of networks, characteristic of certain groups and formed as a result of migration, can be viewed as a mark of differentiation or even of segregation in the same way as is the place of residence. This approach is, nonetheless, not a-spatial, in so far as the intensity of the networks generates phenomena of movement and circulation, which mark and are marked in space and which represent major stakes as regards harmonious cohabitation of populations on an urban scale. The frequent observation that the ethnic label given to a neighbourhood does not cover its resident population is important.

Another example of such discontinuous logic can be found in the functioning of the numerous national or regional associations that regroup foreigners; such is the case in Lausanne (Fibbi, 1993). There the network generates spatial configurations which must be studied as 'conjunctions of two logics, a logic of residential space and of processes of territorialisation resulting in natural areas, located and marked on the morphological level, and a logic of public space, and of the process of communication between

74 *Studies in Segregation and Desegregation*

territories defined as regions of dislocated and fragmented signification' (Joseph, 1984).

In this perspective, the use that André Piette (1990) proposes for, the concepts of *accommodation* and *interstice* appears particularly interesting as a new approach to problems of interethnic co-existence and intercultural communication. Rather than represent a simply transitory step in this process of racial relations that should result in cultural assimilation, accommodation would designate the political process permitting the 'symbiotic' co-existence of multiple ethnic communities who are not only adapted and integrated into said process, but who also maintain their own identity, their own culture, even their own territory within the greater cosmopolitan order.

Thinking about the Relationship to the Other in Terms of Space

The discussion soon focusses on the necessity of imagining and enhancing those in-between spaces in the city, those interstices that A. Piette (1990) puts into three categories:

- The 'full' interstice where 'one is at home, while keeping the other at a certain distance',
- the 'empty' interstice, or neutral space marked by the absence of real collective communication and the impossibility for public interaction, where 'one is neither at home nor with the other', as in the case between Spanish immigrants and the French population in the XVth *arrondissement* in Paris,
- the 'transparent' interstice, whose structure permits heterogeneous elements to dispose of a perfect code of translation, 'where one is perfectly at home there, foreigners and locals'.

According to A. Piette, the definition of the transparent interstice seems a central concept since 'the transparent interstice, as a place of full translation and transposition between different cultural codes, makes use of the coexistence of these heterogeneous elements that one is striving to promote so that they become the essential resource of the area. Furthermore, in this definition there appears the forceful idea of interculturality and not only of pluriculturality'. It is clear that the idea of a transparent interstice constitutes an ideal: it is possible that we may never find any places of this type.

The idea of interstices of communication or translation interstices that are necessarily transparent finally refer to an essential attribute for urban life and one of the key attributes of the Biblical vision of a New Jerusalem. The prefix *trans* in the sense of 'by, beyond, across' also refers to 'transaction', the act of carrying out transactions, to 'transactional', to 'transcode', to 'transcribe' or 'transcription', to 'transform', and lets reality appear clearly, that which expresses truth without altering it, to the limpidity of *parere*, in the original sense of the apocalypse. It is also the end of *anathema*, of the ban, of the 'interdict'. It raises the possibility of the return to paradise: an urban - and pluriethnic - paradise (Racine, 1992).

It is this transparency that our societies so badly need in the city and elsewhere in our various portions of urban space. It needs to be established in a prefabricated city made of multiple territories. Such transparency needs to be placed between here and there, between me and the other, in consideration of the fact that the one does not go without the other. This is possible, thanks to mutual codes and to the metabolising of a certain similarity without extracting, as A. Medam put it recently, the similar from the different while respecting origins, memories and eccentricities within the same nationality, as is the case between disciplines, between human beings, between men and women or between our different forms of spirituality. In other words, we should aspire not to focus on the *dis*, as in 'dissimilar, distance, disjointed and disappear' but on those places with the suffix *co*, places of convergence, of connivance, of communion, of conformity, of co-ordination, of conviviality and of community.

Perhaps we can go even further than A. Piette, who speaks of 'pluri-ethnic' spaces and try to understand how the exchanges between communities, individuals and cultures interact in space, how this space is perceived and experienced, how eventually this space can be modified by the behaviour of the immigrants and locals, what distortions arise in the experience and life projects of these individuals. This returns us to thinking in spatial terms of the relation to the 'other'.

76 *Studies in Segregation and Desegregation*

In Search of 'Hybrid' Places: Social and Cultural Ties and Representations of Interculturality: The Role of Places of Interculturality

It was in both theoretical and pragmatic contexts that research was undertaken at the University of Lausanne to ascertain the role played by some 'intercultural places' in Lausanne broadly defined as locations of reception, exchange and transaction where the actors and socio-ethnic variables seemed to be better suited than elsewhere to foster intercultural exchanges and cohabitation while maintaining diversity. The fact remains, however, that before even defining the 'ins' and 'outs' of this everyday life network in the inter-cultural city it was hypothesised that there existed in these 'hybrid places', in urban centres in particular, something which could enhance 'cultures of mixture'.

The questions to be answered in regard to these places concerned both their role in the creation of a migrant frame of reference and their perception by the local population. Were they more or less recreational spots of interculturality where people coming from different social milieus and cultures had the opportunity to mix and perhaps to get to know one another? Or did they remain places of exclusion, of refuge, ethnically marked, where natives and non-natives rub elbows without 'seeing' one another? Contrary to the perspective which tends to consider these places as sites of refuge, it is perhaps in these 'bridging' spaces, perhaps spaces of translation (Remy, 1990) or of 'transduction' (Medam, 1995), that the ties of a multi-cultural society are formed. They can be spaces for playgrounds where there is some room for 'interplay': '*des lieux où il y ait du jeu*'.

Our contribution emphasised 'places' in relation to the development of social ties. The understanding of the relationship between the non-native status of the population and the space required taking into account much more than quantitative indications. However, this path of research takes into account the fact that a neighbourhood becomes ethnic once it is *felt* to be such by certain population groups whether they are residents or not. It is also necessary to take into account the sense given by the actors to the phenomena to which they are party as well as the fact that, far from being 'givens', ethnicity, integration or segregation are constantly being recreated (Smith, 1992).

The research conducted by the University of Lausanne on 'places of interculturality' was explicitly based on the process through which socio-cultural groups are formed and coexist in space and, thus, to some degree, on the manner in which these groups negotiate relationships of proximity.

This research highlights the possibility that individual places may emerge where the actors and socio-ethnic variables form an integral unit. These places are more suitable than others for intercultural communication, and this is true whatever the problems that may come to light are, be they in terms of social or spatial relationships or in terms of rifts or tensions. These places could influence the strategic use of ethno-cultural attributes by the immigrant populations, or they might be places which play a role in the mutual understanding – or incomprehension – of the different actors. These are places about which we could question the conditions which help to make the actors – within that continuum where normally we distinguish situations of assimilation, integration, separation, marginalisation or even exclusion – better instruments to facilitate cohabitation in diversity. The project was an attempt to answer these questions by studying more precisely the context in which such places emerge, their history and the discourse which supports them. This approach of placing the emphasis on representations and on the construction of meaning and on the manner by which space is structured was designed to lead to a better understanding of these places, their role within the city and the intercultural relationships that may emerge.

To understand the role of associations, restaurants and ethnic businesses in the creation and functioning of a multi-cultural society, it is necessary to try to determine a field of spatial study in which the different aspects and the dynamics of the phenomenon can be grasped. Our agglomerations offer the possibility of studying this phenomenon in a sufficiently large spatial framework that encompasses a large collection of associative networks, ethnic businesses (approximately half of the grocery stores which do not belong to the large, national chains are run by persons of foreign origin or ethnic characteristics) and an ever-increasing number of foreign speciality restaurants. In the case of Lausanne, for example, this phenomenon is prominent. It is a city where the foreign population (not including naturalised citizens) is greater than 30% and where foreigners also represent nearly 35% of the active population.

The Ethnic Dimension in Lausanne's Social Space

For the moment, besides the qualitative studies undertaken by Marina Marengo (1999a), two kinds of quantitative analyses have been realised on all the potential 'intercultural' places in Lausanne, regrouped in three categories, which are provisional partly because they are based on 'official'

78 *Studies in Segregation and Desegregation*

criteria: places having a formal foreign connotation, places with a mixed explicit cultural vocation and places without any particular affectation but potentially open to 'interculturality'. The first step was a *spatial analysis,* which sought to find a model of distribution by first asking the question, 'Is the distribution of these places random or not?' and then to demonstrate a configuration of places linked to the effects of centrality. In the second step, a *contextual analysis* was undertaken to try to link that distribution to the factorial ecology of the city (Racine & Mager, 1999). The results generally reflected the classic socio-demographic-ethnic structure of social space with its own local specificities. Socially, Lausanne is not organised according to a classic concentric, centro/peripheral, geographical logic related to demographic status but follows a sectorial 'pattern', cardinal, in fact, and already largely explored elsewhere (Racine, 1996), where the zone east of the Sauvablin-Ouchy axis would capture the essentials of high revenues, members of higher socio-professional categories and 'acceptable' foreigners (French, German, other Europeans and Americans). A preliminary analysis of principal components conducted on one sole modality – foreign nationality – shows clearly that in the urban space of Lausanne in 1990, two ethnic groups were in confrontation. Our first factor grouped African, Mediterranean, Latin-American and Asian foreigners, and our second factor grouped those 'acceptable' foreigners mentioned above.

At the scale of the agglomeration, the distribution of the different nationalities in space also shows a principal differentiation between people coming from Portugal, Spain, Italy, South America, Africa, and ex-Yugoslavia (Group I), and people from Northern Europe, Germany, France and North America (Group II). In fact, the urban location of the first group depends mainly on the availability and the cost of renting a flat (Piguet, 1994). As rents tend to be lower in the western part of the Lausanne metropolitan area, most of the foreigners from relatively poor Mediterranean countries live there. The second group is linked to the immediate fringe of the main centres and sub-centres, the very rich and residential municipalities around the city as well as to tax levels, very low in the municipalities with that type of foreign population. But even if a form of residential segregation is thus noted, this segregation operates not only between the Swiss and foreigners but at a more general level between different layers of the Swiss population. Clearly, that kind of result is not essential.

Going from exception to exception, the often mentioned demographic spatial 'pattern' of Lausanne appears to be a seductive but questionable shortcut. In other words, the factorial analysis (taking into consideration the distortions and ambiguities and opacity related to the differences in scales) has already enabled us to exclude the purely logical socio-demographic contextuality from the possible explanations concerning the establishment of intercultural places. The characteristics of the population of a sub sector do not determine its capacity to function as a receptacle for potential intercultural places.

Under these conditions if there is a 'centralised' concentration of the chosen places, then the 'objective' research trails which could be suggested in order to find a pertinent explanation should be oriented along two axes. By formulating the hypothesis of a 'chosen' centrality, the first trail should strive to determine the importance of strategies of economic (potential markets, cost/profit analyses) and political location (visibility in the 'city'). The second trail should, on the contrary, think of centrality as 'imposed' (an establishment close to the principal junctions of the public transport system of Lausanne (St-François, Chauderon, Flon-TSOL, Tunnel, Train Station), or along the two axes, which in this perspective are of major importance to the foreign populations who have limited financial means. That is why a second analysis implied a longitudinal study to see the evolution of these associations, clubs and circles. In some cases, the tendency is toward concentration, in other cases toward dispersion and fragmentation. Interviews with those responsible provided very interesting interpretations of the reasons behind each kind of process. Places of interculturality treated by authorities tend to be concentrated, whereas spontaneous places seem to be dispersed. In the case of places without a declared vocation the dispersion is systematic and a common phenomenon for all types of services. However, we do not consider this kind of statistical analysis to be really essential. Much more significant is the passage from issues related to location and form to questions of meaning and intention, thus placing the emphasis on representations, on construction of meaning and on the manner in which space is structured. These new directions were much more effective in leading us to a better understanding of these places, their role within the city and the intercultural relationships that may emerge.

From Forms to Meaning

Even if the first part of our study (Racine, 1999, Racine & Mager, 1999) demonstrated, in the traditional geographical description and analysis of social space (factorial ecologies, etc.), that we found particular groups

80 Studies in Segregation and Desegregation

occupying definite niches in the structure of status, class and power in the local society with some degree of conflict, a question remained. Which terms of negotiation were drawn along ethnic lines? In this context we needed to consider the internal organisation of the ethnic groups, to discover the ways in which a traditional heritage had been maintained, transformed, denied or used to jostle for a position within the larger society and to identify factors that influenced the rate of retention of ethno-cultural traits. Furthermore, we also needed to define what we knew and what we could demonstrate about the specific ways in which ethno-cultural groups eventually contributed to the redefinition of urban character. Some studies (Harney, 1985) on Toronto's ethnic enclaves, which treated the ethnic neighbourhood as 'ambiance' and sought to 'comprehend the group's sense of group' and to assess the concepts of neighbourhood and ethnic networks of various community institutions in terms of their changing significance for the immigrant and each successive generation, were valuable.

Culture has become a central theme in debates touching on immigrant ethnic minorities, if only because the survival of their language and their culture of origin are ordinarily taken as proof of their inadequacy in an advanced industrial society. The dominant groups often tend to see the migrants' culture as primitive and static, even regressive, and assimilation as a necessary condition to integration and social mobility. From this perspective, those who are not assimilated have only themselves to blame if they remain marginalised.

For members of ethnic minorities, on the other hand, the survival of their culture of origin is idealised because it plays a key role as a source of identity and a basis for organising resistance to exclusion and discrimination. It helps people maintain their self esteem and their personal identity in situations where their abilities and experiences are scorned. However, this culture of origin can contribute nothing if it remains static because it will no longer offer any orientation or protection in a hostile evolutionary environment. Migrant or minority cultures are, thus, constantly being recreated, based on the needs and the experiences of the group and its interaction with the host social environment without either the immigrants or the dominant groups being necessarily conscious of the changes. For this reason, immigrants and their descendants do not have a static ethnic culture that is closed and homogeneous but rather one which is multiple and dynamic and influenced by a large variety of cultural, social and gender-related factors.

A person who wants to grasp the day-to-day social life of immigrant communities must examine the places of its day-to-day expression rather than the constant re-creation by the migrants of their culture of origin. One must evaluate the creation by these groups of 'institutions' (in the most general sense of the term). If one begins with the generally accepted idea that all social life implies the setting up by social groups of certain 'dispositions' which often take the form of institutions, one can ask how immigration in a given country is able to create a certain number of institutions in an environment highly constrained by the norms of the society in question. However, in order to understand the diverse dimensions of day-to-day life, the analysis should not be limited to organisations such as friendly sports associations or societies but should extend to include places that can be characterised by the strong relationships they foster with immigrants. Without doubt, ethnic businesses and restaurants should be included in the list of those places that play an important role in the life of foreigners. The question is how they are seen and experienced by the local population.

Towards an Ethno-Methodology for a New Understanding of Places by Competent Actors

In order to attain the objectives proposed in the study, previous knowledge of these locations (necessary in order to choose our sample places) was not sufficient to develop the qualitative part of our work since our knowledge was based on official information or special witnesses as well as to our previous relationships. They were, however, not intended for the purpose of gathering notes or impressions which directly aimed at the interpersonal relationships between different social actors. Therefore, it was necessary to re-evaluate these places from a new point of view, starting from the interactions of mobilised social actors.

To answer the questions that we asked ourselves certainly supposes that we passed from the initial contextual analysis which legitimised the choice of places to the actual observation of these places and to the work within each chosen place. In order to describe and characterise the places chosen for the investigation instead of projecting on them an *a priori* or theoretical definition of ethnicity, it was necessary to explore the way in which the actors conceived the 'ethnicity' of meetings, places and people and the way in which they treated these elements as pertinent. To further the exploration, we asked them to actually intervene in a given context in order to make a situation, an event or a problem intelligible. In other words, we wished to determine how certain – institutional, regulatory and legal –

82 Studies in Segregation and Desegregation

organisms develop and render operational ethnic and intercultural categories, which must go through an analysis of their discourse, the way in which they produce coherence, intelligibility or even have control over social reality. We wished to examine the way in which, historically, these systems of inscribing categories were deposited and coded, the more or less efficient way in which they influence a society and spread among each other (see Marengo's paper in the next chapter).

Let us insist on the fact that the descriptions given of the places will not reveal the abstract knowledge of the investigators but the descriptive activity of the participants. In fact, the social practices of the participants are inseparable from practices of description and interpretation. It is the symbolic elaboration that structures them and gives them meaning while at the same time discovering them. The processes of categorisation are part of these practices, and they not only allow the involved people to identify these known or unknown persons but also to interpret their activities, their positions, their opinions and their relationships as they are linked to the categories. The question then is how the participants themselves choose and make operational those categories which they judge to be pertinent in describing other actors or places frequently visited (Mondada, 1994).

During interviews, it is possible to have the people involved verbalise their point of view, their reactions and their positions. But interviews cannot replace real life situations; the description given by the participants in an interview strives to construct a meaning oriented to the situation in progress, the interview itself. It throws light on descriptive strategies which can be used by the participants when they have to react out of context or in a context with no bearing on ethnic or cultural questions.

In addition to interviews, other methods of observation were employed. These included, on the one hand, participatory observation, limited within the descriptions and field notes of the investigator participating in the field or exploiting the possibilities of how public places are used by unknown persons. They also included, on the other hand, privileged informers who play a role in the field (for example social workers, animators and restaurant owners). The descriptive elements thus obtained can, however, be augmented with audio/video recordings of empirical situations of interaction which took place in the field. The recordings permitted a finer analysis of the processes of interaction; they mainly allowed the study of details which went unnoticed by the participants in order to form a context or a meeting Such details might be a particular tone of voice, the way to interrupt or not interrupt an interlocutor and the linguistic difficulties of the migrant noticed or not by the

Jean-Bernard Racine 83

indigenous people. Whereas the notes taken during non-formal interviews of participatory observation organises the context by describing it, the recordings make it possible to analyse the way in which the people involved, themselves, construct and perceive the context (Mondada, 1996). This observation should also allow one to observe how, in the detail of interactions, processes of 'integration', 'assimilation' or 'segregation' are practically elaborated, which are to be defined not in relationship to academic models but in relationship to the way in which the migrants themselves manage their relationships with the host society, their integration in the various networks, their specific modes of sociability in their daily activity. In this sense, the observation of situations is complementary to the interviews, which requires a decontextualised version or one actually oriented to the context of the interview itself. Marina Marengo's chapter in this collection will give some of the results obtained. This is a necessary step in order to determine if ethnic mobility is undertaken and continues to be undertaken by both parties with a view to integration or segregation.

References

Alpheis, H. (1993), 'La concentration ethnique a-t-elle vraiment de l'importance?' in Blanc M. & Le Bars, S. (eds), *Les minorités dans la cité, Perspectives comparatives*, L'Harmattan, Paris.

André, J.-L. (1994), *Au coeur des villes*, Odile Jacob, Paris.

Barthes, R. (1993), *L'Empire des signes*, Skira, Paris.

Bastenier, A. & Dassetto, F. (eds) (1990), *Immigrations et nouveaux pluralismes, Une confrontation de sociétés*, Editions universitaires, De Boeck, Brussels.

Berry, J.W. & Laponce, J.A. (1994), *Ethnicity and Culture in Canada, The Research Landscape*, University of Toronto Press, Toronto.

Bolzmann, C., Fibbi, R., & Valente, L. (1992), 'Les racines locales des immigrés ou comment inventer une nouvelle citoyenneté', *Espaces et Sociétés*, vol. 68.

Brun, J. & Rhein, C. (eds) (1994), *La ségrégation dans la ville*, L'Harmattan, Paris.

Brun, Jacques & Rhein, Catherine (eds) (1994), *La ségrégation dans la ville*, L'Harmattan, Réseau Socio-Economie de l'Habitat, Paris.

Carre, O. (1994), 'Transculturel et interculturel: le conte comme objet de relations en groupe interculturel', in *Connexions*, vol. 63 (1), pp. 125-144.

Fibbi, R. (1993), 'Stratégies identitaires et participation sociale: les racines locales des immigrés', in *Les Migrations Internationales*, Université de Lausanne, Cours général public 1992-1993, pp. 89-102.

Grafmeyer, Y. (1994), *Sociologie urbaine*, Nathan Université, Paris.

Harney, R. (1985), *Gathering Places: Peoples and Neighbourhoods of Toronto, 1834-1945*, Multicultural History Society of Ontario, Toronto.

Haug, W. (1995), *La Suisse: Terre d'immigration, société multiculturelle. Eléments pour une politique de migration*, OFS, Bern.

84 Studies in Segregation and Desegregation

Joseph, I. (1984), 'Situation migratoire et double appartenance culturelle', in A.M. Kumps, (ed), *Du bon usage de la ville*, Facultés universitaires Saint-Louis, Brussels, pp. 95-110.

Latouche, Daniel (1998), 'Le retour de l'utopie: cosmopolitisme et urbanité en Amérique du Nord', in Emmanuel Eveno (ed), *Utopies urbaines*, Presses universitaires du Mirail, coll. Villes et territoires, Toulouse, ch. 9.

Ley, D., Clarke, C. & Peach, C. (eds) (1984), *Geography and Ethnic Pluralism*, George Allen & Unwin, London.

Lipiansky, E.M. (1992), *Identité, communication interculturelle et dynamique des groupes*, in *Connexions*, vol. 58, pp. 59-69.

Marengo, M. (1993), 'L'immigrée italienne sur le marché du travail suisse. Le cas du canton de Vaud', in *Rev. suisse d'Economie politique et de Statistique*, vol. 129 (3), pp. 385-392.

Marengo, M. (1999a), 'Intercultural Places in Lausanne (Switzerland): The Dialectic of Theoretical Knowledges and Fieldwork Returns', in A. Aguilar & I. Escamilla, *Problems of Megacities, Social Inequalities, Environmental Risk and Urban Governance*, Institute of Geography, Commission of Urban Development and Urban Life, IGU, Mexico, pp. 499-514.

Marengo, M. (1999b), 'Les lieux de l'interculturalité: une image de la complexité urbaine, Actes du Colloque 'Les approches culturelles en géogrpaphie', *Cybergéo*, Internet, Paris.

Marengo, M. & Mager, C. (1999), 'Les lieux de l'interculturalité. Le cas de l'agglomération lausannoise', *Carrefour*, vol. 3.

Medam, A. (1995), *Blues Marseille,* Editions Jeanne Laffitte, Marseille.

Mondada, L. (1994), 'Catégorisation: l'approche de H. Sack', in L. Quere & J. Widmer (eds), *L'enquête sur les catégories*, Editions de l'Ecole des Hautes Etudes en Sciences Sociales, Paris, pp. 129-148.

Mondada, L. (1996), 'L'entretien comme événement interactionnel. Approche linguistique et conversationnelle', in: J.B. Thibaud, & M. Grosjean (eds), *Méthodes d'investigation des espaces publics urbains*, Presses universitaires de Lyon, Lyon.

Olson, S.H. & Kobayashi, A.L. (1993), 'The Emerging Ethno-Cultural Mosaic', in L.S.Bourne & D.E. Ley (eds), *The Changing Social Geography of Canadian Cities*, McGill/Quennes University Press, Montreal, pp. 138-152.

Piette, A. (1990), 'L'école de Chicago et la ville cosmopolite d'aujourd'hui: lecture et relectures critiques', in A. Bastenier & F. Dassetto (eds), *Immigrations et nouveaux pluralismes. Une confrontation de sociétés*, De Boeck-Weasmeal, Brussels, pp. 67-84.

Piguet, E. (1994), 'L'immigration et ses espaces, Géographie des populations étrangères à Lausanne', in *Geographica Helvetica*, vol. 49 (2), pp. 73-80.

Poutignat, P. & Streiff-Fenart, J. (1995), *Théories de l'ethnicité*, PUF, Coll. Le sociologue, Paris.

Racine, J.B. (1992), *La ville entre Dieu et les hommes*, Anthropos, Paris.

Racine, J.B. (1998), 'Proximités urbaines, minorités ethniques et relations interculturelles', in J.M. Huriot (ed), *La ville ou la proximité organisée*, Anthropos, Publication du PIR-Villes CNRS Paris, pp.185-195.

Racine, J.B. (1999), 'Lausanne entre flux et lieux', in N. Commerçon et P. George (eds), *Villes de transition*, Anthropos, Paris, pp. 43-56.

Racine, J.B. & Mager, C. (1999), *The Foreigner and the City*, Institute Géographie (Unpublished Paper).

Racine, J.B. & Marengo, M. (1998), 'Migrations et relations interculturelles: les lieux de l'interculturalité', *Géographie et cultures*, vol. 24.

Raffestin, C. (1979), 'La ville comme métaphore', *Médecine et Hygiène*, Genève, vol. 1352, pp. 3749-3750.

Raffestin, Cl. (1993), 'Autour de la fonction sociale de la frontière', *Espaces et Sociétés*, vol. 70-71, pp. 157-174.

Remy, J. (1990), 'La ville cosmopolite et la coexistence inter-ethnique', in A. Bastenier & F. Dassetto (eds), *Immigrations et nouveaux pluralismes, Une confrontation de sociétés*, Editions universitaires, De Boeck, Brussels, pp. 85-106.

Rudder de, V. & Taboada-Leonetti, I. (1982), 'La cohabitation pluri-ethnique: espace collectif, phénomènes minoritaires et relations sociales', in *Pluriel*, vol. 31, pp. 37-54.

Schnell, I. & Benjamini, Y. (1999), 'Socio-Spatial Lifestyles and Segregation', www.cybergeo.presse.fr, April, 1999.

Smith, M.P. (1992), 'Postmodernism, Urban Ethnography, and the New Social Space of Ethnic Identity', *Theory and Society*, vol. 21, pp. 493-531.

Tarrius, A., Marotel, G, & Peraldi, M. (1988), *L'aménagement à contre-temps. Nouveaux territoires immigrés à Marseille et Tunis*, L'Harmattan, Paris.

Tarrius, A. Marotel, G, & Peraldi, M. (1994), 'Migration et citadinité, L'approche de la ville par la mobilité', *Les Annales de la recherche urbaine*, vol. 64, pp. 86-89.

Touraine, A. (1996), 'Faux et vrais problème', in M. Wieviorka et al (1996), *Une société fragmentée? Le multiculturalisme en débat*, La Découverte, Paris, pp. 291-319.

Touraine, A. (1997), *Pourrons-nous vivre ensemble? Egaux et différents*, Fayard, Paris.

5 Interculturality: A Preferential Path in the Search for a New Urban Social Equilibrium?

MARINA MARENGO

Introduction

In the context of a more general project focussing on cities and intercultural relationships in Switzerland, this paper intends to present certain types of places in which exchange and transaction take place, not only between the immigrant and indigenous populations, but also between the different immigrant ethnic groups inhabiting the Lausanne urban area.[1] It also seeks to examine the context in which these places emerged and the discourses that underlie them by placing the emphasis on the representations that are made of these places and on the construction of sense and the way in which space is structured. Our interest in these 'hybrid places' stems from the notion that immigration in urban centres promotes a 'culture of mixedness' which in itself represents the central issue in the whole question of cohabitation between and integration of different populations at the urban level.

Our preoccupations and reflections can be situated within the larger context of the economy of the 'construction of the individual', of his/her education, personal competencies and material/immaterial well-being. Further, this approach reflects the emergence of a social economy centred on solidarity and on a new sector of production, the third sector, in which public institutions and associative networks of social solidarity intervene simultaneously, even conjointly. These types of possible partnerships are worthy of analysis and discussion.

The consciousness of and the use of a double hermeneutics – of the researcher and the competent protagonist – allowed us to demonstrate an

---

[1] *'Les lieux d'interculturalit?'*, FNRS Project, PNR39 – *Migrations et relations interculturelles*, Bern, FNRS, under the direction of Jean-Bernard Racine with Marina Marengo.

88 *Studies in Segregation and Desegregation*

unexpected and as yet only partially articulated aspect of interculturality (Giddens, 1993; Kilani, 1994). Thus in this presentation we will endeavour to show that the mechanisms of interculturality function far beyond the scope of 'everyday' relationships between the indigenous and non-indigenous populations. While studying this type of relationship constitutes the basis of the main project, we are additionally aware that the problem constituted by attitudes towards change and otherness and towards cohabitation in a context of difference is almost a 'communicational problem' between official and non-official social networks.

Furthermore, an additional result of this type of study is the new awareness of unexpected forms of commitment and mediation by the observer-researcher, who becomes in turn a subject of observation.

We would like to emphasise at this juncture that we have avoided inevitably narrowing definitions of the concepts of segregation, integration and interculturality. In addition, we consider that the categorisation of our study sites as 'intercultural places' is not inherent to them, nor does it depend on the perspectives of or the theoretical choices made by the researchers involved in the project. This categorisation is the product of the protagonists themselves and of their actions. These actions are what constitute the place as it appears (Mondada, 1996). Therefore, instead of an approach which *a priori* defines the concepts of interculturality, we prefer an approach which removes the question of the definition of interculturality from the domain of theoretical discourse and places it in that of those day-to-day practicalities through which the protagonists themselves identify, describe and characterise intercultural situations in their context. The emergence of interculturality, then, is a phenomenon that needs to be studied in the field and not a predetermined theoretical construct. This position contrasts with a certain critical posture regarding interculturality, which stems from a comparison made between different cultural systems and which then decides upon their relative compatibility or incompatibility. As opposed to this approach, we prefer an empirical examination of those forms and practices which are the concrete manifestations of the emergence of intercultural relationships. In order to achieve this, it is essential to first establish an *in situ* observation of the ordinary practices of the protagonists, documented with recordings of their encounters and meetings (Marengo & Mondada, 1997). The case studies will be developed on the basis of the analyses of several semi-directive interviews that were held with a number of competent protagonists on site in a certain number of the places specifically chosen within the overall project to be the objects of more in-depth examination at a later date (Mondada, 1997).

Marina Marengo 89

Within this context, we will endeavour to demonstrate the manner in and extent to which the social protagonists correlate the relative complexity of their relationships towards 'the other' with the relative complexity of the urban environment (Guarrasi, 1996; Marengo, 1997). Our approach will, furthermore, allow us to reveal the contradictions that exist between the two operative social networks that exist in the Lausanne agglomeration, i.e. the 'official' one and the 'unofficial' one.

The Protagonists' Speech or the Discovery of a Fluid, Changing and Complex Universe

Let us move on to the presentation of some of the initial findings of our inquiries. For this we shall be using extracts taken from semi-directive interviews that were undertaken in some of the places chosen for the in-depth analysis.[2] The aim of this paper is to demonstrate how the complexity of day-to-day relationships has appeared in our inquiry into interculturality. The emergence of this component seems all the more significant to us because it was not made apparent to us through our reading or scientific reflection but rather through the social protagonists who were mobilised during the course of our research inquiries.[3] We found ourselves confronted by a field which was at once alive, changing, fluid

---

[2] The places chosen for detailed study are the following: The Spanish Centre 'Garcia Lorca' in Crissier, the Colonia Libera Italiana association in Renens, 'Globlivres', an intercultural library in Renens, the 'Français en Jeu' ('French at Stake') association, the Islamic Centre of Lausanne in the city center, the Recreation Centre in the Bourdonnette neighbourhood (western Lausanne), and the Recreation Centre in the Chailly neighbourhood (eastern Lausanne).

[3] 'By the term 'social protagonist' we refer to all those individuals who contribute in some way to the construction of the places in question. However, the different levels of their respective knowledge of the places in question and the nature of the specific competencies – professional or otherwise – that each of them brings to bear in the field have caused us to distinguish between these protagonists in relation to their level of competence. To mention but one example, the persons responsible for the management of these places exercise their influence over them in a completely different way than the users of the places do. It will be our business to ascertain how and to what extent the different levels of competence proper to the different protagonists contribute to the construction of those places chosen as objects of in-depth analysis' (M. Marengo, J.B. Racine, 'Social Sustainability in the Urban Context. Official and Unofficial Social Patterns: The Case of the Lausanne Agglomeration (Switzerland)', IGU Commission on Urban Development and Urban Life, Sinaia, 18-22 August 1998, p. 5 (in print).

90 Studies in Segregation and Desegregation

and sensitive, and whose level of complexity exceeded all the pre-existing hypotheses (de Béchillon, 1994).

The Individual Pathways: The Expression of a Private Complexity

In the course of the initial interviews with our field informants, we asked them to tell us how they came to commit themselves to the creation of a place of encounter, exchange, leisure or training.

Many of these narrations, often amounting to condensed life histories, enabled us to reach an understanding that there exists – despite the differences of origin, profession, education and social group – a commonality behind the choice of commitment to a place. All our competent protagonists (Swiss or foreign) possess at least a double, and sometimes multiple, cultural affiliation and daily confront otherness and 'others' in their private or professional lives: *My husband is a Muslim and so in my family we have to get on with different cultures and religions* (Français en Jeu).

The necessity of mediating between different language and/or cultural affiliations in order to manage family and professional relationships calmly and harmoniously motivated our informants to go beyond the sphere of family and/or work and to attempt to exploit their individual capacities either in the creation of a place of cultural, social and/or linguistic mediation or by their active participation in an existing place which needed people capable of playing a conciliatory and mediating role among different languages and cultures.

Making available acquired capabilities and the expression of a desire to share personal experience is also a common component in the stories of many of our informants: *In the beginning it wasn't the social centre yet, but just the local community centre. It was in an old laundry on the ground floor of an apartment building. It was tiny but there were always people there and things going on* (Centre Socioculturel de Chailly).

In some cases, sharing personal experiences and making available acquired capacities led our protagonists to become conscious of the kinds of risks necessary in order to set up enterprise initiatives. These risks were often of an economic kind: *And so we started like that, with a few books which had been donated, some books that had been lent to us by the 'Bibliothèque pour Tous'. Then it just got bigger, little by little. We paid for it all ourselves. To begin with we paid for everything ourselves* (Globlivres). But they could also be political in nature: *Some of us were members of left wing parties....In those days the Swiss Communist Party was outlawed but they met anyway. They met from time to time* (Colonia Libera Italiana).

From the private and/or professional sphere to social action, the status of these multiple affiliations and acquired mediation capacities evolved. From individual richness/complexity – even pride in having known how to get by, in having understood how to transcend day-to-day difficulties – gradually there evolved a 'culture of sharing' as well as the indispensable tools necessary to help others unravel the tangle of their different cultural backgrounds and of their family and professional lives, which were often as complicated, if not more complicated to manage than those of the founders of the places in question: *Because of my personal situation, I think I'm able to get closer to the people that come here...perhaps I am able somehow to share their anxieties, but to understand their needs too* (Français en Jeu). Or: *To begin with they felt pretty lost when they came here. But then...finding a book in their own language. Not just on the level of reading...* (Globlivres). This additional complexity arose because the cultural and geographical distances which separate the country of origin from the country of immigration increased significantly with each successive migratory wave that established itself in Switzerland.

The Spatial Establishment

Making available acquired capabilities was not and has never been enough by itself if these same people are to achieve some sort of 'official' recognition as well as a visible profile within the Lausanne area. The principal founding act in all the cases considered was the setting up of an association and the acquisition of legal status from the administrative point of view. In order to be visible and able to establish concrete social relationships with other 'plural' individuals – or at the least to take an interest in plurality and in difference – it was indispensable for them to become figures of stability in the Lausanne environment. In all the cases that we have considered, spatial establishment – i.e. the opening of premises in the association's name – was considered the significant step by those persons who are now responsible and/or by those who initially set up the places under study (Marengo, 1998): *To begin with, in order to have some kind of status, we rented a shop which was free on the other side of the square. It used to be a wine store. We got going like that* (Globlivres) but also...*I was looking for people who could speak my language. In 1961*

92 Studies in Segregation and Desegregation

there weren't too many Spaniards in Renens...there weren't too many. We got to know a few people, and then, in 1963, we set up the association and we opened the Spanish centre in Renens. I was part of it from the beginning (Garcia Lorca).

The spatial establishment implied, and still implies, responsibility, not only towards other members of the association but also towards other people interested in using the premises; this fact was clearly noted by our informants. In the first place, the responsibilities felt to be the most burdensome are the economic ones. It is obvious from what our informants said that the financial responsibilities were, and still are, either a cause of anxiety concerning the management of the place or a sorce of awareness of its durable territorial status. Despite unpaid voluntary labour – which represents the most common type of participatory activity both at the outset of these places and later – an economic investment on the part of the initiators was often necessary in order to get started: *...We paid for it all ourselves. To begin with we paid for everything ourselves* (Globlivres).

Financial problems often cause the responsible persons, particularly the founders, to make real material investments of money as well as free labour in the setting up of the premises: *It was an old house in Renens, rue de la Mebre. A really old house. We painted the doors; we did up the walls inside. That's where we started from* (Colonia Libera). This personal investment led the founders and the other voluntary workers to appropriate the place for themselves sometimes to the point of opposing initiatives from new members.

In some cases, the spatial establishment came well after the setting up of the association. The consciousness of being able to fulfil a societal function, to answer the needs expressed by a particular section of the community was sometimes more important than concern about spatial establishment: *They made room for us at the CSP* [Protestant Social Centre]. *We had just the corner of a table at our disposition. It wasn't easy to manage, to make ourselves known...but it worked with the people* (Français en Jeu). It was only later because of growth and the specific tasks which they needed to do that the need to have premises of their own became imperative: *Later on we got money from grants, and recognition, and the commune* [Lausanne] *offered us these premises. It was wonderful. At last we had a place were we could work properly* (Français en Jeu). In some cases, official recognition and the allocation of grant monies was indispensable for the setting up of a place with which the responsible people could identify and that the users might appropriate.

Marina Marengo 93

Relationships with the Local Authorities: Between the Need for Official Recognition and the Delicate Management of Neighbourly Relations

Relationships with the foreign 'other' are at times difficult to manage. One particular aspect concerns the arbitrary contingencies of the localisation of the places in question. It may present too great a difficulty for the people responsible for the place to deal with, not in the intellectual sense but simply in terms of time and energy. If changes in localisation are frequent in order to accomodate the ever increasing numbers of people interested in a place and in the activities and/or services it provides or because of the evolution in the type and number of activities and/or services being offered, it is not always the case that the quality of relations with the local population (especially when the place is situated in a residential building) and with the local authorities improves: *Because we were a bit noisy - over there we were in a first floor flat, rue du Midi, they threw us out...* And, *...seeing as how we'd been thrown out from the rue du Simplon and we needed to do something ...*(Garcia Lorca). This is particularly the case with places linked to foreign associations. A general attitude of suspicion or even hostility on the part of local authorities is often a cause of tension, particularly in cases where the role played by the associations in the community is not recognised, which is often the case with foreign associations. These tensions may lead to unexpected results to the detriment of other foreigners present in the agglomeration. Early groups of immigrants may reject the last immigrants to arrive when the first group's territorial inscription or particularly their status as stabilised inhabitants is questioned: *They said to us* [the members of the communal council] *that there were too many associations, that there were the Turks and the Tamils...but we've been here for forty years! You can't compare us...*[the President of la Colonia] *I don't have anything against the Turks or any of the others who have arrived here afterwards, but you can't compare us to them* [to the Mayor of Renens] *They arrived here once everything was finished. Us Italians, we made it all. Because we were the first here, before the Spanish, before the Portuguese* (Colonia Libera). The intervention of other local authority figures is sometimes asked for to resolve tensions of this kind. These are usually local worthies who act as mediators between the foreign spokespersons and the local political or administrative authorities: *In the end the owner of the premises, the boss of xxxx phoned me up and said, 'I've fixed a meeting with the Mayor. We're going, me, you and the building supervisor.' We met the Mayor, the communal clerk, a*

94 *Studies in Segregation and Desegregation*

council member... (Colonia Libera). This paternalistic factory boss is a good example of one of these 'alternative' local authority figures. Sufficiently 'enlightened' to be able to become involved in the mediation and find solutions to reconcile the two parties in question, these 'alternative' figures often play a fundamental negotiating role in the management of relations between the people responsible for the places (not only foreigners) and local institutions.

The Place and the Neighbourhood: a Privileged Link?

Our observations in the field – both in the places and in their surrounding neighbourhoods – and more particularly the things that were said by the managers and active members in the two socio-cultural centres that were chosen for the study (in the Bourdonnette and Chailly neighbourhoods) enabled us to understand the extent to which these two places play a crucial role within the neighbourhoods in which they are located – at least so far as those people who use them are concerned. It will obviously be necessary for us to extend our study even further and particularly to take the time to speak at length with the people who frequent the centres as well as with the other inhabitants of the neighbourhoods. Nonetheless, the managers of the centres have already widened our vision of the field.

In the case of the Bourdonnette Socio-Cultural Centre, the responsible people clearly showed that: *This neighbourhood is geographically isolated. It is surrounded by roads, and separated from the rest by these roads....There is a village atmosphere. It feels like one is in a village and not in a town neighbourhood. Everybody knows everybody else and says hello.* The particularity of the neighbourhood (viewed from the outside as problematic or marginal) – along with its geographical location (circumscribed by major traffic arteries on the western edge of the city) – gives additional meaning to the socio-cultural centre which is situated right in the 'heart' of this 'village'. The people responsible for the place are even able to benefit from this environment in their work. The types of relationships that they are able to establish are far closer than in other, less isolated but also less problematical neighbourhoods. The social workers are perfectly well aware of this and realise that in exploiting these 'privileged' relationships they can achieve better results in the accomplishment of their tasks.

In the view of the people responsible for it, the Chailly Socio-Cultural Centre serves a function identical to that served by the Bourdonette centre for a different category of population – especially foreign families recently arrived in Lausanne and in need of a place which can receive and look after their children during the daytime: *...there you are, those are the centre's regulars. This is like home to them. They are not really watched. Sometimes we find it quite hard to get them to go home, as often there's nobody in the house* (Centre Socioculturel de Chailly). At the same time, however, the social workers are well aware that the neighbourhood is 'special' because of the presence of a population belonging to a high level socio-economic group and that this often results in tensions or a lack of communication with the centre's users. On the other hand the people responsible are also conscious of the fact that this place provides an opportunity for both children and parents to have encounters outside the circle of their own social affiliation: *When parents get together, they are only interested in their kids...Here they can meet and talk to people who otherwise they would never get to meet* (Centre de Rencontre de Chailly). As opposed to the Bourdonnette, where the population changes fairly rapidly and where the adults are not very present, there exists a well-established adult presence at the Chailly Centre, constituted particularly of elderly people who have generally spent all their lives in the neighbourhood and sometimes have even been involved in the setting up of the centre. These adults do on occasion have some difficulty in sharing the centre's facilities with the younger people as they have, over a period of decades, come to think of it as theirs: *They've understood now that we don't want to exclude them, that the Foundation[4] is especially aiming at the young people. But it was hard going to begin with...They still have attitudes which are a bit racist, they don't want to be disturbed* (Centre Socioculturel de Chailly).

The Place as a Pretext for Knowledge and Discovery

The links that exist between this type of place and its environment can be strong enough in certain cases to condition the relationships established between our informants in the places themselves and the population living in the surrounding neighbourhood. These relationships can often be rather complex and sometimes contradictory. The difficulties involved in the management of relations with others enables us to understand the intensity of the established links and to better analyse the role that the places chosen for the in-depth study play for the inhabitants of these neighbourhoods.

---

[4]   FASL, Fondation pour l'animation socioculturelle de Lausanne (Foundation for Socio-Cultural Animation of Lausanne).

96 Studies in Segregation and Desegregation

Finally, these difficulties may allow us to understand the manner and the extent to which these places contribute to the establishment of links between the living environment and the social, cultural and religious lives of the immigrant populations as well as promoting contact and exchanges between these immigrant populations and the local inhabitants.

Going beyond the problems and difficulties of management, these places often fulfil the role – a function which is of especial interest to us as geographers – of being a pole of attraction along more or less diversified itineraries within the Lausanne urban area. *Of course, Globlivres is 'the library' but it's a reason to get out of the classroom too. There's the subway trip and exploring the city, the Bourdonnette, the university, Renens...* (Globlivres, a specialised teacher responsible for an integration class and a library user). This would appear to present a new avenue for research. Our collaborators will help us in the exploration and perhaps they will take us even further into this intercultural universe which is becoming more complicated, more fluid and more changeable daily and as a result more difficult to examine and comprehend.

Maintaining Independence: A Complicated Interplay of Balance and Power

The management of relations with local or foreign authorities is one of the most obvious manifestations of the complexity of the role that these places and our collaborators play in the Lausanne urban context. On the one hand, the need to be visible and to benefit from official recognition incites the managers to seek official backing, whether financial or otherwise: *We are not integrated into anything. On the one hand, we've always insisted on the importance of maintaining our independence, because that seems to be indispensable to this work because you need to be free to choose as regards the real requirements.... But, on the other hand, we are neither recognised nor integrated into any stable structure, so the library might have to close in a few months' time if the money runs out* (Globlivres). On the other hand, the desire to maintain a certain independence and to not accept compromises make these relations somewhat ambiguous, and even stormy at times, because the local authorities and the representatives of the foreign authorities (for example, embassies or consulates) in the area get together to elaborate strategies in order to avoid or repress the problem, whether it be of a relational or a financial nature. In some cases, independence in relation to the local and foreign authorities may be thought of as being the

Marina Marengo 97

principal advantage of the place: *Ever since its founding, the centre has always been managed in an autonomous way without any institutional funding – whether it be local or from Muslim countries. We fund ourselves...our members can make whatever contributions they want to and can afford* (Lausanne Islamic Centre).

Maintaining a balance in the management of these places between official recognition and backing on the one hand and independence on the other would seem to be rather a delicate business. Up until the present, our collaborators have firmly emphasised that maintaining their independence in the daily running of their institutions is of fundamental importance. Without this, the social control that the authorities would be able to exercise would, in the opinion of our collaborators, prevent the spontaneity of communication and relationships with 'the other' and would render all the efforts of the management and staff of these intercultural places useless.

The Observer Observed: Volunteer Culture and Politico-Social Culture - Are We Moving towards a Separation of Functions and the Social?

During the past two years of fieldwork in all of the chosen intercultural places, the researchers frequently found themselves confronted by a more and more explicit request for feedback and critical analysis of the data gathered from the mobilised competent protagonists. Even though such feedback was specifically and officially planned in the main project, it was originally intended to be provided at the conclusion of the study when all the data had been collected, collated and analysed. These requests for feedback, however, opened up the prospect within our research of yet another avenue for the comprehension of the way the management of relations with 'the other' is established within the Lausanne agglomeration. Thanks to the protagonists' requests to be allowed an active participatory role, we were led into a network of social operators which allowed us to make further discoveries. Though they have not yet been fully verified, we intend to study and analyse them at a later date.

It seems to us that this request for feedback is chiefly the expression of a need on the part of the protagonists for an outside point of view and opinion which would be without an official role to play in the places in question. This need was created by the researchers themselves though they did not intially realise this. The very fact of interviewing the protagonists within their places made them realise that they needed an opinion from the

98 Studies in Segregation and Desegregation

observing researcher even when, in some cases, the process of critical re-appraisal of the functions and objectives of the places was already under way. The observing researchers, for their part, were slowly integrated into the protagonist group through their participation at internal meetings and staff discussions.

From the moment that they agreed to no longer be merely passive and external observers, the researchers' role changed completely. They in their turn became the objects of observation and began to play an active role although they did not have any official status.

From this moment, the researchers were integrated into the different groups of competent protagonists and, thanks to their knowledge of other places, found themselves fulfilling a role of go-between between certain place managers and different social networks in the Lausanne area.

If this process intially appeared to have been primarily engendered by the researchers' presence in the intercultural places, it subsequently became apparent that the requests for them to become more active was due to a lack of some sort that the competent protagonists were not always willing to openly express. The reason for this was that the protagonists had not been aware that such a lack existed perhaps because the needs of these intercultural places, of their managers and staff and of their users had not been sufficiently and clearly discussed despite the discussions that did take place.

As time passed, the researchers became mediators between the managers of the places, between other competent protagonists functioning in the places and other competent protagonists who met in the places but who functioned in other contexts (teachers of integration classes for foreign children or various professional and voluntary social workers who functioned in other centres and in other professional spheres) (Kilani, 1994).

Does this role which was attributed to the researchers and this need for informal mediation not hide a need for greater official recognition and backing (material, moral, training) for our protagonists from the representatives of the official social networks (administrative and political) as well as the need for greater contact or more mediation between the representatives of an only partially recognised social network such as the ones in which the managers of our places operate and the representatives of officially recognised social networks? The question is relevant because, in point of fact, the competent protagonists, whether they be professional or voluntary, all know each other or know how to contact each other should the need arise (Tabin, 1997).

The gap between the two networks has widened continually since our field research began. At first it was just a matter of an unexpressed impression which the competent protagonists had not yet put into words. After two years in the field, a greater understanding of the different networks has allowed us to grasp the sense of the processes which are under way and to understand some of their mechanisms.

By all accounts an 'intercultural communications' problem seems to exist between a voluntary and a socio-political position. The problem appears to be due to the different statuses accorded the official and non-official networks as well as to the ever widening divergence of their respective social projects.

Social Networks in Deadlock

How can the communication problem between the two social networks be resolved or alleviated? Protagonists who function in the non-official network are expressing their needs and lacks more frequently as a result of the numerous new problems and difficulties that have become apparent as users of the intercultural places make more and more diverse requests (Voyé, 1995).

In some cases the difficulties are of a financial nature as requests for services and new types of social assistance increase. In response to the ever increasing range of problems that need to be solved, the managers of the places are only able to provide satisfactory solutions for a percentage of those making requests, even where they are in a position to benefit from partial or total official social network funding.

In other cases it is a need for training in the management of day-to-day operations which is requested from the representatives of the official social networks. The competent protagonists, voluntary or professional, find themselves more and more often in a position wherein they must confront problems and answer questions for which they were not trained. In some cases, the users of a given service seem to believe that the protagonists must be able to provide an answer or a solution to all their problems or requests. These paradoxical situations are becoming more and more frequent, yet the requests of our competent protagonists to the representatives of the official network go unheeded.

It would seem that official and non-official networks are continually evolving at different speeds and in different directions. Whatever the case may be, the non-official network seems to be running out of steam. The

100 *Studies in Segregation and Desegregation*

events created by the managers of the different intercultural places, therefore, constitute an 'appeal to the authorities', which do not, however, elicit either concrete propositions or even partial solutions. Without the backing of an official network, the unofficial network will not be able to advance or even to respond to the current social demand. Without concrete assistance in the areas of training and funding, the whole non-official network is in danger of collapsing. Even when the 'authorities' do give their support it is often at the price of imposing relatively strict conditions, so that, if the competent protagonists initially congratulate themselves on having been finally attended to by the authorities, they quickly realise that they have in the process lost a significant part of their maneuverability in the field where the real problems and needs have to be met. The non-official social network requires large measures of flexibility and independence, qualities that the official social institutions are not always happy to allow. Yet without independence, they are not able to go forward and develop at their 'natural' speed, i.e. as dictated by the new needs as they become apparent in Lausanne's society (Vincent, 1996).

In the cases of both the foreign associations examined,[5] their managers are more and more aware that the authorities of the countries of origin will no longer be – as they have been until now – the best placed to assist them in the solving of new problems as they arise or to support them in new initiatives. In expressing their desire to officially integrate the researchers into their intercultural places, they were conscious of their need for mediators who, though close to them from the point of view of their origins and culture, operated in a different domain: *We need some one who knows how to say these things and who knows who to write to the right people too* (Colonia Libera). The observer's role was not merely transformed into that of a mediator with the outside world but also into that of a person whose function it is to encourage the protagonists to express themselves more openly and to involve themselves in fresh initiatives. The official incorporation of the researchers could then in some way legitimise their taking the initiative and at the same time allow the existence of an 'official' and 'competent' scapegoat in the cases where those initiatives might fail.

Conclusion

By means of this presentation, and through these few examples, we hope that we have been able to demonstrate how the complexities of relations

---

[5] The Spanish Centre 'Garcia Lorca' and the Colonia Libera.

with 'the other' can emerge and even affirm and inscribe themselves lastingly within the urban environment and especially in this case of the Lausanne agglomeration despite the difficulties of managing these relations on a day-to-day-basis. It is clear that the data at our disposal are not only fragmentary but still in the process of collation and treatment; they do not yet allow us to give to our analyses all the confirmation that we believe they deserve.

Nonetheless, by means of these narratives, which show how these intercultural places were constructed and how they continue to develop, it has been possible to gain access to a relational universe whose complexity is not an abstract concept but the concrete materials which our protagonists have learnt to handle and manage on a daily basis.

References

Bechillon, de D. (ed) (1994), *Les défis de la complexité. Vers un nouveau paradigme de la connaissance?* L'Harmattan, Paris.

Besnier, J.M. (1996), 'L'altérité comme argument de communication', in K. Fall, R. Hadj-Moussa & D. Simeoni (eds), *Les convergences culturelles dans les sociétés pluriethniques*, Presse de l'Université de Québec, Québec.

Blomart, J. & Krewer B. (1994), *Perspectives de l'interculturel*, L'Harmattan, Paris.

Caldeira, A., Marengo, M. & Turki, M. (1999), 'Chercheurs et praticiens: des enjeux interculturels communs? Réflexions sur une expérience lausannoise en cours', *VIIe Congrès international de l'ARIC*, Paris, 29 juin-3 juillet 1999 (in print).

Camilleri, C. (1993), 'Le relativisme, du culturel à l'interculturel', in F.Tanon & G. Vermes (eds), *L'individu et ses cultures*, L'Harmattan, Paris.

Chambon, A. & Bellamy, D. (1995), 'Ethnic Identity, Intergroup Relations and Welfare Policy in the Canadian Context: A Comparative Discourse Analysis', *Journal of Sociology and Social Welfare*, vol. 22(1).

Garfinkel, H. (1967), *Studies in Ethnomethodology*, Prentice Hall, Englewood Cliffs.

Geertz, C. (1993), *The Interpretation of Cultures: Selected Essays*, Fontana Press, London.

Giddens, A. (1993), *New Rules of Sociological Method: A Positive Critique of Interpretative Sociologies*, Polity Press, Cambridge.

Guarrasi, V. (1996), 'Les dispositifs de la complexité: métalangage et traduction dans la construction de la ville', *3ème Cycle Romand de Géographie 'Géographie et Culture(s)'* Lausanne 11-13 mars 1996 (ronéo).

Gumperz, J.J. (1992), 'Interviewing in Intercultural Situations', in P. Drew. & J. Heritage (eds), *Talk at Work: Social Interaction in Institutional Settings,* Cambridge University Press, Cambridge.

Kilani, M. (1994), 'Du terrain au texte - sur l'écriture de l'anthropologie', *Communications*, vol. 58.

Ley, D. (1988), 'Interpretative Social Resarch in the Inner City', in J. Eyles (ed), *Research in Human Georgraphy*, Basil Blackwell, Oxford.

102 Studies in Segregation and Desegregation

Liberman, K. (1990), 'An Ethnomethodological Agenda in the Study of Intercultural Communication', in D. Carbaugh (ed), *Cultural Communication and Intercultural Contact*, Erlbaum, Hillsdale.

Marengo, M. (1997), 'La donna nei luoghi di immigrazione', in C. Brusa (ed), *Immigrazione e multicultura nell'Italia di oggi. Il territorio, i problemi, la didattica*, Angeli, Milano.

Marengo, M. (1998), 'Les lieux d'interculturalité: lieux d'échange, de construction et reconnaissance des identités', *Colloque 'L'habitat au regard des relations interethniques'*, Grenoble 26-27 mars 1998 (in print).

Marengo, M. (1999), 'Les lieux d'interculturalité: une image de la complexité urbaine', *Colloque 'Les Approches culturelles en Géographie'*, Cybergeo, Paris (Internet address: www.cybergeo.presse.fr).

Marengo, M. (1999), 'Intercultural Places in Lausanne (Switzerland): The Dialectic of Theoretical Previous Knowledge and Fieldwork Return', in A. Aguilar & I. Escamilla (eds), *Problems of Megacities: Social Inequalities, Environmental Risk and Urban Governance*, Institute of Geography, Universidad Nacional Autonoma de Mexico, Commission of Urban Development and Urban Life –IGU.

Marengo, M. & Mondada, L. (1997), 'Les lieux de construction de l'interculturalité: le cas de la bibliothèque Globlivres de Renens (Vaud)', *Colloque 'Multilinguisme et multiculturalité De la recherche aux applications'* Fribourg 16-17-18 octobre 1997 (in print).

Marengo, M. & Racine, J.B. (1998), 'Social Sustainability in the Urban Context. Official and Unofficial Social Patterns: The Case of the Lausanne Agglomeration (Switzerland)', IGU Commission on Urban Development and Urban Life, Sinaia, 18-22 August 1998 (in print).

Mondada, L. (1994), 'Catégorisation: l'approche de H. Sacks', in L. Quere & J. Widmer (eds), *L'enquête sur les catégories*, Editions de l'Ecole des Hautes Etudes en Sciences Sociales, Paris.

Mondada, L. (1996), 'Processus de catégorisation et construction discursive des catégories', in D. Dubois (ed), *Actes du Colloque 'Catégorisation, représentation des connaissances et systèmes symboliques'*, Kimé, Paris.

Mondada, L. (1997), 'L'entretien comme événement interactionnel', in J.P. Thibaud & M. Grosjean (eds), *L'espace urbain en méthodes*, Parenthèses, Marseille (in print).

Mondada, L., Söderström, O. (1993), 'Lorsque les objets sont instables: les faits culturels comme processus', *Géographie et cultures*, vol. 8.

Oriol, M. (1995), 'Les relations interculturelles. Aspects situationnels et aspects structuraux', in M. Abdallah-Pretceille & A. Thomas (eds), *Relations et apprentissages interculturels*, Armand Colin, Paris.

Racine, J.B. (1996), *Lausanne entre flux et lieux*, Travaux et Recherches de l'Institut de Géographie, Lausanne.

Racine, J.B. & Marengo, M. (1998), 'Migrations et relations interculturelles: les lieux de l'interculturalité, *Géographie et cultures*, vol. 25.

Rinaudo, C. (1999), *L'ethnicité dans la cité. Jeux et enjeux de la catégorisation ethnique*, L'Harmattan, Paris.

Roberts, C. (1992), *Language and Discrimination: A Study of Communication in Multi-Ethnic Workplaces*, Longman, London.

Sacks, H. (1973), 'Tout le monde doit mentir', *Communications*, vol. 20.

Schutz, A. (1987), *Le chercheur et le quotidien*, Méridiens Klincksieck, Paris.

Tabin, J.P. (1997), *Bénévolat et État social*, École d'Etudes Sociales et Pédagogiques, Lausanne.

Vincent, G. (1996), 'Formes et fonctions du bénévolat dans le travail social. Prévention spécialisée et lutte contre l'exclusion. La situation française', *Revue suisse de sociologie*, vol. 22 (1).

Voye, L. (1995), 'Pour revisiter le bénévolat. Propos hétérodoxes', *Revue suisse de sociologie*, vol. 21 (2).

Part 2:
Segregation and State Policies

6 Ethnic Segregation and the Welfare State

TINEKE DOMBURG-DE ROOIJ AND SAKO MUSTERD

Introduction

Today, in urban social debates, considerable attention is given to residential segregation issues. Not just the ethnic and socio-economic contrasts among different groups in society but particularly the spatial dimension tend to appeal to a wide audience. Although there is insufficient knowledge about the consequences of segregation, it is presumed that residential segregation is undesirable and that it is a major cause of social problems in cities. People assume that clear segregation prevents full participation in society and, therefore, fear spatial inequality, especially if it is rigid. Following this line of reasoning it appears logical that several countries have taken measures to resolve spatial inequalities. However, if solutions for 'segregation problems' are sought, the 'causes' should be known and understood. Without a proper understanding of the mechanisms related to segregation there cannot be an appropriate response to segregation. Here, we will offer a contribution to such understanding by presenting part of an empirical analysis of a broader international comparative research project that deals with segregation and the welfare state.

Many scholars discuss economic restructuring, globalisation and the impact of international migration as important factors, which cause polarisation and subsequent segregation (Sassen, 1991). Others focus on cultural differences (Waldinger, 1996), while yet others refer to welfare state arrangements (Musterd & Ostendorf, 1998). The ideal research situation would be to consider the impact of all of these dimensions within the framework of one international comparative research project. That, however, for the moment is beyond our abilities. We have to try to extend our knowledge by small steps. In this contribution, we will focus attention in two ways. First, we will consider the relationship between segregation and the welfare state and try to determine whether there are – at least hypothetical – arguments for assuming that there is a relationship between segregation and the type of welfare state. Secondly, we will look at ethnic

108 *Studies in Segregation and Desegregation*

segregation in particular, knowing that there is a connection, although not a one-to-one correspondence, between ethnicity and socio-economic status. After a short discussion of the concept of segregation and the question of what motivates people to pay so much attention to it (section 2), we will consider the theoretical explanation of segregation as is presented in the literature (section 3). Then we will describe variations in ethnic segregation (section 4) as well as variations among welfare states (section 5). Finally, (section 6), we will present some interpretative conclusions.

The Concept of Segregation and Why It Receives So Much Attention

The term segregation is frequently used, having various meanings, measured on various scales and appearing with various phenomena. Since it is useful to be as specific as possible, in this section we will clarify the parameters of our definition and discussion. Segregation can be regarded as a situation as well as a process. Here, the focus is on the structure that exists on the situation as it is. Segregation can be measured on different geographical levels. In this contribution we will try to compare segregation levels on the neighbourhood level. Finally segregation can be described for a wide variety of phenomena. We will concentrate on the ethnic dimension, but some reference to the socio-economic dimension is unavoidable and even required. There are at least two reasons to do so. First, the dimensions explaining ethnic segregation partly run parallel to the dimensions that explain social segregation. Second, the attention given to ethnic segregation is, for various reasons, frequently linked to people's supposedly weak economic position. Their economic position often is one of the most important reasons why people are concerned about ethnic segregation in the first place. Although there can be many reasons for paying attention to the issue, in the literature the disadvantages of residential segregation receive prime attention. Usually, the concentration of ethnic minority groups is regarded as undesirable because it is identified with all kinds of disadvantages for the people who live in these concentrations and who are supposed to have few socio-economic opportunities. The literature uses such terms as 'cultures of poverty', 'states within the state', 'cultures of segregation' and 'lack of integration' (Morris, 1987; Wilson, 1987; Massey & Denton, 1993; Schill, 1994; Santiago & Galster, 1995; O'Loughlin & Friedrichs, 1996; Musterd & Ostendorf, 1998). Some say that segregation prevents individuals from improving their situation. Claims are made that segregation blocks opportunities for social mobility. Others clearly fear for their own secure position. The negative effects of ethnic residential segregation are especially emphasised where segregation has a strong link with poverty. And, although the relationship between 'race' and 'class' is not one-to-one, there is considerable worldwide evidence that such a relationship exists, at least partially. Research done by Clark (1998), for example, provides support for the idea that recent immigrants to the US have lower level skills and education than earlier migrants and the indigenous population. According to Massey and Eggers, urban poverty is most concentrated among African-Americans and Puerto Ricans.... (in Massey, Grass & Shibuya, 1994, p. 425). It is suggested these associations are more or less structural. In France similar associations were found: 'At the metropolitan level, foreigners have been shown to be concentrated in the blue collar stratum, while French heads and most spouses are concentrated in the professional/managerial stratum and at a growing rate.' (Rhein, 1998, p. 445). With regard to the Netherlands, Musterd et al. (1998, p. 185) refer to literature on the basis of which it can be concluded that most areas with a concentration of immigrants from non-industrialised countries are characterised by low-income households, high unemployment figures and sometimes by poor social and physical conditions in their neighbourhoods. In other countries, such as Sweden, Belgium, Great Britain and Germany, similar experiences have been described (Andersson, 1998; Kesteloot, 1994; Peach, 1996; Haussermann & Sackmann, 1994).

However, we should not treat these associations between ethnic segregation and weak socio-economic status, between ethnicity and poverty, as if they are absolute and always negative, as if they always block upward social mobility. First, there are sufficient examples of successful immigrants, which blur the association. Secondly, new immigrants, who may indeed have a weak economic position, can acquire positive experiences from a certain segregation. Boal (1976), for example, pointed to the advantages of culturally homogeneous areas and applied concepts such as the 'colony' where people cluster voluntarily to be able to help each other in their first steps in the new society. Others have also drawn attention to the positive aspects of segregation. The advantages of ethnic segregation include social, cultural, economic and political atmospheres, such as social contacts of 'like-minded' people, economic and socio-cultural support for special services as shops, schools and religious institutions (Polanyi, 1944; Peach & Smith, 1981; Ostendorf & Vijgen, 1982; Portes & Sensenbrenner, 1993; Boal, 1976 & 1998).

Perhaps there are several negative effects of ethnic segregation, and perhaps there are several positive effects of ethnic segregation. It is clear

110 *Studies in Segregation and Desegregation*

that the effects of segregation vary and depend on such variables as the level of choice people have, the length of stay, the level of discrimination and the rate of economic transformation. However, it is clear that a better understanding of the reasons why segregation develops as it develops is required.

The Interpretation of Residential Segregation: Towards a Hypothesis

With regard to the process of residential segregation, economic restructuring and globalisation processes dominate the discussion (Sassen, 1991; Fainstein et al., 1992). These two factors are closely related. The first includes processes of structural economic changes, whereby employment expands in the producer and consumer services and declines in traditional manufacturing. The internal organisation of companies changes as well. Globalisation is a more complicated concept and is related to many aspects of society, not only to the economy. Usually, however, only the structural trend of the formation of a global economy is emphasised. In the words of Marcuse (1996: 4): 'Globalisation is an international process and its components are: internationalisation of activities, technological advance, concentration of economic ownership and control, and weakening of democratic public control'.

According to the 'social polarisation thesis' (Sassen, 1991) globalisation, connected international migration and economic restructuring are inevitable results of social polarisation of the occupational and income structures, with an absolute growth at both top and bottom ends of the distribution and expense in the middle. Several studies stress that the lower end of the scale is predominantly occupied by immigrants from (former) third world countries. The social polarisation thesis has been heavily criticised (Murie, 1993; 1998; Murie & Musterd, 1996; Silver, 1993; Hamnett, 1994; 1996a; 1996b; 1998; Thrift, 1994; Kloosterman, 1996; Musterd & Ostendorf, 1998). One point of criticism is that in some cases economic restructuring can have many more widespread effects in the entire society than in others. Hamnett detected a 'professionalisation' process for almost all classes of society he studied (1994, 1996a, 1996b, 1998). Others pointed out that the polarisation thesis focusses on immigration and economic processes and that it neglects other factors, such as national welfare state provisions or demographic structure, which could have mediating roles. The outcomes of these processes do not always yield the same results. Therefore, there are discussions about the extent to which polarisation and segregation processes in cities are straight and inevitable results of globalisation, immigration and economic restructuring processes. These processes are as manifest in Europe as they are in the US; the outcomes, however, are clearly different. Critics tend to ascribe these differences to, on the one hand, cultural differences that are related to different population compositions (Waldinger, 1996) and histories of population and urban development (Burgers & Musterd, forthcoming) and, on the other hand, the national context in which the processes occur. Usually they refer to the different institutional context, the welfare state, which influences the extent in which macro-processes have repercussions on society and on segregation (Musterd & Ostendorf, 1998). Research in which the welfare state receives prime attention (Esping-Andersen, 1990; Leibfried, 1991) suggests that the type of welfare state may have various effects upon the daily life of households. The type of welfare state has repercussions in several spheres of life and, thus, also in the sphere of residential segregation processes, which are partly related to socio-economic factors. Therefore, it makes sense to investigate the relationship between segregation and the welfare state. Until now, the knowledge about that relationship has been insufficient. As far as we know, there is no empirical study that systematically relates segregation with the type of welfare state. That is sufficient reason to focus attention on this relationship. If we deal with the connection between segregation and the type of welfare state, we could pay attention to socio-economic dimensions as well as to ethnic dimensions. In both spheres states may or may not try to bridge gaps. Probably the efforts to integrate people into the wider society will encompass both dimensions, although different weights may be attached to the various instruments that are applied to reach the objectives in the ethnic and in the socio-economic spheres. Ethnic integration objectives, may perhaps require more attention to housing policies, while socio-economic integration objectives may perhaps require more attention to social policies. The ideal would be to deal with both spheres of segregation and integration simultaneously. In our international comparative framework, however, this was impossible. For the purpose of this contribution, we decided, as we have stated, to focus on the relationship between ethnic segregation (and integration) and the type of welfare state. Although there is no doubt that other factors also affect the segregation of population, we will confine the description and analysis to these two dimensions only. Our purposes are to describe the variations in both dimensions across countries and cities as well as their bi-variate association. By doing this we hope to provide a small contribution to the

112 *Studies in Segregation and Desegregation*

testing of hypotheses that can be formulated about the role of the welfare state with regard to segregation.

The central hypothesis with which we start our analysis is that welfare states have effects on the degree of socio-economic inequality and the position of low income-groups and ethnic minorities. In general the motivating goal of welfare states is to protect minimum standards of living, but welfare states differ in that some respond to urgent needs of only a small part of the population (residual or rudimentary), while others are more universally oriented and provide some kind of help to integrate all members of the society. We assume that more universal government intervention will better prevent sharp inequalities and divisions between residents, compared to residual or rudimentary intervention. (A broader discussion about the application of these concepts will follow in section 5.)

The hypothesis that more developed welfare states will have only moderate levels of segregation is assumed to have its basis in social, labour, housing and health care policies. With regard to social policy, the residual model is supposed to result in sharper differences between socio-economic and ethnic groups than the universal model, where due to welfare state arrangements the distribution of affluence is more equal and sharp inequality is prevented. Provisions such as minimum income, state pensions, disability benefits and unemployment benefits are universal and at a high level. They do not only prevent people from being poor but also have redistributive effects that to some extent may also bridge the gaps between ethnic groups. Regarding labour market policy, some countries have an active policy to stimulate labour market participation for all, while others have a more passive, compensating policy. The latter cases are typified as 'welfare without work' (Esping-Andersen, 1996) with a low level of labour market participation. It is supposed that having a job will have positive effects on integration into society. The residual model is characterised by a passive and compensating labour market policy, while the relatively universal models have more active policies to stimulate participation in the labour market.

Different systems of health care financing also have different effects on socio-economic position. The degree of progress in health care financing systems influences the distribution of income (Wagstaff et al., 1997). A universal model has the most egalitarian effects because health care is financed by direct taxes, which are a progressive source of finance in all countries. Insurance systems in universal models also display a degree of progress (Van Doorslaer, 1998). Privately financed systems are the most regressive and will have the least egalitarian effects.

Although housing also influences socio-economic inequality via subsidy-systems, the impact of the government will especially influence segregation and residential distribution of the population. The organisation and nature of the housing market have an important impact on the spatial distribution of population according to socio-economic and household position. In both the comprehensive and the universal model the government plays an extensive role in the housing market, which, as a result, is dominated by social housing. Cities with large social housing areas may provide better opportunities to realise socio-spatial mixes of population. However, that will only be possible if certain conditions are met: the social area has to be spatially de-concentrated and the supply of housing has to be sufficient to meet the needs of lower class households. Furthermore, social inequality should not be too large (Musterd, 1994, p. 187). With a declining social sector and increasing social inequality residential segregation is likely to be more prominent; the social rental housing sector will be dominated by the lowest income groups. Danermark and Jacobson (1989) show that a more market oriented housing policy and less 'mixed housing' will cause stronger residential segregation. In Britain, where the structure of the housing market has changed in the last few decades, there is a loss of social mix and an increasing concentration of the poorest sections of the population in the social rented sector (Murie & Musterd, 1996).

In market oriented societies economic position, housing and participation in the labour market are strongly connected to each other (for example, the United States), but in societies with a well-developed welfare state these relationships are much weaker due to welfare state arrangements (Musterd & Ostendorf, 1994). These welfare states guarantee an acceptable minimum level with respect to income and housing, irrespective of participation in the labour market. Consequently, there will also be a weaker link between the type, quality and location of housing and the income of households.

Before we look at the empirical relationship between the type of welfare state and the level of segregation, we will first describe the levels of ethnic segregation (section 4), and the types of welfare state (section 5).

Ethnic Segregation

International comparative research into ethnic segregation is complicated by several factors. We would particularly like to mention two of them. The first is that each country has its own definition and registration of ethnic minorities. We have tried to select definitions that are as comparable as possible, but the reader is warned to be cautious. A second problem refers to the scale for which the data are available and to the measures used in various studies. We have tried to use comparable spatial units as well as comparable measures. Accordingly we have selected the index of segregation (IS), which offers information on the spatial separation of one group compared to the rest of the population, and the index of dissimilarity (ID), which offers information on the spatial separation of one group compared to another group. Comparing segregation in cities in different countries is not possible without the acceptance of some methodological problems with regard to definitions, scale and period of measurement. Besides, there are many different ethnic groups: immigrant workers, colonial immigrants, asylum seekers and immigrants from richer countries. Within these groups there are also differences with regard to the period of immigration. They all have different socio-economic positions in society and different residential patterns. In short, there are a variety of pitfalls when comparing these phenomena internationally. Keeping all this in mind, we will still make an effort. Basically, what we have done is to collect indices for a considerable number of cities that represent the variety of welfare states that can be distinguished. Several sources were used. We have constructed a large table to include all the indices (Table 6.1).

Table 6.1 Index of segregation (IS) or index of dissimilarity (ID)

City	IS/ID	Year	Remarks	Source
NETHERLANDS				
AMSTERDAM				
Ethnic minorities	32	1995	93 neighbourhoods	Musterd et al. (1998)
Turks	41	1995	93 neighbourhoods	Musterd et al. (1998)
Turks	42	1994	369 neighbourhoods (avg. 2,000 inh)	Musterd (1998, p. 25)
Turks	45	1994	1216 grids (avg. 500 inh)	Musterd (1998, p. 25)
Moroccans	39	1995	93 neighbourhoods	Musterd et al. (1998)

City	IS/ID	Year	Remarks	Source
Surinamese	35	1995	93 neighbourhoods	Musterd et al. (1998)
ROTTERDAM				
Ethnic minorities	44	1993	Neighbourhoods	Breebaart et al. (1996, p. 47)
Turks	53	1993	Neighbourhoods	Musterd (1998, p. 25)
Moroccans	50	1993	Neighbourhoods	Breebaart et al. (1996, p. 47)
Surinamese	30	1993	Neighbourhoods	Breebaart et al. (1996, p. 47)
THE HAGUE				
Ethnic minorities	51	1992	Neighbourhoods	Breebaart et al. (1996, p. 47)
Turks	51	1996	Neighbourhoods	Musterd (1998, p. 25)
Moroccans	47	1996	Neighbourhoods	Musterd (1998, p. 25)
Surinamese	36	1996	Neighbourhoods	Musterd (1998, p. 25)
UTRECHT				
Ethnic minorities	35	1991	Neighbourhoods	Breebaart et al. (1996, p. 47)
Turks, Moroccans, South Europeans	43	1991	Neighbourhoods	Breebaart et al. (1996, p. 47)
Surinamese + Antillean	25	1991	Neighbourhoods	Breebaart et al. (1996, p. 47)
BELGIUM				
BRUSSELS				
Foreigners	40	1991	Brussels capital region, neighbourhoods	Breebaart et al. (1996, p. 54)
Moroccans	59	1991	Brussels capital region, neighbourhoods	Breebaart et al. (1996, p. 54)
Turks + Moroccans	61	1991	587 quarters (avg. 1.600 inh)	Musterd (1998, p. 25)
GERMANY				
FRANKFURT				
Non-Germans versus Germans	17	1994	Ortsteile	Breebaart et al. (1996, p. 71)
Turks	17	1995	45 Ortsteile (36715 pers)	Freund (1997)
Moroccans	21	1995	45 Ortsteile (9157 pers)	Freund (1997)
Italians	14	1995	45 Ortsteile (16609 p.)	Freund (1997)

116 *Studies in Segregation and Desegregation*

City	IS/ID	Year	Remarks	Source
Yugoslavians	23	1994	Ortsteile	Breebaart et al. (1996, p. 71)
Spaniards	21	1994	Ortsteile	Breebaart et al. (1996, p. 71)
Dutchmen	21	1995	(1146 pers)	Freund (1997)
Frenchmen	23	1995	(3558 pers)	Freund (1997)
Americans	23	1995	(4378 pers)	Freund (1997)
British	25	1995	(3646 pers)	Freund (1997)
Greek	29	1995	(8781 pers)	Freund (1997)
Korean	45	1995	(783 pers)	Freund (1997)
Japanese	56	1995	(1885 pers)	Freund (1997)
DÜSSELDORF				
Foreigners	19	1994	Stadtteile	Breebaart et al. (1996, p. 84)
Turks	30	1994	Stadtteile	Breebaart et al. (1996, p. 84)
Moroccans	27	1994	Stadtteile	Breebaart et al. (1996, p. 84)
Japanese	56	1994	Stadtteile	Breebaart et al. (1996, p. 84)
FRANCE				
PARIS				
Foreigners	11	1990	Department 75	Breebaart et al. (1996, p. 139)
Foreigners	20	1990	Agglomeration	Breebaart et al. (1996, p. 139)
Algerians	23	1990	Department 75	Breebaart et al. (1996, p. 139)
Portuguese	12	1990	Department 75	Breebaart et al. (1996, p. 139)
LILLE				
Non-French	22	1990	district level	Kruythoff and Baart (1998, p. 21, 54)
Non-French	25	1990	LMCU (zone level)	Kruythoff and Baart (1998, p. 34, 54)

Tineke Domburg-De Rooij and Sako Musterd 117

City	IS/ID	Year	Remarks	Source
ITALY				
TURIN				
Non-Italian residents[1]	32	1991	2 zona statistica	Petsimeris (1998)
Non-Italian non-residents	42	1991	92 zona statsitica	Petsimeris (1998)
MILAN				
Non-Italian residents	20	1991	144 zona statistica	Petsimeris (1998)
Non-Italian non-residents	41	1991	144 zona statistica	Petsimeris (1998)
GENOA				
Non-Italian residents	36	1991	76 zona statistica	Petsimeris (1998)
Non-Italian non-residents	68	1991	76 zona statistica	Petsimeris (1998)
GREAT BRITAIN				
LONDON				
Non-White			Greater London,	Peach (1996, p. 222)
	35	1991	ward level	
	40	1991	Greater London, enumeration district	
Black Caribbean			Greater London,	Peach (1996, p. 222)
	45	1991	ward level	
	49	1991	Greater London, enumeration district	
Black African	41	1991	Greater London, ward level	Peach (1996, p. 222)
Bangladeshi	63	1991	Greater London, ward level	Peach (1996, p. 222)
Indian	49	1991	Greater London, ward level	Peach (1996, p. 222)
Pakistani	49	1991	Greater London, ward level	Peach (1996, p. 222)
BIRMINGHAM				
Non-White	52	1991	ward level	Peach (1996, p. 223)
	56	1991	enumeration district	
Black Caribbean	42	1991	ward level	Peach (1996, p. 223)

[1] Residents are persons who are registered at both police office (and hold a permit to stay) and the city registry office. Non-residents may hold a permit to stay; they are not registered at the city registry office.

118 *Studies in Segregation and Desegregation*

City	IS/ID	Year	Remarks	Source
	48	1991	enumeration district	
Black African	36	1991	ward level	Peach (1996, p. 223)
Bangladeshi	68	1991	ward level	Peach (1996, p. 223)
Indian	50	1991	ward level	Peach (1996, p. 223)
Pakistani	66	1991	ward level	Peach (1996, p. 223)
MANCHESTER				
Non-White	56	1991	Greater Manchester, ward level	Breebaart et al. (1996, p. 104)
Non-White	43	1991	Borough Manchester, ward level	Breebaart et al. (1996, p. 104)
Blacks	55	1991	Greater Manchester, ward level	Breebaart et al. (1996, p. 104)
Blacks	46	1991	Borough Manchester, ward level	Breebaart et al. (1996, p. 104)
Indian continent	64	1991	Greater Manchester, ward level	Breebaart et al. (1996, p. 104)
Indian continent	51	1991	Borough Manchester, ward level	Breebaart et al. (1996, p. 104)
Bangladeshi	63	1991	ward level	Peach (1996, p. 224)
Pakistani	54	1991	ward level	Peach (1996, p. 225)
LEEDS				
Bangladeshi	79	1991	ward level	Peach (1996, p. 224)
Pakistani	61	1991	ward level	Peach (1996, p. 225)
Black Caribbean	66	1991	ward level	Peach (1996, p. 226)
SHEFFIELD				
Bangladeshi	71	1991	ward level	Peach (1996, p. 224)
Pakistani	70	1991	ward level	Peach (1996, p. 225)
Black Caribbean	48	1991	ward level	Peach (1996, p. 226)
SWEDEN				
14 MUNICIPALITIES				
Foreign-born (before 1985)	25	1995	14 municipalities	Andersson (1998, p. 416)
Foreign-born (after 1985)	47	1995	14 municipalities	Andersson (1998, p. 416)
Turks (after 1985)	69	1995	14 municipalities	Andersson (1998, p. 416)
Iranians (after 1985)	58	1995	14 municipalities	Andersson (1998, p. 416)
Iraqis (after 1985)	68	1995	14 municipalities	Andersson (1998, p. 416)

City	IS/ID	Year	Remarks	Source
Finns (before 1995)	30	1995	14 municipalities	Andersson (1998, p. 416)
Finns (after 1985)	41	1995	14 municipalities	Andersson (1998, p. 416)
NORWAY				
OSLO				
Third world immigrants	29	1998	(13% of population in 1998, in Norway 1%)	Brevik (f c)
CANADA				
TORONTO				
Minorities	42	1991	475 census tracts	Breebaart et al. (1996, p. 155)
British	23	1991	475 census tracts	Breebaart et al. (1996, p. 155)
Blacks	40	1991	475 census tracts	Breebaart et al. (1996, p. 155)
Portuguese	64	1991	475 census tracts	Breebaart et al. (1996, p. 155)
Chinese	48	1991	475 census tracts	Breebaart et al. (1996, p. 155)
Italians	51	1991	475 census tracts	Breebaart et al. (1996, p. 155)
UNITED STATES				
CHICAGO				
Black versus white	91	1980	Central city	Massey and Denton (1993, p. 71)
CLEVELAND				
Black versus white	88	1980	Central city	Massey and Denton (1993, p. 71)
LOS ANGELES LONG BEACH				
Black versus white	83	1980	Central city	Massey and Denton (1993, p. 71)
NEW YORK				
Black versus white	83	1980	Central city	Massey and Denton (1993, p. 71)
NEWARK				
Black versus white	85	1980	Central city	Massey and Denton (1993, p. 71)

120 *Studies in Segregation and Desegregation*

City	IS/ID	Year	Remarks	Source
PHILADELPHIA				
Black versus white	84	1980	Central city	Massey and Denton (1993, p. 71)
ST. LOUIS				
Black versus white	84	1980	Central city	Massey and Denton (1993, p. 71)
ATLANTA				
Black versus white	80	1980	Central city	Massey and Denton (1993, p. 71)
BALTIMORE				
Black versus white	79	1980	Central city	Massey and Denton (1993, p. 71)

The table shows that there is considerable variation within the different metropolitan areas. When looking at the table, one has to consider that the aggregate categories hide some variation at the level of the individual category of ethnic minorities. High scores of segregation are reached in Brussels. Turkish and Moroccan nationals live segregated with indices above 60. The overall index of 40 for Brussels could be considered as relatively low, in view of the numerous foreign diplomats and professionals who live in upper class neighbourhoods. In Manchester the index of segregation is also relatively high, despite the relative low number of immigrants. In London the index is somewhat lower, but the aggregate index of London hides a high level of segregation for the ethnic Bangladeshi group – which is close to 70.

Segregation in both the German cases – Frankfurt am Main and Düsseldorf - is remarkably low, except for the Japanese in Düsseldorf who live in highly segregated conditions (indices above 60). Dutch and Italian cities occupy intermediate positions between the German and British cases, although the non-Italian people living in Genoa tend to be relatively segregated. In Scandinavia, the picture is hard to perceive. Ethnic segregation in Oslo appears to be moderate; in Sweden, the figures are hard to compare. In the case of Paris there are also some methodological problems that complicate the calculation of the index of segregation. The levels of ethnic segregation in Lille (France) are moderate.

Canadian figures resemble the UK figures, whereas the USA data clearly express the sharp ghetto-like divisions we encounter there. The overall picture seems to be: high values in the USA, followed by Canada, the UK, Belgium, Italy, the Netherlands, France, Sweden, Norway and Germany. The question now is whether this order corresponds to the welfare state model of the countries involved.

Welfare States

To examine the relationship between the welfare state and segregation, it is useful to have a solid typology of welfare states to see if particular characteristics of welfare states go together with a particular degree of segregation. Most investigations regarding the welfare state refer to the typology of Esping-Andersen (1990). His typology will not be used here because it is only based on some limited factors of the welfare state and fails to cover other significant factors. It does not pay any attention to housing and environmental/spatial planning, for example, which are very important aspects of welfare states with regard to residential segregation. Therefore, this section will elaborate the classifications of welfare states to discover if there is a more useful typology, which is based on other aspects of the welfare state that are relevant to the segregation debate as well. Over the last decades several typologies of welfare states have been developed to include the diversity that exists. However, a problem with typologies is that they are idealised models and do not exist in reality. Therefore, they should be handled with caution since welfare states, which belong to one type, are not entirely similar. Furthermore, typologies generally present a picture at a given moment in time; when a welfare state changes, it sometimes better fits another type. Another major critical point is that most existing typologies are based on only a few aspects of the welfare state, generally in one particular policy area, while they pretend to give a complete picture. They suggest more uniformity than actually exists. After all, welfare states consist of various aspects, which all have different features, histories and intentions (Van der Veen, 1994, p. 75). Those different parts do not automatically fit the same type. Pierson also warns of the 'danger in generalising about the welfare state which is, after all, a concept covering a range of disparate public policies' (1994, p. 5). An all-embracing typology that also focusses on the variety within welfare states is practically impossible. These remarks should be kept in mind here as well when we present a 'typology' of welfare states.

Typologies of welfare states can be made on the basis of a particular policy area, on the basis of the content of policy and on the basis of

122 *Studies in Segregation and Desegregation*

institutional characteristics such as who is involved and what is the relationship between state and market. As said, in existing typologies the welfare state is frequently reduced to just one particular policy area, usually to social policy and income-supporting programs. However, there are also typologies based on other policy areas. This section concentrates on typologies of social policy, housing and health care. These policies will or will not have impacts upon the social divisions and the housing opportunities in society.

Most typologies of welfare states are based on social insurance and income-supporting programs. This is not surprising since they are some of the most important aspects of the welfare state. Usually, the origin of the welfare state is set at the provision of social security regulation by law. Frequently quoted typologies in studies about the welfare state are those from Titmuss (1974), Therborn (1986), Esping-Andersen (1990), Leibfried (1991), Becker (1996) and Abrahamson (in Kleinman, 1996). They all classify the welfare state on the basis of social policy and are sometimes associated with employment policy.

The health policy of the welfare state is also an important element, and it can tell us something about the politics of welfare states more generally (Immergut, 1992, p. 2). The literature (Roemer, 1991; Immergut, 1992; Collaris & Bakker, 1994) distinguishes three different health care systems with respect to the relationship between state and market and to the form of organisation and financing: a private system, a national health insurance system and a universal health system.

Although the housing policy lies at the intersection of social and economic policy, in comparative welfare state analysis it is almost ignored as an element of welfare. Wilensky does not include housing in his study on welfare states because of measurement problems and since '... a bewildering array of fiscal, monetary and other policies that affect housing directly and indirectly - even remotely - have made the task of comparative analysis of public spending in this area nearly impossible' (1975, p. 7). There are just a few theoretical studies, which explicitly connect housing to welfare. Kemeny produced one of them: 'housing is even a particularly important link between the welfare state and wider society' (1992, p. 119). Kleinman (1996, pp. 1-2) also considers housing policy a significant part of the welfare state: 'By studying housing policy, one can therefore also discover much about the direction of public policy as a whole, about the balance between economic and social goals in public policy, and about the relative weights given to the free markets and state intervention in different countries'. Harloe sees housing as the 'wobbly pillar of the welfare state'

(1995, p. 11) because it is neither fully part of the welfare state, nor fully part of the free market. Such authors as Harvey, Kemeny, Donnison and Barlow and Duncan have made typologies of housing systems (Doling, 1997). In one way or another, they also focus on the relationship between state and market.

For each of these three policy areas a few typologies exist. All these different typologies of elements of the welfare state all have in common the fact that they concentrate on the relationship between state and market, i.e. on the degree of government intervention in the different policy areas. Most authors distinguish three or four different types that represent different degrees of government intervention (for example, Esping-Andersen's well-known social policy typology of liberal, corporate and social democratic welfare states). Existing typologies in each of the three policy areas (social, housing and health care) are set side-by-side based on the characteristics given by the authors. These authors all use different names, even though the typologies overlap. We have tried to express the overlap by using general overarching labels which reflect the degree of government intervention: rudimentary, residual, comprehensive and universal. The models are not phases. They are just four generalised models of welfare states, which reflect the relationship between the state and the market. A welfare state may switch to another model, but that need not occur.

In the 'rudimentary' model there is hardly any government intervention. The provisions come into being by traditional forms such as family, church and community. The second model is called 'residual' because in comparison to the others, it contains just a hint of the welfare state. Here the market is central and government intervention is minimal, a last resort for those who can not manage for themselves. The remaining two models are more difficult to distinguish since both are well-developed welfare states. In the 'comprehensive' model the state provisions need some supplements from the private sphere. This model protects the existing status differences. In a 'universal' model there is a higher degree of government intervention. The provisions have higher standards and they are universal. The last three models can be regarded as a continuum, but they do not imply convergence. The welfare states classified as rudimentary tend to have a status of their own.

So far, one might conclude that state and market are completely separate. The opposite is true: state and market have always been inextricably intertwined (Kemeny, 1998, p. 11). The state cannot exist without a market and vice versa. Both are components of one society. Therefore, these typologies of welfare states on the basis of the relationship between state and market should only be regarded as crude subdivisions of

124 *Studies in Segregation and Desegregation*

reality in which state involvement can be more intense or 'different' in one context compared to another.

These four types that can be distinguished for each of the three policy areas presented above has been applied to produce a classification of twelve European countries and the United States (Table 6.2). In filling in the table

Table 6.2 Countries ordered according to the character of social health and housing policies

	RUDI-MENTARY	RESIDUAL	COMPRE-HENSIVE	UNIVERSAL
ITALY	social policy, housing policy	labour market policy		health care policy
UNITED STATES		social policy, labour market policy, housing policy, health care policy		
UNITED KINGDOM		social policy, labour market policy, housing policy		health care policy
BELGIUM		labour market policy, housing policy	social policy, health care policy	
GERMANY			social policy, labour market policy, housing policy, health care policy	
FRANCE		labour market policy	social policy, housing policy, health care policy	
THE NETHER-LANDS		labour market policy	social policy, housing policy, health care policy	
NORWAY			labour market policy	social policy, housing policy, health care policy

SWEDEN	social policy labour market policy, housing policy, health care policy

we have used the examples of the authors who made the more specific typologies, as well as general indications in the literature and OECD-data. As stated, the purpose of this 'classification' is modest; it should *not* be interpreted as a strict multi-class typology but only as a crude way of trying to describe multiple differences among states in one scheme. Although the policy areas are only ordered on the relationship between state and market the table must be regarded as having a multidimensional character in that the welfare state is not seen as a unity but as an interacting compilation of different policy areas which could all fit into a different category.

Two striking things can be seen in this table. The first is that the policy areas show a high degree of overlap; in most of the countries presented the policy areas distinguished tend to fit in the same model. Secondly, rough clusters of countries can be distinguished: South European countries; Anglo-Saxon countries; continental European countries, such as Belgium, Germany, France and the Netherlands; and finally, the Scandinavian countries.

It is interesting that these clusters of countries, on the basis of these policy areas, correspond to the results of a clustering on the basis of economic, demographic and socio-cultural characteristics (data from OECD, 1997; Eurostat, 1984; 1995a; 1995b). Although the table seems to be clear, it is rather generalised. The positioning of the policy areas needs many annotations that underline their specific characteristics.

For example, in the table, housing policy in the United Kingdom is classified as similar to housing in the United States. However housing policy in the United States has many more residual characteristics. Nevertheless, housing policy in the United Kingdom has more residual characteristics than comprehensive ones. Moreover the policy areas are treated as homogeneous entities, but in reality the opposite is true. For example, social policy consists of different parts, which could have fairly different orientations. Furthermore, the table is far from complete: just a few policy areas are considered. It is conceivable that the countries show less similarity when policy areas are examined in greater detail and when other elements of the welfare state are also considered. In short, the table will only be used as an to aid to characterising different welfare states.

126 *Studies in Segregation and Desegregation*

The Relation between the Welfare State and Segregation

An intersection of both tables reveals a clear association (Table 6.3). There appears to be a link between the level of inequality or ethnic spatial division and the level of intervention of the welfare state. Concerning ethnic segregation, the United States and the United Kingdom as well as Brussels have relatively high scores while the German cities have relatively low levels of segregation. So, in the more residual welfare states the ethnic segregation is higher than in others except for Belgium. The specific position of housing policy in the Belgium context most certainly plays a role, which is only a marginal one.

Altogether, the central hypothesis that wide and deeply involved government intervention – especially through welfare arrangements – will prevent sharp patterns of segregation, that the welfare state matters and that social processes cannot be ascribed only to economic restructuring and globalisation processes seems to be supported. It was assumed that universal welfare states would have lower degrees of segregation while the so-called residual welfare states would have higher degrees of segregation.

This empirical exercise does not reject the idea that the more comprehensive welfare states have prevented sharp patterns of segregation by making use of different (welfare state) arrangements, such as income distribution, social security, control of the housing market and compensating policies.

Table 6.3 Cities according to welfare state classification and index of ethnic segregation

IS: 0-20	IS: 20-40	IS: 40-60	IS: 60-100
UNIVERSAL WELFARE STATES			
Sweden	Sweden 14 municipalities: foreign-born (before 1985), Finns (before 1985)	Sweden 14 municipalities: foreign-born (after 1985), Iranians (after 1985), Finns (after 1985)	Sweden 14 municipalities: Turks (after 1985), Iraquis (after 1985)
COMPREHENSIVE WELFARE STATES			
The Nether- Lands	The Netherlands	The Netherlands	The Netherlands

	Amsterdam: Ethnic minorities, Moroccans, Surinamese	Amsterdam: Turks	
	Rotterdam: Surinamese	Rotterdam: Ethnic minorities, Turks, Moroccans	
	The Hague: Surinamese	The Hague: Ethnic minorities, Turks, Moroccans	
	Utrecht: Ethnic minorities, Surinamese, Antilleans	Utrecht: Turks, Moroccans, South-Europeans	
Belgium	Belgium	Belgium Brussels: Foreigners, Moroccans	Belgium Brussels: Turks, Moroccans
Germany Frankfurt: Turks, Italians	Germany Frankfurt: Moroccans, Yugoslavians, Spaniards, Dutchmen, Frenchmen, Americans, British, Greek	Germany Frankfurt: Korean, Japanese	Germany
Düsseldorf: Foreigners	Düsseldorf: Turks, Moroccans	Düsseldorf: Japanese	
France Paris: Foreigners, Portuguese	France Paris: Algerians	France	France
	Lille: Non-French		

RESIDUAL WELFARE STATES

Great Britain	Great Britain London: Non-White	Great Britain London: Black Caribbean, Black African, Indian, Pakistani	Great Britain London: Bangladeshi

128 *Studies in Segregation and Desegregation*

	Birmingham: Black African	Birmingham: Non-White, Black Caribbean, Indian Manchester: Non-White, Blacks, Pakistani	Birmingham: Bangladeshi, Pakistani Manchester: Indian Continent, Bangladeshi Leeds: Bangladeshi, Pakistani, Black Caribbean
		Sheffield: Black Caribbean	Sheffield: Bangladeshi, Pakistani
United States	United States	United States	United States
			Chicago: Blacks Cleveland: Blacks Los Angeles: Blacks New York: Blacks Newark: Blacks Philadelphia: Blacks St. Louis: Blacks Atlanta: Blacks Baltimore: Blacks
RUDIMENTARY WELFARE STATES			
Italy	Italy Turin: non-Italian residents Milan: non-Italian residents	Italy Turin: non-Italian non-residents Milan: non-Italian non-residents Genoa: non-Italian residents	Italy Genoa: non-Italian non-residents

Based on Tables 6.1 and 6.2.

References

Andersson, R. (1998), 'Socio-Spatial Dynamics: Ethnic Divisions of Mobility and Housing in post-Palme Sweden' *Urban Studies*, vol. 35 (3), pp. 397-428.

Becker, U. (1996), 'Over de typologie van welvaartsbestellen. Esping-Andersens theorie in discussie', Beleid en Maatschappij 1996 (1), pp. 19-30.

Boal, F.W. (1976), 'Ethnic Residential Segregation', in D.T. Herbert, & R.J. Johnston (eds), *Social Areas in Cities, Vol.1, Spatial Processes and Form*, London, pp. 111-158.

Boal, F.W. (1998), 'Exclusion and Inclusion: Segregation and Deprivation in Belfast', in S. Musterd, & W. Ostendorf (eds), *Urban Segregation and the Welfare State. Inequality and Exclusion in Western Cities*, Routledge, London, pp. 94-109.

Breebaart, M., Musterd, S. & Ostendorf, W. (1996), 'Etnische segregatie en beleid', AME, Amsterdam Study Centre for the Metropolitan Environment, Universiteit van Amsterdam, Amsterdam.

Brevik, I. (forthcoming), 'Income Inequalities and Socio-Economic Segregation in Oslo', in J. Burgers, & S. Musterd (forthcoming).

Clark, W.A.V. (1998), 'Mass Migration and Local outcomes: Is International Migration to the United States Creating a New Urban Underclass?', *Urban Studies*, vol. 35 (3), pp. 371-383.

Collaris, J.W.M. & Bakker, W.E. (1994), 'Naar een Europese gezondheidszorg?', in G. Engbersen, A.C. Hemerijck & W.E. Bakker (eds), *Zorgen in het Europese huis. Verkenningen over de grenzen van nationale verzorgingsstaten*, Boom, Amsterdam, pp. 173-188.

Danermark, B. & Jacobson, T. (1989), 'Local Housing Policy and Residential Segregation', *Scandinavian Housing and Planning Research*, vol. 6, pp. 245-256.

Doling, J. (1997), *Comparative Housing Policy. Government and Housing in Advanced Industrialized Countries*, Macmillan Press Ltd., London.

Doorslaer, E.K.A. van (1998), *Gezondheidszorg tussen Marx en markt. Oratie*, Erasmus Universiteit Rotterdam, Rotterdam.

Esping-Andersen, G. (1990), *The Three Worlds of Welfare Capitalism*, Polity Press, Cambridge.

Esping-Andersen, G. (ed) (1996), *Welfare States in Transition. National Adaptations in Global Economies*, Sage, London.

Eurostat (1984), Basisstatistieken van de Europese Unie. Vergelijking van de belangrijkste partners van de Unie. Luxemburg. 23ᵉ uitgave.

Eurostat (1995a), Basisstatistieken van de Europese Unie. Vergelijking van de belangrijkste partners van de Unie. Luxemburg, 33ᵉ uitgave.

Eurostat (1995b), *Eurostat Jaarboek '95*, Een statistische blik op Europa 1983-1993. Luxemburg.

Fainstein, S.S., Gordon, I. & Harloe, M. (eds) (1992), *Divided Cities. New York & London in the Contemporary World*, Blackwell, Oxford, UK.

Freund, B. (1997), 'Staatsbürger aus entwickelten marktwirtschaftlichen Ländern in Frankfurt am Main und Umgebung', *Frankfurter Statistische Berichte*, vol. 59 (1).

Hamnett, C. (1994), 'Social Polarisation in Global Cities: Theory and Evidence', *Urban Studies*, vol. 31 (3), pp. 401-424.

Hamnett, C. (1996a), 'Why Sassen Is Wrong: A Response to Burgers', *Urban Studies*, vol. 33 (1), pp. 107-110.

130 *Studies in Segregation and Desegregation*

Hamnett, C. (1996b), 'Social Polarisation, Economic Restructuring and Welfare State Regimes', *Urban Studies*, vol. 33 (8), pp. 1407-1430.

Hamnett, C. (1998), 'Social Polarisation, Economic Restructuring and Welfare regimes', in S. Musterd, & W. Ostendorf (eds), *Urban Segregation and the Welfare State. Inequality and Exclusion in Western Cities*, Routledge, London, pp. 15-27.

Harloe, M. (1995), *The People's Home? Social Rented Housing in Europe and America*, Blackwell, Oxford, UK.

Haussmann, H. and Sackmann, R. (1994), 'Changes in Berlin: The Emergence of an Underclass?', *Built Environment*, vol. 20 (3), pp. 231-241.

Immergut, E.M. (1992), *Health Politics. Interests and Institutions in Western Europe*, Cambridge University Press, Cambridge.

Kemeny, J. (1992), *Housing and Social Theory*, Routledge, London.

Kemeny, J. (1998), 'Narrative, Sagas and Social Policy. State and Market in Housing Research', Paper presented at ENHR-Conference in Cardiff, 7-11 September 1998.

Kleinman, M. (1996), *Housing, Welfare and the State in Europe. A Comparative Analysis of Britain, France and Germany*, Edward Elgar, Cheltenham.

Kloosterman, R.C. (1996), 'Double Dutch: Polarization Trends in Amsterdam and Rotterdam after 1980', *Regional Studies*, vol. 30 (5), pp. 467-476.

Kruythoff, H.M. & Baart, B. (1998), *Towards Undivided Cities in Western Europe. New Challenges for Urban Policy, Part 6*, Delft University Press, Lille, Delft.

Leibfried, S. (1991), *Towards a European Welfare State? On Integrating Poverty Regimes in the European Community*, Arbeitspapier No. 2, Bremen University: Zentrum fur Sozialpolitik.

Marcuse, P. (1996), *Is Australia Different? Globalization and the New Urban Poverty*, Australian Housing and Urban Research Institute.

Massey, D.S & Denton, N.A. (1993), *American Apartheid. Segregation and the Making of the Underclass*, Harvard University Press, Cambridge.

Massey, D.S., Gross, A.B. & Shibuya, K. (1994), 'Migration, Segregation, and the Geographic Concentration of Poverty', *American Sociological Review*, vol. 59 (June), pp. 425-445.

Morris, L.D. (1987), 'Local Social Polarization: A Case Study of Hartlepool', *The International Journal of Urban and Regional Research*, vol. 11, pp. 331-350.

Murie, A. (1993), *Cities and Housing after the Welfare State*, AME, Amsterdam Study Centre for the Metropolitan Environment, Universiteit van Amsterdam, Amsterdam.

Murie, A. (1998), 'Segregation, Exclusion and Housing in the Divided City', in S. Musterd and W. Ostendorf (eds) *Urban Segregation and Social Exclusion in Western Welfare States*, pp.110-125.

Musterd, S. (1994), 'A Rising European Underclass?', *Built Environment*, vol. 20 (3), pp. 185-191.

Musterd, S. (1998), 'Uimtelijke segregatie in Europese steden: achtergronden, symptomen en dynamiek', in H. Priemus & E. Philipsen (eds), *Naar een ongedeelde stad. Volkshuisvestingsbeleid als wapen tegen ruimtelijke segregatie*, Delft University Press, Delft, pp. 21-36.

Musterd, S. & Ostendorf, W. (1994), 'Affluence, Access to Jobs, and Ethnicity in the Dutch Welfare State: The Case of Amsterdam', *Built Environment*, vol. 20 (3), pp. 242-253.

Musterd, S. & Ostendorf, W. (eds) (1998), *Urban Segregation and the Welfare State. Inequality and Exclusion in Western Cities*, Routledge, London.

Musterd, S., Ostendorf, W. & Breebaart, M. (1998), *Multi-Ethnic Metropolis: Patterns and Policies*, Kluwer Wolters Publishers, Dordrecht.

Tineke Domburg-De Rooij and Sako Musterd 131

OECD (1997), *Employment Outlook, July 1997*, OECD, Paris.

O'Loughlin, J. & Friedrichs, J. (eds) (1996), *Social Polarisation in Post-Industrial Metropolises*, Walter de Gruyter, Berlin & New York.

Ostendorf, W. and Vijgen, J. (1982), 'Segregatie en sociale integratie. De spreiding van bevolking binnen dynamische stadsgewesten', *Geografisch Tijdschrift*, vol. 16 (4), pp. 368-379.

Peach, C. (1996), 'Does Britain Have Ghettos?', *Transactions of the Institute of British Geographers*, vol. 21, pp. 216-235.

Peach, C. and Smith, S. (1981), 'Introduction', in C. Peach, V. Robinson & S. Smith (eds), *Ethnic Segregation in Cities*, Croom Helm, London, pp. 9-22.

Petsimeris, P. (1998), 'Urban Decline and the New Social and Ethnic Divisions in the Core Cities of the Italic Industrial Triangle', *Urban Studies*, vol. 35 (3), March, pp. 449-465.

Pierson, P. (1994), *Dismantling the Welfare State. Reagan, Thatcher and the Politics of Retrenchment*, Cambridge University Press, Cambridge (reprinted 1996).

Polanyi, K. (1944), *The Great Transformation*, Rinehart, New York.

Portes, A. & Sensenbrenner, J. (1993), 'Embeddedness and Immigration: Notes on the Social Determinants of Economic Action', *American Journal of Sociology*, vol. 98 (6), pp. 1320-1350.

Rhein, C. (1998), 'Globalisation, Social Change and Minorities in Metropolitan Paris: The Emergence of New Class Patterns', *Built Environment*, vol. 20 (3), pp. 429-447.

Roemer, M.I. (1991), *National Health Systems of the World, Volume 1, The Countries*, Oxford University Press, New York.

Santiago, A.M. & Galster, G. (1995), 'Puerto Rican Segregation in the United States: Cause or Consequence of Economic Status?', *Social Problems*, vol. 42 (3), pp. 361-389.

Sassen, S. (1991), *The Global City. New York, London, Tokyo*, Princeton University Press, Princeton, New Jersey.

Schill, M.H. (1994), 'Race, the Underclass, and Public Policy', *Law and Social Inquiry, Journal of the American Bar Foundation*, vol. 19 (2), pp. 433-456.

Silver, H. (1993), 'National Conceptions of the New Urban Poverty: Social Structural Change in Britain, France and the United States', *International Journal of Urban and Regional Research*, vol. 17 (3), pp. 336-354.

Therborn, G. (1986), *Why Some Peoples Are More Employed than Others*, Ashgate, London.

Thrift, N. (1994), 'Globalisation, Regulation, Urbanisation: The Case of the Netherlands', *Urban Studies*, vol. 31 (3), pp. 365-380.

Titmuss, R.M. (1974), *Social Policy. An Introduction*, George Allen and Unwin Ltd., London.

Veen, R. van der (1994), 'De wankele verzorgingsstaat. Een vergelijkende analyse van verzorgingsstaten in het licht van internationaliseringsprocessen', in G. Engbersen, A.C. Hemerijck & W.E. Bakker (eds), Zorgen in het Europese huis. Verkenningen over de grenzen van nationale verzorgingsstaten, Boom, Amsterdam, pp. 58-88.

Wagstaff, A., van Doorslaer, E., van der Burg, H., *et al.* (25 authors) (1997), *Equity in the Finance of Health Care: Some Further International Comparisons*, ECuity Project Working Paper, No. 11. Erasmus Universiteit Rotterdam, Rotterdam.

Wilensky, H.L. (1975), *The Welfare State and Equality. Structural and Ideological Roots of Public Expenditures*, University of California Press, Berkeley.

Wilson, W.J. (1987), *The Truly Disadvantaged, the Inner City, the Underclass and Public Polity*, University of Chicago Press, Chicago.

7 Urban Poverty in Germany[*]

ANDREAS FARWICK, BRITTA KLAGGE AND
WOLFGANG TAUBMANN

Introduction

Problems linked with poverty - specifically urban poverty and social exclusion - have become central issues not only in Germany but also in many other EU member states. More than one quarter of all Europeans - depending on their own income - are regarded as 'poor', which means they receive less than 50% of the national average in the country where they reside.

There are at least four different problem areas in modern social and economic development that are relevant to increasing poverty. First, there is the well known discussion about the consequences of globalisation and industrial restructuring for the labour market. Secondly, it has been suggested that the ongoing labour market segmentation results in social exclusion. Thirdly, the weakening of welfare state functions in areas such as social security systems, education, health and housing provision mainly affect the poorer groups in society. The fourth reason is to be found in socio-demographic and structural changes in modern societies, which are also responsible for the 'new risks of poverty'. Simplified, this development can be described as an individualisation and pluralisation of life styles or as tendencies towards disintegration of the traditional household and family structures.

Poverty is a difficult issue both from a methodological and theoretical point of view. The concept of poverty always has to be discussed and defined within an appropriate social context.

---

[*] This contribution is based on two research projects on urban poverty in Germany, supported by the German Research Foundation (Deutsche Forschungsgemeinschaft) and the University of Bremen.

134 *Studies in Segregation and Desegregation*

How Can Poverty Be Measured and Defined?

'Absolute' poverty, threatening the very existence of men, can no longer be found in Germany and other industrial nations. However, absolute poverty is still a central problem in many countries of the third world, as the latest report by the 'Development Program of the United Nations' (UNDP) has shown.

In contrast to poverty as defined in countries of the third world and defined mainly on the basis of material deficiency, the present discussion on poverty in countries of the first world uses a relative poverty definition that is derived from the socially defined degree of under-supply.

In this discussion we will use the so-called resource or economic concept of poverty, i.e. insufficient income, because in all countries with a free market economy the 'accessibility to chances and perspectives in life is primarily regulated by the availability of income'.

Besides the resource-theoretical concept, the 'life-situation orientated theory' tries to analyse the supply in all spheres of life: work, education, dwelling and health. It also considers participation in various realms of life in order to define the degree of insufficient supply and deficient participation in social life as a measure of poverty. So far it has not been possible to practically apply this second concept of poverty with regard to indicators or different levels of insufficient supply.

In the following, resource-orientated concepts are taken as the basis for approaching the question of how poverty could develop and which groups are specially concerned. The concept 'income' is central because of the availability of sufficient statistical data.

On the one hand, the concept of resource uses as an indicator dependency on public assistance - as a rule so-called permanent help with the cost of living outside of institutions (*laufende Hilfe zum Lebensunterhalt ausserhalb von Einrichtungen*). On the other hand, certain poverty lines are considered and calculated as shares of an average income.

Recipients of Public Assistance as Indicator of Poverty

By using both indicators, a short overview of the development of poverty in Germany's old federal states can be provided. Official statistics concerning social assistance serve as a source, which registers the so-called 'poverty addressed by the state by social means'. In spite of weaknesses and taking the official statistics for social security as an indicator of poverty, we see

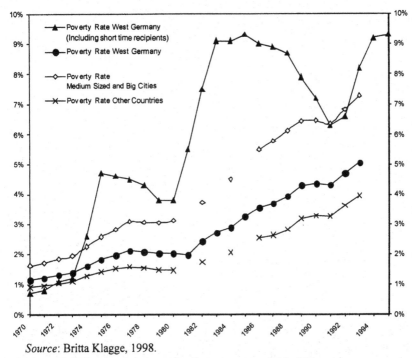

Source: Britta Klagge, 1998.

Figure 7.1 Unemployment and poverty rates in West Germany, 1970-1993/94

that since 1970 the number of recipients of social support has grown by more than four (Figure 7.1).

In 1970 more than 1% of the population received social assistance, and in 1994 the figure was over 5%. These so-called cumulative statistics, however, are higher than the statistics at the end of the year which include only those persons who received social support on December 31st of the year. At the end of 1993, for instance, 2.45 million recipients received permanent help, while the cumulative number of recipients within the year came to 3.33 million. The difference between these two figures reveals a relatively high percentage of people that were supported for only a short time. Since 1980 the poverty rate of foreigners has been increasing rapidly, i.e., the rise of the total poverty share is mainly caused by the growing share of foreign recipients. While the share of foreigners dependent on welfare stood at 9% in 1980 (old Lander), it ran to 23% in 1997 (Statistisches Jahrbuch für die BRD, 1999).

Whatever figure we take, the number of recipients of social assistance has increased considerably since the beginning of the 80s and has again since 1991, after a slight decline in 1990. In 1970 many old people received social support, but in 1994 the risk of poverty among groups 65 years of age and older was at its lowest compared to all German age groups.

In contrast, the poverty risk of younger age groups - mainly young

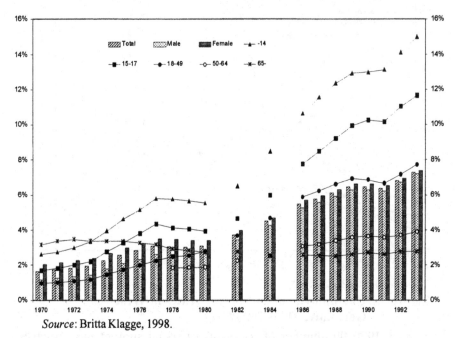

Source: Britta Klagge, 1998.

Figure 7.2 Poverty rates by gender and age in West German medium-sized and large cities, 1970–1993

people between 15 and 18 years and children below 14 years - has grown considerably. As Figure 7.2 shows, this is especially true in medium-sized and large cities. In 1994 every tenth child in non-German households received social assistance. This 'infantilisation of poverty addressed by the state' can mainly be explained by the increasing number of so-called residual families, particularly the growing number of households with single mothers. In other words, children often become paupers, because a single parent, due to divorce or separation from a partner, has to live on social support. It can be supposed, that the increasing disappearance of the classical model of a 'normal' family leads to new risks of poverty.

Besides, the poverty risk for foreigners, which is more than double that of the German population, another group with a high risk of poverty is, quite naturally, the unemployed. In 1993 30.8% of all recipients of public assistance were at the same time recipients of unemployment benefits.

In general, the statistics for persons dependent on welfare demonstrate that the poverty risk of the unemployed, children and single parents as well as foreigners is well above the average. With regard to these partly new groups living in poverty, sociologists speak of a 'heterogeneisation of poverty'.

Poverty Lines as Defined by Different Relative Incomes

Beside the statistics concerning social assistance, the data of the Socio-Economic Panel (SOEP) are also used to analyse poverty. The SOEP - a wide-ranging representative longitudinal study of private households since 1984 - analyses the living conditions in a sample of almost 6,600 households (about 12,700 persons in 1998) and marginally shows the problems of poverty. Since 1990 an approximate 2,200 households (ca. 4,450 persons) in the new federal states have also been included in the annual survey (Statistisches Bundesamt, 1997).

The concept of poverty used in the survey operates on three different threshold figures to define the relative lines of poverty: 'Severe' income poverty exists if a person has less than 40% of the average net income; usually people are described as 'poor' when their so-called net equivalence-income is below 50% of the average income, a level quite common in the EU; with 60% of the average income one speaks of an income position 'close' to poverty. The SOEP data for the period between 1984 and 1995 show a quite surprising result for the population in the 'old' federal republics (Figure 7.3).

In contrast to the general impression as well as to the data of the statistics concerning social security, the number of people whose income was less than 40, 50 or 60% of the average income of a reference population remained more or less stable in the second half of the 80s and even went slightly down at the beginning of the 90s. Only since 1993 has there been an increase in the number of people affected by poverty. Between 1984 and 1993 the number of welfare recipients increased by 75% (1984: 2.9%; 1993: 5.1% of the population), whereas according to the data of the SOEP the percentage of the '50%-income poor' during the same period of time remained at 11% (compare Figure 7.3).

This discrepancy seems to be difficult to explain because of the lack of any obvious reasons for the difference. It is, however, likely that the latent or 'hidden' poverty in about one decade changed into open poverty. At the beginning of the 80s there was quite a considerable number of people (of undisclosed cases), who in spite of their right did not apply for social

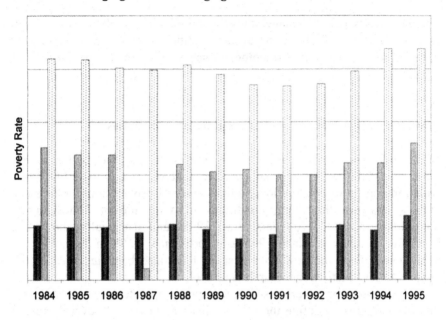

■ Severe Poverty (40 %)   ▦ Poverty (50 %)   ▧ Close to Poverty (60 %)

Figure 7.3 Poverty in West Germany, 1984–1995 (SOEP 1997)

assistance out of shame or for other reasons; nowadays the number of those who know how to use their entitlements has grown conspicuously. The bashful poor no longer predominate, and those with growing self-awareness are increasing in number. A further reason might be the increase of the above-mentioned social transfers which prevent a growing number of poor persons. In Germany the percentage of the '60%-income poor' would have amounted to 24% without public assistance, which reduced it to 18% in 1998 (Süddeutsche Zeitung, Oct. 14, 1999).

For the period between 1984 and 1995 the SOEP data show the following details: The percentage of people, living in 'severe poverty' during the decade between 1984 and 1994 was between 4 and 5% of the population; in 1995 it increased to 6.1%. Between 10 to 12% of West German inhabitants lived below the poverty line of 50%; the poverty rate in this group also increased in 1995 and reached 13%. Since 1984 about one fifth of the population has had to live on an income that was below 60% of the average income.

When seen against the background of the distribution of income and the poverty quota, the result of the sample survey could lead to the conclusion that we are far from a 'two-third society'. However, when we regard its material situation and living condition, the data so far do not prove that one-third of the population will permanently be excluded from taking part in the social life of the country. In opposition to this social model and on the basis of empirical data, sociologists have developed the concept of the '70-20-10 society': 70% live in a situation without poverty; 20% are periodically in a position close to poverty; and 10% live below the 50% poverty line.

One of our assumptions was that increasing poverty might be linked to growing spatial disparities between poor and non-poor populations. This process was looked into at two levels. Firstly, the development of poverty was compared in 78 cities in West Germany, and secondly, intra-urban segregation with regard to poverty was analysed in selected cities (Bielefeld, Bremen, Düsseldorf, Essen, Frankfurt, Hannover, Stuttgart) and expanded by longitudinal research in Bielefeld and Bremen.

Poverty and Welfare Recipients in West German Cities: Interurban Disparities

As in the whole country, in West German cities (above 50,000 residents) poverty based on the number of recipients of welfare, has also increased rapidly since the early 1970s. In 1970 the rate was 1.6 % and in 1993 7.3%. In both years poverty was significantly above the West German average (see Figure 7.2).

At the beginning of the 1970s poverty among the aged was more severe than among children, who since the early 1980s have been increasingly affected.

Regional disparities are large, including a significant North-South gap. In the cities of the northern federal states (Laender) the average percentage of poverty ran to 7.6% in 1993, while it ran to only 5.6% in the southern federal states (Bavaria, Rhineland-Palatinate, Baden-Württemberg).

One explanation for these disparities might be found in the general economic situation and the intensifying processes of polarisation within a market economy, which leads to lower unemployment or technologically advanced industries in the southern part of Germany.

With the help of different regression models it is possible to isolate four explanatory factors which explain the growing variances of inter-urban poverty rates in 1988 and 1993. Regression models including at least three of the following variables explain up to 60% of the intra-urban disparities

140 *Studies in Segregation and Desegregation*

of the German and total population and almost completely explain the North-South disparity.

Table 7.1 Regression analysis to explain the variance of poverty rates among West German cities for the years 1988 and 1993 (Partial regression coefficient of the standardised variables)

	Dependent Variable							
	Poverty Rate 1988				Poverty Rate 1993			
Independent Variable	Model 1	Model 2	Model 3	Model 4	Model 1	Model 2	Model 3	Model 4
Unemployment Rate 1987 resp. 1993	0.64 (7.20)	0.52 (6.27)	0.52 (6.59)	0.74 (8.91)	0.61 (6.65)	0.49 (5.74)	0.65 (7.89)	0.77 (8.81)
Rate of Tertiarisation 1988 resp. 1993			0.23 (2.89)	0.34 (4.41)			0.25 (3.10)	0.34 (3.98)
Share of Children 1987 resp. 1992								
Share of Foreigners 1987 e.g. 1992				0.40 (4.78)				0.38 (4.43)
Share of Church Affiliation 1987		-0.39 (-4.75)	-0.36 (-4.50)			-0.40 (-4.67)	-0.32 (-3.99)	
R^2 Corrected	0.401	0.488	0.534	0.546	0.368	0.462	0.577	0.523
F-Value	51.8	37.7	30.4	31.9	44.2	33.2	33.7	27.7
N	77	78	78	78	75	76	73	74
Excluded Outliers (Licence Plate)	OF	–	–	–	MA, OF, WI	MA, WI	FL, NMS, MA, OF, WI	FL, NMS, MA, WI

[a] The partial correlation coefficients of the standardised variables and the F-values are significant at the 1%-level. As outliers were excluded those cities showed a standardised residual value above 3.
[b] Unemployment rate = Unemployed persons in percent of all employed persons working under the social insurance system plus of all unemployed (in percent).
[c] Rate of tertiarisation = Employed persons in the tertiary sector in percent of all employed persons (under the social insurance system).
[d] Share of children = Persons below 18 years old in percent of the total population.
[e] Share of foreigners = Foreigners in percent of the total resident population.
[f] Share of church affiliation = Members of the Protestant or Catholic church in percent of the total population.
Source: Calculated by Britta Klagge 1997. Based on data from Bundesanstalt für Arbeit, Statistisches Bundesamt, Statistische Landesamter.

Differences in the unemployment rates are the most significant factor in explaining the variance of poverty rates. This is not surprising, as unemployment is the most important cause of poverty.

The share of tertiary employment as an indicator of the modernity of the economic structure of cities is an additional factor. At constant unemployment rates, a higher share of tertiary rates predict higher poverty rates. This result confirms the hypothesis of increasing social polarisation in cities with a 'modern' economic structure.

The number of foreigners in the total population is also positively correlated with poverty rates. There are different underlying reasons: A large, but not identifiable number of foreigners on welfare are persons seeking asylum that in most cases are welfare recipients by law. Recent legal changes have excluded asylum seekers from welfare so that future data will better describe the situation of the 'regular' foreigners. These 'regular' foreigners are over-represented in those categories that carry the highest poverty risk (children and unemployed persons). Therefore, a poverty quota among immigrants of about 30% can be observed (Bedau et al. 1996).

In cities with a more conservative milieu – indicated by larger membership in the two main Christian churches in Germany – poverty rates are lower, if unemployment rates are kept constant. This result confirms the 'behavioural' hypothesis which states that in conservative milieus there is a share of poor household that are eligible for but do not seek welfare, possibly due to traditional values and family structures. The significance of behavioural issues shows that poverty rates based on welfare do not necessarily correspond with poverty rates based on income indicators.

In a third step we can ask which consequences rising poverty rates in German cities have for inner urban development in terms of social segregation.

Selected German Cities: Intra-Urban Disparities

As we have seen above, the number of poor people, especially in cities, has increased as they have in other Western countries. In relation to this phenomenon a debate on the emergence of an urban underclass and of social exclusion has developed.

It has been argued that with the increase in poverty the spatial separation of poor and non-poor people in large cities has been growing. Investigations in various West German cities have shown that the poor are

142 *Studies in Segregation and Desegregation*

especially concentrated in run-down and not yet gentrified inner-city neighbourhoods and in the peripheral public housing estates of the sixties and seventies. With the growing concentration of poverty in some areas of the city the extent of stigmatisation and discrimination has gone up. Because of social as well as spatial exclusion people often react with apathy, resignation and other deviant behaviour. More and more it is argued, that spatial exclusion in highly concentrated poverty areas leads to long term poverty and to a vicious cycle of poverty and welfare dependence. A development towards a socially and spatially excluded population to which one could refer as an urban underclass is becoming more and more possible.

Facing these developments and referring to the situation in Germany two empirical questions can be derived from the debate:

- Does the increase in poverty in large German cities lead to an increasing intra-urban spatial polarisation of poverty?
- Do poor neighbourhoods make their residents poorer? Do these poor neighbourhoods reduce the chance of terminating poverty?

In the following, the term 'poverty' is again defined as 'publicly administered poverty', that is, by the type of poverty explicitly dealt with by the welfare state through public assistance.

Based on our empirical findings there is no unambiguous answer to the first question. The spatial patterns and especially the development of segregation of the recipients of welfare in the above-mentioned cities only partly correspond to our theoretical assumptions. First, there is no very significant correlation between the general share of recipients of welfare and the extent of inner-urban segregation. It is, however, of interest that cities with a higher share of foreigners show lower indices of segregation in connection with both the German and foreign population. Second, the index of segregation – a relative measurement – did not increase significantly during the observed period of time, despite on overall increase of the poverty level. At least this was true for the cities in Table 7.2 for which we had sufficient data to make comparisons.

Measured in absolute terms, the increase in the total number of persons dependent on public assistance in these cities has led to a very high growth of the number of recipients of welfare in those districts where already in 1980 a high proportion of poor people had been observed.

Table 7.2 Comparison of indices of segregation (Duncan/Duncan) of recipients of welfare in the middle of the 1980s and in 1997

Table 7.2a Bremen, break down of the total effect of an increase in the poverty rate in poverty areas (1994-1997)

City division	Rec. 94 (a_{t0})	pop. 94 (p_{t0})	rec.-r. 94 (r_{t0})	rec. 97 (a_{t1})	Pop. 97 (p_{t1})	rec.-r. 97 (r_{t1})	rec. 97 with pop.97 (a_{fbt1})	Rec. 97 with pop.94 (a_{fbto})	$a_{t1}-a_{to}$ (z_1)	$a_{fbt1}-a_{t0}$ (z_2)	$a_{fbto}-a_{t0}$ (z_3)	z_1-z_2 (A)	z_3-z_2 (B)	z_1-z_3 (C)
Poverty areas	9010	76809	11,7	10547	76430	13,8	10172	10222	1536	1161	1212	375	50	324
Other areas	34324	474258	7,2	41210	471749	8,7	41585	41807	6886	7262	7483	-376	221	-597
Bremen total	43334	551067	7,9	51756	548179	9,4	51756	52029	8422	8422	8695	0	273	-273

Table 7.2b Bielefeld, break down of the total effect of an increase in the poverty rate in poverty areas (1992-1996)

Neighbourhood district	Rec. 92 (a_{t0})	pop. 92 (p_{t0})	rec.-r. 92 (r_{t0})	rec. 96 (a_{t1})	pop. 96 (p_{t1})	rec.-r. 96 (r_{t1})	rec. 96 with pop. 96 (a_{fbt1})	rec. 96 with pop. 92 (a_{fbto})	$a_{t1}-a_{t0}$ (z_1)	$a_{fbt1}-a_{t0}$ (z_2)
Poverty areas	1473	33658	4,4	3099	35244	8,8	2187	2088	1626	714
Other areas	6671	286801	2,3	10943	286122	3,8	11886	11914	4272	5215
Bielefeld total	8144	320459	2,5	14042	321366	4,4	14042	14002	5898	5898

144 *Studies in Segregation and Desegregation*

Despite the generally stable extent of segregation because of poverty, a comparison of the analysed cities reveals that the spatial patterns of segregation do not follow a general model but are largely determined by specific local circumstances, that is historical, structural, socio-demographic or economic development as well as by different policies, e.g. low-income housing.

These results show that we need a complex pattern of attempted explanations. In the following section, a further attempt is made, to partially answer the two above mentioned research questions through a detailed examination of the situation in the cities of Bremen and Bielefeld.

The Example of Bremen and Bielefeld: Intra-Urban Disparities and the Risk of Entering the Underclass

In this example the number of welfare recipients is again used as an indicator of the extent of poverty since data for the number of welfare recipients in the two cities are available at a small-scale spatial level and –

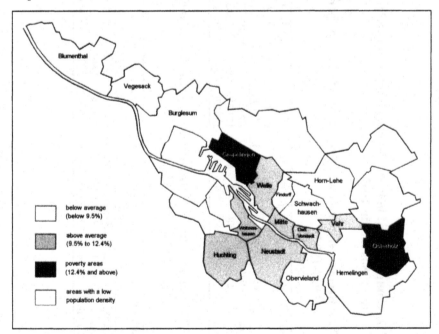

Figure 7.4 Bremen, rate of social assistance recipients in city divisions, 1997

what was decisive for the discussion of the second research question – longitudinal data sets exist for the recipients of social assistance.

A first look at a map showing the social assistance rates of the districts in Bremen for 1997 confirms an uneven spatial distribution of poverty (Figure 7.4). This is a common spatial pattern, which could be found in all the cities we analysed.

In some areas of Bremen the number of welfare recipients was more than one standard deviation above the average value of all city districts. In the following, areas with poverty rates of more than one standard deviation above the mean value are defined as poverty areas. In Bremen at the level of city districts (areas with an average of 30,000 inhabitants), there are two poverty areas: Grepelingen and Osterholz. Unfortunately, for Bremen there are no new data available on the level of neighbourhood districts (areas with on average 6,500 inhabitants). However, for 1988, a map showing the distribution of poverty at the level of neighbourhood districts reveals that the city district of Osterholz is very heterogeneous (Figure 7.5). Poverty is mainly concentrated in public housing estates, whereas in Grepelingen - a

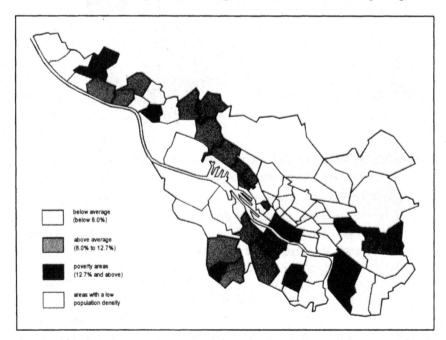

Figure 7.5 Bremen, rate of social assistance recipients in neighbourhood districts, 1989

traditional working class district near the harbour - a relative high number of poor people can be found in all neighbourhood districts.

For the city of Bielefeld, there are new data obtainable for small neighbourhood districts. As in Bremen, Figure 7.6 shows a strong uneven distribution of recipients of welfare. Poverty areas here consist of traditional working class areas, public housing estates and unattractive inner city regions.

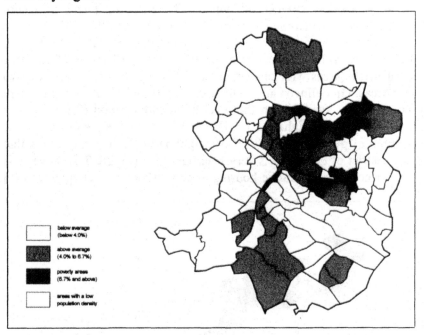

Figure 7.6 Bielefeld, rate of social assistance recipients in neighbourhood districts, 1996

Regarding the development of the rate of social assistance in both cities it can be seen that in poverty areas the rate of welfare recipients has grown faster than in other areas of the city (Figure 7.7). These findings of an above average increase in the poverty rate of areas which are already characterised by poverty indicate that there has indeed been a polarisation process of poverty in these two cities (Farwick, 1996; Farwick, 1998b).

When looking for the reasons for the above average increase of the social assistance rate in poverty areas we have to consider that the development of the rate of welfare recipients in an area is dependent on the change in the number of welfare recipients and/or the total population of this area. Using a method similar to the shift-and-share analysis, we first divided the effect of an above average increase in the poverty rate (A) into an effect of a change in the total population of the poverty area (B) and second, into an effect of a change in the number of persons dependent on welfare (C) (Tables 7.3a and 7.3b).

The outcome of this analysis is that the above average increase of the poverty rate in poverty areas is mostly due to an increase in the poor population and only to a smaller extent to the decrease in the total population of these areas (for a more detailed description see Farwick, 1996; Farwick 1998b).

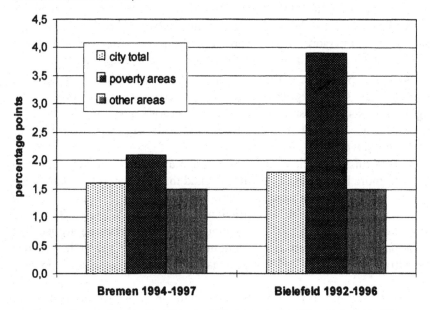

Source: Bremen Longitudinal Sample of Social Assistance Files, University of Bremen.

Figure 7.7 Increase in poverty rate in different types of residential areas for the cities of Bremen and Bielefeld

There are four possible factors which can lead to an increase in the number of welfare recipients in a specific district:

- a move of welfare recipients into potential poverty areas;
- an increased impoverishment of the resident population in the poverty areas;
- an above-average administrative allocation of German immigrants and persons seeking political asylum who were in many cases eligible for social assistance;

148 *Studies in Segregation and Desegregation*

- an accumulation of long-term welfare recipients in these areas.

The determination of which of these four factors can explain the above average increase in recipients of public assistance in poverty areas was addressed by analysing the data concerning the historical events of welfare recipients' lives. The conclusion of these analyses was that the above average increase of welfare recipients in poverty areas cannot be explained by the influx of poor persons (Farwick, 1996; Farwick, 1998b). It is rather caused by an increased impoverishment of the resident population in the poverty areas and an above average administrative allocation of German immigrants and persons seeking political asylum. To some extent it is also caused by a cumulative increase of long-term welfare recipients.

We have pointed out that at least in the two cities of Bremen and Bielefeld, a spatial polarisation of poverty in poor, segregated neighbourhoods can be shown. However, the second question has still to be answered: Do segregated poor neighbourhoods affect the chances of terminating poverty?

Within this discussion the role of space as a factor of deprivation is more and more being considered. It is argued that the features of segregated poverty areas reduce the chance of terminating poverty, thereby increasing the risk of social exclusion. In particular, James Julius Wilson (1987) paid some attention to the role of a neighbourhood effect when he argued that the formation of an underclass is - among other factors - due to the absence of positive role models and social isolation in highly segregated poverty areas.

There are three factors which can explain an impact of the respective neighbourhood on terminating dependency:

- social learning (the adoption of norms, values and roles);
- structural effects (lack of jobs, poor public transportation, poor social infrastructure such as schools);
- discrimination and stigmatisation of the residents from outside the poverty areas.

Data for investigating the impact of a neighbourhood consist of different cohorts of cases, which received public assistance in the cities of Bremen and Bielefeld for the first time. These data allow us to analyse patterns of welfare use from the point at which recipients first receive public assistance to the end of recipiency.

Patterns of welfare use could be observed for two Bremen cohorts for a

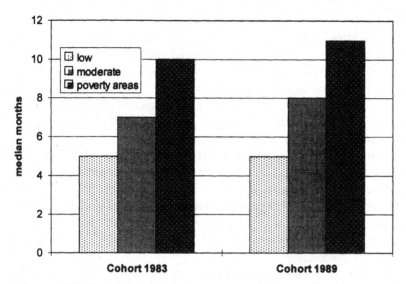

Figure 7.8 Bremen, median duration of dependence on social assistance by residential areas

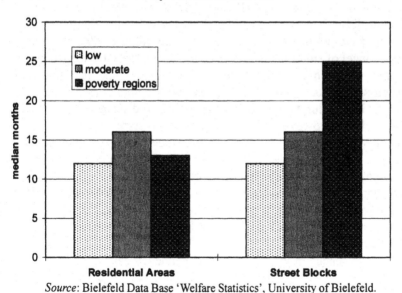

Source: Bielefeld Data Base 'Welfare Statistics', University of Bielefeld.

Figure 7.9 Bielefeld, median duration of dependence on social assistance by different classifications of residential areas (Cohort 1993)

150 *Studies in Segregation and Desegregation*

time period of 69 months, one starting in 1983 and the other in 1989 as well as for one Bielefeld cohort for 60 months, starting in 1992. Important in this approach is a consideration of residential mobility. However, in the Bremen cohorts nearly 75% of recipients did not move during the time they received assistance. Roughly 16% changed their place of residence only once, and only 9% moved twice or more. In Bielefeld the mobility was even lower: 92% of all recipients did not change their place of residence, 7% moved once, and only 1% moved twice or more.

To analyse the neighbourhood effect on the chances of terminating dependency on social assistance, we can, as a first step, describe the period of dependency and differentiate neighbourhoods at different poverty levels. In the following section, low poverty means a rate below the average, moderate poverty means a poverty rate above the average, and a 'poverty area', as we mentioned earlier, refers to a poverty rate of one standard deviation above the average.

For the city of Bremen it can be seen both for the 1983 and 1989 cohorts, that recipients in neighbourhood districts with moderate poverty rates and especially so in poverty areas are dependenct on social assistance for a significantly longer time (Figure 7.8). For Bielefeld the picture is somewhat different; on the level of neighbourhood districts there is a longer duration in areas with a moderate poverty rate (Figure 7.9). But on the small-scale level of street blocks we see again a significantly longer time of dependence in the highly segregated poverty areas. The fact that most poverty street blocks are located in areas with a moderate poverty rate explains the longer duration in these neighbourhood districts.

These charts, however, give only a rough picture of the process of social exclusion. Therefore, we took a closer look at the survival curves of the different cohorts of recipients (Figure 7.10). These figures show that in poverty areas the rate of recipients who are dependent on welfare for three years and longer is significantly higher. In Bremen, the difference between the types of residential areas for the 1989 cohort is smaller. But again in the Bielefeld case for street blocks, the rate of long term recipients is extremely different than in other areas.

These differences in the duration of dependency can so far not be due to a neighbourhood effect. Rather, they may have been caused by an over-representation of specific groups with characteristics of a long duration of dependency, such as single mothers or elderly householders. However, regardless of the type of household, for most groups again a significantly longer duration of dependency on social assistance could be found in poverty areas (Figure 7.11 and Figure 7.12). The short duration of

Andreas Farwick, Britta Klagge and Wolfgang Taubmann 151

dependency in the case of the resident foreigners can be interpreted, on the one hand, to close social networks within the communities of migrants who can help in locating work. On the other hand, it might be explained by the fact that resident foreigners who are unemployed or dependent on social assistance tend to return to their home countries.

Due to the significantly longer duration of dependency on welfare in poverty areas, a multiple deprivation of the poor in these areas can be expected. This result now supports the assumption of a neighbourhood effect (Farwick, 1998a).

To prove the hypothesis of an impact of segregated neighbourhoods in a more elaborate way, we estimated the effect of 'living in a poor neighbourhood' by controlling for important individual variables in a so-called 'event history' model. Based on this model, the neighbourhood effect was estimated as a time dependent co-variable, controlling for up to two residential moves during the time period of dependency (Farwick & Voges, 1997; Farwick, 1998b). First, we controlled for individual characteristics and attributed as much variance as possible to these individual characteristics. In a second step we controlled for different types of residential areas.

The result of these analyses was a significant negative effect of living in a poor neighbourhood on the chances of terminating welfare dependence. Living in a poor neighbourhood district in Bremen (1989 cohort) reduces the chances of terminating dependence by 28% compared to neighbourhoods with a low poverty rate (Figure 7.13). The chance of terminating poverty in the Bielefeld poverty street blocks is reduced by 37% (Figure 7.14). Individual characteristics such as being single and elderly or ill during the time of dependence do clearly have a major impact on the risk of being dependent on welfare. However, the results support the assumption of a neighbourhood effect as well.

152 *Studies in Segregation and Desegregation*

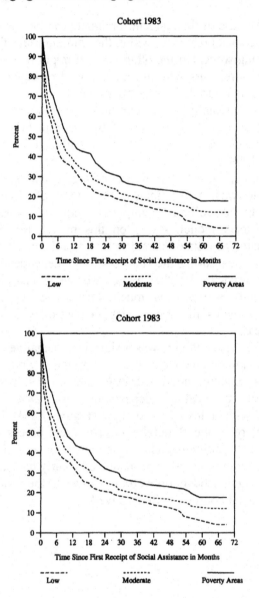

Figure 7.10 Bremen, duration of social assistance by the extent of segregated poverty in different residential areas

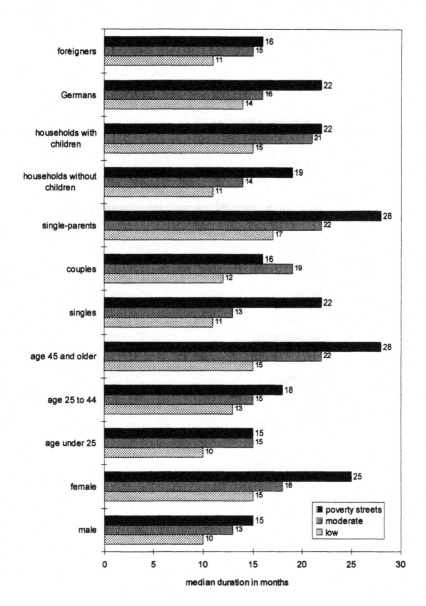

Source: Bremen longitudinal sample of social assistance files.

Figure 7.11 Bremen, median duration of welfare dependency by type of household and residential area (Cohort 1989)

154 *Studies in Segregation and Desegregation*

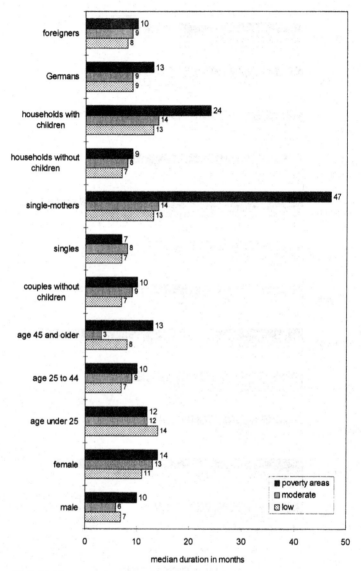

Source: Bielefeld Data Base 'Welfare Statistics', University of Bielefeld.

Figure 7.12 Bielefeld: median duration of welfare dependency by type of household and residential area (Cohort 1993)

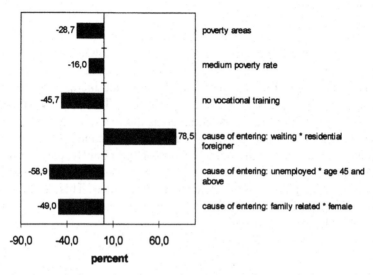

Source: Bremen longitudinal sample of social assistance files.

Figure 7.13 Bremen, relative risk of dependency on social assistance (Cohort 1989)

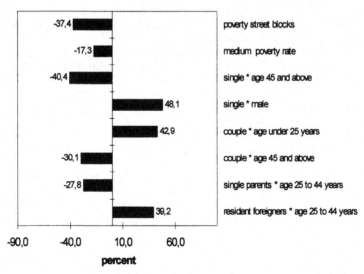

Source: Bielefeld Data Base 'Welfare Statistics', University of Bielefeld.

Figure 7.14 Bielefeld, relative risk of dependency on social assistance (Cohort 1993)

156 *Studies in Segregation and Desegregation*

Final Remarks

In times of increasing poverty in the city as a whole the spatial separation of poor people in poverty areas seems to be growing. Even if a process of increasing segregation, measured in relative terms, could not be found in the majority of cities we analysed, the absolute increase of the poor in so-called poverty areas is a cause for concern. Thus, it makes sense to ask whether or not in these residential areas the risk of becoming dependent on welfare for a longer period of time is significantly higher than in non-poverty areas. Though characteristics of the poor do play a major role in determining the risk of longer-term dependency on social assistance, the nature of neighbourhoods is also of importance. This result should have important consequences for urban policies to allocate poor persons or persons to urban quarters.

References

Bedau, K.D. (1996), Zuwanderung vergreüert Einkommensungleichheit und Einkommensarmut geringfügig. Neue Ergebnisse des Sozio-Ekonomischen Panels (SOEP), in: DIW-Wochenbericht 50/96.

Buhr, P., Leisering, L. Ludwig, M. & Zwick, M. (1991), Armutspolitik und Sozialhilfe in vier Jahrzehnten, Blanke, B./H. Wollmann (Hg.):Die alte Bundesrepublik. Kontinuitet und Wandel, pp. 502 - 545 (Leviathan-Sonderband).

Bundessozialhilfegesetz: Lehr- und Praxiskommentar (1994), 4. Aufl., Baden-Baden.

Dering, D., Hanesch, W. & Huster, E.U. (1990), Armut im Wohlstand. Frankfurt (edition suhrkamp 1995).

Farwick, A. (1996), Armut in der Stadt - Prozesse und Mechanismen der raumlichen Konzentration von Sozialhilfeempfangern, Arbeitspapier Nr. 25, ZWE Arbeit und Region, Universitat Bremen.

Farwick, A. (1998a), Soziale Ausgrenzung in der Stadt. Struktur und Verlauf von Sozialhilfebedürftigkeit in stadtischen Armutsgebieten, in: Geographische Rundschau, Heft 3, S. 146-153.

Farwick, A. (1998b), Soziale Ausgrenzung in der Stadt. Das Beispiel Bielefeld. Arbeitspapier, ZWE Arbeit und Region, Universitat Bremen.

Farwick, A., Nowak, F. & Taubmann, W. (1993), 'Marginale Gruppen auf dem Wohnungsmarkt', Das Beispiel Bremen (Sonderforschungsbereich 186, Arbeitspapier Nr. 20).

Farwick, A. & Voges, W. (1997), Segregierte Armut und das Risiko sozialer Ausgrenzung. Zum Einfluü der Nachbarschaft auf die Verstetigung von Sozialhilfebedürftigkeit, Arbeitspapier Nr. 27, ZWE Arbeit und Region, Universitat Bremen.

Hanesch, W. et al. (1994), Armut in Deutschland. Reinbek bei Hamburg (rororo aktuell 13420).

Hauser, R. (1995), Das empirische Bild der Armut in der Bundesrepublik Deutschland - ein überblick, in: Aus Politik und Zeitgeschichte, B 31 - 32/95, pp. 3-13.

Andreas Farwick, Britta Klagge and Wolfgang Taubmann 157

Jencks, C. & Mayer, S.E. (1990), 'The Social Consequences of Growing Up in a Poor Neighborhood', in L.E. Lynn & M.G. McGeary (eds.), *Inner-City Poverty in the United States*, Washington D.C., pp. 111-186.

Klagge, B. (1998), Armut in westdeutschen Stadten, in: Geogr. Rundschau, Jg. 50, H. 3, pp. 139-145.

Klagge, B. (2000), Disparitaten der Sozialhilfedichte in westdeutschen Staten: Entwicklung, Ausmaü und Hintergründe, Forschungsbericht Band 12, ZWE Arbeit und Region, Universitat Bremen.

Klein, P., Leibfried, S. & Priester, T. (1991), Chancengleichheit in der 'Hilfe zur Arbeit'? Die Werkstatt Bremen - eine Fallstudie. In: Nachrichtendienst des Vereins für Effentliche und private Fürsorge, H. 71, pp. 386-391.

Leibfried, St. et al. (1995), Zeit der Armut. Lebenslaufe im Sozialstaat. Frankfurt a. M.

Leisering, L. (1995), 'Zweidrittelgesellschaft oder Risikogesellschaft?', in K.-J. Bieback, H. Milz (Hrsg.), *Neue Armut*, Frankfurt a. M./New York, pp. 59-92.

Leisering, L. & Zwick, M. (1990), Heterogenisierung der Armut, in: Zeitschrift für Sozialreform, 36. Jg., H. 11/12, pp. 715-745.

Projektgruppe Das sozio-Ekonomische Panel' (Hg.) (1991), Lebenslagen im Wandel: Basisdaten und Analysen in den Neuen Bundeslandern. Frankfurt a. M./New York.

Statistisches Bundesamt (Hrsg.) (1997), Datenreport 1997. Zahlen und Fakten über die Bundesrepublik Deutschland, Bonn (Bundeszentrale für politische Bildung, Schriftenreihe Bd. 340).

Taubmann, W. (1992), 'Armut in Industrienationen - gibt es eine Zwei-Drittel-Gesellschaft', *Geographie und Schule*, vol. 14, Jahrgang, H. 76, pp. 13-19.

Taubmann, W. (1997), 'Armut im Reichtum. Armut in Deutschland und anderen Industrienationen', Geographie heute, H. 156, pp. 2-8.

Weber, A. (1997), Sozialhilfe im sozialstrukturellen Wandel. Sozialhilfeempfanger in den 80er Jahre. Diss. rer. pol. Universit t Bremen.Wendt, H. (1995): Asylbewerber in Deutschland, in: Geogr. Rundschau 47, H. 7-8, pp. 443-446.

Wilson, W.J. (1987), *The Truly Disadvantaged. The Inner City, the Underclass, and Public Policy*, University of Chicago Press, Chicago.

8 Segregation and Urban Policies in the Netherlands

WIM OSTENDORF

The Dark Sides of Segregation in Literature

In international literature the dominant view is that residential segregation has negative consequences, in particular for poor people. These views are heavily influenced by the stereotype of the American black ghetto. The situation of the American-born poor black population is historically connected to long-lasting oppression and discrimination and is maintained by a set of institutional arrangements, all of which have caused the special characteristics of the spatial concentrations of these residents. At first sight this seems to justify the notion that the American black ghetto will not manifest itself very easily elsewhere, for instance, in Europe. As an example, in the United States, the percentage of blacks in areas identified as black ghettos appears to be over eighty percent. In Europe the concentrations are much lower, and in the United States other poor population categories do not show such high concentrations, either. European immigrants in the United States, for instance, hardly concentrate in particular areas; the Irish ghetto of Burgess contained only three percent of the Irish population in Chicago, while the black ghetto contained 93% of the black population of that city (Musterd, 1996).

Nevertheless, the American black ghetto is always the point of reference, when discussing segregation, and the negative consequences of spatial segregation of poor residents is constantly pointed to. The work of Oscar Lewis appears early in this discussion. He pointed out that long-term unemployment might cause the emergence of a 'culture of poverty'. He referred to slum-like areas where unemployment is particularly persistent and connected to a chronic lack of money and prospects of social mobility (Lewis, 1966). A culture of poverty can also apply to those with low-income jobs and without prospects of improvement. Oscar Lewis saw the culture of poverty as an adaptation and reaction to the marginal position of the poor in societies that are strongly individualised and subdivided into social classes. Subsequently, such a culture of poverty can develop in an

160 *Studies in Segregation and Desegregation*

independent manner that adds to the social problems of the population involved.

Some ten years ago Wilson (1987) activated the discussion on the negative effects of segregation by stating that the inhabitants of a ghetto do have extra social problems just because they live in a ghetto. For the cause of the existence of a ghetto, Wilson points to the process of economic restructuring fuelled by global competition, but the concentration of poverty in a ghetto is seen as having an effect of its own, whose results are polarisation and the formation of an underclass. The economic restructuring leading to a post-industrial society asks for more highly educated workers, and the labour market will, therefore, be subject to a process of continuous upgrading. This relates to the emergence of a potential underclass consisting of people living in inner cities who are too poorly educated to acquire the increasing qualifications asked for by a post-industrial economy. Apart from their lack of education, these people face the problem of living in inner cities where, more than in other locations, unskilled industrial work that they qualify for has decreased. So, those living in the inner cities fall victim to a double mismatch: they do not qualify in terms of education for available work and they live far away from places where there still are remnants of the industrial era and the work they can do. Blacks are often subject to this, because they used to work in industry. Because the black middle-class is able to escape from the ghetto, the concentration of poor blacks in the ghetto increases. This situation isolates the ghetto-population from mainstream society in which jobs and job-stability are the norms and further reduces their chances for upward social mobility. For those growing up it easily results in adopting inappropriate values for mainstream society and further decreases their integration in society. According to Wilson this process causes the emergence of the black 'underclass'.

Many people have endorsed this view. In their book, *American Apartheid*, Massey and Denton (1993) did even more than that. In their view, too little attention has been paid to residential segregation as a separate factor. They state that Wilson and other scholars have failed to point to the detrimental impact of segregation with respect to social and economic processes: 'Residential segregation is the principal organisational feature of American society that is responsible for the creation of the urban underclass' (p. 9). Referring to the concept of a 'culture of poverty', they introduce the concept of a 'culture of segregation'. In their view segregation creates the structural conditions for the emergence of a counterculture, in which education, work and family-life are no longer central values. Actual behaviour is often hostile to success in mainstream society. The lack of sufficient successful role-models in a segregated environment and the notorious name of a neighbourhood add to the continuing concentration of poverty. In an experiment Massey and Denton successfully showed that increasing segregation of poor households results in a decreasing chance for these households to meet other, well-to-do households. This also holds true when the share of poor households in the urban region is constant. Empirical research shows that growing up in a ghetto increases the chances of becoming a school-drop-out, entering inferior schools and leaving school to work, while it also increases the chances of having a low income as an adult, having a child out of wedlock and being a single parent.

Interesting in this connection is Massey and Denton's reaction to the much-discussed and criticised views of Charles Murray. Murray hypothesised that generous social security benefits would discourage the search for a job, lead to having children out of wedlock, undermine stable family relations and generally make the situation of poverty permanent. Massey and Denton state that social security benefits only have such detrimental effects when the people involved live in spatially concentrated areas. In such a situation receiving social security benefits becomes the norm and encourages poverty for future generations. In the words of Schill (1994, p. 443) '...this concentration of poverty generates attitudes, behaviours, and values that impede the ability of residents to grasp whatever opportunities exist for social mobility'.

This view that the segregation of poverty is an independent factor in the chances for social success is clearly based on the American situation but is adopted by many European politicians and journalists as well as by scholars. According to Robson (1988), the determinants of the well being of households are not only the characteristics of the individual people but the contextual circumstances of their place of residence, as well. In short, 'place as well as people matters' (p.7). De Lannoy & Kesteloot (1990) state the following:

> The residential differentiation is not only the result of the class-relations within a society but is also the cause of the maintenance and the reproduction of this class-structure. Living in a specific area is an important factor in the availability of public amenities, the norms of the residents, their behaviour and their ambitions in society. Residents of underprivileged neighbourhoods possess few chances for upward social mobility and there is a great possibility that their poverty will be

162 *Studies in Segregation and Desegregation*

transferred to the next generation (Translated by the author, 1990, pp. 143-144).

However, there is reason to be careful in translating these neighbourhood-effects to the context of European cities, especially to the Dutch cities. Firstly, research concerning the effects of segregation in European cities is alarmingly scarce. Secondly, in Europe the level of segregation is much lower. And thirdly, there is justification in assuming that the type of welfare state has an effect (Musterd & Ostendorf, 1998b). In liberal welfare states in which the role of the market is stressed, there indeed exists a strong relationship between having a job and other social indicators such as income, education and quality of housing. In such a situation unemployment leads to low income, and this results in a bad housing situation together with other unemployed in a specific low quality part of the urban housing market. Segregation with respect to housing is then reflected in social participation in other spheres, and a rise in segregation may be connected with a waning participation in other spheres of life.

In European welfare states, where the state is more pervasive, the impact of unemployment is offset by all kinds of welfare state arrangements. So, the relation between residential segregation, education, work and income is much weaker (van Amersfoort, 1992; Musterd & Ostendorf, 1994). In addition, income inequality is lower in European welfare states. As a consequence, it seems plausible not to expect a European copy of the American ghetto.

The Effects of Segregation: Empirical Results in The Netherlands

In line with the ideas referred to above, many discussions on urban problems in The Netherlands express the idea in one way or another that the social composition of residential environments is crucial: the composition of the population of neighbourhoods designed as ghettos is expected to have a negative influence on the chances for upward social mobility for the population of that particular neighbourhood. Although, according to many people, the Dutch situation does not justify the use of the word ghetto, the debate on ghettos and the fear of ghettos and ghetto-effects is very much alive. The fear is based on the negative effects that are ascribed to this phenomenon. In fact the debate on ghettos is a debate on the neighbourhood-effect (de Vos, 1997), although this is seldom made clear.

However, this discussion is not based on actual information of neighbourhood-effects in The Netherlands because research on the subject is scarce. This statement sounds matter of fact, but it is rather surprising when one realises how much attention and social concern is directed to the problem. Concern is in sharp contrast with research. It is this lack of research that justifies attention to the research that has been done, although it certainly has limitations. It makes use of a secondary analysis of data in research in Amsterdam that had another purpose. A sample of more than 4,000 persons (Musterd et al. 1999a) was used, and the secondary analysis had the following research-question: How does living in a underprivileged residential environment affect social participation? In other words, does the social environment have an effect on one's chances in society?

Crucial in the conceptual scheme of this research is the definition of underprivileged in the residential environment. There are many possible factors such as the measurement of social participation of the residents with necessary control of relevant elements of social participation, such as age, type of household and education. Another factor is whether or not residents consider themselves underprivileged. Whatever factors are included, central to the concept of being underprivileged is a lack of opportunity for upward social mobility. In policy debates in The Netherlands one usually refers to income as the crucial characteristic. However, this is not a very accurate indicator of chances for upward social mobility. The example of university students having low incomes but generally bright futures underlines the weakness of this indicator. With respect to social mobility, the literature often refers to such central characteristics as education and employment. In our opinion these two characteristics should be combined at the individual level: people are considered underprivileged if they experience a combination of limited education, unemployment and a partner without a job. According to this definition, an unemployed person with sufficient education still has positive prospects; merely having a low income is not decisive for future prospects. All persons not having the combination of limited education and unemployment are not considered underprivileged. This strict definition yields only 179 underprivileged persons in the data, only about 4.5%.

The database also contains the exact location. This gives the opportunity to aggregate the data to any spatial level of analysis with the help of GIS and, as a next step, to link these data to other data describing the housing stock and population.

The first level of analysis to be considered is that of neighbourhoods: some 100 in Amsterdam. For each of these neighbourhoods containing at

164 *Studies in Segregation and Desegregation*

least 25 persons in the sample, the percentage of underprivileged is calculated (Figure 8.1). The picture is rather flat, caused by the low number of underprivileged people in moderate concentrations.

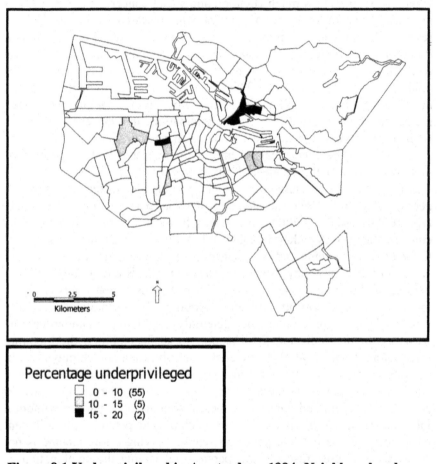

Figure 8.1 Underprivileged in Amsterdam, 1994: Neighbourhoods

Neighbourhoods can be quite large, resulting in an analysis with a lack of precision. With the help of GIS-analysis, even for every respondent the number of underprivileged people in a radius of 300 meters around his or her dwelling can be determined (Deurloo et al. 1998). This procedure results in immediate residential vicinities on an individual basis. For these immediate residential vicinities we know the number of underprivileged people and, thus, to what extent every respondent lives among underprivileged people. The small number of underprivileged people justifies the expectation that the concentrations of underprivileged people will not be high.

This expectation appears to be correct when the database is used for an analysis with more detail than the level of neighbourhoods provides. Therefor a grid of 100 x 100 meters is used, resulting in cells as a second level of analysis. In judging the concentration of the underprivileged in these cells, not only the cell itself is taken into account. The ring of eight surrounding cells and the next ring of sixteen surrounding cells are also considered. These results in small areas with a radius of some hundreds of meters, representing the immediate residential vicinity of the persons

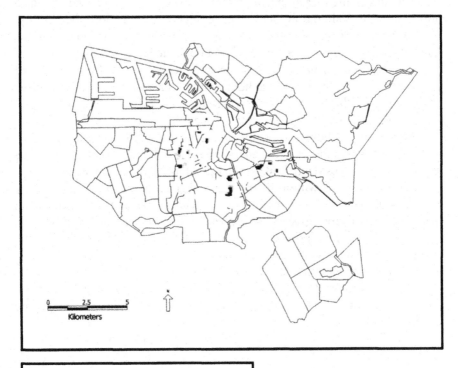

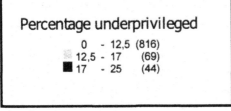

Figure 8.2 The concentration of poverty in Amsterdam

166 Studies in Segregation and Desegregation

involved. In this case the total area of 25 cells should contain at least 25 persons in the sample. For this reason the concentration of poverty can be shown only for a part of Amsterdam (Figure 8.2). In the remainder of Amsterdam the density of the population, given the size of the sample, is too low to meet the requirement of 25 persons in the sample. The concentration is moderate and the picture is dispersed. In the two darker areas more than 12.5% and more than 17% are underprivileged. These areas can be regarded as 'pockets of poverty'. But even in these areas the majority is far from underprivileged.

A second problem for the secondary analysis of the neighbourhood-effect relates to the measurement of social participation. The available data only allow for a simple measurement of social participation: the activity-pattern in two ways. On the one hand, there are the volume and the intensity of social contacts with neighbours, acquaintances, friends and family. Rather independent of these are the measurement of the number of evenings that the person is not at home and the measurement of the number of visits to places of recreational or cultural entertainment. Not unexpectedly, these last two indicators appear to be strongly correlated.

The analysis shows the following results. Above, the relatively low concentrations of underprivileged people was already pointed out. This means that in all residential areas, a large majority of the population is not underprivileged. So, within all the residential areas of Amsterdam many people who are not underprivileged appear to be available for social participation. There appears to be no clear correlation between the concentration of underprivileged people in the immediate vicinity, on the one hand, and the volume and intensity of social contacts with neighbours, acquaintances, friends and family, on the other hand.

Thus, this form of social participation seems to be hardly dependent on the relative concentration of underprivileged people in the immediate vicinity of the people concerned.

This conclusion does not apply to the other indicator of the activity pattern: the number of evenings, that the person is not at home and the number of visits to places of recreational or cultural entertainment. This kind of social participation appears to be dependent on the relative concentration of underprivileged people in the immediate vicinity: a higher number of underprivileged people in the immediate vicinity increased the chances of finding people at home. Personal characteristics such as age, type of household and education are even more strongly correlated to this type of social participation. But it is important to discover that the correlation between the concentration of underprivileged people in the

Wim Ostendorf 167

immediate vicinity and this form of social participation does not disappear when one controls for these personal characteristics.

In conclusion, this analysis points to the fact that the concentration of underprivileged people in the immediate vicinity has an impact on social participation. But the same conclusion is also true for personal characteristics.

This analysis seems to prove that the residential environment has an impact on social participation, even in a welfare state like The Netherlands and even in a city like Amsterdam where the number of underprivileged people is limited and where the spatial concentration of these underprivileged people is relatively low. However, the research of this topic is very limited and requires more extended and profound research. It is, for instance, still uncertain if the same conclusion would apply to another and more extended indicator of social participation. In any case, the same conclusion appeared not to be valid for the volume and the intensity of social contacts with neighbours, acquaintances, friends and family. And because of lack of data, the most important indicator, social mobility, could not be included in this secondary analysis. For the moment it seems correct to conclude that segregation can have an impact on the chances for social mobility but that personal characteristics play an even more important role. This means that there is no good reason, when discussing the problem of ghettos, to focus on the segregation factor and to ignore the position of the involved individuals.

Urban Policies in the Netherlands: A Solid Basis?

In the debate on poverty and segregation in The Netherlands, segregation with respect to income has played an important role in the last several years. The rise of 'income ghettos' is especially feared. This concept is also labelled 'income neighbourhoods', a euphemism for areas that are homogeneous with respect to income. However, the concern is with areas characterised by a concentration of low incomes rather than high incomes. In order to prevent the hypothesised negative effects of income neighbourhoods, a new policy program has been developed, which is aimed at restructuring the urban housing market at the level of neighbourhoods in order to prevent the spatial concentration of people with low incomes (Nota Stedelijke Vernieuwing, 1997). By diversifying housing possibilities, the government hopes to influence the social composition of neighbourhoods. In the case of new housing construction this is to be done by mixing newly

168 *Studies in Segregation and Desegregation*

built houses of different price levels. But in the case of the existing housing, some has to be demolished and replaced with houses of different price levels. In essence this policy of urban restructuring can be stated as 'A physical mix will result in a social mix, and a social mix is the solution for poverty'.

The idea of balanced population structure is not new. It was also present in the seventies (Jobse, 1974). Social integration, however, was less the focus at that time, while a more extended social basis for all kind of provisions was more important. The planner Buit (1977) described the search for balance in those years as follows (translated by the author):

> Always the line of reasoning is that, compared to other neighbourhoods in the city, there are, too many industrial enterprises, too few children or young families, [...] too many guestworkers, etc. and, therefore, planning should give less room to industrial enterprises, more room for children and young families, [...] less room for guestworkers, etc.

He continues:

> Urban renewal tries to correct, with the help of an enormous amount of state-money, these aspects of spatial inequality that are viewed as negative (p. 611).

The search for a balance, for average neighbourhoods, was the main goal. Policies aiming at differentiating the composition of the population are not uniquely Dutch. They are applied in other countries as well (Musterd et al, 1998; Musterd & De Winter, 1998) and also criticised (Kesteloot, 1998; Galster & Zobel, 1998).

Policy in urban restructuring is heavy with the pursuit of more differentiated housing, especially at the level of the neighbourhood so as to consequently increase the social mix of the population, which will result in an undivided city. Predominant is the belief that only mixed neighbourhoods are viable and the way to create social and cultural integration and participation in society. Segregation is considered wrong because it would prevent integration and would result in ghettos (Duivesteijn, 1996). Policy documents and discussion on urban problems stress these points. Physical renewal and restructuring are supposed to change social structures and, thus, prevent the rise of ghettos and happily create an undivided and balanced city. This ambition in The Netherlands is

Wim Ostendorf 169

illustrated in the 'Convenant Grotestedenbeleid' (Covenant of Big City Policy) that states: 'In order to especially prevent spatial segregation, owner-occupied houses and/or expensive houses will be built in existing neighbourhoods, and in new neighbourhoods cheap accommodation will also be built' (p. 19). Restructuring at the level of neighbourhoods, aiming at more differentiation, will solve the problems of decline, downgrading and segregation (Ministerie VROM De Gedifferentieerde Stad, 1996, pp. 17, 27, 30; Nota Stedelijke Vernieuwing, 1997, pp. 76-77).

The plans of the policy of urban restructuring concentrate on diversifying housing. These plans are far more specific than the goals. In the process of actualizing the plans, the goals of reducing segregation and preventing the effects of segregation are easily lost sight of. The scale and accompanying costs of urban restructuring suggest important goals, but these goals are rather vague. This situation of clear plans and vague goals is applicable to many policies and makes evaluation difficult. As indicated above, it is correct to summarise the goal of the policy of urban restructuring as preventing spatial concentration of people with low incomes and, as a consequence, the negative impact of such segregation. In other words, based on the idea of 'mixing as a solution for poverty' the problems of underprivileged households in mixed neighbourhoods are supposed to be reduced. This goal will be used in judging the chances for a successful policy of urban restructuring.

For this purpose attention will be paid to an analysis of the relationship between - again - being underprivileged and characteristics of housing in Amsterdam (Musterd et al. 1999b). As indicated before, the policy of urban restructuring aims at differentiating housing in neighbourhoods in order to reduce the problems of underprivileged households. Thus, the policy presupposes a neighbourhood effect. Evaluating the success of such a policy requires a longitudinal research. This is impossible as it asks for a database that is not available, and it expects patience for several years in order to give the policy of urban restructuring time to prove its results. For the moment, the only solution is to study the present situation and to look for indications that can support the policy.

However, in our opinion the real expectation of the policy of urban restructuring is not based on rectilinear relations, but on curvilinear relations. Figures 9.3 and 9.4 help to explain this. Figure 8.3 shows two theoretical relationships at the level of neighbourhoods, based - as an example on the fact that underprivileged people usually do not live in owner-occupied houses. In the first theoretical line this individual relationship is translated to the level of neighbourhoods and shows that neighbourhoods with more owner-occupied houses have less underprivileged people. This first line is purely based on the individual relationship and does not contain a neighbourhood-effect.

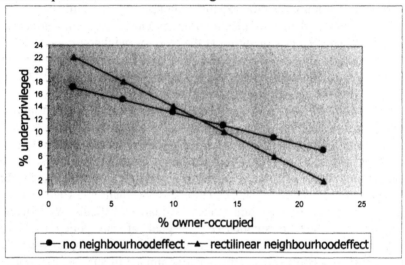

Figure 8.3 A rectilinear neighbourhood effect model

In the second theoretical line a neighbourhood-effect is active. In neighbourhoods with only a small share of owner-occupied houses there are many underprivileged people. The neighbourhood-effect results in an increase of this number caused by the composition of the population; the large number of underprivileged people has a negative impact and leads to even more underprivileged people than might be expected without such a neighbourhood effect. In neighbourhoods with a large share of owner-occupied houses, the opposite happens. Here we already find few underprivileged people, but the neighbourhood-effect results in a decrease of the number of underprivileged people, the large number of wealthy people has a positive effect and leads to less underprivileged people than could be expected based on the individual relationship. So, in neighbourhoods with many owner-occupied houses less underprivileged are found, and in neighbourhoods with few owner-occupied houses one finds more underprivileged people than could be expected on the basis of the individual relationship. As a consequence, the second line, based on the individual effect and a neighbourhood-effect is steeper than the first one, based only on the individual effect.

It is important to realise that this neighbourhood effect does influence the number of underprivileged people in various neighbourhoods (and so the distribution) but that the total number of underprivileged people in the city does not change: negative effects compensate for positive effects. If this neighbourhood effect were to be the result of the policy of urban restructuring, it would be very disappointing because the total result of the policy would be zero. A lot of money would have been spent without a reduction in the number of underprivileged people, which is the ultimate aim of the policy.

Although the documents on the policy of urban restructuring do not pay attention to this issue, it seems safe to state that the aim of the policy has to be based on another model: that of a curvilinear neighbourhood effect (Figure 8.4). This curvilinear neighbourhood effect is also based on the individual relationship but shows a considerable difference between

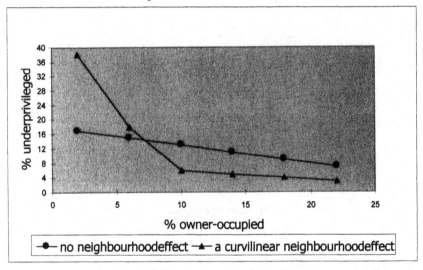

Figure 8.4 A curvilinear neighbourhood effect model

homogeneous low-quality neighbourhoods and 'mixed' neighbourhoods, while the difference between 'mixed' neighbourhoods and high-quality neighbourhoods is much smaller. In this model a serious reduction in the total number of underprivileged people is reached because of the low share of underprivileged people in 'mixed' neighbourhoods. In fact, the policy of urban restructuring needs such a model as a legitimisation: a serious reduction of underprivileged people in low-quality neighbourhoods that are changed into 'mixed' neighbourhoods, while the increase in the numbers of underprivileged people in high-quality neighbourhoods that change into 'mixed' neighbourhoods, is very limited.

This brings us to the question of the extent to which the relationship between the characteristics of available housing, on the one hand, and the

172 *Studies in Segregation and Desegregation*

level of segregation with respect to underprivileged people on the other hand, does show the curvilinear relationship that is required for the success of the policy of urban restructuring. Figures 8.5-8.8 show for both neighbourhoods and cells, how far these curvilinear lines can be recognised. This is calculated for the present situation in Amsterdam with respect to different ideas of mixed housing, based on the following variables: owner-occupied houses, private (i.e. not government sponsored) housing, size and newly constructed housing. Only Figure 8.5, analysing the

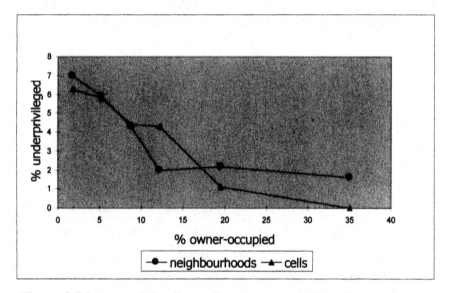

Figure 8.5 Impact of the share of owner-occupied housing

effect of the 'mix' with respect to owner-occupied houses, indicates some idea of a possible curvilinear relationship at the level of neighbourhoods; however, no relationship is indicated at the level of cells. The remaining figures are not at all promising that a mixture of housing types will be successful in reducing the number of underprivileged people.

In summary it can be stated, that thanks to a curvilinear neighbourhood effect, the analysis of the present situation in Amsterdam does not support the idea that the policy of urban restructuring will result in a reduction in the total number of underprivileged people.

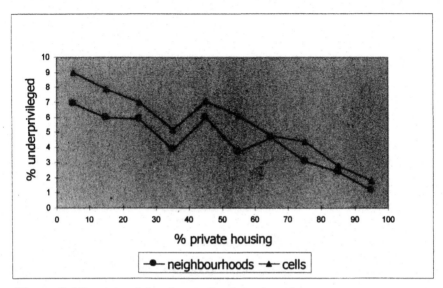

Figure 8.6 Impact of the share of private housing

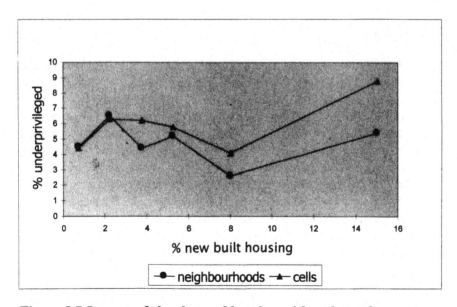

Figure 8.7 Impact of the share of housing with at least three rooms

174 *Studies in Segregation and Desegregation*

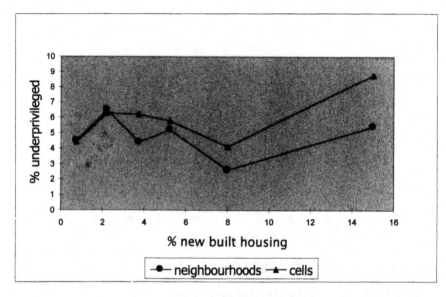

Figure 8.8 Impact of the share of new built housing

Conclusion

The policy of urban restructuring in The Netherlands presupposes a number of things. Firstly, it assumes that a considerable number of underprivileged people live in Dutch cities and that they have to be helped by this policy. In the second place, it assumes that these underprivileged people are concentrated in a few areas. This concentration, if actual, would make it possible to reach the majority of these people by a policy targeting a limited number of neighbourhoods. In the third place, the policy of urban restructuring presupposes a strong relationship between the characteristics of the dwelling and the characteristics of the household. Further, the policy assumes that neighbourhoods with mixed housing are preferable to homogeneous neighbourhoods because – based on the strong relation between household and dwelling – this would result in neighbourhoods that are also mixed, socially. Finally, the policy supposes that socially mixed neighbourhoods would show a considerable decrease in underprivileged people because of the existence of a curvilinear neighbourhood effect.

Above, it is argued that there exist many doubts with respect to all these presuppositions and consequently with respect to the chance for success of the policy of urban restructuring.

In the first place are the underprivileged people themselves. The policy of urban restructuring can only be successful if one really knows the target population, the underprivileged, and their characteristics, abilities, opinions and needs. In this respect there exist serious doubts. Often, income and income-neighbourhoods are referred to. The concept of underprivileged – based on a combination of low education and no job – is to be preferred to one considering only income. Students, for instance, do have a low income but cannot be considered underprivileged. So, the idea of being underprivileged is better related to the prospects of upward social mobility.

The analysis pointed to a small number of underprivileged people in Amsterdam, some 4%. Thus, the policy of urban restructuring, in so far as it is directed at helping underprivileged people by mixing types of dwellings and consequently mixing residents, applies to only a modest category of the population.

Secondly, the spatial concentrations of underprivileged people, at least in Amsterdam, appear to be rather low. Only small pockets of poverty can be found. They are small in the sense of not being large, spatially unbroken areas; moreover, even in these pockets of poverty only small concentrations of underprivileged people are found. So, the policy of urban restructuring has to deal with large sections of the urban environment in order to reach small numbers of spatially dispersed underprivileged people by mixing available housing in their neighbourhoods.

In the third place, the literature (Musterd et al. 1999b) shows that the relationship between dwelling and household indeed exists in The Netherlands but that this relation is not very strong and also changes over time. Increasing social differentiation seems especially to decrease this relationship or at least make it more complex.

In the fourth place, the idea that in The Netherlands a strong neighbourhood effect with respect to poverty can be found lacks an empirical foundation. Moreover, an empirical foundation for the belief that this neighbourhood effect is curvilinear is also lacking, while such a relation is crucial in order to decrease the total number of underprivileged people. The analysis above did not show such empirical evidence. On the contrary, mixed neighbourhoods sometimes showed higher rather than lower concentrations of underprivileged people. In short, in the case of Amsterdam, neighbourhoods or cells with mixed housing do not show a seriously reduced share of underprivileged people. Such a situation also

176 Studies in Segregation and Desegregation

applies to the United States, where Galster and Zobel (1998) find similar results.

These findings support the view that an extended programme of research should be part of the policy of urban restructuring in order to test its presuppositions. Unfortunately, such a programme is lacking. Based on what has been discussed above, there is reason to argue for an adaptation of such research. In essence, the goal of the policy of urban restructuring is to help underprivileged people in an indirect way: the state of being underprivileged is to be alleviated by a mix in the residential environment. It is unclear how this mechanism works. On the other hand, the analysis presented above made clear that a neighbourhood effect in the Dutch situation indeed might exist but also that the individual characteristics appear to be very important for social participation. This means, that being underprivileged is also an individual characteristic indeed partly expressed in the dwelling and in the residential environment but not completely or even largely determined by it. This means, that the solution for tackling the problem of being underprivileged is not solely to be found in the housing market. The approach that deals with personal characteristics via education and employability, seems far more effective. This would make housing market policy much easier. It could concentrate on adapting the supply of accomodation and of residential environments to the demand.

References

Amersfoort, H. van (1992), 'Ethnic Residential Patterns in a Welfare State: Lessons from Amsterdam, 1970-1990', *New Community*, vol. 18(3), pp. 439-456.

Buit, J. (1977), 'Over ruimtelijke ongelijkheid en stadsvernieuwing; enkele kanttekeningen', *Stedebouw en Volkshuisvesting*, pp. 611-618.

De Lannoy, W. & Kesteloot, C. (1990), *Het scheppen van sociaal-ruimtelijke ongelijkheden in de stad*, Werkgroep Mort-Subite, Barsten in België. EPO, Berchem.

Deurloo, M.C., Musterd, S. & Ostendorf, W. (1998), *Pockets of Poverty*, AME/NETHUR. DGVH-NETHUR report no. 2, Amsterdam/Utrecht.

Duivesteijn, A. (1996), 'De stad als spiegel van de samenleving', *Woningraad Magazine*, no. 3, pp. 33-40.

Galster, G. & Zobel, A. (1998), 'Will Dispersed Housing Programmes Reduce Social Problems in the US?', *Housing Studies*, vol. 13(5), pp. 605-622.

Jobse, R.B. (1974) 'Bevolkingssamenstelling en -ontwikkeling in grootstedelijke nieuwbouwwijken: achtergronden en consequenties' *Stedebouw en Volkshuisvesting*, okt. pp. 354-366.

Kesteloot, C. (1998), 'Over de beperkingen van sociale mix als beleidsstrategie', *Planologisch Nieuws*, vol. 18(3), pp. 144-147.

Lewis, O. (1966), 'The Culture of Poverty', in R.T. LeGates & F. Stout (eds), *The City Reader*, Routledge, London/New York, pp. 217-224.

Wim Ostendorf 177

Massey, D.S. & Denton, N.A. (1993), *American Apartheid*, Harvard University Press, Cambridge.

Ministerie van Volkshuisvesting, Ruimtelijke Ordening en Milieubeheer (1996), *De gedifferetieerde stad*, Ministerie van VROM, Den Haag.

Ministerie van Volkshuisvesting, Ruimtelijke Ordening en Milieubeheer (1997), *Nota Stedelijke Vernieuwing*, Ministerie van VROM, Den Haag.

Musterd, S. (1996), *Ruimtelijke segregatie en sociale effecten*, Inaugurele rede, Van Gorcum, Assen.

Musterd, S. & Ostendorf, W. (1994), 'Affluence, Access to Jobs, and Ethnicity in the Dutch Welfare State; The Case of Amsterdam', *Built Environment*, vol. 20(3), pp. 242-253.

Musterd, S. & Ostendorf, W. (1998a), 'The Changing Distribution of Incomes in Dutch Cities: Myth and Reality', *Geojournal*, vol. 46, pp. 29-38.

Musterd, S. & Ostendorf, W. (eds) (1998b), *Urban Segregation and the Welfare State: Inequality and Exclusion in Western Cities*, Routledge, London.

Musterd, S., Ostendorf, W. & Breebaart, M. (1998), *Multi-Ethnic Metropolis: Patterns and Policies*, Kluwer, Dordrecht, Boston, London.

Musterd, S. & Winter, M. de (1998), 'Conditions for Spatial Segregation: Some European Perspectives', *International Journal of Urban and Regional Research*, vol. 22 (4), pp. 665-673.

Musterd, Sako, Deurloo, Rinus & Ostendorf, Wim (1999a), 'Het omgevingseffect, de problematiek van het vaststellen van 'getto-effecten'', in Sako Musterd & Ad Goethals, *De invloed van de buurt*, SISWO-publicatie 404, SISWO, Amsterdam, pp. 14-25.

Musterd, Sako, Ostendorf, Wim & Vos, Sjoerd de (1999b), *Kansarmoedeconcentraties en woningmarkt*, AME/NETHUR, DGVH-NETHUR rapport, no. 6, Amsterdam/Utrecht.

Robson, B. (1988), *Those Inner Cities*, Clarendon Press, Oxford.

Schill, M.H. (1994), 'Race, the Underclass, and Public Policy', *Law & Social Inquiry*, vol. 19(2), pp. 433-456.

Vos, S. de (1997), *De omgeving telt: compositionele effecten in de sociale geografie*, Academische Pers BV, Amsterdam.

Wilson, W.J. (1987), *The Truly Disadvantaged, the Inner City, the Underclass and Public Policy*, University of Chicago Press, Chicago.

Part 3:
A Comparative Perspective

9 National Identity in a Transforming Quebec Society: Socio-Economic and Spatial Segregation in Montreal

CHARLES SMALL

Introduction

Montreal is a city that has been transformed over the last several decades. In fact, in could be argued that this transformation has gained momentum in recent years. It is a city that is the heart of the Quebec economy, a society attempting to choose a path regarding the national question.

The purpose of this paper is to examine social and spatial differentiation in the Montreal urban context, a subject essential in understanding the current conflict in Quebec and Canadian society. This paper consists of three main sections: i) a brief overview of the significance of Montreal, demonstrating the richness of this context for analysis; ii) introductory remarks concerning the current political and economic situation in Montreal as well as an examination of the social formation, with emphasis placed on the socio-economic development of the city; iii) a detailed analysis of social and spatial differentiation in Montreal and the situation between various groups within the city. This section provides insights into existing levels of stratification, which are illustrated in detail.

Despite living in the shadow of the United States in the North American context, Canada's particular history and efforts to address socio-cultural policies and notions of national identity provide a perspective different from that of its large neighbour to the south. For instance, Canada, unlike the United States, has long acknowledged notions of group rights in policy and legislation as a means of fostering integration. It is a perspective often overlooked by the international community of scholars and provides a context with different processes and realities in terms of understanding issues of socio-economic and spatial differentiation in the city. In addition,

182 *Studies in Segregation and Desegregation*

Montreal constitutes an excellent case study for several other reasons. It is a truly multicultural or cosmopolitan city. In fact, one region of the city, Cotes des Neiges, is purported to have one of the most diverse populations in the world (Shahar, 1991, p. 4). Perhaps more significant, since the politics of 'culture' has played such a crucial role in the development and sustaining of Canada as an entity, it is fitting to assess the city which characterises those developments and personifies the contemporary contradictions of Canadian society. In its urban and cultural space, Montreal embodies the legacies and influences of socio-cultural policies from two different perspectives: those represented more generally in Canadian society by Ottawa (English) and Quebec City (French). Montreal, therefore, is useful for assessing differing effects in the areas of social integration. Does language, culture, race, or ethnicity dominate in the drive to achieve successful integration in Canadian and Quebecois society? Clearly, Montreal provides a dynamic case study for addressing questions and the ramifications of social policies in relation to urban differentiation.

Consequently, this article intends to make a contribution to the literature through the exploration of a case study that is vital to the Canadian national project and has been often overlooked. Through the analysis of urban differentiation in Montreal, levels and forms of segregation are depicted, which is different than that which exists in the United States, as well as in other major Canadian cites. Given the unique socio-economic history of Montreal, original observations and insights can be offered to this field of study.

The Significance of Montreal

Montreal is a valuable location for examining the complex mixture of spatial and cultural issues pertaining to urban socio-economic differentiation. Montreal embodies the essence of the Canadian national experience. It is a unique city in terms of its population composition and socio-economic development and is representative of the Canadian national experiment. Inherent in the history of Montreal is the very nature of the Canadian attempt to remain unified and to forge harmony among the competing interests of both the French and English, as well as the 'others', within the Federation of Canada. Montreal, the dominant city for most of Canadian history and the centre of these tensions and at times conflicts is indicative of this national experiment.

Charles Small 183

Montreal has been a bilingual city of English and French speakers since New France was conquered by the British in 1760. Between 1830 and 1850 a large group of immigrants from Britain temporarily created an English majority in Montreal. It was the only time in the history of the city that the English constituted a majority. In every census since 1871, however, French speakers have been in the majority, accounting for at least 60 percent of the population, (Levine, 1990, p.1). For more than a century, Montreal has been one of the largest French speaking cities in the world, second only to Paris. Despite this fact, for much of the last one hundred years Montreal has been dominated by the English minority in terms of socio-economic indicators, politics and culture. Reflecting this dominance, that clearly existed at least until the 1960s, Jacobs (1980) asserts that Montreal appeared '... to be what it had been for almost two centuries: an English city containing many French speaking workers and inhabitants' (Levine, 1990, p. 1).

The reason for the 'English feel' to the city was due to the unchallenged dominance, particularly economic, of Anglophone residents. Much of the Canadian national economy was controlled and directed from the headquarters of many major corporations located in Montreal, and the city was the most important urban setting in Canada until the 1970s. It is important to realise, that until the mid 1970s, Montreal led the economic, financial (capital accumulation), political, social and cultural development of Canada as a whole (Levine, 1990, p. 3).

During the 1950s and 1960s, Quebec entered an era of change, in which the predominantly Catholic population underwent a process of modernisation. This period, the 'quiet revolution', witnessed the decline of the Church's influence in the lives of the vast majority of French speaking Catholic Quebecois, while the modern welfare state replaced its authority. The French Quebecois became more educated and entered sectors of the labour markets once entirely controlled by the English. With the nationalisation of many large corporations, such as Hydro Quebec, and the expansion of the bureaucracy the (provincial) state offered the French Quebecois employment and career opportunities never before available. These processes led to a generation of French Quebecois, with a greater ability to control their own destinies in a socio-economic, political and cultural sense. This period also saw the growth and development of a capable nationalist movement. This nationalist element forms the context in which all current considerations and decisions are made in Quebec as well as in the rest of Canada.

184 *Studies in Segregation and Desegregation*

Throughout the history of relations between Canada and Quebec, Montreal has been the focal point of the majority of conflicts and tensions as well as attempts at rapprochement. In terms of social policies concerning cultural issues, Montreal provides the crucial urban context especially in relation to the Canadian national question. From the time of confederation in 1867, when the English and French negotiated the unity of the nation, Montreal has been a centre of power and influence. During the 1940s and 1950s when notions of Anglo-conformity began to wane, it was the intellectuals and politicians from Montreal who shaped post-World War II society so as to reflect the pluralistic composition of Canadian society. Since they reflected the interests of a powerful component of the confederation, they were able to fulfil many of their national objectives. Towards the end of the 1960s, a group of young French Canadian intellectuals and politicians went to Ottawa and joined the Liberal Party of Canada, ultimately taking over its leadership. Led by Pierre Trudeau, this group had great influence in shaping the future of Quebec and Canada. To this day many of the same people are still influential actors, their legacy profoundly influential in the contemporary political reality of Canada.

Background

Montreal has changed during the last several decades in socio-economic and political terms. This shift can be categorised as a general decline. This is reflected in the general state of social relations. Perhaps this is particularly true in the wake of the October 1995 referendum on Quebec sovereignty when Quebec society split over its future status and direction. The results of the referendum by popular vote was 50.6% in favour of remaining in Canada and 49.6% in favour of sovereignty (Small, 1996, p. 410). Montreal is the center of Quebec's economy and home to the vast majority of the province's minority communities. It is in this urban context that the socio-economic fallout over the political question has had its greatest impact.

Within Montreal visible signs of economic and political decline are evident. The rate of bankruptcies is up, is the highest in the country and growing at an alarming rate. Many individuals are selling property and moving assets out of Quebec (Small, 1997, p. 3). The West End of the city, home to many minority communities, seems to be particularly hard hit. The mood in Montreal has changed, and there is an increase in political and social tensions. Recently released census statistics by the federal government confirmed what has been apparent to Montreal's population; the flight from the city by residents has accelerated substantially over the last year in the aftermath of the referendum. In fact, the exodus of Quebecers during the first six months of 1996 was approximately three times greater than for the same period in 1995. According to an opinion poll conducted by Alliance Quebec, more than 30 percent of the English speaking population intended to leave in the near future. The numbers in similar polls indicate that a higher percentage of Montreal's Jewish Community intend to leave Quebec. This is also true of other minority communities, particularly the African-Canadian (Small, 1996, p. 374). Recently, Premier Lucien Bouchard, when asked why he felt so many Quebecers were leaving, simply stated; 'Your guess is as good as mine.' (Small, 1998).[1] Statements such as this indicate that *'les autres'* are not a pressing concern for the Premier.[2]

Many youth, particularly minority youth, are leaving Quebec, mainly due to the economic situation and the general uncertainty. Experts, community leaders and lay people have expressed concern over the future viability of minority communities in Quebec. Youth unemployment crises in Quebec are prevalent among minority communities, especially the

---

[1] It should be noted that in the aftermath of the referendum and Premier Jacques Parizeau's racist comments blaming minorities for the nationalists loss, which forced him to resign, several episodes served to increase social tensions with minority communities in Montreal. These events increased concern in minority communities, in particular the Jewish community which bore the brunt of most of the attacks, and among those involved in human rights in Quebec (Small, 1996).

[2] As Quebec changes and gains greater economic and political control over its affairs, its very notion of identity and integration is being transformed. In the realm of socio-cultural policy, for example, this has a particular effect. The Federal policy of multiculturalism finds its roots in the British approach to identity, promoting integration with an emphasis on ethnic or group identity. The Quebec policy of inter-culturalism promotes integration into the dominant society and culture at the individual level, not on the group level. Inter-culturalism, can be understood to be more closely affiliated to the French 'Republican' model. Both approaches have rich colonial legacies. The multicultural, or group approach, can contribute to segregation or highlight differences. Conversely, the French inter-cultural model could promote intolerance through forced assimilation. As Quebec society changes, what will be the place of the minority communities? Some in Quebec, perceive the very notion of 'community' to be antagonistic to the Quebec approach. Ottawa's multiculturalism has been seen to be an attempt to augment the Federalist cause in Quebec and to offset nationalist aspirations by promoting differences among Quebecers and supporting minorities. Will minorities be pressured to assimilate into the dominant Quebec culture, or will differences be respected? Will there be a back-lash against multiculturalism and *'les autres'*, in the future (Small, 1996, p. 335; McAndrew, 1996, p. 23)?

186 *Studies in Segregation and Desegregation*

African-Canadian population. Among Haitian youth in Montreal, for example, unemployment figures have reached approximately 30 to 40 percent. The unemployment figures for 'Black' Anglophone youth in Montreal are even higher, at a staggering 50 percent. This can only cause further suffering and instability within the community and for Montreal as a whole. The exodus of Jewish youth from Quebec in search of employment and political stability is also a serious issue, threatening the very future of the community itself (Small, 1998).

Social Formation of Montreal: A Brief Examination of Economic Development

The period from the mid-1800s to the early 1960s witnessed the rise and fall of Montreal as Canada's economic centre. During its preeminence, it ushered in confederation, and was at the forefront of national modernisation during the post-World War II era. Its dominance coincided with Anglo hegemony over the city. With the Frenchification of Montreal and the political upheavals it precipitated, combined with the construction of the St. Lawrence Seaway in the late 1950s and the subsequent loss of economic preeminence to Toronto, its socio-economic status in Canada declined from metropolis to provincial centre, (Small, 1996, p. 352).[3] The growth of Montreal's industrial sector during the mid and late 1800s, occurred within a framework of the development of a Canadian transportation infrastructure, a waged labour force, rural specialisation and growing state intervention. The transportation network created, integrated and expanded the national market. It attracted foreign capital, generated a fixed infrastructure and established spin-off effects throughout the economy (Palmer, 1983, pp. 9-10).

The St. Lawrence River is a vital east/west transportation link, enabling shipping to gain access to the North American interior from the Atlantic Ocean to the Great Lakes. In the 1880s it played a central role in the economic development of Montreal, as the centre of ocean-going shipping during the ice-free months, (McNaught, 1988, pp. 80-81). It was, therefore, the key entrepot of eastern Canada. Modifications were completed on the river in 1848, making Montreal a warehousing centre for staple products for trade throughout the North American interior. By the

---

[3]   Frenchification refers to the political and socio-economic changes emerging out of the 'Quiet Revolution'. French Quebecois cultural symbols and power replaced those developed by the English (refer to Levine, 1990).

Charles Small 187

1960s, however, it ultimately contributed to the city's economic decline (Small, 1996, pp. 350-351).[4]

During the mid- to late 1800s Montreal emerged as Canada's major urban economic centre and consolidated the place of English in the city's economy (Levine, 1990, p.19). During this period, Montreal was under English and Scottish Protestant hegemony.[5] The migration of Britain's dispossessed also meant that Anglophone Montreal no longer consisted solely of a handful of wealthy merchants and became more diverse along class and ethnic lines. By the 1840s, the Irish constituted 20% of Montreal's working class (Levine, 1990, p. 8).[6]

The 1920s witnessed a large influx of investment capital, due to diminishing natural resources and the steady rise of labour costs in the northeastern US (McRoberts & Posgate, 1980, p. 38). During World War II an economic renewal occurred, facilitating development in Quebec's interior. Quebec's raw materials contributed to Canadian economic development. Since 1935, the industrialisation of Quebec has been

---

[4] During the 1950s the Canadian and Quebec Governments agreed to build a deep water route through the entire St. Lawrence with the US. Officially opened in 1959, the Seaway is only frozen for three months a year. The project advanced the integration of the U.S. and Canadian economies, marking the end of reliance on Montreal's warehouses. Trade bypassed Montreal to Ontario and US cities along the Great Lakes. Combined with the 1959-1961 recession and rising nationalism, Montreal's decline began (Small, 1996, p. 351). It was the last occasion in which the Queen would officiate at a ceremony on Quebec soil (McNaught, 1988, pp.292-293). The opening of the St. Lawrence made it possible to exploit Quebec's mineral resources, essentially benefiting Ontario and US industry (Fitzmaurice, 1985, p. 87).

[5] Montreal's English businessmen were continental economic actors, promoting Montreal as a central transportation link in Canada's expanding agricultural commodity export markets. Conversely, Francophone merchants were mostly small businessmen, conducting their activities in a regional market. The English consistently blocked French attempts to penetrate continental oriented economic sectors. Subsequently, by the early nineteenth century, economic development had produced discernible linguistic divisions of labour in Montreal. By 1840, for example, more than 70 percent of Montreal's merchants were English, while the French were over represented within the working class. More than a century later, even though Montreal has become a major metropolis, the pattern of linguistic hierarchy remains (Levine, 1990, p. 19).

[6] The fur trade created an indigenous entrepreneurial class that switched to other staples when the fur trade collapsed in the 1820s and bankrupted Montreal merchants. The merchants were primarily English and pro-British (Tulchinsky, 1977, pp. 4-5). The British mercantile system disintegrated in the 1840s. Montreal was dependent on mercantile exchange and petty commodity production at this time. Merchants focussed on export trade and finance and were unwilling to invest in industry since return on capital was slow. Some manufacturing was ventured by artisans for local markets (Lewis, 1985, p. 52; Levitt, 1970, p. 49).

188 *Studies in Segregation and Desegregation*

characterised by a rapid development of industries related to natural resources, further developing its natural resources and expanding secondary and tertiary activities (Milner & Milner, 1973, p. 38). Agriculture, once a major source of employment, diminished in importance due to mechanisation, though it generated higher levels of revenue. Resources were transported mainly by railway and through the St. Lawrence Seaway (McRoberts & Posgate, 1980, pp. 38-39). During the second half of the twentieth century hydroelectric power and mining became the two major contributors to Quebec's economic growth. Hydroelectric power was cheap and plentiful and derived from the interior of the province. It was a crucial factor in the growth of processing industries, such as pulp and paper and aluminum smelting and manufacturing. Prior to the Liberal government establishing the Quebec Hydroelectric Commission in 1944, power production had been entirely controlled by private monopolies, mostly US corporations. In 1963 all hydro electricity was nationalised (McRoberts & Posgate, 1980, p. 38).

Unlike the primary activities, manufacturing is concentrated in Montreal, itself. Manufacturing in Montreal was historically dependent on primary extractive industries, and played a crucial role in economic development. Smelting and refining, aircraft production, textiles, clothing, and tobacco products followed pulp and paper, the most important manufacturing industry. Many of these sectors had roots in small, labour intensive operations, characteristic of Quebec industry before the growth of highly capitalised resource based industries (McRoberts & Posgate, 1980, p. 39).

From the 1960s to the 1990s, Montreal's economic development centred on activities in the service sector, such as banking, insurance and tourism (Levine, 1990, pp. 202-203). Structural changes contributed to the post-Frenchified Montreal economy. In the late 1960s the economic focus shifted away from Canadian markets towards the Quebec region. The displacement of Montreal as Canada's preeminent urban economic centre accelerated after the 1960s as growing numbers of Canadian corporate head offices and US branch plants moved, mostly to Toronto (Levine 1990, p. 202). Montreal's manufacturing investment slightly exceeded Toronto's in 1961. By the 1970s, Toronto's stock exchange surpassed Montreal's in volume and value. At this time, Toronto clearly became Canada's national economic heart, while Montreal functioned increasingly as the urban node of the Quebec regional market (Levine, 1990, p. 202).

It is also important to note that in Quebec and Canada, capital is linked to ethnic differences. This is expressed within the federal political party

Charles Small 189

structure and development strategy (Ornstein, 1985, p. 137; Small, 1996, p. 318). A deeper understanding of Canada's ruling elite groups can be reached if the perspective includes the acknowledgment of a fragmented bourgeoisie with a solid Anglo-Saxon fraction as the hegemonic partner (Niosi, 1983, p. 117). As assessed in the next section of this report, these socio-economic cleavages play a central role in the development of Quebec's economy and the ongoing conflict.

The Historical Formation of Montreal's Population

Urbanisation in Quebec, mirroring its economic development, was dominated by Montreal and Quebec City. Montreal became the centre of trade and commerce, while Quebec City remained a smaller administrative and educational centre. Montreal became the focal point of industrialisation, attracting rural French labourers. The city's population tripled between 1861 and 1891 to 265,000 then doubled again to 530,000 by 1913 (Small, 1997, p. 7; McRoberts & Posgate, 1980, p. 28).

As early as 1831, Montreal had a British majority. According to the 1851 census, 55 percent of the city's 60,000 residents were of British ethnic origin (Levine, 1990, p. 8). The French Quebec population, however, remained less urbanised than English Canada's. Even as late as the beginning of the twentieth century the vast majority of Francophones were rural, and the Roman Catholic Church still dominated (Small, 1996, p. 287). However, in the 1860s, Montreal's linguistic balance changed significantly and, demographically, the city became French speaking. The economic crisis in rural Quebec, combined with the dynamic growth of Montreal's industrial economy, attracted thousands of rural Francophones to the city (Hamelin & Roby 1971, p. 76). Montreal grew from 90,000 to 800,000 between 1861 and 1931 (Levine, 1990, p. 9).

Table 9.1 Percentage of Quebecois living in Montreal: 1871-1961

YEAR	% OF QUEBEC ANGLOS	% OF QUEBEC FRANCOS
1871	22.6	8.9
1901	39.3	17.4
1931	61.4	26.6
1961	74.3	39.3

Source: Levine 1990, p.10.

190 *Studies in Segregation and Desegregation*

From 1871 to 1961, significant changes occurred in the demographic composition of Montreal. In 1871, only 22.6 percent of Quebec's Anglophones lived in Montreal, while in 1931, 61.4% lived in the city, and 74.3% lived there by 1961. By the 1960s, Montreal had become the demographic centre of both Quebec Anglophone and Francophone populations, a phenomenon that today contributes to increased linguistic tensions and conflict (Levine, 1990, p. 9).

At the beginning of the twentieth century, French Canadians emerged with a strong ideological and political belief in cultural survival, pertaining to their relationship with the rest of Canada. This became especially relevant with regard to the radical legacy of Papineau and remained an integral aspect of Quebec's politics throughout the 1900s (Small, 1996, p. 345; McRoberts & Posgate 1980, p. 35). The processes of urbanisation and industrialisation of Quebec and the growing awareness of social and economic conditions affected the collective social and political consciousness of French Canadians (Small, 1996, p. 354).

Table 9.2 Ethnic composition of Montreal: 1871-1961

YEAR	% OF FRENCH	% OF BRITISH	% OF OTHERS
1871	60.3	38.1	1.6
1902	63.9	31.6	4.5
1921	60.7	27.3	12.0
1941	62.6	24.5	12.9
1951	63.8	22.2	14.0
1961	62.0	18.1	19.9

The distinction between the Two Founding Fathers of Confederation or the Charter Groups and their competing interests shaped the history of Canada from colonial times to the present (Small, 1996, p. 231).[7] Throughout Canadian history, Montreal was the focal point of these tensions and the centre of economic and political power (Small, 1997, p. 3). The conflict was mainly played out in Montreal due to the competing

---

[7] The notion of the 'Two Founding Fathers of Confederation' is used in the B and B Report, the foundation of multiculturalism. It refers to the British and French ethnic groups (B and B Report, 1969, pp. 3, 10). This terminology, which is problematic in terms of gender issues, has also been criticised for its ethnocentricity. It collapses Canada's history in terms of the contribution by the 'others'. Most notable, the First Nations (Small 1996, p. 229).

Charles Small 191

interests within the city, first between the English and French, then later the 'others'. Montreal is unique in terms of its population composition, though it actually reflects and embodies the central contradictions of the Canadian Federal experiment.[8]

After 1900, Montreal's ethnic and linguistic balance was affected by new sources of international migration. As late as 1901 Montreal's population still consisted essentially of British and French. Only 4.5% of the residents were not of French or British stock. Between 1901 and 1961 Montreal became a multi-ethnic city, due to two significant waves of immigration. In 1931, with the migration of predominately Jews and Italians, 13.5% or 135,000 of Montreal's population was not of French or British stock. By 1961, as the post-world war II immigration accelerated from southern and Eastern Europe, the non-French, non-British population reached 350,000 or nearly twenty percent of the total (Levine, 1990, pp. 9-10). For the first time 'others' outnumbered the British on the Island of Montreal (Small, 1996, p. 349). In fact, if the current trends continue, '*les autres*' or non-Francophone Quebecois will become the majority on the Island of Montreal during the first decade of the twenty-first century.

As early as the 1940s, the new ethnic amalgam began to influence Montreal's linguistic dynamics. Until then, Anglophone Montreal was still vastly British. However, as non-Anglophone and non-Francophone immigrants arrived and chose English as their new language, 'Anglophone' Montreal became multicultural (Small, 1996, p. 386). By 1971, as Jews, Italians, Greeks, Portuguese, Caribbeans and 'others' joined the English speaking community, British Montrealers comprised only 61% of the Island's Anglophone population and only 37% of Montreal's entire non-Francophone population (Levine 1990, p. 10).

The multiculturalisation of English-speaking Montreal had two important effects: i) as immigrants opted for English, they bolstered the demographic strength of the English in Montreal; ii) the ethnic diversification of English Montreal transformed 'Anglophones' into a statistical category instead of a communal social grouping (Small, 1996, p. 386; Levine, 1990, p. 11). By 1960, English speaking Montreal was a collection of sub-communities: a British community from Quebec,

---

[8]   Montreal embodies the central contradictions of the Canadian federal experiment in the sense that it historically has the two founding ethnic groups residing in the city. They have competed for dominance in Montreal for several centuries. The resulting tensions have had both negative and positive consequences, much as in Canada as a whole. In addition, the arrival of a substantial 'other' population also reflects the more contemporary questions related to notions of integration and the place of minorities in society.

192 *Studies in Segregation and Desegregation*

consisting of English, Scottish and Irish; English-speakers from elsewhere in North America; Jews and Italians, southern and eastern Europeans and Caribbeans. The existence of these sub-communities meant that so-called 'Anglophones' often fought among themselves. For example, British Protestants discriminated against Jews (Levine, 1990, p. 11).[9] It took the politicisation of the language question during the 1960s and 1970s to generate a common linguistic community out of these diverse groups (Levine, 1990, p.11). Traditionally, Quebec and its institutions did not absorb as many immigrants as did the other parts of Canada. Since 1946, Quebec has received 20.7% of the total of Canadian immigrants. Only 12 to 13% of the immigrants came from French-speaking countries. Of these French-speaking immigrants, 90% integrated into the English community of Quebec (Hawkins, 1988, p. 218).

Table 9.3 Enrolment in Montreal public schools: 1970-1990 by language of instruction (in percentages)

YEAR	FRENCH	ENGLISH
1970-71	63.2	36.8
1974-75	59.7	40.3
1976-77	58.8	41.2
1977-78	58.5	41.5
1982-83	64.9	35.1
1987-88	69.7	30.3
1989-90	71.0	29.0
1991-92	72.0	28.0

During the 1970s, especially with the 1976 Parti Quebecois Government, an effort was made to integrate immigrants into the French milieu. A move away from bilingualism to Frenchification occurred during this time. This phenomenon was created by law: Bill 63 (1969) created the watchdog Office de la Langue Francaise; Bill 22 (1974), the Official Language Act, instituted the primacy of French in schools and places of

---

[9] The history of discrimination against the Jewish community by English Montrealers is abundant. This includes quotas at McGill University for Jewish students, which only ended in the 1960s. Jews were not permitted to purchase homes in Hampstead, the Town of Mount Royal or Westmount. They could not enter Anglo-owned ski resorts or golf clubs (see Anctil, 1992; Small, 1996; Levine, 1990).

Charles Small 193

work; and Bill 101 (1977) made French the official language of Quebec to the exclusion of English (Brown, 1986, p. 263; Small, 1996, p. 267).

Bill 101 had a profound effect on the educational system and the non-Francophone community in Montreal. It accomplished its goal of turning English education in Montreal into a privilege for a narrowly defined community of Anglophones, not a system that integrated immigrants. This has been perceived by Montreal Anglos as threatening to its continuity (Levine, 1990, p. 141).

The language issue, especially pertaining to education, was central to the Frenchification of Quebec. The focus of the linguistic conflict was Montreal. Successive Quebec governments, from the late 1960s to the 1990s, understood that the future of a French Quebec was based on the school system (Brown, 1986, p. 264). English instruction for the children of Anglophone Quebecers was not at issue. The right of newcomers, however, to have their children educated in the English school system was firmly restricted legislatively (Brown, 1986, p. 264). Since 1977, immigrants to Quebec must send their children to French language schools. Substantial levels of enrolment for English language schooling has been lost as many Anglophones leave the province and a significant number of those who remain decide to send their children to French schools even though they are eligible for English education (Small, 1997, p. 43).

Table 9.4 Distribution of allophone students by language of instruction Montreal: 1970-88 (in percentage)

YEAR	FRENCH	ENGLISH
1970-71	7.9	92.1
1973-74	11.4	88.6
1976-77	22.3	77.7
1983-84	45.4	54.6
1984-85	51.3	48.7
1985-86	54.0	46.0
1986-87	60.0	40.0
1987-88	66.2	33.8

Source: Levine 1990, p.139.

194 *Studies in Segregation and Desegregation*

Using Canadian Census Surveys to Measure Differentiation

This section of the present paper examines social and spatial differentiation in Montreal. It relies on raw data provided by Canadian census surveys to provide an in-depth picture of Montreal's social and spatial population distribution. This section offers an empirical examination of Montreal and should be understood within the context of both the historical and conceptual.

The Canadian census material provides an excellent source of data not found in other countries. This is especially true since 1981 when the wide availability of computerised data makes it possible to conduct a systematic analysis of issues pertaining to ethnic origin and class at the basic level of individuals. In fact, Canadian censuses provide the most extensive and widely used data source for studies in ethnic stratification and inequality (Li, 1988, pp. 4, 61).

Studies that examine US social and spatial segregation do not enjoy the same type of detailed information. They are forced, for example, to rely on the category of Russian origin, in order to calculate levels of Jewish segregation (Lieberson & Waters, 1984, pp. 10-11). This situation is based on the fact that large numbers of Russian immigrants to the US, during the early twentieth century were Jewish. This source for measuring Jewish dissimilarity, which is the best available in the USA is clearly prone to misconceptions. First, of the Russians who immigrated, many were not Jewish. Secondly, the majority of the US Jewish community does not come from Russia, but from other countries. Thirdly, there is an assumption that most of the Jews from Russia would identify themselves in a census questionnaire as Russian. At the very least, a considerable numbers of Jews of Russian origin might not identify themselves as Russian. This could be due to a strong Jewish identity or not wanting to be viewed as Russian in their new anti-communist and anti-Soviet society. Jews of Russian origin may have also wanted to dissociate themselves from Russia and the painful memories associated with their past (Lieberson & Waters, 1984, p. 11).

In fact, Nancy Denton, who examines issues pertaining to social and spatial segregation in the US, was astonished at the levels of Canadian differentiation, particularly regarding the Montreal Jewish population. This is due to the widely held belief that levels of segregation are largely economically determined. Her presumption is based on the US experience of the heavily segregated and impoverished African-American population. Experts assume that once African-Americans gain economic status, there will be less segregation and more integration. However, when taking into

Charles Small 195

account levels of Montreal Jewish segregation, this premise must be critically re-examined. In Montreal, the Jewish community possesses the economic ability to integrate or live freely within most areas of the city. Yet, despite the economic mobility to do so, they remain the most highly segregated group. This reinforces a central contention that there is a need to provide a conceptual examination of the social construction of national identity and race within a socio-economic and historical context. Given Canadian socio-cultural policies and the history of racism, integration for the Jewish population has not been a viable option.[10]

Despite the wealth of information that the Canadian census surveys provide, weaknesses exist. The criteria used by *Census Canada* for assigning origin to respondents, for example, have been ambiguous pertaining to race, ethnicity, mother tongue and birthplace. Historically, definitions assigned to groups change. It is, therefore, problematic to compare ethnic groups from one census to another (Li, 1988, pp. 61-62).

During the 1971 census survey of non-official language groups, for instance, respondents were asked to indicate their ethnic or cultural group based on the male side of their family. Since ethnic origin in the 1981 and 1986 census surveys are based on paternal descent, the data are not directly comparable (Li, 1988, p. 62). In addition, some cultural groups, such as the Jewish community, trace their religious descent matrilineally, causing some difficulties with the categorisation itself. Furthermore, ethnic origin was established on a subjective measurement. The census question stated, 'To which ethnic or cultural group do you feel you now belong?' (Boyd et al. 1985, p. 534). Pineo and Porter discovered that an overwhelming majority of second and third generation Canadians, selected 'Canadian' as their response to the above question (1985, p. 359).

The ethnic categories used by *Census Canada* vary from one study to another. There has been a tendency to focus on European origins and ignore non-white minorities (Li, 1988, p. 63). In studies of ethnic inequalities within Canadian society, the omission of non-whites is a serious flaw, especially given racial discrimination in the labour market (Royal Commission, 1984, p. 14). Satzewich and Li (1987) assert that there is a need to include more non-white immigrant groups in census surveys,

---

[10] Refer to Omi and Winant, 1986, pp. 10-11; Brown, 1981, p. 198; Freedman, 1984, p. 147; Hall (1980) for analysis of the weaknesses of the ethnic paradigm and notions of integration without assessing socio-economic conditions in a systematic fashion. In addition, Hall (1980) and CCCS associates assert the need to examine different social contexts and the manifestation of different 'racisms', which aptly apply to the Montreal context.

196 *Studies in Segregation and Desegregation*

and studies of stratification arising out of census data. This is especially pertinent since the source of immigrants has shifted from Britain and other European countries to 'developing' nations (Li, 1988, p. 63).

Throughout the analysis of this section, *Census Canada* (1986) defines a 'single' origin for a respondent who answered the census question, concerning 'ethnic' origin, with only one ancestry. Multiple origin is designated if respondents stated that they were of an additional ancestry to the origin in question. A person who did not provide an origin or reported ancestry not included in the census survey is considered a 'non-response' (Kralt, 1986, p. 17).

Population Composition

As discussed, in terms of its economy and population, Montreal is the second largest Canadian city. It, however, holds the key to national unity and the viability of Canada as a nation. The total Canadian population is approximately thirty million. The majority of Canadians are of British descent, followed by French, Italian, Jewish, Greek, 'Black', Portuguese and 'others'. The total Quebec population is 6,532,460. The majority of Quebecers are of French origin, followed by British, Italian, Jewish, Greek, 'Black', Portuguese and 'others' (Choiniere, 1990, p. 8). The total population of Montreal is 2,036,745. From 1981 to 1986, the city's population remained steady with an increase of only 0.4 percent or an additional 7,550 inhabitants (Small, 1998, p. 14).

Table 9.5 Population of the Montreal region and the rest of Quebec: 1966-1986

CENSUS YEAR	MONTREAL REGION	REST OF QUEBEC
1966	2,119,266	3,661,579
1971	2,188,570	3,841,515
1976	2,116,850	4,118,140
1981	2,029,195	4,409,265
1986	2,036,745	4,495,715

Source: Choiniere,1990, p. 9.

Cartographical Analysis

The historical linguistic divisions in Montreal are clearly reflected in the city's social geography. Montreal is a divided city. In macro terms, the east of the city is Francophone and the west is fundamentally Anglophone. Figure 9.1 illustrates that the eastern part of Montreal is highly represented by the French population in relation to its percentage of the city as a whole.

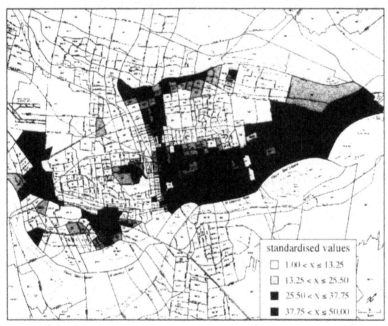

Figure 9.1 Francophone areas in Montreal

The east-west division of Montreal is explicitly demarcated along St. Lawrence Boulevard, the traditionally and popularly perceived dividing line. Figure 9.2 demonstrates British representation. It is essentially the mirror image of Figure 9.1 with British highly represented in the West End of Montreal. Recently, there has been some young professional Francophone migration to the established Anglophone areas of Notre Dame du Grace (N.D.G.) with some concentration evident on Figure 9.1. Young Anglophones have recently established themselves in the extreme western edge of the city, in Dollard des Ormeaux and Kirkland.

Figure 9.3 demonstrates extremely high concentration levels of the Jewish community in the Middle Western section of the city. They are clearly the most highly segregated group in Montreal. The 'Black'

198 *Studies in Segregation and Desegregation*

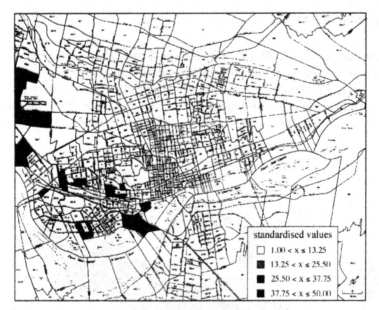

Figure 9.2 Anglophone areas in Montreal

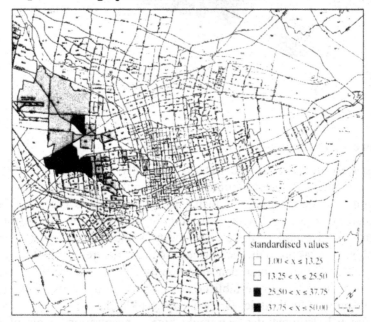

Figure 9.3 Jewish areas in Montreal

community, on the other hand, is spread out with extremely low levels of concentration (Figure 9.4). The next section of this paper will examine levels of segregation in a detailed manner.

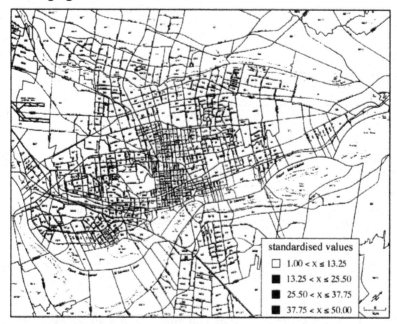

Figure 9.4 Black areas in Montreal

Levels of segregation in Montreal are striking since they are substantially different from those typically found south of the border in the US. The two Montreal majority groups, the French and British, have levels of dissimilarity that are double the levels of white groups in the US, as demonstrated by Leiberson (1980). Conversely, the degree of Black segregation in Montreal is less than half that found in the US Jewish segregation in Montreal, on the other hand, reaches levels associated more closely with African-Americans in the US.

Levels of dissimilarity are also significantly higher in Montreal in comparison to other Canadian cities (Kralt, 1986, pp. 22-24). Kralt (1986), in his analysis on behalf of *Census Canada*, using the 1981 census survey and the Gini Coefficient Model, demonstrates that Montreal's level of differentiation is higher than Toronto's.[11] The dominant French population

---

[11] The Gini Coefficient measures residential concentration for each ethnic group. It summarises the extent to which the cumulative percent of the ethnic group can be compared with the cumulative percent of the total population in a given number of census tracts and may have a range of values from 0 to 1 (Kralt, 1986, p. 22). Duncan and Duncan (1955) demonstrate that the ID and Gini models are quite similar. The

200 *Studies in Segregation and Desegregation*

in Montreal had a differentiation level of 0.159, based on the Gini Coefficient Model, while the differentiation level of the British majority in Toronto was 0.121. The British in Montreal reached 0.477 while the French in Toronto were 0.213 (Kralt, 1986, pp. 22-24).[12]

Table 9.6 Index of dissimilarity in Montreal by census tracts

	Brit	Fren	Ital	Jew	Greek	Black	Portu	Other	Total
British	0.0								
French	52.9	0.0							
Italian	66.2	54.2	0.0						
Jewish	72.6	86.9	90.0	0.0					
Greek	69.7	73.9	78.5	77.1	0.0				
Black	56.1	55.2	51.8	76.2	67.8	0.0			
Portuguese	71.1	56.7	65.2	87.7	73.1	67.4	0.0		
Other	40.6	47.0	58.9	69.7	53.7	42.0	60.1	0.0	
ID	41.5	18.0	49.0	77.6	64.7	46.1	54.1	32.3	0.0
IS	45.5	44.9	53.9	81.5	63.7	47.0	54.9	36.7	--

*Source:*1986 *Census Canada*, 20 percent survey; Calculations by Small, 1996.[13]

The high levels of differentiation of the French population must be understood in relation to the historical domination of Quebec by the British, the late urbanisation and modernisation of the French Catholic population and the political discourse of nationalism. In a real sense the majority French population possesses social patterns and behaviour more typical of a minority group (Weinfeld, 1986, p. 85).

The group with the highest level of dissimilarity or the group most segregated in Montreal is the Jewish population. The ID for the Jewish population is remarkably high at 77.67, while the IS figure is 81.54. In comparison to New York in 1910, for example, the Montreal Jewish

---

    Gini model measures dissimilarity on a scale from 0 to 1, while the ID uses a scale from 0-100 (Duncan & Duncan, 1955, pp. 51-54).

[12] It should be noted that the index of segregation (IS) offered in this section measures levels of segregation more effectively when assessing the dominant groups of a given population. Consequently, the analysis in this section is deeper than that offered by Kralt (1986). See Peach and Rossiter (1996).

[13] The index of segregation (IS) is a variant of the ID. It compares the level of difference between a given population and the total population minus itself. The tables demonstrate that the ID and IS are similar for most groups except those that constitute a large majority, in this case the French population. The IS is calculated by dividing the ID for the target group by 1 minus the target population divided by the total population of the city (Peach and Rossiter, 1996, in print).

Charles Small 201

dissimilarity is unique since Russian (Jewish) ID was only 34 (Lieberson 1980, p. 266). Interestingly, Italians in Chicago during the 1930s and 1950s, another minority group, had ID levels in the 50s (Duncan & Lieberson, 1959, p. 367).[14] In comparison to Toronto, according to Kralt's Gini Coefficient Model based on the 1981 census survey, Jews in Toronto scored 0.816, while in Montreal it was somewhat higher at 0.895 (Kralt, 1986, p. 24). Darroch and Marston (1972) examined dissimilarity in Toronto and demonstrated that the ID level for the Jewish population was 75, similar to the above findings, though Montreal was moderately higher (Darroch & Marston, 1972, p. 115).[15]

Given anti-Semitism historically in Montreal and throughout Quebec by both the British and French, this phenomenon is understandable.[16] According to Weinfeld (1986), classical sociologists contend that this type of social phenomenon is essentially due to a response to exclusionary behaviour on the part of the majority group. He, however, suggests that this segregation is also partially voluntary, since many Montreal Jews, signify their identity by socialising with other Jews (Weinfeld 1986, pp. 94-95). Here again, it is essential to examine Quebec history critically, the treatment of the Jewish community and other minority groups, as well as the socio-cultural issues in order to understand differentiation in its proper context.

Jewish segregation is even more striking when the diversity within the community itself is considered. Approximately seventy percent of the Montreal Jewish population is of Ashkenazi descent, while 25% is Sephardi. The remaining five percent includes various other groups, such as the largest Diaspora Ethiopian Jewish community (Elazar & Waller, 1990, p. 74; Shahar, 1991, p. 2). Of the Jewish population approximately 55% list

---

[14] Italian ID in Montreal at 49.08, and the IS at 53.95 are comparable to Duncan and Lieberson's (1959) figure.

[15] Darroch and Marston (1972) examine the Jewish population as a 'religious' entity as opposed to an ethnic group (Darroch & Marston, 1972, p. 115).

[16] According to Weinfeld (1986), ninety percent of the adult Montreal Jewish population agreed that all or most of their friends were Jewish, 53 percent agreed that all or most of their neighbours were Jewish, while more than one third agreed that all or most of their business associates and clients were Jewish. Jewish economic segregation is widespread with only thirty percent of Montreal Jewish households employed by essentially non Jewish firms. The majority of Jews are self-employed or work for wholly or largely Jewish owned firms. Interestingly, economic segregation is equally prevalent among foreign and native born, religiously observant and less observant Jews (Weinfeld, 1986, p. 95). See the socio-economic calculations provided in this section, based on the two percent sample survey of Montreal, demonstrating Jewish economic segregation.

202 *Studies in Segregation and Desegregation*

English as their mother tongue, 25% list French, 11.3% indicate Yiddish, and the remaining 20% list other languages (Shahar, 1991, p. 7). With the high degree of diversity within the Jewish population, the levels of dissimilarity compared to non-Jewish groups are that much more striking.[17]

The Montreal Jewish community has a reputation of being one of the best organised in the Diaspora. This is reflected in the amount of Jewish education received by members of the community. On average, 80 percent of the Jewish population receive some formal Jewish education. One hundred percent of Montreal Jews between the ages of 18 to 29, according to the survey by Shahar (1991), receive some formal Jewish education; 76 percent of those thirty years and over obtain Jewish education. This suggests that among young adults, in particular, there is a keen interest for receiving Jewish education. Interestingly, Jewish education increases with the level of household income. 87.1% of Jewish households with incomes over $80,000 receive Jewish education, while 78.4% of households with incomes below $40,000 acquire Jewish education (Shahar, 1991, pp. 40-41).[18]

According to the survey by Shahar (1991), anti-Semitism appears to be a major concern within the Jewish community. When asked to identify reasons for leaving Quebec, 72.9% refer to the political situation, 66% mention the economic situation, 65.2% claim anti-Semitism, 53.4 percent refer to the language policy, 35.2% list a wish to join family and 28% claim a desire for a better education (Shahar, 1991, p. 12). In terms of anti-Semitism, it seems that Jewish Montrealers are quite concerned. In fact, indicative of the instability of Montreal in general and the Jewish community specifically, more than 40% of the Jewish population between the ages of 18 to 29 think that they will leave the province permanently within the next five years, while the figure for the entire Jewish population is 20% (Shahar, 1991, pp. 10-11).

During the late 1980s and early 1990s violent anti-Semitism re-emerged in Montreal as a serious phenomenon. Between 1987 and 1991, anti-Semitic incidents increased by two hundred percent (Small 1996, p.

---

[17] It should be noted, however, that the Jewish community has a high level of language proficiency. Nearly 75% of Jewish English speakers are fluent in French, while 70% of Jewish French speakers are fluent in English. In addition, 55% of the Jewish population is proficient in Hebrew to some extent, while 62% are proficient in Yiddish to some degree (Shahar 1991, p. 9).

[18] The fact that Jewish education increases with the level of household income is consistent with the general trend in Montreal's differentiation. It seems that with economic mobility groups turn to their community. In a society that promotes 'ethnic' identities, success appears to encourage the ability to practise this Canadian ethos.

263). In 1992 a total of 196 incidents of anti-Semitic vandalism and harassment was reported. This represents a 22% decrease over the previous year, mainly due to a rash of anti-Semitic acts attributed to the Gulf War in 1991. The 1992 findings, however, represent an 11% increase from 1989. The 1992 League Report placed blame for the increase on the rise of the political right.

In 1990 an estimated 400-600 neo-nazi 'racist' skinheads were based in Montreal (Shipman & Kagedan, 1990, p. 5; Prutschi, 1989, p. 2). Montreal has become a centre for skinheads and contains numerous fascist and white supremacist organisations. Skinheads maintain a high level of visibility in the east end of Montreal and 'hang out' at 'le Cargo' bar on rue St. Denis and 'Foufounes Electroniques' on Ste. Catherine Street (CCRP, August, 1991, p. 8). Among their contemporaries, Montreal neo-nazis, have the reputation for being the most violent in the country (McFarlane, 1994, p. 11). Despite their violent activities they face little interference from law enforcement agencies (La Ligue des Droits et Libertes, 1989, p. 1).

An escalation of attacks against minority communities throughout Canada, and specifically in Montreal, has occurred during the last several years. While the Jewish community is the prime target, African-Canadians, Asians and gays, have also been the victims of skinhead violence (Shipman & Kagedan, 1990, p. 6). In 1992, in central Montreal's Angrignon Park, for example, skinheads brutally beat to death a man 'suspected' of being gay (CCRP, June, 1993, p. 15).

Notably, the Black population is not as highly segregated as one would suspect, especially in comparison to the US. The Black ID in Montreal is 46.11, while the IS is 47.04. This is remarkably low. In Chicago, for instance, ID levels for the Black population, during the 1930s and 1950s were in the 80s (Duncan & Lieberson, 1959, p. 367). Black differentiation, according to Kralt's Gini Coefficient Model based on the 1981 census survey was higher in Montreal at 0.573 than in Toronto at only 0.452 (Kralt, 1986, p. 23). Given the well-documented social problems experienced by African-Americans in highly segregated US society, one might consider this a positive phenomenon. We do not since the Black community of Montreal does not have a strong sense of place. There are several areas of Montreal, in which the Black population is spread, and they are consequently far from one another.

There are several reasons why Black 'ghettoisation' has not occurred in Montreal. First and most relevant, in keeping with the general socio-historical trend, the African-Canadian community, like the city's

204 *Studies in Segregation and Desegregation*

population in general, is divided along linguistic lines.[19] Secondly, the Black population is diverse. There is the old established Black community founded over three hundred years ago as well as immigrants from the US the Caribbean, Africa and Europe. The census definition of Black does not account for these different subgroups whose members tend to live in close proximity to one another.[20] Thirdly, socio-economic status and religious affiliations play a role in the dispersal of the population. Fourthly, racial discrimination, particularly in Montreal's housing market, significantly affects and distorts the typical patterns of social mobility and spatial location in comparison to other immigrant populations. In addition, state sponsored accommodation in Montreal is usually located in areas outside districts often inhabited by the African-Canadian community (Williams, 1989, pp. 109-110).[21]

Currently, racism directed against the African-Canadian community is structured into Montreal society (Foster, 1991, p. 15). Racism affects Black socio-economic mobility and remains a serious obstacle for the community. At the institutional level, racism marginalises Blacks away from the mainstream of society (Williams, 1989, p. 111).

In housing, racial discrimination against the Black community is widespread, posing a rampant structural problem. Research in this area, however, is limited (Cambridge & Roberts, 1986, p. 9). Garon (1988) demonstrated the existence of high levels of racial discrimination in Montreal housing by measuring responses of landlords to visitations of potential white and Black tenants (pp. 30-31). According to Berube and Teitelbaum (1981), racism in the Montreal housing market against non-whites is not directly related to socio-economic position. Attainment of a minimum level of economic stability does not ensure that similar gains will be acquired outside the workplace. Berube and Teitelbaum conclude that there are high levels of racial discrimination in Montreal housing (pp. 63-

---

[19] It seems that the Jewish population although possessing linguistic and socio-economic differences are an exception. They live in close proximity to one another, especially in comparison to other groups. See location quotient figures.

[20] English-speaking subgroups and their institutions are primarily centred in the west and south of Montreal, while Francophone subgroups are essentially based in the north and east of the city. Consequently, the two communities are separated from one another. Within the Francophone and Anglophone associations, subgroups exist, especially within the Caribbean communities, with networks and affiliations significantly based on island of origin. This differentiation is demonstrated within the figures indicating location quotients.

[21] The fact that there are few African-Canadian 'ghettos' throughout the country contributes to the popular perception that there is little racism in Canada, especially in comparison to the US. This assumption is not accurate.

Charles Small 205

64). However, there exists little information on issues of discrimination in the Montreal housing market.

Within the educational system African-Canadian students are disproportionately placed in vocational courses (Brand & Bhaggiyadatta, 1986, pp. 53-54). In employment, Blacks are also discriminated against and enjoy less social mobility than do others. In 1983, the Ontario Human Rights Commission discovered that throughout the country African-Canadians earn twenty-five percent less then whites for the same work (Walker, 1985, p. 21).

In the early 1980s a major scandal emerged in Montreal's taxi industry. It involved four companies and reflects the state of racism in the city. The companies attempted to avoid hiring Black drivers, particularly Haitians. They treated their Black employees poorly by not sending them clients, giving them wrong addresses of clients and refusing them permission to use certain taxi stands. The companies claimed, with a degree of truth, that their clients felt uncomfortable driving with Black drivers (Commission des droits de la personne du Quebec, 1984, p. 21).[22] The Quebec Human Rights Investigation (1984) uncovered blatant racism in the industry and sanctioned companies guilty of practising discrimination (Commission des droits de la personne du Quebec, 1984, pp. 12-17).

In Montreal, as in other major North American or European cities, the criminalisation of young African-Canadians is endemic.[23] Police have been accused by the Montreal African-Canadian community and human rights groups of harassment, false arrests and blatant expressions of racism. One of the results in the last several years has been police shootings of numerous young Black men. As of 1990, there were only six Black police officers in the entire Montreal force of more than 4,500 (Levine, 1990, p. 218).[24]

The coroner's report, prepared by Judge Yarosky for the inquest into the 1991 police shooting death of Marcellus Francois, was critical of the force. Yarosky (1992) concluded that racism played a role in the shooting and that there was '... the continued presence within the Montreal Urban

---

[22] Under Quebec law it is illegal to discriminate. Clients are not permitted to request drivers by ethnicity (Quebec Human Rights Commission, 1984, pp. 3-4).

[23] In 1980 Hall argued that in order to undermine welfare rights, notions of citizenship and the freedom of organised labour, police powers are used to criminalise parts of the Black community. Gilroy saw criminalisation in terms of constructing a narrowing nationalism (in Keith, 1993, p. 199).

[24] Ethnic minorities in the Montreal municipal and Quebec provincial bureaucracies consist of less than two percent of the workforce in both (Small, 1998, p. 24).

206 *Studies in Segregation and Desegregation*

Community Police Department of an attitude toward members of the black community that is completely unacceptable' (Yarosky, 1992, p. 72).[25]

In 1987, Anthony Griffin, a young African-Canadian man, was shot to death by police officer Allan Gossett while he was in custody. He was detained for a dispute arising from a five dollar taxi fare. Gossett was tried and acquitted of manslaughter. Several thousand Montrealers marched in protest, prompting the formation of a commission to investigate police treatment of racial minorities (Levine, 1990, p. 219). The commission discovered that there was widespread discrimination by the police and that Blacks were much more likely to be arrested than whites (Human Rights Commission of Quebec, 1988, pp. 9-12).

Real or Perceived Differentiation

As mentioned, the French and British are the least segregated in comparison to other groups in Montreal. Interestingly, the Black population with the lowest level of differentiation follows them. The Black population possesses the lowest level of differentiation among minority groups. Given the racial tensions and their poor economic ranking in Montreal, they are not able to control urban space in the Montreal area. The Jewish population with considerable socio-economic success and a strong sense of community in a society that exhibits anti-Semitic tendencies has been able to control their own space and create a sense of place for themselves.

Philpott (1978) reveals that immigrant ghettos are often fictitious in both urban studies and mythology.[26] In US cities, most European groups, did not actually live in immigrant ghettos. The Irish ghetto, for example, assessed by Burgess in 1933, was discovered by Philpott in 1978 to actually consist of only 3% of Chicago's entire Irish population (in Massey

---

[25] Radio communication by the police on the day of Francois' murder, was filled with racist slurs (Yarosky, 1992, pp. 64-65). Police racism is a serious issue, threatening the security of the Montreal African-Canadian community, particularly its young men. Little research has been carried out on this topic in the Montreal context. It is vital that critical analysis be carried out since the criminalisation of a sector of the population could have profound ramifications.

[26] See Small (1995) for an analysis of the US ghetto and issues concerning real and perceived differentiation. It also offers an assessment of US differentiation and socio-economic factors affecting the ghettoisation of the African-American community and discusses weaknesses in the analysis by the Chicago School, which does not provide a comprehensive socio-economic historical analysis.

Charles Small 207

& Denton, 1993, p. 34).[27] The Black ghetto, however, comprised 82 percent of the city's total Black population, which constituted an important distinction in comparison to other so-called group 'areas'. Only a quarter of the total Irish population was, by comparison, within the Irish area (Massey & Denton, 1993, p. 32).

Table 9.7 Index of dissimilarity in comparison to expected levels of dissimilarity in Montreal

GROUPS	EXPECTED I.D	OBSERVED I.D	% EXPECTED OF OBSERVED
British	0.57	41.55	1.4
French	0.66	18.05	3.7
Italian	3.16	49.08	6.4
Jewish	4.72	77.67	6.1
Greek	2.89	64.70	4.5
Black	8.38	46.11	18.2
Portuguese	2.07	54.16	3.8
Others	0.63	32.35	2.0

Source: 1986 Census Canada, Twenty Percent Census Tract Survey.
Calculations: Small, 1996.[28]

---

[27] Lieberson (1980) confirms Philpott's critique of Burgess's work by examining the spatial isolation of various ethnic groups and comparing them to the African-American population in several US cities. His findings demonstrate that African-American levels of isolation are higher than other ethnic groups. These factors illustrate weakness in Park and Burgess's argument as well as in the Chicago School in general (in Massey & Denton, 1993, p. 33).

[28] The approach of comparing observed with expected levels dissimilarity was developed by Taueber and Taeuber (1964). They attempt to illustrate the component of social segregation that is due to economic factors. Their model utilises indirect standardisation of available census data. They delineate the status of a residential area in terms of, for example, income distribution. For each community area they apply city wide percentages to the observed income distribution, thus obtaining the number of the different ethnic group families expected if income alone determines residential locations of ethnic groups. They compute the expected number of ethnic group members in each area. Then they determine the index of residential differentiation between expected numbers of each ethnic group's members. This index can be regarded as the amount of ethnic residential segregation attributed to patterns of residential differentiation of income groups. It is admittedly a rough measure of ethnic residential segregation to income (Taueber & Taeuber, 1975, pp. 130-131).

208 *Studies in Segregation and Desegregation*

In Montreal, the popularly perceived Jewish area of Cote St. Luc, Hampstead and parts of Snowdon and Outremont, have in actuality heavily concentrated Jewish populations.[29] Commonly perceived Anglophone Black areas, such as Little Burgundy and Cote des Neiges/Snowdon have significant numbers of Blacks, though they also possess concentrations of other groups. The Francophone Black population is more concentrated, although significant levels of other groups also live in the same vicinity. High levels of Jewish concentration and Black dispersal are depicted in the figures using the location quotient. This is interesting, given the striking differences of the two groups' spatial distribution in the city. In the case of real differentiation of the Montreal Black population Philpott's argument that ghettos are often fictitious clearly applies (Massey & Denton, 1993). In the case of real Jewish segregation, however, high levels of differentiation obviously exist.

Dissimilarity, in comparison to expected levels of dissimilarity, within the urban context of Montreal demonstrates important social phenomena. As previously shown, although the Jewish population is highly segregated, only 6.1% of the differentiation is due to economic factors. In other words, 93.9% of Jewish differentiation is for other reasons. This certainly points to issues, such as socio-cultural policies and the place of minorities in Quebec and Canadian society, historically. In the past, French and British tensions were played out at the highest level of intensity in Montreal and considerably affected the Jewish population. Anti-Semitism and nationalism, which the Jewish community is sensitive to, given their Diaspora experience and was exposed to longer than any other minority group in Quebec, caused the community to react and create its own space within the city.[30] This concrete example illustrates the legacy of Quebec

---

[29] During the last decade or so, Hasidic Jews have moved into Outremont, a traditional immigrant enclave combined with an old wealthy French Canadian community. As the Hasidic community expands, this has caused tensions. The mayor of Outremont recently refused to issue permits for synagogues, claiming there were too many Jews and that they take up too much space.

[30] Bonacich (1973) examines 'middlemen' minorities in various social formations and the economic roles they play. Jews, perhaps, are the epitome of this role, often occupying it throughout much of Europe, at least since the Enlightenment (Bonacich, 1973, p. 583). In Quebec, with its history of anti-semitism and nationalism, Jews are popularly understood as playing the middleman's role. First, Jews, like other minorities, are resented since they are seen as pawns in Ottawa's 'multiculturalism' policy, which is perceived as designed to undermine Quebec nationalism. Secondly, Jews occupy a highly visible economic position, typical of Bonacich's notion of the middleman. This generates resentment from the French majority population, especially from nationalists, who perceive Jews as not quite Quebecois. In fact, many studies of

society's non-acceptance of its Jewish Quebecois population. Certainly, the Montreal Jewish population has inherent and positive reasons to be closely affiliated within their community and culture. Nevertheless, high levels of dissimilarity in comparison to US cities and Toronto point to the uniqueness of Montreal, as examined earlier, particularly the excluding nature of its Catholic society.

In comparison to all the groups in Montreal, the most significant proportion of Black differentiation is due to economic factors. 18.2% of the dissimilarity of the Black population is due to economic considerations. Black differentiation, taking into account the 'percentage of the expected and observed', is incredibly low in Montreal. In a society that places high value on the promotion of ethnic identity, the Black population fails to meet this Canadian ethos and, based on these standards, represents a failure. This is undoubtedly due to the complex social phenomena of racism and diversity within the Black population even though the complete opposite transpires in the US with a highly segregated Black population. Segregation in the US is often blamed for widely known, negative socio-economic ramifications.

This points to other issues, such as racism in the labour market and education. Since high levels of Black differentiation are due to economic factors combined with low levels of ID, especially in comparison to the US and to some extent, Toronto, the ID in Montreal is most striking.

Among the French and British population of Montreal, only 3.7 and 1.4%, respectively, of dissimilarity are due to economic factors. These are the lowest levels of any groups in Montreal and demonstrate the British and French dominance of the city and their satisfaction at living separately from 'les autres'. It is important to understand that the Quebec context is unique in many ways. French levels of segregation are remarkably high, especially in comparison to dominant groups elsewhere. In a sense the French Quebecois, in terms of dissimilarity, act as a minority. They are, after all, a minority in the North American context, a notion constantly upheld in social and political discourse. It is subsequently important, as previously stated, to recognise that Quebec does not possess classic minority-majority relations. The dominant French group is unusually marked by minority characteristics (Weinfeld, 1986, p. 85). The high levels of French segregation point to this.

Quebec's economy depict the supposed control and influence of the Jewish community. (For example, see Fitzmaurice, 1985.) This easily supports the stereotypes of Jews. Combined with nationalism, it creates a potentially volatile combination, a situation, which clearly applies to Bonacich's (1973) analysis.

210 *Studies in Segregation and Desegregation*

Socio-Economic Dissimilarity in Montreal: The Two Percent Extended Census Survey

This section of the paper provides further, detailed empirical data regarding socio-economic differentiation in Montreal based on ethnicity. This in-depth statistical information provides an abundance of socio-economic indicators based on the Census Canada 'Two Percent Extended Survey' of Montreal. It is designed to enhance the understanding of spatial dissimilarity in Montreal, partially described in the previous section. The analysis in this section is brief so as not to repeat the earlier material but does give a more detailed picture of the Montreal context.

The statistical calculations regarding household income by ethnicity are pertinent on several levels. The Jewish population is highly represented in the $50,000 to $100,000 income range. Yet they are under-represented in the range from $25,000 to $49,000, the middle income range. They are also well represented in the range of less than $10,000 to $24,999. These figures dispel the stereotypical myth that all Jewish people are wealthy and disproportionately control societal resources. Levels of Jewish household income, however, demonstrate the general economic success of the community and confirm their ability to create their own space in Montreal, a notion that was examined in the previous section. According to Shahar and Torczyner (1991), 17.1% of the Jewish population in Montreal are poor, while 6.6% are very poor (p. 10). This level is higher than the average for Montreal as a whole.[31]

In terms of household income and in comparison to all groups, the Black population has achieved the least. This includes the indigenous population, dismissing a widely held belief that although the Black population is poor, it is not as impoverished as the original population.[32] This fact reinforces the view examined in the preceding section that the

---

[31] The acceptance of the stereotype of the Jew as affluent is detrimental. First, the Jewish homeless, unemployed and poor, have difficulties being absorbed by institutions geared to servicing the destitute. Secondly, Jews themselves are largely unaware of the Jewish poor since many of them have internalised the popularly perceived notion (Tobin, 1985, p. 25; Torczyner, 1981, p. 11).

[32] Aboriginal People in Montreal are, nevertheless, extremely poor. This is significant in relation to the colonial legacy. Matters pertaining to the 'First Nations' in the Canadian urban context are often overlooked as most attention focusses on the 'reserves'. Mohawks in the Montreal area fought to control their land, against the Canadian Armed Forces and the Surete de Quebec. During the summer of 1990 social relations reached a dangerous point, especially regarding 'indigenous' peoples and other minorities in Montreal (Small, 1991).

Charles Small 211

Black Montreal population is economically weak and unable to control its own space as a community.

Interestingly, the British and French are both distributed quite equally in all income groups. The British are slightly better represented in the upper income categories, while the French are somewhat more incorporated in lower areas. This demonstrates the socio-economic and political change of the last several decades. The French have improved their standards due to the 'quiet revolution', while British dominance has diminished. A wide range of the 'newer ethnic' groups fare extremely well.

Within Canadian 'race relations' literature, particularly federal government documents, the notion and category 'visible minority' has been widely used since the late 1980s. The findings of this study, however, call into question the validity of the separate 'visible minority' classification. It must be stressed that people who are visibly perceived as 'other' in Canadian society, in terms of race or ethnicity, experience specific forms of discrimination. There are, nevertheless, large discrepancies between people of African decent and others who have been placed in the visible minority category by Census Canada, other government documents and scholarly publications.[33] In fact, these figures could be used to conceal the African Canadian experience and portray supposed progress made by people of 'colour'. When assessing the Black group separately from the visible minority category, large disparities are evident. According to the 'visible' and 'non-visible' classification, differences exist but are not nearly as large as when examining the Black group in comparison to others.

The Jewish population has the lowest level of unemployment at 4.2 percent. This could be attributed to the effects of communal assistance. However, a large part of the Jewish population, 40.3%, is not considered a part of the labour force. This is likely due to the aging population since many young productive Jews are leaving the city (Small, 1998, p. 35). The Black population has the highest level of unemployment at 14.7%. This is in keeping with the general trends previously discussed and is consistent with the structural effects of racism. British and French unemployment levels are similar to each other although the British manage slightly better at 6.4 percent compared to 7.0% for the French.[34] Visible minorities are

---

[33] The West Asian and Arab groups, for example, in comparison to the Black population achieve higher levels in terms of household income although both are classified as 'visible minorities'.

[34] Interestingly, the Filipinos are highly successful. This could be due to the fact that there are several wealthy entrepreneurs among them. Yet there is a significant proportion who are documented as being domestics. If they are 'live-in maids' in a wealthy home, are they counted as part of that household in the survey? Officials at

212 *Studies in Segregation and Desegregation*

considerably more unemployed in comparison to the non-visible group. Clearly, high levels of Black unemployment affect the visible minorities' overall average. Black unemployment is higher than any other group classified as a visible minority.

Examining occupation by ethnicity is pertinent since it illustrates prominent levels of dissimilarity in the labour market. The Jewish population is highly concentrated in manufacturing and sales, seemingly traditional Jewish occupations.[35] They have no farming representation, which is historically consistent with the general Jewish Diaspora experience, and are not represented in primary industries. The Jewish and Black populations are both highly represented in medicine and health. This is most likely due to a high proportion of Jewish doctors and Caribbean nurses and orderlies. Historically, Jews were not permitted to practise medicine in Montreal. As a result the Montreal Jewish community created the Jewish General Hospital, providing Jewish doctors with a place to work (Anctil, 1992, p. 3). It eventually became one of the leading medical institutions in North America. Many Caribbean immigrants came to Canada as skilled labourers, a considerable number of whom were nurses. The Black population is poorly represented in management, however, they are prominently represented in the service sector. Service sector employment is often poorly paid.

The visible minority segment of the population, in comparison to the non-visible group, is most notably under-represented in management and administration. They are highly represented in natural sciences, engineering and maths as well as medicine and health, previously mentioned.

The most successful groups in terms of educational achievement are the Filipino, Scandinavian, West Asian/Arab, Jewish, East/South Asian, and South Asian groups. Consistent with other socio-economic indicators, the Black population does not fare well. This most certainly reflects racism

---

Census Canada were unable to provide me with a satisfactory answer. The major post-WW II immigrant groups, the Italians, Greeks and Portuguese seem to reflect the general patterns for the entire population of Montreal. The Portuguese group ranks slightly above the other two groups and the Montreal averages although there is over representation of Italians in the highest income category.

[35] It is important to note that the manufacturing of clothes and textiles in Montreal was detrimentally affected by the recent NAFTA Accord. Many companies went bankrupt as a result, and numerous larger firms moved to Mexico to enjoy the benefits of cheaper labour. This also has had spin off effects in sales, also highly represented by the Jewish population. Sales is an occupation with high visibility, as textile salesmen, for example, travel throughout the province selling their wares. This contributes to the notions of Jews as the middleman, examined by Bonacich (1973). See Arthur Miller's *Death of a Salesman* for insight into the Jewish North American experience.

Charles Small 213

and is associated with streamlining students. Surprisingly, however, the Portuguese population is the least successful and has extra representation in the category of less than grade five education. They are also over-represented in the three lowest categories.

Aboriginal people have also not met with much success. Their numbers drop off at grade nine to thirteen. Interestingly, this is the time in which aboriginal children must leave schools in the reserves to pursue education in the Montreal region. East Asians, who perform well at the university level, also have high rates of those who obtain less than a grade five level of education.

Compared to the non-visible group, visible minorities have much more success in the category of university education. They actually do better in all categories, except at the lowest end of the scale in the category of less than a grade five education.

Groups with high levels of dwelling values are the Jewish population, Scandinavians, South Asians, Filipinos and Chinese. The Jewish group is well represented in the highest category of $150,000 and over. In comparison to the total group average for Montreal, all of these mentioned groups do well in the three highest groupings of $80,000 plus. Once again the Black and aboriginal populations are well below the average for Montreal.

Comparing visible and non-visible groups regarding the value of dwellings once again calls into question the validity of the category. Visible minorities have a greater proportion living in the highest valued homes. This is especially true in the three wealthiest categories. Consequently, they perform better than the non-visible population. It is interesting, however, to note that at the bottom of the scale, the visible minorities also score higher than the non-visible group. This illustrates the levels of poverty experienced by a significant segment of the Black population.

Inherent in these patterns is the assumption that a low amount of money spent on rent usually indicates a high level of income or wealth. Interestingly, a large number of Portuguese, Filipinos and Italians spend the least on rent, or less than 15% of their income. Conversely, the West Asians/Arab and Scandinavians spend the largest total of their income, more than 60%, on rent.

Visible minorities are most different from the non-visible group, at the extreme ends of the categories. In the lowest category of less than 15%, and highest 60% or more, visible minorities are consistently more represented than the non-visible group, while they seem quite similar in the middle.

214 *Studies in Segregation and Desegregation*

Similar to the table examining levels of rent, the same groups spend the least amount of their income on mortgage payments. The least amount of mortgage payments is understood to mean that the group has disposable income. These groups are Scandinavian, some of the Eastern Europeans, Jewish, Croats/Serbs and Ukrainians, who seem to be the most successful. The group that fares worst in this category is, once again, the Black population.

Visible minorities do not achieve as well as the non-visible group. Discrepancies in this area are quite wide. Perhaps these points to a problem of visible minority groups receiving support from financial institutions for mortgages and loans, combined with the problems generally associated with low income, education, and racism, examined previously.

Conclusion

This paper set out to define and examine the levels of social and spatial dissimilarity in Montreal. Through calculations, using the rich data provided by the 'Twenty Percent Survey of Montreal' by Census Canada, degrees of differentiation were clearly demonstrated. The empirical data offers a detailed picture of Montreal and its social formation.

Based on the 20% census survey, and utilising the ID, IS and the expected versus the observed models, levels of dissimilarity were firmly established. The findings illustrate that Montreal is severely segregated. The differentiation was found to be atypical in terms of its high degrees, and the social and spatial differentiation patterns of certain groups were found to be unique in comparison to Toronto and other cities, particularly in the US.

It was ascertained that levels of spatial dissimilarity in Montreal were extremely high for the French and British groups. In the case of the French it was most striking, in comparison to other dominant groups in the US and Toronto since their patterns of dissimilarity are rather indicative of a minority group. This phenomenon is a product of Canadian and, particularly, Quebec's societal historical development.

Of all the Montreal groups, Jewish dissimilarity was the highest. Despite its general economic success, the Jewish group is heavily segregated from the rest of the population. This is certainly due to the history of anti-Semitism and nationalism in Quebec. Having the economic capacity, the Jewish community developed a highly organised community. Only a small portion of Jewish differentiation is due to economic factors.

Charles Small 215

Montreal Jewish dissimilarity, compared to the levels found in the US and Toronto, is significantly higher.

The Black population is the least segregated minority group, according to the ID in Montreal. In comparison to US cities and partially to Toronto, Black Montreal differentiation is extremely low. Of the differentiation, however, a significant segment is due to economic factors. In fact, in comparison to any other group, Black differentiation is mostly the result of economic factors. This is certainly the result of the Black population's poor economic standing, as ascertained in the two percent extended survey. Blacks are unable to create their own space in the city in a similar fashion to other groups. The economic deprivation of the Black community is in large measure due to racism structured throughout Canadian society and certainly manifested in the Montreal context on many levels.

In light of the above mentioned issues, Montreal serves as an important and insightful context for a case study. It embodies the importance of issues such as national identity, socio-cultural policies and immigration. Certainly the concepts 'race', 'ethnicity' and 'racism', all directly influence social and spatial dissimilarity.

References

Anctil, P. (1992), 'Interlude of Hostility: Judeo-Christian Relations in Quebec in the Interwar Period, 1919-39', in A. Davies (ed), *Antisemitism in Canada: History and Interpretation*, Wilfrid Laurier University Press, Waterloo, Ontario.

Berube, L. & Teitelbaum, B. (1981), 'La discrimination raciale dans le logement a Montreal', Mouvement Quebecois pour combattre le racisme, Montreal.

Bonacich, E. (1973), 'A Theory of Middleman Minorities', *American Sociological Review*, vol. 38, (October) pp. 583-594.

Boyd, M. (1985), *Ascription and Achievement: Studies in Mobility and Status Attainment in Canada*, Carleton University Press, Ottawa.

Brand, D. & Bhaggiyadatta, K. Sri (1986), *Speaking of Racism: Rivers Have Sources, Trees Have Roots*, Cross Cultural Communication Centre, Toronto.

Brown, K. (1981), 'Race, Class and Culture: Towards a Theorisation of the "Choice/Constraint" Concept', in P. Jackson & S. Smith (eds), *Social Interaction and Ethnic Segregation*, Academic Press, London.

Brown, M. (1986) *Jew or Juif?: Jews, French Canadians, and Anglo Canadians, 1759-1914*, The Jewish Publication Society, New York.

Cambridge-Roberts, P. (1986), *A Compilation and Review of Literature on Discrimination and Segregation in Housing and Identification of Affirmative Actions, Measures and Programmes Being Advanced*, Commission des droits de la personne du Quebec, Quebec.

Canadian Centre on Racism and Prejudice (CCRP) (1991), *The Presence of the Ku Klux Klan in Quebec: A Background on History and Ideology*, Special Bulletin #1, August, Montreal.

216 *Studies in Segregation and Desegregation*

Canadian Centre on Racism and Prejudice (CCRP) (1993), *From the Oka Crisis to the White Warriors*, Bulletin, Nos. 3-4, April, Montreal.

Canadian Centre on Racism and Prejudice (CCRP) (1993), *Lydon Larouche: Fascist*, Bulletin, June, Montreal.

Census Canada (1986), *Twenty Percent Survey of the Canadian Population*, Minister of Supply and Services Canada, Ottawa.

Choiniere, R. (1990), 'La situation demographique et socio-economique de la population du Montreal metropolitain: principaux resultats du recensement de 1986 par CLSC et DSC,' Departement de sant ecommunautaire hopital general de Montreal, Montreal.

Commission des droits de la personne du Quebec (1984), *Investigation into Allegations of Racial Discrimination in the Montreal Taxi Industry: Final Report*, Montreal.

Commission des droits de la personne du Quebec (1988), *Investigation into Relations between Police Forces, Visible and Other Ethnic Minorities: Excerpts from the Final Report: Recommendations*, November, Montreal.

Darroch, A.G. & Marston, W.G. (1972), 'Ethnic Differentiation: Ecological Aspects of a Multidimensional Approach', in A. Richmond (ed), *Reading in Race and Ethnic Relations*, Pergamon Press, Oxford.

Driedger, L. (1987), *Ethnic Canada: Identities and Inequalities*, Copp Clark Pitman, New York.

Duncan, O.D. & Duncan, B. (1955), 'Residential Distribution and Occupational Stratification', in C. Peach (ed), *Urban Social Segregation*, Longman, London.

Duncan, O.D. & Leiberson, S. (1959), 'Ethnic Segregation and Assimilation', *American Journal of Sociology*, vol. 64, January, pp. 364-374.

Duncan, O.D. & Leiberson, S. (1975), 'Ethnic Segregation and Assimilation', in C. Peach (ed), *Urban Social Segregation*, Longman, London.

Elazar, D. & Waller, H. (1990), *Maintaining Consensus: The Canadian Jewish Polity in the Postwar World*, The Jerusalem Centre for Public Affairs, University Press of America, Jerusalem.

Fitzmaurice, J. (1985), *Quebec and Canada: Past, Present and Future*, C. Hurst and Company, London.

Foster, C. (1991), *Distorted Mirror: Canada's Racist Face*, Harper Collins Publishers, Toronto.

Freedman, C. (1984), 'Overdeterminations: On Black Marxism in Britain', *Social Text*, vol. 8.

Garon, M. (1988), *Une experience de testing de la discrimination raciale dans le logementa Montreal*, Commission des droits de la personne du Quebec, Quebec.

Hall, S. (1980), *Race Articulation and Societies Structured in Dominance*, UNESCO, New York.

Hamelin, J. & Roby, Y. (1971), *Histoire economique du Quebec: 1851-96*, Fides, Montreal.

Hawkins, F. (1988), 'Canadian Multiculturalism: The Policy Explained', in A.J. Fry & C. Forceville (eds), *Canadian Mosaic: Essays on Multiculturalism*, Free University Press, Amsterdam.

Henry, F. (1989), *Housing and Racial Discrimination in Canada: A Preliminary Assessment of Current Initiatives and Information*, Multiculturalism and Citizenship Ontario, Toronto.

Innis, H.A. (1960), *The Fur Trade in Canada*, University of Toronto Press, Toronto.

Charles Small 217

Keith, M. (1993), 'From Punishment to Discipline? Racism, Racialisation and the Policing of Social Control', in M. Cross & M. Keith (eds), *Racism, the City and the State*, Routledge, London.

Kralt, J. (1986), *Atlas of Residential Concentration for the Census Metropolitan Area of Montreal*, Minister of Supply and Services Canada, Ottawa.

La ligue des droits et libertes (1989), *Le mouvement skinhead et l'extreme-droit*, La ligue des droits et libertes, Montreal.

League For Human Rights, B'Nai Brith Canada (1992), *1992 Audit of Anti-Semitic Incidents*, B'Nai Brith Canada, Montreal.

Levine, M. (1990), *The Reconquest of Montreal: Language Policy and Social Change in a Bilingual City*, Temple University Press, Philadelphia.

Levitt, K. (1970), *Silent Surrender: the Multinational Corporations in Canada*, Macmillan Canada, Toronto.

Lewis, R. (1985), *The Segregated City: Residential Differentiation, Rent and Income in Montreal, 1861-1901*, unpublished masters thesis, Department of Geography, McGill University, Montreal.

Li, P. (1988), *The Chinese in Canada*, Oxford University Press, Toronto.

Li, P. (1988), *Ethnic Inequality: In a Class Society*, Wall and Thompson, Toronto.

Lieberson, S. (1980), 'A Societal Theory of Race and Ethnic Relations', in J. Goldstein & R. Bienvenue (eds), *Ethnicity and Ethnic Relations in Canada*, Butterworths, Toronto.

Lieberson, S. & Waters, M.C. (1984), *From Many Strands: Ethnic and Racial Groups in Contemporary America*, Russell Sage Foundation, New York.

Massey, D. & Denton, N. (1988), 'The Dimensions of Residential Segregation', *Social Forces*, vol. 67 (2) December, University of North Carolina Press.

Massey, D. & Denton, N. (1993), *American Apartheid: Segregation and the Making of the Underclass*, Harvard University Press, Cambridge, MA.

Matas, D. (1987), 'The Ethnic Dimension to the Nazi War Criminal Issue: Some Reflections on the Deschenes Commission Report', *The Review of Anti-Semitism in Canada*, League for Human Rights, B'Nai Brith Canada, Toronto.

McAndrew, M. (1996), 'La redifinition des politiques publiques de gestion du pluralisme au Canada et au Quebec: vers quelle citoyennet? L'Immigration et metropoles', CEETUM, Universite de Montreal.

McFarlane, P. (1994), 'Home-Grown Hate: Canadian Racists Getting Together to Spew Venom', *The Gazette*, 2 April, Montreal.

McNaught, K. (1988), *The Penguin History of Canada*, Penguin Books, London.

McRoberts, K. & Posgate, D. (1980), *Quebec: Social Change and Political Crisis*, McClelland and Stewart, Toronto.

Milner, S.H. & Milner, H. (1973), *The Decolonization of Quebec*, McClelland and Stewart, Toronto.

Niosi, J. (1983), 'Continental Nationalism: The Strategy of the Canadian Bourgeoisie', in R. Brym (ed), *The Structure of the Canadian Capitalist Class*, Garamond Press, Toronto.

Omi, M. &. Winant, H (1986), *Racial Formation in the United States*, Routledge, New York.

Ornstein, M. (1985), 'Canadian Capital and the Canadian State: Ideology in an Era of Crisis', in R. Brym (ed), *The Structure of the Canadian Capitalist Class*, Garamond Press, Toronto.

Palmer, B. (1983), *Working Class Experience: The Rise and Reconstitution of Canadian Labour: 1800-1980*, Butterworths, Toronto.

218 *Studies in Segregation and Desegregation*

Peach, C. (1983), 'The Dissolution and Growth of Ethnic Areas in American Cities', in J. Patten (ed), *The Expanding City*, Academic Press, London.

Peach, C. & Rossiter, D. (1996), 'Level and Nature of Spatial Concentration and Segregation of Ethnic Minority Populations in Great Britain: 1991', in P. Ratcliffe (ed), *Social Geography and Ethnicity: Spatial Concentration and Internal Migration*, Office of Population Census and Surveys, HMSO, London.

Pineo, P. & Porter, J. (1985), 'Ethnic Origin and Occupational Attainment', in M. Boyd et al (eds), *Ascription and Achievement: Studies in Mobility and Status Attainment in Canada*, Carleton University Press, Ottawa.

Prutschi, M. (1989), *Hate Groups and Bigotry's Fellow Travellers: An Overview*, Toronto Cares Conference, August 23, Toronto.

Shahar, C. (1991), *Montreal Jewish Community: Attitudes, Beliefs and Behaviours*, Allied Jewish Community Services, Community Planning Department, Montreal.

Shahar, C. & Torczyner, J. (1991), *The Jewish Poor in Montreal: Demographic and Planning Perspectives*, Allied Jewish Community Services, Montreal.

Shefman, A. (1987), 'Manifestations of Anti-Semitism in Canada: The 1986 Survey of Incidents', *The Review of Anti-Semitism in Canada*, The League For Human Rights of B'Nai Brith Canada, Toronto.

Shipman, L. & Kagedan, M. (1990), *Skinheads in Canada: And Their Link to the Far Right*, League for Human Rights of B'Nai Brith Canada, Toronto.

Small, C. (1991), 'The Oka Uprising', *The Woodstock Editorial*, No. 7, Spring, Oxford.

Small, C. (1995), 'Montreal, Nationalism and a Divided City', *Jewish Chronicle*, London, November.

Small, C. (1996), *Social Theory: An Historical Analysis of Canadian Socio-Cultural Policies, 'Race' and the 'Other': A Case Study of Social and Spatial Segregation in Montreal*, Ph. D. Dissertation, University of Montreal.

Small, C. (1997), 'National Identity in Quebec Society and Social and Spatial Differentiation in Montreal', paper presented at INCORE Conference of the Ethnic Studies Network, June 26-28, 1997, Derry, Northern Ireland.

Small, C. (1998), *Youth Unemployment in Montreal: An African-Canadian and Jewish Response to a Changing City and Rising Nationalism*, Secretariat of State, Ottawa.

Supply and Services Canada (1969) Royal Commission Report on Bilingualism and Biculturalism, Ottawa.

Supply and Services Canada (1984), *Royal Commission Report on Equality in Employment*, Ottawa.

Tobin, G. (1985), *Jews on the Edge: An Essay on Economically Marginal Jews and Unemployment*, Council of Jewish Federations and the National Association of Jewish Vocational Services, New York.

Torczyner, J. (1981), 'To Be Poor and Jewish in Canada', in M. Weinfeld, W. Shaffir & I. Cotler (eds), *The Canadian Jewish Mosaic*, John Wiley and Sons, Toronto.

Tulchinsky, G. (1977), *The River Barons: Montreal Businessmen and the Growth of Industry and Transport: 1837-1853*, University of Toronto Press, Toronto.

Tulchinsky, G. (1992), 'Goldwin Smith: Victorian Canadian Antisemitism', in A. Davies (ed), *Antisemitism in Canada: History and Interpretation*, Wilfrid Laurier University Press, Waterloo, Ontario.

Walker, J. (1985), *Racial Discrimination in Canada: The Black Experience*, Historical Booklet No. 41, The Canadian Historical Association, Ottawa.

Weinfeld, M. (1986), 'The Jews of Quebec: An Overview', in R. Aigen & G. Hundert (eds), *Community and the Individual Jew*, Reconstructionist Rabbinical College Press, Philadelphia.

Williams, D.W. (1989), *Blacks in Montreal 1628-1986: An Urban Demography*, Yvon Blais Inc., Cowansville, Quebec.

Yarosky, H. (1991), *Coroner's Report Following an Inquest into the Death of Mr. Marcellus Francois Which Occurred on July 18, 1991, at the Montreal General Hospital as a Result of Injuries Received in the Course of a Police Operation Carried Out by the Montreal Urban Community Police Department*, Bureau du Coroner, Gouvernement du Quebec, Quebec.

10 Segregation in the Ruhr
LUDGER BASTEN AND LIENHARD LÖTSCHER

Introduction

Segregation is very much back on the agenda of urban social research. Theoretical reflections about societal change during the current phase of globalization and post-modern development and its impact on the urban social fabric have fuelled empirical work in recent years. Much of this research has focussed on issues related to segregation: socio-economic polarization (Dangschat, 1996, 1999), the role of the welfare state (Musterd & Ostendorf, 1998), changing mechanisms and patterns of segregation and the function of large cities and metropolitan areas as 'integration machines' for immigrants (e.g., Heitmeyer, Dollase & Backes, 1998 or the diverse contributions to the Canadian Metropolis projects).

In Germany, recent studies on segregation and desegregation have primarily focussed on specific cities – e.g. Berlin, Hamburg, Frankfurt, Cologne and Düsseldorf. While some of the studies have approached the socio-economic aspects of segregation and the links between segregation and poverty (Friedrichs, 1998; Dangschat, 1996), a great number have looked at ethnic segregation (Thieme & Laux, 1996; Glebe, 1997; Tharun, 1997), partly reflecting the shocking incidents of violence against foreigners and political debates which have increasingly caught the public eye since German reunification.[1] Many of these studies, however, in spite of using place-specific empirical data, have treated their individual cities as more or less indicative of general trends in German urban society. And while many findings do indeed produce congruent results that seem to indicate some general trends, we would argue that this may partly be a result of research focus and that a more historical angle might well produce relevant insights into the mechanisms and spatial patterns of segregation. It might also lead to a reassessment of the importance of specific local or regional conditions.

---

[1] It should, however, be noted that in the German context, statistics and most empirical studies do not really refer to ethnicity but rather to citizenship, distinguishing between 'Germans' and 'foreigners' (i.e., those who do not hold German citizenship).

222 *Studies in Segregation and Desegregation*

In this paper we concentrate on a specific part of Germany, the Ruhr. We want to investigate patterns and processes characterizing segregation in this metropolitan region which we consider rather unique in Germany, in terms of its historical and spatial configuration. Can we simply use the results and insights produced by other, more general studies on segregation in German urban society or other German cities and, thus, explain experiences in the Ruhr? Or, to phrase the question differently, what importance do socio-geographical factors play in explaining urban segregation in Germany? What are the roles of locality and milieu?

What we suggest is that the practices and patterns of segregation in the Ruhr do not simply reflect more general trends in Germany. In fact, we would argue that there are some marked differences between the Ruhr and the experiences of cities like Hamburg, Berlin, Frankfurt or Düsseldorf. And we would suggest that these differences are largely due to the specific historical context of industrialization and urbanization in the late 19th century, when the Ruhr first emerged from a sleepy pre-industrial and largely non-urban past into a multi-centred urban region.

This paper is divided into four parts. First, we provide a very brief introduction to the history of industrialization and urbanization of the Ruhr and explain why and how it emerged as an industrial and urban agglomeration in the west of Germany. This is required as background to the second part of the paper, which describes and explains segregation in the Ruhr at that time. We look at the practices, the mechanisms and the resulting spatial outcomes of segregation during the late 19th and early 20th century and, thus, highlight the very specific circumstances, which made the Ruhr notably different from other German cities or urban agglomerations. Part three analyses the changes that have taken place in these processes and patterns approximately during the last half-century. We note that there are both tendencies towards desegregation as well as towards persistence of segregation or even re-segregation, and we link them to a period of industrial and social change. Some 'old' mechanisms of segregation have virtually disappeared, and others have changed very little although the population groups experiencing segregation are different ones today. At the same time, patterns and possibilities for measuring segregation are different today, and we show how this is related to processes of urbanization and, partly, to urban forms. Finally, in the last part of our paper, we try to bring these insights together and to put the experiences of the Ruhr into the perspective of more general trends in German cities.

The Historical Background: Urbanization of the Ruhr

Central to the understanding of practices and patterns of urban segregation in the Ruhr area is the realization that there was no urban region here before the latter half of the 19th century. Since medieval times there had been a number of small towns in the actual Ruhr river valley and some slightly larger urban centres along the west-east trade routes known as the 'Hellweg', which followed the slightly higher terrain of the cretaceous escarpment that roughly formed the northern edge of the valley. These towns and cities – Essen and Dortmund being the largest ones – had grown on trade and local or regional craft production, but their progress had been intermittent and hampered by territorial disunity, political instability and, at various times, wars. Early iron and steel industries had emerged to the south, in the central German uplands where deposits of iron ore were coupled with abundant water power and wood for fuel. In contrast, the poor quality coals that had surfaced in the Ruhr valley could only be used as a rather inferior source of energy for home heating. It was only later technological developments that allowed the exploitation of the deeper, high-grade coals further north.

During the first half of the 19th century, favourable socio-political circumstances (the creation of a German customs union and market deregulation) met with important technological developments to spur the beginnings of industrial growth in the existing towns and cities of the Ruhr. Improvements in the technology of steam engines allowed water control in mine shafts, the successful penetration of the limestone escarpment gave access to the deeper, high-grade coals through deep shaft mining, and the development of coke allowed the use of this coal for efficient, large-scale industrial production. And, finally, the construction of the railways introduced both a new and efficient means of transport and, even more important, a rather reliable consumer of a variety of iron and steel products.

Economic and urban development followed a regional or zonal pattern, due to the geology of coal. Industrial development moved north in line with the progressive exploitation of the coal seams, which dipped towards the north. Rapid population growth ensued, and while this experience, especially after 1870, was not exceptional, since other industrial cities in Germany also went through unsurpassed expansion, its pace and scale were, nevertheless, remarkable. Up to 1839 most growth took place in the Ruhr valley, then it shifted to the towns and cities along the 'Hellweg', and then it moved still further north to the zone along the river Emscher (Wiel, 1970, p. 7).

224 *Studies in Segregation and Desegregation*

Table 10.1 Population growth in the Ruhr

1816/18	219,600
1837/39	289,200
1852	374,400
1871	703,100
1885	1,085,600
1895	1,555,800
1905	2,568,500
1925	3,768,000

Source: Wiel, 1970, p. 13.

What was unusual about this expansion of the Ruhr was that growth did not primarily occur within the urban fabric of existing cities and towns. Most other urban centres in Germany grew out of existing towns and cities, acting as seedbeds for industrial growth (e.g. Berlin, Hannover, Cologne). While there was some of this in the Hellweg-cities of the Ruhr - e.g. industrial complexes like Krupp in Essen – much or even most of this industrial growth was initially divorced from the urban fabric or rather actually initiated urban development, especially in the northern parts of the Ruhr, where there were virtually no pre-industrial urban centres of note. Likewise, the first railway line through what is now the Ruhr - built in 1846/47, when there was very little industrial development as yet - deliberately chose a track far to the north of pre-industrial urban centres like Essen, Mülheim or Bochum, in order to minimize land costs and gain financially from land speculation. The railway line soon became a prime factor in the location of new industries and the consequent growth of settlements.

Elsewhere in Germany, local manufacturers and craftspeople turned into industrialists, and their burgeoning industrial complexes outgrew medieval cities and led to rapid urban expansion. In the Ruhr, it was different; industry was the prime city-builder in the first place, and, thus, rather ill-defined, industrial age cities emerged from a melange of pre-industrial urban centres, industrial complexes, mines, housing complexes, old village cores and railway stations. In the northern zones of the Ruhr, towns and cities were incorporated only in the late 19th century (e.g. Oberhausen in 1874, Gelsenkirchen in 1875 and Herne in 1897), and they owed their sense of identity more to such administrative acts of incorporation and amalgamation than to any historical core or established and popular sense of place. It is in these northern parts of the Ruhr that segregation and desegregation appear to be the most unique and specific.

Industrialization, Urbanization and Segregation

If we consider the forces and mechanisms that produce segregation in urban landscapes, it is quite obvious that these very much depend on the existing societal order. Feudal, medieval societies had legal mechanisms controlling residential choices. When Germany started to shed its feudal system, economic rationale gained in power and slowly began to replace other established mechanisms for social control. In a rapidly industrializing region like the Ruhr during the last three decades of the 19th century, the clash between the old and the new orders and the enormous potential of the forces of modern industrial development became very notable. In this emerging era, segregation was primarily an outcome of market forces, most particularly through the workings of the housing market. It is, thus, imperative to take a closer look at housing in the Ruhr if we want to understand the processes and resulting patterns of segregation towards the end of the 19th century.

As described above, economic development was rapid and led to a massive influx of population into the emerging industrial region (Table 10.1). Obviously, existing urban centres, which in the northern stretches of the Ruhr were practically nonexistent, were unable to accommodate this kind of population growth. An enormous need for additional housing arose so new housing was built and hitherto agricultural lands were converted to industrial and settlement uses. In spite of the influx of industrial workers from other parts of Germany, industry tended to grow at such a rapid pace - especially after the foundation of the German Reich in 1871 and during the boom phase of the early 1890s - that it sometimes experienced severe shortages of labour and felt a constant need to improve both the quantity and the quality of its workforce.

One symptom of these problems was fluctuation. Expansion caused a constant demand, most notably for skilled workers, and largely outran supply. With numerous positions available, workers often and quickly changed jobs if they considered a move to be advantageous in terms of wages, working conditions or fringe benefits. In 1900 the various coal mines of the Gutehoffnungshütte in Oberhausen experienced a fluctuation rate of 78.2% (Hundt, 1902, Tab. IV, p. 38). Fluctuation caused a need for constant training of new employees (which was costly), uneven skill levels and, therefore, less than maximally productive work groups. It also resulted in a lack of shared experience and trust between management and workforce. Poaching was a widespread practice; workers were enticed to

226 *Studies in Segregation and Desegregation*

change jobs by other companies trying to increase and improve the quality of their own workforce.

Clearly, industrialists were keen to reduce fluctuation rates and create a stable, loyal and contented workforce with close ties to a particular company. Having such an employment base would also make recruitment of additional workers easier, partly through recommendations but also through family ties. Not surprisingly, given the settlement situation described above, industrialists recognized the improvement of housing conditions as a strong element in any kind of solution to these problems. Housing being in short supply and, thus, both expensive and generally of rather poor quality, the construction of company housing for workers became one of the most common reactions of industry. This was a multi-faceted strategy. Firstly, the provision of decent housing at rents considerably lower than those paid on the open market (20-30% lower on average, according to Schmitz, 1987, p. 53)[2] attracted new workers to a particular company and kept them content. Fluctuation rates were reduced; compared to the general fluctuation rate of 78.2% quoted above, the fluctuation rate of Gutehoffnungshütte miners living in company housing was only 1.57 % in 1900 (Hundt, 1902, Tab. IV, p. 38). The more loyal and satisfied the workers, the more likely their sons, other relatives and friends would be to sign on with the same company. Secondly, lower rents and the provision of garden land in these housing projects enabled companies to pay lower wages since families could supplement their income through vegetable gardening.[3] Thirdly, housing contracts were tied to work so if a worker wanted to change his employer, he would automatically need to find a new home as well. Employers hoped this would not only reduce fluctuation rates but also strikes or temptations by the agitation and recruitment of socialists or trade unions. Supervision by company officials or police was a further element of this strategy of direct social control. In all these ways, the provision of housing was supposed to support the development of a stable and loyal workforce.

Whatever the intentions, the strategy was commonly adopted. Mining and manufacturing companies built their own housing projects and bought up existing housing stock. In this way, company housing - and most of it was new and purpose-built - became a significant part of the housing

---

[2]   Hundt (1902), to whom Schmitz (1987) refers, lists detailed comparisons for the different mining areas of the Ruhr. Tab. IV, p. 33 shows that the price differential was even significantly greater for many mining company housing projects.

[3]   In this way, female labour was indirectly integrated into the production process since the garden was generally the responsibility of the wives.

market, especially from the 1890s onwards. While its relative importance varied from one town, city and mining company to the next, there is no doubt that a large and increasing number of workers in the Ruhr found homes in company housing (Steinberg, 1978, p. 35).

Table 10.2 Miners and mining company housing in the Ruhr, 1893-1914

	1893	1914	% growth 1893-1914
Miners	152,851	368,284	141
Mining company housing units	10,376	70,045	575
Miners in company housing	18,482	114,085	517
Miners in company housing as % of all miners	12.1	31.0	

Source: Schmitz 1987, p. 87, tables 28, 29; authors' calculations.

By 1914, almost a third of all miners lived in housing supplied by their employers.[4] If we add to this the very common practice of taking in one or more unmarried miners to acquire additional family income from rent, we can conclude that the percentage of miners living in company housing was even larger –though the practice slowly became less common towards the First World War. Even though the above data includes only coal miners, the increasing significance of company housing in the Ruhr was universal, not least since other industries, like steel production and related manufacturing, were competing for employees in a common labour market and so developed their own company housing. Furthermore, vertical integration often led to common ownership of mines and steel plants, so both followed common company policy.

The widespread building of company housing was partly a reaction to a lack of alternatives. With few and only small established urban centres there was very little in the way of an established bourgeois or capitalist elite. Accordingly, speculative construction of housing for workers was not a common occurrence, especially not on a large scale. Such construction activity, so characteristic of the urban development of other industrializing cities in Germany in the late 19th century (e.g. Berlin or Hannover), was

---

[4] The fact that one household often had more than one active miner (father and sons) explains the difference between lines two and three in Table 10.2.

228 *Studies in Segregation and Desegregation*

largely missing in the Ruhr. The financial potency of industrial capital was much better developed than that of the construction industry, and most surplus capital was plowed back into industrial expansion.

To what degree did this peculiar situation of the housing market influence segregation in the Ruhr? The answer to this question depends on the different dimensions of segregation we distinguish. These are, however, interrelated. In particular, the socio-economic and the ethnic dimensions of segregation had a common basis in the Ruhr, increasingly so over the two decades around the turn of the century. Furthermore, the question of segregation also requires a distinctly spatial view, a close consideration of scale as well as spatial configuration of the emerging urban fabric.

As we have seen, industrial development initially led to the growth and spatial expansion of the pre-industrial towns and cities on the 'Hellweg' (e.g. Essen or Dortmund) in the south of the region. Since, originally, there was some housing available and population growth was not as extreme as later, early company housing was built in relatively small projects which were integrated with or attached to existing settlement cores; sometimes existing houses were bought up. But closer towards the end of the century, industrial development and, consequently, population growth moved further north into a landscape with few settlement beginnings. As described above, industry here did not follow urban development; it largely caused it. There was hardly anything, which could be called urban, and industry pillaged what was – in industrial and urban terms – a virtually virgin landscape. Coal mining took hold wherever it was easy to get at the coal, and manufacturing industries chose their locations based on the availability of cheap land (for plants and workers' housing) and on accessibility, which increasingly came to mean railways. It was in this northern zone of the Ruhr, during the most rapid decades of expansion, and in an area where there was very little housing stock to begin with, that company housing acquired particular significance. Projects increased in size, and their design tended to favour village-like layouts. They were not, as a rule, integrated into an existing urban fabric but placed wherever it was cheapest to build – mainly adjacent to mines and plants and, thus, often in unfavourable locations: behind railway lines and next to slag heaps. This reduced land costs as well as the distance between home and work.

For the factory workers this meant a rather clear geographic separation from the 'indigenous' population. Spatial distance came to coincide with social distance, since the small numbers of long-term townsfolk were predominantly small-scale craftspeople or even farmers and socially quite distinct from the increasingly proletarian class of industrial labourers. What emerged was a strongly socio-economic segregation which closely coincided with the segregation between long-term residents and in-migrants (and soon the former were no longer a numerical majority). The spatial patterns of this segregation were often very marked and distinct due to the emerging settlement pattern.

These patterns were also quite closely related to ethnic dimensions of segregation, and this can be explained by the patterns of in-migration into the Ruhr. The early phases of industrialization in the Ruhr were fuelled by workers from regions rather close by: rural Westfalia, the Rhineland and Hesse (Kleßmann, 1978, p. 37). Their migration was largely distance-related and initially often seasonal.[5] Non-German immigrants, mainly from the Netherlands and Italy, were skilled labourers - miners, bricklayers, etc. - specifically recruited by industrialists in the Ruhr. The relatively small absolute numbers of in-migrants, their cultural proximity to the resident population and their spatial integration in the 'Hellweg' cities explains the observation that segregation between established and incoming population groups was not particularly strong (Wührl, 1994, p. 42).

This changed, however, over the last decades of the 19th century, especially from the 1890s onwards, when during a phase of rapid economic growth, immigrant numbers grew and ethnic backgrounds became more distinct from the local population. Predominant among the new immigrants were the Poles. These has Prussian citizenship since they had been living in what had become the eastern provinces of Prussia after the partition of Poland, but most of them were Polish-speaking.[6] While there had been some immigration of skilled Polish miners from Upper Silesia in the early 1870s, most of them had returned home during phases of economic recession. Now, in the 1890s, Polish immigration into the Ruhr became far more substantial: by 1910 almost half a million people had migrated from the four eastern provinces (Kleßmann, 1978, p. 260).[7] Most of these immigrants were unskilled labourers from rural backgrounds, who had been

---

[5]   E.g. early on, small-scale iron and steel works often employed rural farm labour during the winter. These then returned to agricultural employment after a seasonal campaign of industrial production, which only lasted for a few months.

[6]   Of course, they did not form a uniform group. While most Poles were Catholic, people from 'Masuren' (part of the province of East Prussia) were generally protestants, often spoke German as well as their Polish dialect and tended to view themselves as distinct from the other Poles. There was also a certain degree of segregation between these two groups of eastern immigrants – often actively fostered by nationalistic Germans.

[7]   Polish emigration had also been aimed at North America, but after 1893 westward migration within Germany became dominant since the USA restricted the free distribution of land and German industry went into a phase of rapid expansion (Kleßmann, 1978, p. 38).

230 *Studies in Segregation and Desegregation*

left in an increasingly precarious economic situation by the modernization of agricultural production and an excess availability of agricultural labour.

In large measure, labour was actively recruited in the eastern provinces by agents working for the mining and manufacturing industries in the Ruhr. They promised employment in state-of-the-art facilities with high wages and, as an added incentive, provided descriptions of modern and spacious company housing in healthy, rural surroundings, that could be rented at relatively cheap rates. Furthermore, they stressed that company housing included garden land and a little stable so that families could supplement their income by vegetable gardening and the keeping of some animals. This kind of description was clearly targeted at a rural farm population, hinting at the possibilities of at least partially maintaining a more rural way of life.

When the Polish immigrants came into the Ruhr, coal mining had already moved north of the pre-industrial cities in the south. Therefore, most of the new immigrants found themselves, not in the older urban centres but in the as yet undeveloped northern parts of the region. Since new shafts were created in rural surroundings and company housing was built next to the mines, the picture of rural surroundings painted by company recruiting agents was not totally off the mark. However, growth was so rapid, that industry was constantly looking for good workers, and, at the same time, the demand for company housing far outran supply. It is striking, how early and clearly company officials identified the provision of company housing as a key factor in attracting employees and keeping them, thereby hoping to create a contented and stable workforce.

Although the evidence is only indirect, there are clear indications that the majority of Polish immigrants lived in company housing projects. To start with, Polish workers were concentrated in only a few sectors of the labour market, especially in mining. In 1902, 80.1% of all industrial employees of Polish origin worked in mining, and only 19.9% worked in other industries (Kleßmann, 1978, p. 276).[8] Even though this figure declined slightly over the years, the dominance of mining employment remained stable. Additional evidence shows that the Poles were overwhelmingly manual labourers, most notably in those industries where their absolute numbers were highest - in mining and steel production:

---

[8]   This data refers to the province of Westfalia, not the Ruhr as such. However, Polish immigration into Westfalia was virtually exclusively into the Ruhr as the prime industrial area. The figures for the western part of the Ruhr, which belonged to the Rhineland province would likely be quite similar.

99.3% in 1907 (Stefanski, 1984, p. 22, quoting Murzynowska, 1979). In other words, most Poles in the Ruhr were miners.

During the 1890s and 1900s it was mainly the mining companies that built new company housing, and sizable proportions of their work force were Polish. Between 1893 and 1915 the percentage of all mining employees varied between 25 and 38% (with the maximum in 1908) (Kleßmann, 1978, p. 265).[9] These are average figures, and in some mines percentages were significantly higher, especially in the newer mines in the northern stretches of the Ruhr. Most of the so-called 'Polenzechen' (Polish mines), where more than 50% of the work force was Polish-speaking, lay in this newly industrialized part of the Ruhr, in cities like Gelsenkirchen (57.4% of miners were Polish-speaking in 1900) or Herne (53.2% were Polish-speaking in 1912). The attractions which company housing projects held for Polish immigrants were quite clear. Rents were a lot cheaper than on the open market, the garden land and stable allowed for additional food production to partly offset the high costs of living and allowed workers to retain some vestiges of a previously agricultural way of life. Lastly, families could achieve additional income through taking in one or more boarders, a practice which was particularly widespread among the Poles (Kleßmann, 1978, p. 49). For most Polish immigrants, these advantages seemed to outweigh negative points such as tight control or supervision by the mining companies and the link between work and housing contracts. Kleßmann concludes that 'the largest share of the Poles and the immigrants from the east overall lived in mining company housing' (1978, p. 45).

However, it is more difficult to assess whether these residential choices differed markedly for the non-Polish immigrants who migrated to the Ruhr at the same time, that is, whether segregation was predominantly ethnic in nature or a question of established vs. new arrivals. We, therefore, need to examine whether the Poles were actually concentrated or even in a majority in these company housing projects. Unfortunately, data of this kind is very difficult to find, especially on an aggregate level. There is, however, indirect evidence. Stefanski, (1984, p. 49) studied various housing projects by checking for the occurrence of Polish family names through an analysis of address books, and these analyses indicate that the housing projects showed large proportions of Polish households. This is also supported by various accounts of former residents of such housing projects that speak of a clear concentration of Polish immigrants (Braßel, 1998, p. 26).

---

[9] The figures, strictly speaking, refer to workers with German citizenship from the four eastern provinces, not all of whom were Polish.

232 Studies in Segregation and Desegregation

Furthermore, these analyses also reveal that segregation existed within the company housing projects, i.e. on a smaller geographical scale. Polish families were often concentrated in specific streets of these projects, so that even among the recent immigrants who were socially and spatially segregated from the long-term resident population, there was an added dimension of ethnic segregation which must predominantly be explained by the mining companies' practice of housing allocation and by 'German' families attempting not to live close to concentrations of Polish families (Peters-Schildgen, 1997, p. 72). Accounts of Polish immigrants clearly document incidents of racism in daily affairs (e.g., Stadt Recklinghausen, 1981, p. 25), and there can be little doubt of widespread discriminatory practices.

Company housing projects not only revealed internal ethnic segregation, but socio-economic segregation also appears on this small scale of analysis. Most mining companies built different categories of housing for their employees, depending on their status of employment: clerical workers, pit foremen ('Steiger') or ordinary miners. Pit foremen generally qualified for slightly larger housing units than miners, and their houses were also generally separate, in separate streets or towards the edge of the housing projects. While both pit foremen and miners tended to be housed in cottage-type two or four-family houses, clerical workers were offered apartments in larger buildings. The latter received higher wages, so they did not need gardens to supplement incomes, and they generally aspired to a more bourgeois life style. Their apartment houses tended to be architecturally distinct and spatially segregated within the housing projects. Later on, mining companies often built special housing projects limited to clerical and managerial employees. Given the overrepresentation of Poles in the manual labour category, this practice obviously increased the ethnic segregation already in existence.

The picture of segregation in the Ruhr that emerges is thus complex with different dimensions of segregation closely interrelated. In the northern parts of the region, there was strong segregation between new arrivals and the established population, and, on a smaller scale, a separation of foremen or clerical staff from manual labourers. Both led to a segregation between Polish and German-speaking groups due to the numerical dominance of the Poles among the immigrants in the late 19th century. And yet, these factors do not explain the full extent of ethnic segregation that existed. Discriminatory practices were common and accentuated by nationalistic policies of the German government. While primarily directed against possible Polish nationalism in the eastern provinces, these policies also had repercussions for Polish population groups in the Ruhr. Especially noteworthy was legislation concerning language use at work. Ironically, these policies initially seemed to produce counter-effects. In the early 20th century the Polish immigrants began to organize themselves through Catholic parishes and cultural clubs. Later they even formed a Polish trade union. In this way, positive aspects of segregation for the minority group became more noticeable and contributed to the general perception of a segregated Polish population.

The rather clear geographical pattern of segregation certainly owes a great deal to the specific time and processes of urbanization that characterized the Ruhr from the 1890s onwards. It so happened, that in this phase economic expansion took place in the northern parts of the region where urbanization virtually had to start from scratch. Hence, company housing projects were spatially very separate from one another and from pre-existing settlements. This was also a reflection of a lack of planning controls since towns and cities only came into existence over the decades of industrialization. While the initially rural counties had neither the administrative capacity nor the technical ability to introduce and enforce effective planning controls, most cities were very recent administrative constructs. Their powers of control over urban development and industry in general were rather limited, and the general absence of an established bourgeois elite left political power largely in the hands of the industrial companies. The net result was a fragmented and non-integrated urban fabric, a patchwork of older, largely agricultural settlement cores, industrial and mining areas and new housing projects where it was cheap and convenient for industry to build them. Hence, spatial separation increased social distance, thereby strengthening the social and political processes of ethnic segregation of Polish immigrants.

Changing Processes and Patterns of Segregation

The Ruhr at the end of the 20th century looks rather different from the industrial area that it had been at the end of the 19th century. Structural economic change, which has transformed economies on all geographical scales, has also had a profound influence on this urban region. Due to its specialized and poorly differentiated economic structure, however, the trajectory of change has been rather different from many or even most German cities, and this holds true both for the phase of economic recovery and prosperity after World War II as well as for the prolonged phase of

234 *Studies in Segregation and Desegregation*

crisis and adjustment since the late 1950s. But the Ruhr today not only possesses a markedly different economic structure. Social patterns and spatial configurations have also changed and produced an urban landscape where old and new coexist side by side. We will try to sketch some implications these changes have had on questions of segregation.

One initial observation concerns the segregation of the Polish population. Looking through present-day telephone books of the Ruhr, the Polish ancestry of many of its residents is still blatantly obvious, but their story has largely become one of integration and assimilation. Ethnic segregation of this population group is no longer an issue as the social distance between them and ethnic Germans has virtually disappeared. We have already hinted at state policies that institutionalized discrimination against the Polish population in Prussia before World War I and which, at least initially, increased their national awareness and sense of identity. However, the virtual impossibility for ethnic Poles to buy land in the eastern provinces eventually increased the willingness of the Poles in the Ruhr to see their futures in western Germany. Similarly, insistence on German language use at school and in official institutions contributed to cultural integration, especially of second and third generation Poles. Furthermore, the reestablishment of a Polish state after World War I and the necessity to choose between German or Polish citizenship (Peters-Schildgen, 1997, p. 258) required a conscious decision whether to return to Poland, to migrate further (especially into France) or to stay in the Ruhr. The net result was that those who stayed – and at least a third did (Braßel, 1998, p. 31) – largely accepted cultural integration and Germanification. While throughout Prussian times a number of Poles had always applied for changing (i.e., 'Germanifying') or abandoning their Polish family names,[10] this became even more common throughout the Nazi period as pressure to blend in increased significantly (Peters-Schildgen, 1997, p. 218).

If ethnic segregation became less prominent, this was largely caused by political and societal changes. Economically, the function of the Ruhr as the leading coal mining area in Germany was strengthened after both world wars since economic recovery greatly depended on coal as a source of energy. In this way, the socio-economic characteristics of the Ruhr, including patterns of socio-economic segregation initially showed a high degree of persistence. A rapid expansion of coal and steel production

---

[10] The tendency to do so revealed one difference between the people from 'Masuren' and the other Poles. The former were generally pro-Prussian (and Protestant) and loyal to the German emperor; many of them did not want to be associated with 'the Poles' but preferred to be recognized as Germans (Peters-Schildgen, 1997, p. 218 f.).

depended on more workers moving into the area and, thus, on the urgent provision of housing. This now became a state concern; government was involved and devised specific programmes to support the construction of housing for workers. Between 1920 and 1945 state-sponsored schemes financed the construction of some 32,000 housing units for miners. Rental housing built under the scheme was reserved for miners (including invalids and widows) for a period of twenty years (Boll, 1988, p. 263).[11] Similar programmes after World War II supported the reconstruction and expansion of housing specifically earmarked for miners. Government-controlled housing in Germany is generally built by investors using state subsidies. They, in turn, then subscribe to rent-control regulations and to varying degrees of public control over allocation for several years. Eligibility for housing units financed through these mining trust funds depended on both family income and mining employment – if there were no interested miners, housing units would be treated as normal subsidized housing.[12] Most of these housing units were built in the 1950s by the THS and the increasingly independent housing divisions of mining or steel companies (Boll, 1988, p. 264). Therefore, the importance of housing for miners, first directly financed by the mining companies, then increasingly subsidized by government through housing programmes, explains the peculiar pattern of socio-economic segregation which emerged in the Ruhr over decades of industrial growth.

It was structural economic change that caused this pattern of growth to falter and eventually led to a significant erosion and restructuring of this long-established social landscape. In the late 1950s mining in the Ruhr was struck by a heavy and unexpected crisis leading to pit closure and layoffs. Throughout the 1960s restructuring caused the closure of small and relatively unproductive mines, especially in the southern zones of the Ruhr, and finally led to the amalgamation of smaller, private mining companies into a large and unified mining company, the 'Ruhrkohle AG' (RAG) in 1969. As steel crises followed the coal crises, the heavy industrial economic base was gradually eroded, and lack of innovation and technological rejuvenation turned the Ruhr into an 'old industrial region'. In this context, we wish to discuss four particular aspects of the structural

---

[11] Through a partnership between mining companies, trade unions and the state, a trust fund was set up, financed through a special levy on every ton of coal produced. The so-called 'Treuhandstelle für Bergmannswohnstätten' (THS) was founded to become the housing company to administer these funds (Boll, 1988, p. 263).

[12] In Northrhine Westfalia 235,000 housing units for miners were built in this way between 1952 and 1981, most of them in the Ruhr (Boll, 1988, p. 264).

236 Studies in Segregation and Desegregation

economic change over the last decades. The first two aspects reveal a tendency toward social (and partly ethnic) desegregation, while the latter two tend toward increasing segregation or even toward a specific process of re-segregation. As a result, the Ruhr today presents a very complex and varied picture.

The first aspect of change concerns the increasing privatization of subsidized housing in the Ruhr. 254,000 miners' housing units were included in the RAG restructuring deal in 1968/69; the units retained their dual character as miners' and social housing, at least for a period of 20 years (Boll, 1988, p. 264). It is important to note that there were and are no uniform, centrally administered guidelines for decisions on allocation (and upkeep) of these housing units. Rather, decision-making processes vary greatly from one pit to the next, but pit-specific committees which include local trade union representatives often play a significant role (Korte, 1984, p. 85). We will discuss the effect this has had on re-segregation below.

While most of these housing units remained in the control – though not necessarily ownership – of the RAG, some 38,000 housing units were transferred onto the open market. Throughout the 1950s many mining companies had already privatized or sold off at least some of their housing. This was partly a question of location since with mining moving ever further north and southern pits closing, housing units in these locations were given up as no longer relevant to the mining companies (Boll, 1988, p. 264). Partly, however, this was a consequence of the reduced economic vitality and dominance of mining. With the state having taken over some of the responsibility for the provision of housing and with the number of jobs declining, mining companies and later the RAG sought to reduce expenditure and to mobilize some of the capital tied up in housing. This could mean privatization by selling units to renters or by selling whole housing projects to specialized housing companies. It could also mean redevelopment schemes carried out in-house (by the development divisions of increasingly diversified companies) or by professional developers after purchase from the mining companies. The RAG itself also privatized housing units. Furthermore, allocation of housing units to non-miners (paying higher rents) increased, and rents were slowly adjusted to the open market. By 1988, only 190,000 housing units were still contractually tied to mining, compared to 300,000 units in 1968 (Boll, 1988, pp. 265-267). In the 1990s this number fell further with ongoing privatization of the housing units. Many more general social housing units, not only company housing, have now come to the end of the rent-control period. Coupled with changes and especially reductions of state programmes to subsidize social housing projects, the publicly and rent-controlled housing sector in the Ruhr has seen a very notable reduction over the last two decades.

The net effect has been a trend towards occupational desegregation. The greatly reduced number of miners, the increased allocation of non-miners to miners' housing and the privatization of such housing units have led to the almost complete disappearance of 'proper' miners' housing projects. This indicates, however, more general processes of socio-economic desegregation. Privatization of housing units and whole housing projects have produced a gentrification of formerly homogeneous workers' quarters (e.g., in Bochum-Hordel). After active miners, family-members of RAG miners, were given priority rights to purchase, and this change, which is basically generational, has often led to occupational change since the sons and daughters of former mining households are no longer in mining or even industrial employment. Privatization has invariably led to modernization of the housing units, and it has often increased unit sizes through amalgamation of more than one unit or through other extensions (i.e., roof-space conversions). As a result, both the quality of former and present miners' housing as well as the socio-economic composition of such projects have become more 'average' and less 'outstanding'. They have blended into a social landscape which - on this spatial scale - tends to be less segregated today, even though society at large has become more differentiated in terms of occupation, income and class - if indeed this last category is still applicable.

There is a second aspect of structural change that has also led to desegregation in the Ruhr and which is more overtly spatial in nature. If the rapid population growth of the late 19th century had initially created industrial villages and detached company housing projects, continuing growth (and time) eventually, albeit belatedly,[13] led to the development of functionally more complete towns and cities. Commercial centres grew as economies started to diversify, infrastructure was developed, civic institutions emerged and, of course, new housing was added. All of this caused spatial in-fill, a not always very orderly process. In-fill began early in the 20th century and continued without interruptions after World War II. Between 1953 and 1993 the percentage of open space in the city of Bochum declined from 68.2% to 45.5%, in Gelsenkirchen from 63.4% to

---

[13] To stress this time lag, Reif (1993) entitles his history of Oberhausen 'The Belated City'.

238 *Studies in Segregation and Desegregation*

40.4% and in Oberhausen from 53.2% to 37.9%.[14] Urban in-fill was not primarily fuelled by population growth. In fact, growth rates of areas taken up by housing, commerce or infrastructure clearly exceeded those of population, especially after the war. As a result, detached housing projects or former industrial villages slowly became engulfed in a more continuous urban area.[15] Altogether, this led to decreasing spatial isolation of socially and ethnically segregated quarters. A new urban landscape emerged: a more heterogeneous mosaic, rather different in form and spatial organization from most German cities with their clear orientation towards a central core and decreasing densities towards the margins. If nothing else, this has made it more difficult to find meaning in quantitative measurements of segregation since the statistical spatial units do not correspond very well to the natural areas of social area analysis.

The story of the Ruhr, however, is not simply one of integration and desegregation. The third aspect of structural economic change is again related to housing – more particularly to suburbanisation. This has tended to increase both socio-economic and ethnic segregation. Urban in-fill was partly new housing, as rising living standards led to an increase in the demand for more spacious and modern housing (especially for detached single family housing). With a growing availability and ownership of private motor cars, new housing areas in more remote locations also became attractive. Hence, while the cities of the Ruhr could accommodate some growth within municipal boundaries - i.e. the above-mentioned in-fill - suburbanisation also took hold beyond the previously urbanized area and spread to the rural counties surrounding towns and cities. Since the early 1960s, the urban centres of the Ruhr have lost population as the surrounding rural counties gained new inhabitants. Certainly, suburbanisation has been a general trend in Germany from that time, and even if the polynucleated landscape of the Ruhr caused this phenomenon to be less noticeable initially than in other, core-centred German cities, the process introduced socio-economic re-segregation just as it had elsewhere.

---

[14] Data derived from mappings of real land use by the Kommunalverband Ruhrgebiet; personal communication from Johannes Flacke, Ruhr-University Bochum, Department of Geography.

[15] Some patches of company housing still remained secluded, especially where physical barriers (railway lines, slag heaps, canals etc.) led to spatial isolation. These quarters today are often the home of more segregated population groups than other, more integrated quarters (e.g., Gelsenkirchen-Schüngelberg).

It was the richer, middle-class families who could afford the larger plots of land, the single-family housing and the cars to commute.[16]

This pattern closely coincided with the ethnic dimension of segregation since the concentration of foreigners in the cities of the Ruhr closely mirrors the areas of low socio-economic status (Strohmeier & Kersting, 1996, p. 463). Those who were 'left behind' in the core regions were the poorer and the foreigners, the latter thus being concentrated in the heavy industrial centres of the Emscher-zone (Thieme & Laux, 1996, p. 148). Suburbanisation, therefore, has been the spatial expression of a general trend towards increasing socio-economic polarization. The division between the private housing market (especially owner-occupied) and the social housing market increased, and this division also found a clearer spatial expression – even if privatization of company housing and gentrification also redirected some of this demand for private housing into some of the old company housing projects. With many former social housing projects being integrated into the open market, however, those that retained their character as social housing projects increasingly concentrated their population groups at the lowest rungs of the social ladder.

The fourth and arguably most important aspect of structural economic change since the late 1950s has been a new phase of immigration and ethnic re-segregation. The 'economic miracle' following the war had produced labour shortages to which governments and industry again reacted with recruitment drives: the so-called guest workers ('Gastarbeiter') appeared in the industrial centres of Germany. For the Ruhr, we want to stress the significance of a particular group of immigrants, namely, the Turks.[17] A large proportion of Turkish guest workers in the Ruhr found employment in the mining industry, filling positions no longer taken up by Germans, as non-mining employment became more attractive (and secure) and intergenerational recruitment within German mining families failed.[18] 80% of all non-German employees of the RAG are Turkish, and most of them arrived in Germany between 1969 and 1974 (Korte, 1984, p. 13), many expecting to work in Germany only for a number of years before returning home. Not surprisingly, it was initially the men who came to

---

[16] Socio-economic polarization has also found expression in the formation of high-class residential suburbs of some cities in the Ruhr, e.g., in Essen-Bredeney or Bochum-Stiepel – typically located at the 'green' southern edge of the Ruhr-valley.

[17] 45.5 % of all foreigners in the Ruhr are Turkish, so they form the largest national group by far (1996 data; Kommunalverband Ruhrgebiet, 1998, p. 51).

[18] With some 13% foreigners employed, the energy and mining sector is still the industrial sector with the highest foreign component of the total labour force (1996 data; Kommunalverband Ruhrgebiet, 1998, p. 117).

240 *Studies in Segregation and Desegregation*

Germany, who were either unmarried or without their families which remained at home in Turkey. Their housing needs were largely met by RAG company housing. Turkish miners - and their families, as they gradually also moved to Germany – were attracted to company housing for similar reasons as had been the Polish miners of the late 19th century: it was close to work, it was cheap, allowing for the accumulation of savings (to be transferred home), and it also provided garden land for growing vegetables. As a result, the majority of Turkish miners came to live in RAG company housing.[19] At the same time, the unfamiliarity with the German housing market and the necessity of forming internal Turkish support networks led to further spatial concentration.

Ethnic discrimination, however, also played its part, and it clearly worked within the system of RAG company housing down to the small-scale patterns of segregation within individual housing projects. Studies from the early 1980s reveal very clearly that Turkish families were housed in the oldest company housing available, that they found themselves in the lowest standard of housing (no or little modernization) and that they had less floor space per family member - even controlling for household size (which was generally larger than in German families) (Korte, 1984, p. 34 ff.). The argument that Turkish families actually preferred the low end of the housing market in order to accumulate more savings was certainly no longer valid by the early 1980s (if it had ever been true) when Turkish families were generally willing to pay higher rents for better and more spacious housing but were not allocated to such units. In fact, though Turkish families in RAG housing paid less rent in absolute terms, controlling for size, standard and age of housing reveals that they paid higher relative rents than German families (Korte, 1984, p. 40). It is important to note that these data refer to RAG company housing, not to the free housing market. Hence, the described processes of discrimination worked and arguably still works through the system of allocation.

As indicated above, RAG housing is allocated through local committees with elected representatives of the workforce having a strong say. For historical and organizational reasons the mineworkers' union with its relative overrepresentation of German miners tends to dominate these committees, and shop stewards need to be very sensitive to the opinions and feelings of their clientele if they want to be re-elected (Korte, 1984, p 85). If these committees have few or no standardized rules and

---

[19] The parallels don't end here. The sectoral concentration in mining and, occupationally in physical labour, even more specifically below ground are also similar to the situation of Polish immigrants in the late 19th century.

procedures for the allocation of housing, local decision-making can lead and has led to discrimination.

There is an inherently spatial outcome of these practices of discrimination. The concentration of Turkish families in the oldest, smallest and least modernized housing units has led to their overrepresentation in certain housing projects. These are the older and non-modernized ones, often scheduled for demolition and redevelopment by RAG. Often these are found in unattractive locations, spatially separated from other housing and close to active or former industrial land uses.[20] On a smaller spatial scale, there are also patterns of concentration within individual projects, much as has been shown for the segregation of Polish families in the early 20th century. This is largely due to the fact that company housing projects were often built and expanded in phases, adding streets or quarters to existing projects at a later date and that they show a similar pattern of internal differentiation of housing units based on the occupational hierarchy of the mine (see above). If there are German and Turkish families within housing projects, more German than Turkish families tend to occupy the larger units formerly built for pit foremen.

In other words, the allocation mechanisms for miners' housing have reproduced a pattern of ethnic segregation in which Turkish families are allocated old, small and poor-quality housing units and located in housing projects where many housing units show these characteristics. Turks are actively kept out of newer, more modern and more attractive housing units or housing projects. And, to stress the process dimension of ethnic segregation, Germans have shown a noticeable tendency to vacate houses and streets in which more Turkish families rent housing units. In other words, discrimination exists, not just through the practices of housing allocation but also through the negative location choices of German households. Obviously, such discriminatory practices also work in the private housing market, but Glebe (1997, p. 151) stresses the importance of company housing in explaining the comparatively high level of segregation in Duisburg. The patterns and processes of ethnic segregation in the Ruhr, which had their roots in the particular context of the late 19th century, have been reproduced to a large degree in the second half of the 20th century in spite of different economic and political conditions and different ethnic minorities.

---

[20] E.g., Gelsenkirchen-Schüngelberg, Duisburg-Bruckhausen, etc. Though the latter is not RAG, but steel company housing, similar processes and conclusions apply.

242 *Studies in Segregation and Desegregation*

Putting the Ruhr in Perspective

Our discussion of the Ruhr and its experiences of urban segregation, based on socio-economic or ethnic characteristics, has stressed the historic and spatial context that have influenced both patterns and processes. This context is very different from most other German cities, and it can, to a large degree, explain the different experiences of segregation to this day. The formerly heavy industrial economy of the Ruhr created its own landscape of segregation, and this has been reproduced through the workings of the labour and housing market. Furthermore, the spatial pattern that took shape owes much to the peculiar spatial nature of settlement and urban growth in the emerging industrial area. Nowhere else in Germany did there emerge a comparable industrial landscape out of quiet rural surroundings. Nowhere else was company housing predominantly built in small, cottage-type houses, often in village-like projects. The fragmentary and non-integrated urban form that first emerged in the late 19th century is still clearly visible in the Ruhr today. It still shapes small-scale spatial patterns – and people's perceptions – of segregation today. This also helps to explain why indices of segregation tend to show relatively high values in the cities of the Ruhr.[21]

Other old industrial centres in Germany also reveal a close correlation of the socio-economic and ethnic dimensions of segregation. Nowhere else, however, has company housing played such a significant part in housing the immigrants during periods of industrialization and immigration. Elsewhere, expansion of private rental housing through speculative investment in large-scale apartment blocks has been far more pronounced. Nowhere else was there such a concerted effort by whole industries at providing company housing. Nowhere else was government support generated as it has been in the Ruhr since the end of World War I. And through the creation of this important sub-market of the general housing market, the system of housing allocation affected and, to a lesser degree today, still strongly affects the patterns of ethnic segregation.

The segregation indices in the Ruhr are also high when compared to cities with more dynamic economies.[22] More post-Ford cities have more

---

[21] This also hints at the methodological difficulties of applying such quantitative measurements of segregation based on administrative delineations of cities. The validity of the concept 'city' makes decidedly less sense when dealing with Gelsenkirchen or Oberhausen than when one considers Cologne, Berlin or Hamburg.

[22] The 1992 segregation indices, based on voting districts, are 52.1 for Duisburg and 44.7 for Düsseldorf. Based on blocks (i.e., smaller units of analysis), they are 62.7 for Duisburg and 55.3 for Düsseldorf (Glebe 1997, p. 152).

open labour and housing markets which seem to create rather distinct landscapes of segregation, as studies of Frankfurt (Noller & Ronneberger, 1995; Musterd, Ostendorf & Breebaart, 1998) or Düsseldorf (Glebe, 1997) have shown. Their differentiated, service-oriented economies have fuelled further immigration of foreigners throughout the 1990s so these cities tend to show higher shares of foreigners among the residential population than the cities in the Ruhr (Gans, 1997). Heightened socio-economic polarization has led to stronger processes of spatial differentiation, leaving the poor and the foreigners behind in the central cities. However, while the parallel dynamics of economic development and the spatiality of socio-economic/ethnic polarization can explain these differences to some degree, Glebe has also stressed the importance of the company housing market and its allocation mechanisms in understanding the high segregation indices for a city like Duisburg (Glebe, 1997, p. 151).

It must be noted, that patterns of segregation and immigration have been quite strongly changed by political developments since the late 1980s. The fall of the iron curtain and German reunification caused a new wave of immigration in the early 1990s, and, together with the tightening of regulations regarding political asylum, this has led to significant changes in the national composition of foreigners entering Germany. In particular, the number of immigrants from Eastern Europe – and especially from former Yugoslavia – has grown (Musterd, Ostendorf & Breebaart, 1998, p. 67). These immigrants have tended to locate in the large and most dynamic cities, not in the Ruhr.[23] The relative growth of the foreign population in the Ruhr is thus no longer a result of ongoing immigration but largely one of natural population growth (Gans, 1997, p. 403). Therefore, pressure on the housing market has in general been less in the Ruhr than in other German cities. If the ongoing privatization of the company housing units gradually reduces ethnic segregation caused by discriminatory practices of housing allocation, it will probably also lead to increasing socio-economic polarization. Given the fragmented urban form of the Ruhr, this may well cause an increase of ethnic segregation on a smaller geographical scale.

---

[23] Munich 23.9% foreigners, Stuttgart 24.6%, Frankfurt 27.4%, Cologne 18.3% – apart from Duisburg all the Ruhr cities had less than 15% foreigners (1994 data; Gans, 1997, p. 401).

244 *Studies in Segregation and Desegregation*

References

Boll, Joachim (1988), '... ein wenig Licht ins Dunkel. Der stille Strukturwandel in der berg-bauverbundenen Wohnungswirtschaft des Ruhrgebiets', *RaumPlanung*, No. 43, pp. 262-269.

Braßel, Frank (1998), 'Die polnische Hauptstadt Westfalens – Zur Geschichte der Ruhrpolen in Herne und Wanne-Eickel', in Ralf Piorr (ed), *Eine Reise ins Unbekannte. Ein Lesebuch zur Migrationsgeschichte in Herne und Wanne-Eickel*, Klartext, Essen, pp. 22-33.

Dangschat, Jens S. (1996), 'Zur Armutsentwicklung in deutschen Städten', in Akademie für Raumforschung und Landesplanung (eds) *Agglomerationsräume in Deutschland: Ansichten, Einsichten, Aussichten* (Forschungs und Sitzungsberichte, 199) Akademie für Raumforschung und Landesplanung, Hannover, pp. 51-76.

Dangschat, Jens S. (ed) (1999), *Modernisierte Stadt – gespaltene Gesellschaft. Ursachen von Armut und sozialer Ausgrenzung*, Leske + Budrich, Opladen.

Faist, Thomas & Häußermann, Hartmut (1996), 'Immigration, Social Citizenship and Housing in Germany', *International Journal of Urban and Regional Research*, vol. 20, pp. 83-98.

Friedrichs, Jürgen (1996), 'Intra-Regional Polarization: Cities in the Ruhr Area, Germany', in John O'Loughlin & Jürgen Friedrichs (eds), *Social Polarization in Post-Industrial Metropolises*, de Gruyter, Berlin, New York, pp. 133-172.

Friedrichs, Jürgen (1998), 'Social Inequality, Segregation and Urban Conflict. The Case of Hamburg', in Sako Musterd & Wim Ostendorf (eds), *Urban Segregation and the Welfare State. Inequality and Exclusion in Western Cities*, Routledge, London, New York: pp. 168-190.

Gans, Paul (1997), 'Ausländische Bevölkerung in Großstädten Deutschlands. Regionale Trends und Wirtschaftsstruktur', in *Geographische Rundschau*, Vol. 49, No. 7/8, pp. 399-405.

Glebe, Günther (1996), 'Immigration, Labor Market and the Dynamics of Urban Residential Patterns and Segregation of Ethnic Minorities in Germany', in Klaus Frantz & Robert A. Sauder (eds), *Ethnic Persistence and Change in Europe and America. Traces in Landscape and Society*, The University of Innsbruck, Innsbruck, pp. 135-164.

Glebe, Günther (1997), 'Housing and Segregation of Turks in Germany', in Sule Özüekren & Ronald van Kempen (eds), *Turks in European Cities: Housing and Urban Segregation, (Comparative Studies in Migration and Ethnic Relations 4)* European Research Centre on Migration and Ethnic Relations, Utrecht University, Utrecht, pp. 122-157.

Häußermann, Hartmut (1998), 'Zuwanderung und die Zukunft der Stadt. Neue ethnisch-kulturelle Konflikte durch die Entstehung einer neuen sozialen "underclass"?, in Wilhelm Heitmeyer, Rainer Dollase & Otto Backes (eds), *Die Krise der Städte. Analysen zu den Folgen desintegrativer Stadtentwicklung für das ethnisch-kulturelle Zusammenleben* (= Kultur und Konflikt, edition suhrkamp 2036) Suhrkamp, Frankfurt, pp. 145-175.

Heitmeyer, Wilhelm, Dollase, Rainer & Backes, Otto (eds) (1998), *Die Krise der Städte. Analysen zu den Folgen desintegrativer Stadtentwicklung für das ethnisch-kulturelle Zusammenleben* (= Kultur und Konflikt, edition suhrkamp 2036), Suhrkamp, Frankfurt.

Hundt, Robert (1902), *Bergarbeiter-Wohnungen im Ruhrrevier*, Julius Springer, Berlin.

Kesteloot, Christian, van Weesep, Jan & White, Paul (1997), 'Minorities in West European Cities. Introduction to the Special Issue', *Tijdschrift voor Economische en Sociale Geografie*, vol. 88(2), pp. 99-104.

Ludger Basten and Lienhard Lötscher 245

Kommunalverband Ruhrgebiet (eds) (1998), *Städte- und Kreisstatistik Ruhrgebiet 1997*, Kommunalverband Ruhrgebiet, Essen.

Korte, Hermann (ed) (1984), *Wohnsituation ausländischer Mitarbeiter der Ruhrkohle AG* (= Schriftenreihe Landes- und Stadtentwicklungsforschung des Landes Nordrhein-Westfalen, Wohnungsbau – Kommunaler Hochbau, Band 3.033) Institut für Landes- und Stadtentwicklungsforschung des Landes Nordrhein-Westfalen, Dortmund.

Marcuse, Peter (1998), 'Ethnische Enklaven und rassische Ghettos in der postfordistischen Stadt', in Wilhelm Heitmeyer, Rainer Dollase & Otto Backes (eds), *Die Krise der Städte. Analysen zu den Folgen desintegrativer Stadtentwicklung für das ethnisch-kulturelle Zusammenleben* (= Kultur und Konflikt, edition suhrkamp 2036) Suhrkamp, Frankfurt, pp. 176-193.

Musterd, Sako & Ostendorf, Wim (eds) (1998), 'Urban Segregation and the Welfare State', *Inequality and Exclusion in Western Cities*, Routledge, London, New York.

Musterd, Sako, Ostendorf, Wim & Breebaart, Matthijs (1998), 'Multi-Ethnic Metropolis: Patterns and Policies' (= *The GeoJournal Library*, vol. 43) Kluwer Academic Publishers, Dordrecht.

Noller, Peter & Ronneberger, Klaus (1995), *Die neue Dienstleistungsstadt. Berufsmilieus in Frankfurt am Main* (= Studienreihe des Instituts für Sozialforschung Frankfurt am Main), Campus, Frankfurt/M., New York.

N.U.R.E.C.-Institute Duisburg e.V. (1998), 'Strukturen und Strukturentwicklung sanierungsbetroffener Stadtteile. Stadtteil-Monitoring Marxloh 1996 bis 1998 und sozialräumliche Strukturanalyse Duisburg 1998' (= Monitoring kleinräumiger Entwicklungsprozesse, Bericht 4) Duisburg: N.U.R.E.C.-Institute Duisburg e.V. & Stadt Duisburg, Amt für Statistik, Stadtforschung und Europaangelegenheiten.

O'Loughlin, John (1987), 'Chicago an der Ruhr or What? Explaining the Location of Immigrants in European Cities', in Günther Glebe, & John O'Loughlin (eds), *Foreign Minorities in Continental European Cities* (= Erdkundliches Wissen 84) Steiner, Stuttgart, pp. 52-69.

O'Loughlin, John & Friedrichs, Jürgen (eds) (1996), *Social Polarization in Post-Industrial Metropolises*, de Gruyter, Berlin, New York.

Peters-Schildgen, Susanne (1997), *'Schmelztiegel' Ruhrgebiet. Die Geschichte der Zuwanderung am Beispiel Herne bis 1945*, Klartext, Essen.

Reif, Heinz (1993), *Die verspätete Stadt. Industrialisierung, städtischer Raum und Politik in Oberhausen 1846-1929* (= Landschaftsverband Rheinland, Rheinisches Industriemuseum, Schriften Bd. 7) Landschaftsverband Rheinland, Köln.

Stadt Recklinghausen (1981), *Kohle war nicht alles. 100 Jahre Ruhrgebietsgeschichte* (= Hochlarmarker Lesebuch) Asso, Oberhausen.

Steinberg, Heinz Günter (1978), 'Bevölkerungsentwicklung des Ruhrgebietes im 19. und 20. Jahrhundert' (= Düsseldorfer Geographische Schriften, 11) Geographisches Institut der Universität, Düsseldorf.

Strohmeier, Klaus Peter & Kersting, Volker (1996), 'Sozialraum Ruhrgebiet – Stadträumliche Differenzierungen von Lebenslagen, Armut und informelle Solidarpotentiale', in Rainer Bovermann, Stefan Goch & Heinz-Jürgen Priamus (eds), *Das Ruhrgebiet – Ein starkes Stück Nordrhein-Westfalen. Politik in der Region 1946-1996* (= Schriftenreihe des Instituts für Stadtgeschichte, Beiträge Bd. 7) Klartext, Essen, pp. 451-475.

Tharun, Elke (1997), 'Foreign Residents, Housing Market and Local Government Strategies', *Tijdschrift voor Economische en Sociale Geografie*, vol. 88(2), pp. 135-146.

Thieme, Günter & Laux, Hans Dieter (1996), 'Between Integration and Marginalization: Foreign Population in the Ruhr Conurbation', in Curtis C. Roseman, Hans Dieter Laux &

246 *Studies in Segregation and Desegregation*

Günter Thieme (eds), *EthniCity. Geographic Perspectives on Ethnic Change in Modern Cities*, Rowman & Littlefield, Lanham, London, pp. 141-164.

Türken in Deutschland (= ZEIT Punkte Nr. 2/99) Die Zeit, Hamburg.

van Kempen, Ronald & Özüekren, A. Sule (1998), 'Ethnic Segregation in Cities: New Forms and Explanations in a Dynamic World', *Urban Studies*, vol. 35(10), pp. 1631-1656.

Wiel, Paul (1970), *Wirtschaftsgeschichte des Ruhrgebietes. Tatsachen und Zahlen*, Siedlungsverband Ruhrkohlenbezirk, Essen.

11 New Perspectives on Urban Segregation and Desegregation in Post-Resolution South Africa

ANDRÉ HORN

Introduction

In post-resolution South Africa the analysis of urban segregation and desegregation faces new problems and challenges. Not only is there a gradual shift in direction from segregation to desegregation, but the official classification of the population into 'races' and 'ethnic groups' has been nullified by new legislation. In addition, the spatial mix of races and ethnic groups has been lowered in the order of priority of the new government in relation to the transfer of political and economic power and the breaking down of class structures.

The assessment of spatial segregation and desegregation in South Africa is further complicated by an apparent global mind shift on urban segregation issues. Recent published international literature continues to carry references to Park's race cycle framework, the notion of social closure and concentrations of capital reproducing oppression. In this literature, familiar terms such as 'social polarisation', 'gentrification', 'invasion', 'succession', 'redlining' and 'block busting' are still encountered. But there is also a new discourse in which the views of the socio-biologists, the Chicago school, the neo-Weberian school and the neo-Marxist theorists are no longer crucial. It has become clear from this contemporary debate that segregation now displays a range of new characteristics.

The contemporary international discourse shows that urban segregation is on the increase worldwide (van Kempen & Özüekren, 1998; Musterd & de Winter, 1998) and that globalisation has added a new dimension (Kemper, 1998; White, 1998). In addition, segregation is

248 *Studies in Segregation and Desegregation*

becoming a regional, rather than a primarily local phenomenon (Champion, 1994; Musterd & de Winter, 1998), resulting in spatially differentiated trends (Daley, 1998; Fortuijn et al., 1998; Friedrichs, 1998; Kesteloot & Cortie, 1998; Musterd & de Winter, 1998; Phillips, 1998; van Kempen & van Weesep, 1998). Moreover, there is general agreement that urban segregation is no longer only a racial or ethnic issue. It is also closely linked to urban processes such as sub-urbanisation and ex-urbanisation, as well as the polarisation of income, class and status (Galster, 1990; Goering et al., 1997; Anderson 1998; Carter et al., 1998; Petsimeris, 1998; Rhein, 1998). New forms of segregation and concentration are emerging (Marcuse, 1997; Deurloo & Musterd, 1998; van Kempen & Özüekren, 1998; White, 1998), and due to the sheer number of foreigners now flocking to developed countries, the liberal philosophy of 'assimilate to become like us' and the 'politics of sameness' in these previously immigrant-friendly environments are being challenged by increasing hostile attitudes and the 'politics of difference' (Anderson, 1998; Dunn, 1998; Murdie & Borgegard, 1998). Lastly, it seems that the existing frameworks for the analysis of ethnic segregation such as the culturalist, culture-racist and structural perspectives no longer provide convincing explanations for contemporary manifestations of urban segregation (Anderson, 1998). More dynamic strategies are called for that take into account contextual as well as individual factors and developments to explain segregation trends (van Kempen & Özüekren, 1998).

The view that the characteristics of segregation have changed leads to a question concerning South Africa. If present-day segregation differs so markedly from its earlier types, what is the significance of the South African experience in this regard?

First, the formal programme of ethnic segregation in South Africa, commonly known as apartheid, was originally marketed as a positive and progressive doctrine. However, in the reality of a multi-ethnic society, it meant division and oppression. The logic is simple: just as the complexities of South Africa made it impossible to implement apartheid positively, so the nature of globalisation will make it impossible to implement new politics of difference elsewhere. It is of great importance that we be reminded again that the experiment has already been conducted and has failed.

Second, South Africa represents a case of extremes of social engineering. Between 1948 and 1990 the implementation of a deliberate programme of urban segregation was a high priority of the government. Today, the redistribution of people, wealth and opportunity is a priority of

André Horn 249

the present South African government. In both these instances South Africa represented and now represents a highly controlled laboratory of segregation and desegregation policies.

Third, desegregation in the South African context means that concentrations of minority groups (15% of the total population) are expected to accommodate the majority group. Depending on the position of a group in the social hierarchy, a specific community may be invading a better-positioned community or group while at the same time defending itself against other groups. It is clear that the study of segregation and desegregation in the context of a new South Africa offers unusual challenges in terms of methodology, analysis and explanation that may lead to better understanding of these phenomena elsewhere.

Accordingly, this article pays only brief attention to the implementation and outcomes of urban segregation in South Africa during the apartheid era while focussing on adaptive desegregation during the political struggle and emerging patterns and trends of desegregation after political resolution.

A Tradition of Urban Segregation in South Africa

The formation of urban centres as it is understood in the global context is a fairly recent phenomenon in South Africa. Cape Town was established in 1652 by the Dutch East India Company and remained the only sizeable town for almost two centuries. By 1911 there were only 336 urban settlements of which only one in ten housed over 5,000 inhabitants and only two, Johannesburg and Cape Town, over 100,000 inhabitants (Christopher, 1984). Only in 1946, for the first time did the urban non-white population outnumber the urban white population.

The absence of pre-colonial towns of any magnitude gave rise to the idea that towns were the domain of the white settlers of mainly European origin, and from the very beginning the principle of urban segregation was widely practised in cities and towns. Up to the year 1900 segregation in cities and towns was based on social and economic divisions between white settlers on the one hand, and indigenous and imported labour on the other. However, in the Cape, Natal, the Orange Free State and the Transvaal the colonial authorities were free to order society within their own jurisdiction (Davenport, 1991. At the turn of the previous century the inter-colonial Native Affairs Commission (South Africa, 1905) proposed separate residential locations for non-whites as a general principle.

250 *Studies in Segregation and Desegregation*

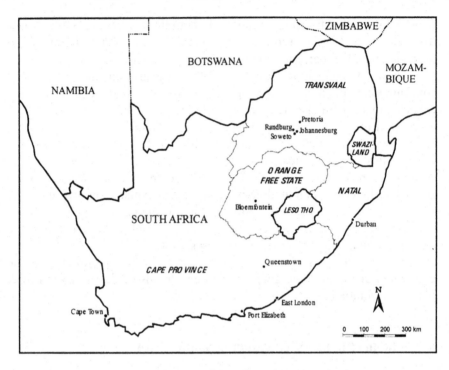

Figure 11.1 Apartheid South Africa: Provinces and selected towns

The first government of the Union of South Africa drafted the Urban Areas Bill in 1912, but it was more than a decade later, in 1923, that the Native (Urban Areas) Act was introduced to remove blacks from defined areas of a city. Racial control in the urban areas was also administered by way of a compendium of other legislation, including the Housing Act (1920) and the Slums Act of 1934. The rapid influx of non-whites into the cities during the Second World War resulted in the Natives Urban Areas (Consolidation) Act (1945) aimed at controlling access and regulating the spatial organization of cities.

Although the segregated South African city (until 1950) was based on a simplistic, dual city concept, the reality was more complicated (Davies, 1981). It exhibited an irregular pattern of comparatively integrated urban cores and largely segregated peripheral suburbs as well as a mixture of leasehold and freehold land systems.

Christopher (1991a) has used the index of dissimilarity to assess the spatial distribution of the various population groups in South Africa in 1951. Table 11.1 indicates high levels of spatial dissimilarity between Indians and blacks, and between whites and all other groups. The index of dissimilarity between coloureds and Indians is relatively high on a national basis and particularly high in the Transvaal, while that between coloureds and blacks is relatively low (47.7) on a national basis, and particularly low in the Orange Free State (22.1). Indices of dissimilarity for 1951 were also calculated by Kuper et al. (1958) for Durban (white-Indian: 91; white-coloured 84; white-black 81, and black-Indian 81), and by Davies (1971) for Port Elizabeth as 89 for whites-others and 80 for blacks-coloureds.

Table 11.1 Indices of dissimilarity in South Africa, 1951

Groups compared	West Cape	East Cape	Natal	Orange Free State	Transvaal	South Africa
White-Coloured	66.0	73.6	44.8	91.2	77.1	75.9
White-Indian	76.3	69.1	61.5	*	75.1	71.5
White-African	72.2	85.1	57.9	87.0	70.7	78.0
Coloured-Indian	47.0	66.3	34.7	*	81.5	68.9
Coloured-African	51.1	46.7	53.7	22.1	51.0	47.7
Indian-African	84.2	90.1	56.4	*	87.1	85.5

* No Indian communities of over 25 members were enumerated in the Orange Free State
Scale of Index of Dissimilarity: 0.0 – completely integrated 100 – completely segregated
Source: Christopher (1991a).

Before 1948 the liberal-minded United Party government failed to deal with the very real problem of urban planning for a multiracial society (Mabin, 1992), thus, putting this government in a paradoxical position because while it rejected racial integration it regarded complete segregation as totally impractical. The opposing National Party branded the segregation policies of the time as 'negative' racism and proposed 'positive' apartheid as an alternative. Although positive apartheid was propagated as the intention to eliminate white domination and to establish equitable geographical partitioning (Cronje et al., 1947), Sparks (1990) contends that the main intention was to save the white race from being swamped and to protect its members from black economic competition. Parnell and Mabin (1995) have contributed to the debate, arguing that urban apartheid was not so much about race as about power and control. Be that as it may, the National Party's victory in the 1948 general elections and its reversion to strict segregation policies represented the instinctive expression of white fear and prejudice (Pirie, 1984).

Apartheid was a grand scheme of social and spatial engineering and

252 *Studies in Segregation and Desegregation*

concerned the micro-scale of interpersonal relations, the meso-scale of urban areas and the macro-scale of regional settlement (van den Berghe, 1965). It started from the premise of marginalisation, if not exclusion, of the non-white races from the political process. The first batch of apartheid laws was aimed at controlling social interaction between the races and included the Prohibition of Mixed Marriages Act (1949), the Immorality Amendment Act (1950) and the Population Registration Act of 1950. For the last piece of legislation the population was divided into blacks, coloureds, Indians, and whites. Attempts to further divide the coloured group into Chinese, Cape Malay, Griqua and Cape coloured were eventually abandoned.

The second batch of apartheid laws focused on urban re-organization aimed at the segregation of residential and commercial areas, transport services, recreation and public amenities. The Group Areas Act of 1950 was the cornerstone of urban segregation. This act made provision for the setting aside of separate residential areas for whites, coloureds and Indians in terms of the Population Registration Act. Blacks were considered temporary sojourners who would eventually be accommodated in black homelands (Fair & Schmidt, 1974). The proclamation of segregated black townships such as Soweto was regulated by further measures, including the Native Laws Amendment Act (1952). Total urban segregation was further supported by the Prevention of Illegal Squatting Act (1951), the Reservation of Separate Amenities Act (1953) and the Group Areas Development Act (1955), which was later incorporated into the Community Development Act of 1966. Soon, the notion of an ideal apartheid city crystallized, and local municipalities competed with one another to reconstruct their cities accordingly. This was the era of mass forced removals and the destruction of communities such as District Six in Cape Town, Sophiatown in Johannesburg, and Lady Selbourne in Pretoria.

From 1953 to 1991, mostly before 1970, a total of 1,750 areas comprising 1,062,000 hectares were declared group areas (Christopher, 1991b; 1992). By 1985 whites, representing only 34% of the urban population of South Africa (excluding the homelands), had been allocated 87% of the total land in group areas (Lemon, 1991). On June 30, 1991, the date on which formal racial zoning legislation was removed from the statute book, the number of the relevant population group members per hectare of urban land zoned for the group was 45 blacks, 22 coloureds, 16 Indians, and 6 whites (Christopher, 1992). It is estimated that about 1.5 million South Africans were moved as a result of group-area proclamations and urban planning schemes. Black urban life in particular was ' ... deeply

André Horn 253

penetrated by bureaucratic regulation that in essence (had) required non-whites to live their lives by permit and (had) caused many to be labeled as criminals for transgressions of such regulations' (Davies, 1986:7).

According to Davies (1981) the apartheid City displayed the following characteristics:

- a dominant white central business district and a segregated coloured or Indian business area;
- white-owned industrial sectors which functioned as communal working areas and at the same time served as buffers between segregated areas;
- strongly segregated residential areas separated by buffer zones;
- concentrations of low income blacks on the urban periphery and on the borders of black homelands close to industries.

Table 11.2 Indices of segregation for South Africa, 1911-1985

Year	White	Indians	Coloureds	Blacks
1911	54.7	*	42.9	64.7
1921	59.6	54.0	36.5	59.7
1936	67.7	57.4	44.3	65.2
1951	74.8	70.5	49.3	68.6
1960	81.4	77.1	54.1	76.2
1970	91.7	87.2	77.8	82.9
1985	92.8	89.2	82.9	87.9

In 1911 Indians were enumerated as coloureds.
Scale of Index of Segregation; 0.0 – complete integration 100 – complete segregation.
Source: Christopher (1990).

Table 11.2 indicates that segregation levels in South African urban areas were remarkably high and rose consistently as a result of the various schemes of spatial and social engineering introduced during the twentieth century. Particularly after 1960 the full impact of urban apartheid became evident as segregation levels increased. Also, from 1963 the number of resident domestic servants was limited to one per household. As a result most white suburbs experienced relative black depopulation (Hart, 1976), particularly in the lower-income areas. By 1985 the apartheid programme had resulted in two-thirds of the population living in cities with segregation

254 *Studies in Segregation and Desegregation*

index levels over 90.0 (Christopher, 1989). Regional variations, nevertheless, occurred. Half the towns in the Orange Free State, for example, recorded white indices of segregation greater than 95.0, but only a sixth of those in the Transvaal and only one in Natal exhibited such high levels of segregation. However, no 'model' apartheid city emerged where everyone lived in their designated area. In 1985 some 10% of the urban population lived outside its designated group areas (Table 11.3).

Table 11.3 Concentrations of South African urban populations in group areas, 1985

Group	Total	Group area of residence				% Outside Group area
		White	Coloured	Indian	Black	
White	4092067	4078634	6353	2339	4741	0.33
Coloured	2232591	189033	1978257	17263	48038	11.39
Indian	767545	44818	10839	710208	1680	7.47
Black	4898270	820208	24140	25552	4028390	17.59
Total	11990493	5132693	2019589	755362	4082849	9.97

Source: Christopher (1989).

In Pretoria, the administrative capital, 10.2% of the population resided in the wrong group area. In Johannesburg, the largest city, the figure was 8.7%, while in Cape Town it was only 5.0%. In the smaller towns the deviation varied from anything between 3% to almost 40%. According to Christopher (1990:439) '... the philosophy of apartheid was not only morally flawed, but impossible to implement in practice.'

Adaptive Desegregation Up to 1990

Adaptive change of the overall apartheid system, implying in urban areas a movement away from segregation under conditions of incremental social and political pressure started in the 1970s (Rhoodie & Le Roux, 1983). It can be argued that the real aim of the policy shift was not to end apartheid but to modernise it (Simon, 1989).

In 1974 the Johannesburg City Council removed 'whites only' signs from park benches. A year later the first non-racial, sit-down restaurant was established at the Carlton Centre in Johannesburg. In 1976 the first 'international' (i.e. multiracial) hotel facilities were approved. In 1983

André Horn 255

open, i.e. desegregated hotels, numbered 74, while 34 restaurants had 'international' licenses (McCarthy, 1990).

Permanent permits for mixed audiences in theatres were first granted in 1978. In 1983 applications for multiracial cinemas were successful for the first time. Two years later a total of 78 cinemas had multiracial permits. The functional desegregation of beaches was started in Cape Town in 1980 with other main coastal cities such as Durban, Port Elizabeth and East London soon following. The first city to desegregate its municipal bus services was Cape Town (1977). One of the last to do so was Pretoria, where 10 blacks had been arrested in 1990 attempting to board a 'whites only' municipal bus (Beeld, 1989). In 1982 an investigation in Randburg showed that about 57% of the white residents in this city indicated some form or other of acceptance of desegregated public amenities, but only 12.7% indicated that they would welcome such a situation (Rhoodie & Le Roux, 1983).

Regulation of the occupation and ownership of urban land for professional and commercial purposes was one of the main functions of the Group Areas Act. Separate coloured and Indian business districts was one of the main characteristics of the apartheid city (Davies, 1981). In 1977 the Act was amended to give coloured and Indian business people more freedom to trade outside group areas, and the prosecution of offenders ceased altogether in 1978. The feasibility of desegregating central business districts (CBDs) was investigated by the apartheid government in 1981, and from 1984 local authorities were permitted to apply for 'free trading zones'. By the end of 1986 a total of 29 such areas had been declared, a figure, which increased to 62 in 1988. The ensuing desegregation of formal business and trade (Bähr & Jürgens, 1990) coincided with a process of hawker deregulation that opened new economic niches and geographical space for the urban poor (Rogerson, 1989). While Pretoria was one of the last big urban centres to apply for a free-trade CBD (January, 1990) the city councils of Johannesburg, Durban and Queenstown moved to declare their entire municipal areas free-trade zones.

A process of unauthorised residential desegregation - greying - started in places such as Hillbrow (Johannesburg) in the late 1970s (Beavon, 1998). By the mid-1980s pockets of racially mixed neighbourhoods had become characteristic of many larger South African towns and cities. Examples included the suburbs of Salt River, Landsdowne, Wynberg, Observatory and Woodstock in Cape Town; North End and Korsten in Port Elizabeth; Albert Park, Clairwood and Greyville in Durban; and Hillbrow, Berea, Joubert Park and Mayfair in Johannesburg. According to Schlemmer

256 Studies in Segregation and Desegregation

& Stack (1990a) the development of such grey areas was the result of various factors catalyzing the movement of non-whites into white areas and state reluctance or failure to enforce the principle of group areas.

During the period of greying De Coning et al. (1986) conducted a study of socio-political perceptions in the densely populated and cosmopolitan inner city areas of Hillbrow, Berea and Joubert Park in Johannesburg. The population of about 62,000 included some 30,000 white South Africans, 20,000 black, coloured and Indian South Africans as well as about 10,000 Europeans and 1,000 black foreigners.

Fifty percent of the white respondents of South African origin already living in grey areas accepted the sharing of apartment blocks with other population groups and at least 42% were in favour of the repeal of the Group Areas Act (Table 11.4). The clear message of this survey was that the first-hand experiences of whites already living in densely populated multiracial conditions were not as negative as expected.

Table 11.4 Views on residential desegregation in the inner city of Johannesburg, 1986 by population category

Population category	Yes, Share flat buildings %	Yes, Legalise grey areas %	Yes, Mixed settlement improved relations %
White SA	50	42	27
White foreigners	68	24	24
Coloureds	90	88	63
Blacks	91	100	57

Source: De Coning et al. (1986).

Further, it became apparent that the attitudes of whites to the issue of urban segregation were changing when the Afrikaans newspaper *Rapport* in 1986 published findings comparing the views of whites in 1981 with their views five years later (Table 11.5).

The *Rapport* survey showed that support for the maintenance of the Group Areas Act had fallen below 50% among whites. The percentage of white respondents hoping to keep all-white schools closed to other races had dropped from 48% to below 36%, and the percentage in favour of the desegregation of all schools in the country had risen from about 11% in 1981 to 24% in 1986.

The suburb of Mayfair, an established area with low-density detached housing units relatively close to the Johannesburg CBD, represents a clear

André Horn 257

example of the erosion of the group area principle during the mid-1980s. This area had been targeted by members of the Indian community for resettlement from about 1983, and soon Indians represented 21% of the Mayfair population. Four years later Indian residents represented close to 50% of the population while whites (43%) were forced into a minority position (Fick et al., 1988).

Table 11.5 Comparison of the views of whites on aspects of desegregation 1981/1986

Maintain GAA, apply strictly, allow limited exceptions		Communities, local governments to be excluded from GAA		Keep all white schools closed to other races		Open all schools to all races	
1981	1986	1981	1986	1981	1986	1981	1986
62.9%	44.4%	36.6%	54.4%	47.9%	34.5%	10.7%	23.9%

Source: Rapport (1986).

It appeared that during 1986 the provincial attorney generals had been instructed to cease prosecutions for infringements of the Group Areas Act. In the following year 1,243 complaints of contravention of this Act were investigated, but only three parties were charged and prosecuted. Also in 1987 the Transvaal Provincial Administration approved 956 out of 1,025 applications it received from non-whites to live in white areas. The process of residential greying quickly gained momentum and became a national phenomenon (Pickard-Cambridge, 1988; Hart, 1989; Rule, 1989; Bähr & Jürgens, 1990; Elder, 1990; Cloete, 1991; Bähr & Jürgens, 1993; Maharaj & Mpungose, 1994).

In 1986 the principle of urban influx control, as embodied by Section 10 of the Natives Urban Areas (Consolidation) Act, 1945 (amended), was abolished and replaced by a strategy of orderly urbanisation. In addition, apartheid measures such as the Mixed Marriages Act (introduced in 1949) and Article 16 of the Immorality Act (dating back to 1957) were repealed.

In an attempt to control the process of greying, the government introduced the Free Settlement Areas Act under the terms of which an area could be proclaimed a multi-racial residential zone. On the other hand, the government appointed boards to police the Group Areas Act in remaining racially zoned areas, but although the police investigated 1,249 cases of group area contravention between July, 1989 and February, 1990, not a single charge was made.

258 *Studies in Segregation and Desegregation*

A number of opinion surveys from 1989 to 1990 (e.g. Schlemmer & Stack, 1990a; Retief & Kelbrick, 1990; Horn et al., 1991) indicated that although white respondents were receptive to the idea of racial desegregation in designated areas they were still opposed to the lifting of group area restrictions in all areas. On the other hand, non-whites remained sceptical of the government's intention to repeal group area restrictions even after the process of reconciliation was set in motion in 1990.

The South African urban scenario in 1990 can be summarised as follows:

- illegal desegregation of inner-city neighbourhoods;
- illegal desegregation of some white suburbs;
- illegal squatting on urban fringes in areas zoned for whites;
- growing black townships;
- establishment of some legal desegregated areas or free settlements;
- gradual change of white attitudes;
- growing scepticism amongst non-whites.

Desegregation after Apartheid

Although limited desegregation had already begun in the 1970s, it can be safely assumed that desegregation on a broad scale was only set in motion in 1990 with the announcement of political reform. Before analysing the spatial trends and outcomes of desegregation during the first decade of post-apartheid urban transformation, let us briefly consider the meaning of non-racialism, integration and desegregation in the present South African context, as well as the forces that influence urban desegregation.

Non-Racialism, Desegregation and Integration

It is generally assumed that spontaneous spatial segregation within national boundaries implicitly includes some degree of social intolerance. Reversed segregation, on the other hand, involves two complementary processes, one social and one spatial. Social integration is a process that should lead to greater social equity; it should also facilitate mutual understanding and foster tolerance. While integration is, therefore, seen as a social process, desegregation is seen as a mere spatial or mechanical process.

In post-resolution South Africa two complementary processes, nation

André Horn 259

building and reconstruction, have been set in motion to achieve the dual aims of integration and desegregation. It is clear, even at this early stage, that the abolition of mechanical apartheid and the introduction of constitutional equality will not of themselves bring about an integrated nation.

President Thabo Mbeki's recent remark that 'South Africa is not one nation but rather a country of two nations – one white and relatively prosperous and the other black and poor' has caused the evaporation of the euphoria of Nelson Mandela's 'rainbow nation'. It is apparent that the lingering problem of race and racism has once again pushed through to the top of the country's agenda, colouring many major issues (*Pretoria News*, 1998). From the political platforms whites are being accused by the ruling African National Congress of not becoming part of the South African nation. The reply of the white minority is that they are being politically alienated and economically marginalised. Ethnic identities are also coming to the fore with complaints of dominance of the Nguni, particularly the Xhosa, over non-Xhosa and non-Nguni; people who once claimed to be black have, since the 1994 elections, started to refer to themselves as Indians and coloureds (Cullinan, 1998). The present government's affirmative action programme has a strong racial, ethnic and political bias and is perceived to be the main cause of racial and ethnic re-polarisation.

A recent nationwide survey has revealed that the majority of whites, coloureds and Indians believe that race relations in South Africa will not improve on the basis of present government policies (*Pretoria News*, 1999a). The *Pretoria News* (1999b) illustrates the difference in views concerning reconciliation: 'Reconciliation can only happen when black people stop blaming whites for everything' (white respondent), and 'We will only have reconciliation when black people have the same as whites' (black respondent).

These differing views about what is needed to bring about reconciliation is the crucial issue in post-apartheid South Africa and is also reflected in the interpretation of the meaning of non-racialism by political groupings. The minority parties - whites and non-whites - view non-racialism as individual equity either through a 'salad bowl' or 'melting-pot'. The view of the ruling party is that non-racialism is about relations of power, attending to the material inequality in society, and the emancipation and renaissance of African people in particular.

In view of the above, let us now ask whether the process of mechanical desegregation gathered further momentum during the 1990s, and whether desegregation in urban South Africa during this period created areas of

260 *Studies in Segregation and Desegregation*

demographic succession and/or areas of shared space.

In answering these key questions it is fundamentally important to first assess the forces presently shaping and re-shaping South Africa's cities.

Urban Dynamics During the 1990s

The mechanical process of post-1990 urban desegregation in South Africa started with the repeal of the legislation that had upheld urban apartheid for so many years. This process was set in motion in mid-1990 with the repeal of the Reservation of Separated Amenities Act. Then, in June 1991, the Abolition of Racially Based Land Measures Act repealed the bulk of the remainder of the apartheid segregation laws. In addition, a host of other laws were amended. The Abolition of Racially Based Land Measures Act also stated that any residential by-laws, which discriminate on the grounds of race, colour or religion or which are grossly unfair shall no longer have force or effect.

Prior to and at the beginning of the transformation process a number of people presented their visions of structural changes in post-apartheid South African cities. Some (e.g. Beavon, 1992) based their vision on the realities at the time, others (e.g. Schlemmer & Stack, 1990b; Saff, 1995) made projections on the desegregation process in the USA and yet others referred to desegregation and changes in other southern African post-colonial cities such as Harare, Zimbabwe (e.g. Davies, 1992), Windhoek and Namibia (e.g. Cilliers, 1990).

However, the dynamics of development and transformation in the South African urban sphere since 1990 have gone way beyond even the most imaginative predictions. Some of these changes are highlighted below.

Inner-city transformation During the process of transformation the central city has emerged as a major area of urban change. As early as 1992 calls were made for a high-level investigation into the causes of inner-city decay (South Africa, 1992a).

While most inner-city residential areas had at that stage not deteriorated beyond repair, living there had become problematic for many people as a result of the magnitude and tempo of the influx of people. For example, approximately one-third of the estimated 100,000 black people living in the Johannesburg inner-city by 1995 had arrived between 1991 and 1992 (Crankshaw & White, 1992; Dauskardt, 1993). This caused the demographic profile of the inner-city areas to change from a younger,

André Horn 261

single white and older, single white population to a young, black single and young, black-family population (Prinsloo, 1998).

The physical decline of the Johannesburg inner-city, for example, has been radical (Morris, 1997; Crankshaw & Parnell, 2000), and since 1990 all the graded hotels in the Johannesburg CBD have closed. Beavon (1998: 30) describes the situation in the Johannesburg centre as follows: 'Property owners have abandoned their premises, had the water and electricity supplies disconnected and the buildings are now used as slum living quarters. Others have bricked up their buildings but in many cases those barriers are broken and the building is simply taken over by homeless people desperate for shelter.'

White flight and decentralization Sub-urbanisation, ex-urbanisation and decentralisation have affected the main cities of South Africa from the late-1970s. The global trend of decentralisation, strengthened by residential white flight in South Africa, has led to the formation of edge cities such as Sandton in the greater Johannesburg area and Centurion in the greater Pretoria area. The phenomenon of white residential flight to suburban and ex-urban locations is epitomized by the construction of security villages in high-income sectors of the city (Donaldson & van der Merwe, 1999).

The commercial sector soon followed on the heels of white residents. In 1970 there were only 12 planned shopping centres in the country with total combined floor space of about 200,000 sq. m. By the end of 1999 there were 230 shopping centres and malls each of more than 10,000 sq. m. Most were located in the suburbs (Prinsloo, 1999). At present, retail space in the Johannesburg CBD is occupied mainly by small shops selling low-order goods and serving an increasingly black-dominated clientele (Beavon, 1998). Of the top 169 industrial and other commercial head offices in Johannesburg, only 48% are still located in the inner-city, while 52% are now located in Sandton and the surrounding northern suburbs (Prinsloo, 1998). For every unit of office space being built in the Johannesburg CBD there are currently about four units under construction in the suburbs (Beavon, 1998).

Transformation of local government Urban segregation and apartheid policies caused the dismembering and disintegration of non-white urban communities (Atkinson, 1991). The non-white local authorities administering the townships were perceived by the majority of non-whites who formed civic associations (civics) to be politically illegitimate institutions. These civic associations had a strong social and political

262 *Studies in Segregation and Desegregation*

agenda and led an organized country-wide struggle against the government beginning in 1982.

In 1989, negotiations on local administrative and social issues were initiated between some local white authorities and the civic associations. This led to the establishment of a national Local Government Negotiating Forum. Urban re-unification started in 1993 with the promulgation of the Local Government Transition Act. This effectively meant the amalgamation of formerly racially based local government structures. In the case of Pretoria, for example, it meant that the townships of Atteridgeville and Mamelodi (black), Eersterus (coloured) and Laudium (Indian) were amalgamated with the Pretoria Metropolitan Sub-Structure (which existed alongside the Akasia and Centurion sub-structures as the Greater Pretoria Metropolitan Structure). The Local Government Transition Act (1993) made provision for the election (on the basis of existing wards) of racially representative Transitional Local Councils (TLCs). These elections took place during 1994/5, and most towns, cities and metropolitan structures are now governed by a black-majority council. In the case of the larger cities and metro's the transitional councils have also evolved into permanent local councils.

Since the publication of the White Paper on Local Government (South Africa, 1998) the process of transformation of local government has entered its final phase. In terms of the constitution an independent Municipal Demarcation Board (MDB) has been established. The MDB tabled its proposals for municipal demarcations at the end of 1999 and these are presently being reviewed by local communities. The final step will be to demarcate new election wards to ensure a fully representative metropolitan council.

The main challenge laid before these new urban management structures is to create integrated cities and towns '... where the poor are not locationally disadvantaged or socially excluded' (South Africa, 1998:178).

New perspectives on urban development and planning A major paradigm shift is taking place in urban planning in South Africa. The main challenge to official planning departments is the pressing need to alleviate the anomalies and disparities created by decades of segregationist planning and the need for new policies to create more efficient and equitable cities (Urban Foundation, 1990). The notion of post-resolution reconstruction and equity planning is widely advocated in order to address the challenge (Mabin & Smit, 1997; Bollens, 1998). In terms of the new paradigm, space is to become interracial and integrative to reflect the vision of a non-racial society (Robinson, 1997). Planners believe that reconstruction and equity planning can be achieved through focussing on infilling and densification, combating low-density sprawl and upgrading and renewing those parts under stress (Dewar & Uytenbogaardt, 1991; Bollens, 1998).

Through the Local Government Transition Act (1993), the Development Facilitation Act (1995) and the White Paper on Local Government (1998), the government has made it clear that the planning profession must emphasize integrated development planning (IDP) through a process of incremental planning, including the formulation of land development objectives (LDOs). The White Paper (South Africa, 1998) stresses that the roles and responsibilities of urban management systems must focus on city-wide spatial integration and socially inclusive development, as well as the promotion of equity, social justice and economic prosperity.

The concept of spatial integration is the fundamental principle of the new official urban planning strategy. The aim of this strategy is to create more efficient and equitable cities and towns where people, particularly the poor, are not locationally disadvantaged or socially excluded.

Certain changes to the apartheid urban structure can already be noticed:

- expansion and development of black townships;
- expansion or siting of regulated informal settlements on the fringes of or between white suburbs;
- spontaneous establishment of unregulated informal settlements within or between more affluent white suburbs;
- upgrading of spontaneous informal settlements and site-and-services schemes into formal suburbs and ex-urbs by way of government housing schemes; establishment of low-cost housing schemes in the midst of or between relatively more affluent suburbs;
- re-zoning of properties in established white suburbs to allow for sub-divisions and the building of smaller and cheaper houses.

According to the White Paper (South Africa, 1998) the urban integration strategy has a spatial dimension, an economic dimension and a social dimension. At this stage, spatial integration refers to non-white communities (through spatial relocation and upgrading of the infrastructure), the economic integration of non-white communities (through the benefits of a wider tax base) and the breaking down of spatial

264 *Studies in Segregation and Desegregation*

income and class structures in the white areas (by way of planning intervention and the encouragement of mixed-income developments).

Rent boycott The new government of South Africa has established the notion of self-reliant local governments and the notion of individual payment for municipal housing, land occupation and services as basic principles of urban management. On average, a city receives about 60% of its revenue from service charges, another 20% from property taxes and the remainder from regional levies and from an equitable share of national revenue.

During the 1980s civic associations organized a countrywide boycott of municipal payments as part of the political campaign against the then government (Swilling et al., 1991). The campaign was intensified during the early stages of political transition. The main conditions set by the civic associations for ending the municipal rent boycott were a write-off of arrears, the transfer of municipal houses to residents, the upgrading of services, the introduction of affordable service charges, the creation of a single tax base and the establishment of non-racial, democratic municipalities. Although these conditions have already been met in most areas, a culture of non-payment has become entrenched and has lead to a fiscal crisis for many local authorities. As a result the new government launched the Masekane - Let's Build Together - campaign to normalise urban governance and to provide services to all urban communities through the promotion of payment of housing and services rates.

It is clear that the Masekane campaign has failed. Even the introduction of a flat rate of no more than 20% of that in other suburbs has not had the required result in many townships. The White Paper on Local Government (South Africa, 1998) acknowledges that one-third of the 843 municipalities in South Africa are at present facing financial difficulties or administrative problems with their service provision. In July, 1998, for example, it was established that the arrears on municipal accounts in the Pretoria metropolitan sub-structure amounted to R515.5 million. At this stage 90.1% of registered rate payers in the previously white areas were paying their accounts compared with 57.2% in Atteridgeville and 56% in Mamelodi (both black townships where below-cost flat rates were introduced). By December, 1998 the arrears on consumer debt had increased to R604 million and the levels of payment had dropped to 84% in 'old' Pretoria, 49% in Atteridgeville and 50% in Mamelodi. Consumer arrears further increased to R692 million in July, 1999, R723 million in September, 1999, and R743 million in December, 1999. At that stage only 59% of account holders were paying property taxes and service charges.

André Horn 265

The constitutionality of fiscal cross-subsidisation between 'have' and 'have-not' areas has been tested in the courts and is now a well-established principle of local government (South Africa, 1998). The implication of this is that well-to-do non-whites living in new township developments that compare favourably with the best of the formerly white suburbs, and paying (or not paying) a subsidised below-cost municipal account may seriously lack the incentive to move out to the previously white suburbs.

Against this background several studies on various aspects of the desegregation process in South Africa have been conducted on a community or neighbourhood scale. These include studies in Johannesburg (Jürgens, 1993; Bähr & Jürgens, 1996; Rule, 1996; Bähr et al., 1998), in Cape Town (Garside, 1993; Myburg, 1996; Oelofse, 1996; Saff, 1996; Bähr, & Jürgens, 1996; Lohnert et al., 1998), and in Port Elizabeth (Ownhouse & Nel, 1993).

At the national level it was found by Christopher (2000) that on average segregation levels in South African cities and towns in 1996

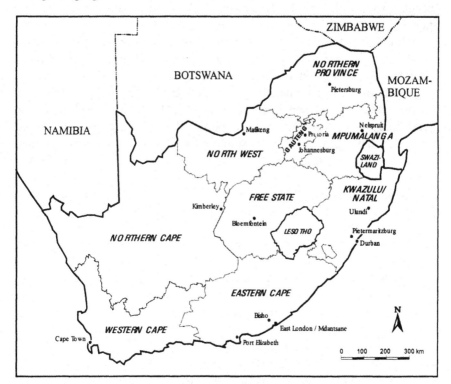

Figure 11.2 Post-apartheid South Africa: provinces and cities

266 *Studies in Segregation and Desegregation*

remained exceptionally high.

However, the remaining sections of this chapter focus on desegregation case studies at the meso-scale of cities as a whole. The first is in two secondary cities, Bloemfontein and Pietersburg, based on residential property transfers. A second case study, also based on residential property transfers, is in the Johannesburg and Pretoria metropolitan areas. A third case study is based on census data and again concerns the Pretoria metropolis.

Desegregation in Secondary Cities

Bloemfontein and Pietersburg can be regarded as secondary cities in the South African urban hierarchy. During apartheid times Bloemfontein was the provincial capital of the Orange Free State, and Pietersburg represented the main regional centre of the northern part of the Transvaal province. After the demarcation of new provinces in 1993/4 both these centres became provincial capitals: Bloemfontein became the capital of the Free State and Pietersburg of the Northern Province.

Although in the past both these cities displayed general characteristics of the classic apartheid city, there were also notable differences. Bloemfontein is located centrally in the heartland of the white farming community of the Free State. Because the closest homeland centres, such as Botshabelo, are more than 100 km. away, it had a typical black township. Pietersburg, in contrast, because it bordered on the Lebowa homeland, instead of having a black township under its jurisdiction, had a huge homeland town, Seshego, in close proximity, about 6 km. from the city centre.

Table 11.6 shows that in the case of Pietersburg, four periods of desegregation have been identified by Donaldson (1999).

Early pioneers: 1992-1993 By May, 1992, ten months after the repeal of the Group Areas Act, 52 residential properties in areas previously occupied exclusively by other races had been transferred to blacks. This represented 1.0% of residential properties in the formerly white, coloured and Indian areas in Pietersburg at that time. Note that figures of property transfers to blacks in the coloured and Indian townships of Pietersburg for the period 1992-1993 were not obtained by Donaldson (1999). By May, 1993, 169 properties, or 3.1% of residential properties in Pietersburg, were owned by blacks. At the end of the first period, the largest numbers of black owners of residential property were concentrated in Central City (23 units), one of

André Horn 267

Table 11.6 Residential desegregation based on property transfers in Pietersburg, 1992-1997

Suburbs		Period 1		Period 2	Period 3	Period 4
		Sept. 1992	May 1993	May 1994	May 1995	May 1996
Low Residential Value Areas						
Annadale	1.	0	0	7	21	13
	2.	(0)	(0)	(1.1)	(1.4)	(1.9)
Westenburg		NA	NA	242	364	364
(previously coloured)				(36.4)	(38.2)	(40.4)
Nirvana		NA	NA	42	44	51
(previously Indian)				(6.7)	(6.3)	(5.2)
Ivy Park		4	11	39	47	31
		(2.2)	(6.1)	(18.5)	(22.3)	(14.9)
Central City		8	23	66	87	18
		(0.6)	(1.6)	(4.0)	(5.3)	(2.2)
Hospital Park /		0	3	9	17	12
Môregloed		(0)	(1.2)	(3.3)	(6.2)	(4.2)
Medium Residential Value Areas						
Eduan Park		0	0	6	7	7
		(0)	(0)	(2.4)	(2.7)	(2.3)
Penina park		10	32	79	92	92
		(3.6)	(11.7)	(24.2)	(28.1)	(26.1)
Capricorn		0	0	5	9	8
		(0)	(0)	(3.0)	(5.3)	(4.7)
Flora Park		14	50	268	400	475
		(1.9)	(7.0)	(21.8)	(26.8)	(23.9)
Medium-to-High Residential Value Areas						
Ster Park		2	5	20	43	6
		(0.8)	(2.0)	(6.8)	(13.4)	(11.3)
Fauna Park		4	17	111	131	44
		(0.7)	(3.0)	(13.7)	(15.7)	(5.4)
Silwerkruin		0	8	11	11	13
		(0)	(9.3)	(7.1)	(6.0)	(4.9)
High Residential Value Areas						
Welgelegen		1	1	7	15	24
		(0.4)	(0.4)	(2.3)	(5.0)	(6.8)
Bendor Park		9	19	78	119	98
		(1.9)	(4.1)	(9.5)	(11.1)	(5.4)
Total		52	169	990	1407	1286
		(1.0)	(3.1)	(10.2)	(12.4)	(10.6)

1. Number of black home-owners. 2. Percentage of black home-owners.
NA - Figures not available.
Source: Donaldson (1999).

the low-value areas; Flora Park (50 units) and Penina Park (32 units) in the medium-value areas; Fauna Park (17 units) in the medium-to-high-value

268 *Studies in Segregation and Desegregation*

areas; and Bendor Park (19 units) in the high-value sector. It is clear that during this period properties across the spectrum of residential values were bought by blacks but particularly in the medium-value areas of Pietersburg, such as Penina Park, where black home-owners numbered more than 10 percent (11.7% to be exact) of the total number of home-owners.

According to Donaldson (1999), estate agents started to refer to Penina Park as the 'black' suburb. Prospective black buyers were also advised by estate agents to avoid politically conservative areas such as Annadale, a suburb of low-property value. The early pioneers mainly fell in an upwardly mobile high-income group within the 30-39 age category, were married, and had a tertiary qualification (Donaldson & Kotze, 1994; Kotze & Donaldson, 1996).

Election period: 1994-1995 Donaldson (1996) indicates that in Pietersburg, an amicable inflow of middle-to-upper income blacks was triggered by the general elections of 1994. By May 1995 there were 990 black home-owners in Pietersburg, representing 10.2% of all home-owners in the city, mostly in Flora Park, a rapidly expanding suburb of medium-value where 268 residential units (21.8% of all units) were then owned by blacks. Previously whites-only suburbs where black home-owners at that stage exceeded 20% of the population were Penina Park and Flora Park, both in the medium-value area.

In May, 1995 the impact of the residential mobility of blacks on the formerly coloured and Indian suburbs was assessed for the first time. Quite astonishingly, 364 residential properties had been purchased by blacks in Westenburg, the coloured suburb, and represented more than one-third (36.4%) of home-owners in this suburb. The impact of black mobility was much less on Nirvana, the Indian suburb where the 42 black home-owners accounted for only 6.7% of home-owners.

Period of increasing desegregation: 1996 By May, 1996, nearly five years after the final abolition of residential apartheid, a total of 1,407 black home-owners had settled in the 15 suburbs of Pietersburg. This was the highest percentage (12.4%) ever in the history of the city. The increase of 2.2% from the previous year can be attributed to the social tranquility that followed the peaceful amalgamation of Pietersburg and Seshego and the successful election of a fully representative local government. Another crucial factor was the new status of the city as provincial capital and the re-deployment of civil servants from the previous homeland governments.

Black home-owners were spread across the property value spectrum,

André Horn 269

but it was Westenburg in the low-value areas and Flora Park in the medium-value areas that were particularly popular. Other suburbs with more than 20% black home-owners now included Ivy Park, and Penina Park.

Period of decreasing desegregation: 1997 There was a small decrease of 1.8 % in the number of black home-owners, from 1,407 to 1,286, for the period between May, 1996 and May, 1997 (Table 11.6).

Since 1991 residential desegregation in Pietersburg has gradually gained momentum, taking the form of dispersion of black home-owners in high-income areas and their concentration in the medium-value white suburbs. Another striking feature is the movement into and concentration of black home-owners in the previously coloured suburb where they now represent nearly half of the home-owners.

Based on the numbers of black and coloured home-owners in previously white neighbourhoods in December, 1995, Kotze and Donaldson (1998) concluded that desegregation in Bloemfontein was proceeding much more slowly than in Pietersburg and showed different spatial features. In December, 1995 there were only 421 black and coloured home-owners in Bloemfontein, which represented 2.3% of all home-owners in the previously white suburbs, compared to 805 in Pietersburg representing 10.8% of all home-owners. In the case of Bloemfontein the non-white home-owners in previously white suburbs were fewer in number and mainly in the white lower-value, lower-income zone between the CBD and the townships located on the opposite side of the CBD to the more affluent white suburbs. In the case of Pietersburg, a significant number of non-white social movers mainly targeted the medium-value and middle-income zone between the CBD and the high-value areas located at the other side of the CBD from the townships and homeland town.

This can be explained by the fact that in Pietersburg the need for housing amongst non-whites in the middle and middle to high income brackets has been addressed by expanding the white suburbs in these categories, whereas in Bloemfontein the strategy has been to expand and improve the existing townships to include houses that, according to Kotze and Donaldson (1998), compare favourably with the houses in middle and high-income neighbourhoods of the previously whites-only areas.

Desegregation in Major Cities

Early trends in the process of residential desegregation in two metropolitan

270 *Studies in Segregation and Desegregation*

areas, Johannesburg and Pretoria, are described below.

For more than a century Johannesburg has been the dominant commercial centre of South Africa and is, with a cosmopolitan population of more than 3 million people, the largest city in South Africa. Included in greater Johannesburg is the largest planned black township in South Africa, Soweto, southwest of the CBD, as well as the black townships of Tembisa and Alexandra in the northeast.

Pretoria, with a population of about 1 million people is South Africa's fourth largest city. Until recently the population could be considered rather conservative and less cosmopolitan than Johannesburg. Pretoria had been the capital of the Transvaal from 1850 and the administrative capital of South Africa from 1910. It lost its provincial capital status in 1994 when Johannesburg became the capital of the new province of Gauteng ('place of gold'). For the time being, however, Pretoria remains the administrative capital of South Africa.

The study by Prinsloo & van Graan (1997), on which this assessment is based, looked into the transfer of residential properties from 1993 to 1996 in selected suburbs in each of the sub-regions of Johannesburg and Pretoria.

Johannesburg By 1993, the high-density flatland area of Hillbrow as well as some of the older inner-residential areas close to the CBD had become predominantly black residential areas, a change accompanied by a general deterioration of the social and structural quality. By contrast, the suburb of Mayfair on the inner-city fringe, no longer predominantly white but mainly Indian, had been upgraded from a below-average residential area to an above-average one. With this as their point of departure, Prinsloo & van Graan (1997) focussed on the transfer of properties in the other formerly whites-only suburbs where levels of black home-ownership hovered between 2% and 4% (Table 11.7).

The south and southwestern suburbs experienced a much higher inflow of black home-buyers than the other areas: 66.5% of all black buyers. On average, one in every five buyers in this sector was black, and in the southwestern suburbs (such as Naturena) two of every three buyers were black. That the south and southwestern suburbs proved to be most popular among black buyers should not be a surprise: these suburbs represent the cheapest, previously white-owned residential properties apart from the already desegregated inner-city areas. They also fall in the same geographical sector as Soweto. On the other hand, the high-value northwestern sector was preferred by more affluent buyers and attracted

André Horn 271

18.0 % of black buyers from 1993 to 1996. The east/northeast sector (medium-value area) attracted 10.8% of black buyers and the northern sector, where the most expensive residential properties are, attracted only 4.7% of black buyers.

Table 11.7 Transfer of residential properties in selected suburbs of Johannesburg, 1993-1996

Area	Selected Suburbs	% Change in Price (1993-1996)	Average Price (R)	Total no. of Sales	No. of Black Buyers
North	Fourways	16.8	357 256	628	12
	Morningside	2.8	366 014	794	18
	Sandhurst	7.8	530 579	41	0
Total				1463	30
Northwest	Newlands	15.6	142 148	619	24
	Fontainebleau	12.2	227 086	147	4
	Fairlands	-0.1	358 217	253	4
	Northcliff	7.7	378 846	779	18
	Bryanston	5.5	437 794	1131	64
Total				2 929	114
East/ Northeast	Bez Valley	5.0	151 023	458	33
	Kensington	5.0	221 699	1 132	28
	Cyrildene	7.0	272 087	180	1
	Norwood	12.5	324 456	323	0
	Observatory	5.8	363 466	187	5
	Houghton	1.7	599 624	287	1
Total				2 567	68
South/ Southwest	Rosetenville	1.7	147 089	563	17
	Naturena	-0.7	161 708	276	175
	Ormonde	16.8	174 161	110	13
	Kibler Park	7.9	178 191	274	64
	Southdale	-1.7	178 711	36	3
	Robertsham	4.0	201 341	285	112
	Glenanda	7.4	209 169	124	12
	Mulbarton	10.2	244 867	376	24
Total				2044	420
Total				9003	632

Source: Prinsloo & van Graan (1997).

There is a slower rate in the increase of house prices where proportionally more black buyers have moved in. However, according to

272 *Studies in Segregation and Desegregation*

Prinsloo and van Graan (1997), this trend is not directly related to the desegregation of these areas but rather to the attributes of the houses and their location.

In Johannesburg, 7.0% of all residential properties sold from 1993-1996 were transferred to blacks. Two trends can be identified: a higher proportion of sales to blacks in the price range R100,000 - R180,000 (low property-value category) and in the price range above R400,000 (high property-value category).

Pretoria In Pretoria the process of greying during the late-apartheid phase was largely absent and the few instances of desegregation that did occur were mainly foreign representatives and their relatives. The demographic transformation of the inner-city regions started in 1993. This consideration together with the transition from a predominantly white to a black state bureaucracy explains the high number of transfers of residential property to blacks in Pretoria (1,955 sales) from 1993 to 1996. During this period a total of 14,207 properties were sold in the 20 suburbs surveyed, 13% of which were sold to black buyers (Table 11.8). The delayed start of the desegregation process resulted in flats being particularly popular among black buyers. Fifteen per cent of flat units sold were to black buyers compared to 11% of detached residential units. The central lower-income flatland areas (Central, Sunnyside, Arcadia), the newer middle-income northwestern part of the metropolis (Karen Park, The Orchards, Theresa Park), some lower to middle-income suburbs in the northeastern area (Silverton, Jan Niemand Park) and some middle to high-income suburbs (Garsfontein, Waterkloof) were the most preferred zones for black purchasers. In those suburbs where average house prices were less than R100,000, up to 21% of sales were to black buyers, and in the price range R100,000 - R200,000, about 11% of all sales were to black buyers.

Based on these observations the following patterns and trends in respect of the purchase of residential property by blacks in formerly whites-only suburbs in Johannesburg and Pretoria are identified:

- influx of black buyers into central flatland areas;
- purchase of residential properties, mostly in the lower-to-medium property-value areas;
- preference for areas close to or in the same geographical sector as existing black townships and former homeland towns;
- significant influx of black buyers into some of the more affluent suburbs.

André Horn 273

Table 11.8 Transfer of residential properties in selected suburbs of Pretoria, 1993-1996

Area	Selected Suburbs	% Change in Price (1993-1996)	Average Price (R)	Total no. of Sales	No. of Black Buyers
West	Wes Park	9.7	108 326	260	14
	Proclamation Hill	4.4	133 772	103	6
	Danville	6.3	107 447	369	21
	Kwaggasrand	9.6	108 700	214	30
Total				946	71
Northwest	Karen Park	-2.7	163 721	155	47
	The Orchards	4.1	141 007	984	335
	Theresa Park	5.8	159 337	439	62
Total				1578	444
Central	Pretoria Central	2.6	83 034	2636	569
(flats)	Sunnyside	-0.2	102 566	3328	397
	Arcadia	2.2	105 732	1147	161
	Hatfield	7.6	119 688	280	6
Total				7391	1133
Northeast	Silverton	7.6	186 644	517	61
	J Niemand Park	1.3	122 978	212	22
	East Lynne	5.4	141 617	243	9
Total				972	92
Southeast	Fairie Glen	3.2	261 849	789	14
	Garsfontein	7.4	216 955	833	58
	Waterkloof	9.8	364 108	1109	135
Total				2731	207
Moot	Mayville	3.5	172 459	112	3
	Gezina	-2.2	201 360	179	3
	Capital Park	8.4	154 956	298	2
Total				589	8
TOTAL				14207	1955

Redistribution of People in Pretoria

Finally, this chapter focusses on an assessment of the redistribution of people in Pretoria from 1991 to 1996, based on an analysis of the data collated by the censuses of 1991 (South Africa, 1992b) and 1996 (South Africa, 1999). The Pretoria metropolitan area comprises approximately 200 suburbs and sub-sections. For the purpose of this assessment, these were

274 *Studies in Segregation and Desegregation*

divided into 19 districts on the basis of geographic location, housing stock and former group area status. The population of Pretoria increased by 11.8% from 830,932 in 1991 to 929,322 in 1996. In 1991 the white population represented 57.3% of the population, blacks 37.4%, coloureds 2.9% and Indians 2.4%. An absolute decrease in the white population from 476,002 in 1991 to 456,476 in 1996 means that whites represented only 49.1% of the Pretoria population in 1996. At that stage blacks represented 44.2%, coloureds 3.0% and Indians 2.7%. It should be noted that a total of 9,216 people or 1.0% of Pretoria residents in the census preferred not to indicate a racial identity.

In 1991, 94.7% of Indians resided in the Laudium township for Indians. Only 4.1% resided in white neighbourhoods, and the segregation index for Indians was 94.5. Some 89.9% of coloureds resided in the Eersterus township for coloureds, 7.0% in white neighbourhoods; the segregation index for this group was 89.8. Some 79.2% of blacks resided in the black townships of Atteridgeville and Mamelodi with almost 20% of non-whites in white neighbourhoods; the segregation index for this group was 79.1, the lowest for all the races. In comparison, the segregation index of whites was 81.8, and 99.9% resided in white neighbourhoods.

Five years later, in 1996, the percentage of Indians residing in formerly white neighbourhoods had increased from 4.1% of the Indian population to 36.5%, with a large group of Indians residing in the West sector of the city. This sector is located adjacent to the Indian suburb Laudiumand and also includes the suburb of Lotus Gardens, originally planned as an Indian suburb cum free settlement area but developed after the scrapping of the Group Areas Act and the Free Settlement Areas Act in 1991. Other concentrations of Indians were established in the Valhalla sector (11.0%), bordering the south of Laudium, and central Centurion (3.5%). As a result of the re-concentration of Indians in areas close to Laudium, the segregation index of this group remained high at 76.0 in 1996.

By 1996, the proportion of coloureds residing in former white areas had increased from 7.0% to 25.7%. One group of coloureds (5.1%) was concentrated in the East sector which includes the suburb of Nellmapius, planned in 1990/91 as a coloured area cum free settlement area but developed only after 1991. The remaining 20.6% of coloureds outside the coloured township of Eersterus had dispersed to sectors such as the Old East, Central, Valhalla, and West. The segregation index for coloureds fell from 89.8 in 1991 to 71.4 in 1996.

The proportion of blacks residing outside the black townships of Atteridgeville and Mamelodi increased from 20.8% in 1991 to 29.1% in

André Horn 275

1996. Significant numbers of blacks moved into mainly three sectors: the affluent Southeast (5.2%), the high-density areas of Central, and the Old East (including the multi-storey blocks of flats in Sunnyside and Arcadia). This resulted in a decline in the segregation index for blacks from 79.1 in 1991 to 71.0 in 1996.

The percentage of whites residing outside traditionally white neighbourhoods was 0.1 in 1991 and just over 0.1% in 1996. The segregation index for whites, nevertheless, fell from 81.8 in 1991 to 71.5 in 1996. This change in the index of segregation is, therefore, not so much the result of dispersal but rather a result of the decrease in the number and proportion of whites in the city and the inflow of non-whites into the formerly white neighbourhoods.

Finally, international research suggests that a residential mix including at least 20% of a different population group represents a desegregation level of some significance. According to the census of 1991, there was only one such area in Pretoria, the sector dubbed Kloof, which includes the older, elite suburbs of Waterkloof, Menlopark, Lynnwood and Groenkloof. This is not a true reflection since many non-whites included in the census were not actual residents but live-in servants. However, by 1996 half of the 19 sectors of the Pretoria metropolitan area accommodated a black population exceeding 20% of the residents: Central (56.3%), Valhalla (36.3%), Southeast (31.8%), Rooihuiskraal (27.0%), Old East (25.0%), West (23.0%), Kloof (22.1%), and Northwest (20.7%).

It can be concluded that significant progress towards spatial integration and desegregation occurred in Pretoria between 1991 and 1996. While the average of the indices of segregation for the four population groups decreased by 13.8 percentage points during this five-year period, the groups displayed different patterns of mobility:

- Indians tended to re-concentrate, albeit in more than one sector of the city;
- coloureds tended to disperse into lower- and medium-income areas;
- blacks re-concentrated in the lower-income flatland areas of Central, Sunnyside and Arcadia, and a significantly large number targeted the most affluent sector of the city (Southeast);
- many whites moved out of the high-density areas (particularly Central, and Sunnyside), yet in none of the 19 sectors of the city did they represent more than 90% of the population.

276 *Studies in Segregation and Desegregation*

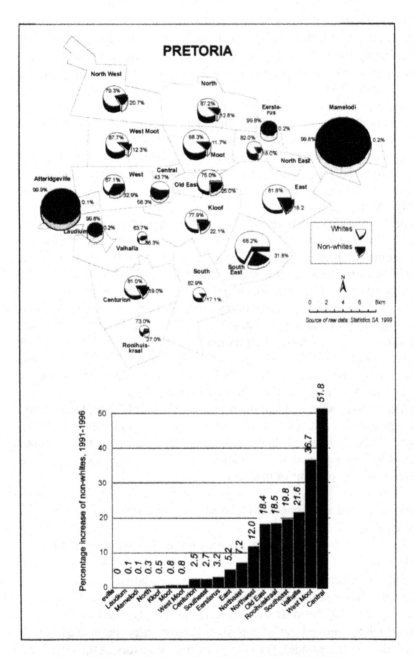

Figure 11.3 Population distribution in Pretoria, 1996

André Horn 277

Conclusion

Urban segregation levels in South African cities and towns remain high and will continue to stay that way for some time to come mainly because the black majority is still compelled to live in peripheral townships. Nevertheless, remarkable desegregation and depolarisation can be observed in at least some of the larger cities. It has emerged from this assessment that urban desegregation in South Africa is particularly influenced by the size and position of a city in the urban hierarchy, by the presence and/or absence of former homeland towns and apartheid townships and by the housing development strategy adopted by the relevant local council.

Also, differentiated mobility trends can be observed: sub-urbanisation and ex-urbanisation by whites, re-concentration in the inner-city areas and limited dispersal into formerly white suburbs by blacks, limited dispersal into predominantly white suburbs by coloureds, and re-concentration in areas of close proximity by Indians. The way in which these trends are influencing segregation levels suggests that, on a conceptual level, one can distinguish between active segregation (segregation, generation, migration and re-concentration), passive segregation as a result of the inability or unwillingness to move out of segregated concentrations, active desegregation resulting from migration and dispersed resettlement and passive desegregation, i.e. the decrease of segregation levels as a result of the inflow of others and decreasing proportional representation.

It is further evident from the outcomes of the above mentioned mobility trends that a clear distinction between social integration, spatial integration and desegregation should be maintained. For example, the demographic succession presently taking place in city centres does not represent desegregation. It represents re-segregation; spatial integration or infilling is also re-segregation rather than desegregation; and mixed densification may increase the level of desegregation but not necessarily facilitate social integration. Spontaneous desegregation resulting from unforced population dispersal and mixing is probably the only process that will ensure both desegregation and social integration of a lasting nature. Spontaneous desegregation and social integration are, however, largely obstructed by continued polarisations of income and class. Therefore, in order to achieve social integration the processes of spatial integration and desegregation must be accompanied by the depolarisation of income and class in any given society.

At present there are different processes at work in South Africa's cities. The first is demographic transformation and re-concentration in city

278 *Studies in Segregation and Desegregation*

centres and other inner-city neighbourhoods. (This is succession, not desegregation.) The second process is spatial integration by way of infilling, creating new concentrations of similar people.(This is segregation, not desegregation.) The third is the destruction of spatial expressions of class through mixed densification. (This may result in desegregation, not integration.) The fourth process is unforced desegregation through individual ability and individual decision-making. Spontaneous desegregation remains the only meaningful way of merging people who originally perceived each other as different. Such a spontaneous process of desegregation, that could very well be the best catalyst for social integration in South Africa, will only be achieved through the broad scale redistribution of power and wealth and the development of class and income categories in the non-white communities.

The complexity of mobility trends and emerging segregation and desegregation patterns in a multicultural society also raises some methodological questions. Is it appropriate to continue to measure desegregation over time as the mere difference in segregation levels in time? Do mono-variate measures, such as the index of segregation, and duo-variate measures, such as the index of dissimilarity, still meet the requirements for assessing segregation and desegregation in a multicultural context featuring differentiated mobility trends and settlement and resettlement patterns? After so many years of using these traditional methods to measure segregation, has the time arrive to devise a multivariate, generally accepted and globally applicable measure for segregation and desegregation levels?

In the specific case of South Africa there are also many questions to be answered. At what stage may a 'post-apartheid' society be regarded as integrated? For how long will desegregation remain a one direction process? Will the development of different income categories and classes amongst non-whites have an impact on the urban landscape? Will spatial integration facilitate a spirit of sameness or entrench the mentality of difference?

While we search for answers to these and other relevant questions, the phenomenon of urban segregation and the process of desegregation in South Africa will undoubtedly remain of wide international interest and concern.

André Horn 279

References

Anderson, R. (1998), ' Socio-Spatial Dynamics: Ethnic Divisions of Mobility and Housing in Post-Palme Sweden', *Urban Studies*, vol. 35, pp. 397-428.

Atkinson. D. (1991), 'One-City Initiatives', in M. Swilling, R. Humphries, & K. Shubane (eds) *Apartheid City in Transition*, Cape Town: Oxford University Press, pp. 271-289.

Bähr, J. & Jürgens, U. (1990), 'Auflösung der Apartheid-Stadt?', *Erdkunde*, vol. 44, pp. 297-312.

Bähr, J. & Jürgens, U. (1993), 'Albert Park, Durban – Mixed-Race Residential Areas during the Phase of Reformed Apartheid', *Geographica Polonica*, vol. 61, pp. 450-470.

Bähr, J. & Jürgens, U. (1996), 'Ethnic Change in Late-Apartheid South African Cities', in C.C. Roseman, H.D. Laux, & G. Thieme (eds), *EthniCity: Geographical Perspectives on Ethnic Change in Modern Cities*, Rowman & Littlefield, London, pp. 223-249.

Bähr, J., Jürgens, U. & Bock, S. (1998), 'Auflösung der Segregation in der Post-Apartheid-Stadt?', Diskutiert anhand Kleinräumiger Wohnungsmarktanalysen im Gro∫raum Johannesburg, *Petermanns Geographische Mitteilungen*, vol. 142, pp. 3-18.

Beavon, K.S.O. (1992a), 'The Post-Apartheid City: Hopes, Possibilities, and Harsh Realities', in D.M. Smith (ed), *The Apartheid City and Beyond: Urbanization and Social Change in South Africa*, Routledge, London, pp. 231-242.

Beavon, K.S.O. (1998), 'Johannesburg, 112 Years of Division: From Segregation to Post-Apartheid Community or Neo-Apartheid City', Paper presented at International Workshop on Divided Cities, February 1998, International Centre for Advanced Studies, New York.

Beeld, A. (1989), 'Tien Vasgetrek by Busse', 31 August, p. 9.

Bollens, S.A. (1998), 'Urban Planning amidst Ethnic Conflict: Jerusalem and Johannesburg', *Urban Studies*, vol. 35, pp. 729-750.

Carter, W.H., Schill, M.H. & Wachter, S.M. (1998), 'Polarisation, Public Housing and Racial Minorities in US Cities', *Urban Studies*, vol. 35, pp. 1889-1911.

Champion, A.G. (1994), 'International Migration and Demographic Change in the Developed World', *Urban Studies*, vol. 31, pp. 653-677.

Christopher, A.J. (1984), *South Africa: The Impact of Past Geographies*, Juta & Co., Cape Town.

Christopher, A.J. (1989), 'Spatial Variations in the Application of Residential Segregation in South African Cities', *Geoforum*, vol. 20, pp. 253-267.

Christopher, A.J. (1990), 'Apartheid and Urban Segregation Levels in South Africa', *Urban Studies*, vol. 27, pp. 421-440.

Christopher, A.J. (1991a), 'Before Group Areas: Urban Segregation in South Africa in 1951', *South African Geographer*, vol. 18, pp. 85-96.

Christopher, A.J. (1991b), 'Changing Patterns of Group-Area Proclamations in South Africa, 1950-1989', *Political Geography Quarterly*, vol. 10, pp. 240-253.

Christopher A.J. (1992), 'The Final Phase of Urban Apartheid Zoning in South Africa, 1990/1', *South African Geographical Journal*, vol. 74, pp. 29-34.

Christopher, A.J. (2000), 'Desegregation in South African Cities', Paper presented at the Human Sciences Research Council Workshop on South African Cities in Transition, January, 2000, HSRC, Pretoria.

Cilliers, S.P. (1990), 'New Neighbours: The Namibian Experience', in A. Bersnstein, & J. McCarthy (eds), *Opening the Cities: Comparative Perspectives on Desegregation*, The Urban Foundation/Indicator Project South Africa, Johannesburg, pp. 23-30.

Cloete, F. (1991), 'Greying and Free Settlement', in M. Swilling, R. Humphries, & K.

280 *Studies in Segregation and Desegregation*

Shubane (eds), *Apartheid City in Transition*, Oxford University Press, Cape Town, 91-107.

Crankshaw, O. & Parnell, S. (2000), 'Race, Inequality and Urbanisation in the Johannesburg Region, 1946-1996', Paper presented at the Human Sciences Research Council Workshop on South African Cities in Transition, January 2000. HSRC, Pretoria.

Crankshaw, O. & White, C. (1992), 'Results of the Johannesburg Inner City Survey', *Report C/PERS 451*, Human Sciences Research Council, Johannesburg.

Cronje, G., Nicol, W. & Groenewald, E.P. (1947), 'Regverdige Rasse Apartheid', Christen Studente Vereniging Boekwinkel, Stellenbosch.

Cullinan, K. (1998), 'Zebra Nation?', *Siyaya*, vol. 2, pp. 7-11.

Daley, P.O. (1998), 'Black Blacks in Great Britain: Spatial Concentration and Segregation', *Urban Studies*, vol. 35, pp. 1703-1724.

Dauskardt, R. (1993), 'Reconstructing South African Cities: Contemporary Strategies and Processes in the Urban Core', *GeoJournal, vol.* 30, pp. 9-20.

Davenport, R. (1991), 'Historical Background of the Apartheid City to 1948', in M. Swilling, R. Humphries & K. Shubane, *Apartheid City in Transition*, Oxford University Press, Oxford, pp. 1-18.

Davies, R.J. (1981), 'The Spatial Transformation of the South African City', *GeoJournal*, Supplementary Issue, vol. 2, pp. 59-72.

Davies, R.J. (1986), 'When! – Reform and Change in the South African City', *South African Geographical Journal*, vol. 68, pp. 3-17.

Davies, R.J. (1992), 'Lessons from the Harare, Zimbabwe, Experience', in D.M. Smith (ed), *The Apartheid City and Beyond: Urbanization and Social Change in South Africa*, Routledge, London, 303-313.

Davies, W.J. (1971), 'Patterns of Non-White Population Distribution in Port Elizabeth with Special Reference to the Application of the Group Areas Act', Series B, Special Publication 1, Institute of Planning Research, University of Port Elizabeth, Port Elizabeth.

De Coning, C., Fick, J & Olivier, N. (1986), *Residential Settlement Patterns: A Pilot Study of Socio-Political Perceptions in Grey Areas of Johannesburg*, Rand Afrikaans University, Johannesburg.

Deurloo, M.C. & Musterd, S. (1998), 'Ethnic Clusters in Amsterdam, 1994-96: A Micro-Area Analysis', *Urban Studies*, vol. 35, pp. 385-396.

Dewar, D. & Uytenbogaardt, R. (1991), 'South African Cities: A Manifesto for Change', University of Cape Town, Cape Town.

Donaldson, S.E. (1996), 'Urban Black Home Ownership Patterns in the Northern Province, South Africa', in R.J. Davies (ed), *Contemporary City Structuring: International Geographical Insights*, Federal Business Communications, Cape Town, pp. 189-199.

Donaldson, S.E. (1999), 'Residential Desegregation and the Property Market in Pietersburg, 1992-1997', Unpublished paper, Vista University, Pretoria.

Donaldson, S.E. & Kotze, N.J. (1994), 'Transformation in the South African Apartheid City – Residential Desegregation in Pietersburg: A Case Study', in G.O. Braun (ed), *Managing and Marketing of Urban Development and Urban Life*, Dietrich Reimer Verlag, Berlin, 267-277.

Donaldson, S.E. & van der Merwe, I.J. (1999), 'Urban Transformation and Social Change in Pietersburg during Transition', *Society in Transition*, vol. 30, pp. 69-83.

Dunn, K.M. (1998), 'Rethinking Ethnic Concentration: The Case of Cabramatta, Sydney', *Urban Studies*, vol. 35, pp. 503-527.

Elder, G. (1990), 'The Grey Dawn of South African Racial Residential Integration',

André Horn 281

GeoJournal, vol. 22, pp. 261-266.

Fair, T.J.D. & Schmidt, C.F. (1974), 'Contained Urbanization: A Case Study', *South African Geographical Journal*, vol. 56, pp. 155-166.

Fick, J. & de Coning, C. (1988), 'Mixed Areas: The US Experience', *South African Foundation Review*, vol. 14, pp. 2-3.

Fick, J., de Coning, C. & Olivier, N. (1988), 'Ethnicity and Residential Patterning in a Divided Society: A Case Study of Mayfair in Johannesburg', Rand Afrikaans University, Johannesburg.

Fortuijn, J.D., Musterd, S. & Ostendorf, W. (1998), 'International Migration and Ethnic Segregation: Impacts on Urban Areas – Introduction', *Urban Studies*, vol. 35, pp. 367-370.

Friedrichs, J. (1998), 'Ethnic Segregation in Cologne, Germany, 1984-94', *Urban Studies*, vol. 35, pp. 1745-1763.

Galster, G. (1990), 'White Flight from Racially Integrated Neighbourhoods in the 1970s: The Cleveland Experience', *Urban Studies*, vol. 27, pp. 385-399.

Garside, J. (1993), 'Inner City Gentrification in South Africa: The Case of Woodstock, Cape Town', *GeoJournal*, vol. 30, pp. 29-35.

Goering, J., Kamely, A., & Richardson, T. (1997), 'Recent Research on Racial Segregation and Poverty Concentration in Public Housing in the United States', *Urban Affairs Review*, vol. 35, pp. 723-745.

Hart, G. (1989), 'On Grey Areas', *South African Geographical Journal*, vol. 71, pp. 81-88.

Hart, T. (1976), 'Patterns of Black Residence in the White Residential Areas of Johannesburg', *South African Geographical Journal*, vol. 58, pp. 141-150.

Horn, A.C., Hattingh, P.S. & Smit, C.F. (1991), 'Points of View of the Residents of the Pretoria Metropolitan Area on the Opening of the Amenities and Deracializing of the City (October 1990)', University of Pretoria, Pretoria.

Jürgens, U. (1993), 'Mixed-Race Residential Areas in South African Cities – Urban Geographical Developments in the Late and Post-Apartheid Phases', *GeoJournal*, vol. 30, pp. 309-316.

Kesteloot, C. & Cortie, C. (1998), 'Housing Turks and Moroccans in Brussels and Amsterdam: The Difference between Private and Public Markets', *Urban Studies*, vol. 35, pp. 1835-1853.

Kemper, F. (1998), 'Restructuring of Housing and Ethnic Segregation: Recent Developments in Berlin', *Urban Studies*, vol. 35, pp. 1765-1789.

Kotze, N.J. & Donaldson, S.E. (1996), 'Desegregation in Pietersburg after the Repeal of the Group Areas Act', *Development Southern Africa*, vol. 13, pp. 119-127.

Kotze, N.J. & Donaldson, S.E. (1998), 'Residential Desegregation in Two South African Cities: A Comparative Study of Bloemfontein and Pietersburg', *Urban Studies*, vol. 35, pp. 467-477.

Kuper, L., Watts, H. & Davies, P.J. (1958), *Durban: A Study in Racial Ecology*, Jonathan, Cape Town.

Lemon, A. (1991), 'The Apartheid City', in A. Lemon, (ed), *Homes Apart: South Africa's Segregated Cities*, Paul Chapman, London, pp. 1-25.

Lohnert, B., Oldfiels S. & Parnell S. (1998), 'Post-Apartheid Social Polarisations: The Creation of Sub-Urban Identities in Cape Town', *South African Geographical Journal*, vol. 80, pp. 86-92.

Mabin, A. (1992), 'Comprehensive Segregation: The Origins of the Group Areas Act and Its Planning Apparatuses', *Journal of Southern African Studies*, vol. 18, pp. 405-429.

Mabin, A. & Smit, D. (1997), 'Reconstructing South Africa's cities? The Making of Urban Planning

282 *Studies in Segregation and Desegregation*

1900-2000', *Planning Perspectives*, vol. 12, pp. 193-223.

Maharaj, B. & Mpungose, J. (1994), 'The Erosion of Residential Segregation in South Africa: The Greying of Albert Park in Durban', *Geoforum*, vol. 25, pp. 19-32.

Marcuse, P. (1997), 'The Enclave, the Citadel, and the Ghetto: What Has Changed in the Post-Fordist U.S. City', *Urban Affairs Review*, vol. 33, pp. 228-264.

McCarthy, J.J. (1990), 'The Divided City: Group Areas and Racial Segregation', in A. Bernstein, & J.J. McCarthy, *Opening The Cities*, An Indicator SA Issue Focus, The Urban Foundation, Johannesburg, pp. 7-14.

Morris, A. (1997), 'Physical Decline in an Inner-City Neighbourhood: A Case Study of Hillbrow, Johannesburg', *Urban Forum*, vol. 8, pp. 153-175.

Murdie, R.A. & Borgegård, L. (1998), 'Immigration, Spatial Segregation and Housing Segmentation of Immigrants in Metropolitan Stockholm, 1960-95', *Urban Studies*, vol. 35, pp. 1869-1888.

Musterd, S. & de Winter, M. (1998), 'Conditions for Spatial Segregation: Some European Perspectives', *International Journal for Urban and Regional Research*, vol. 22, pp. 665-673.

Myburgh, D.W. (1996), 'The Transformation of Social Space in Tygerberg, Cape Town', in R.J Davies (ed), *Contemporary City Structuring: International Geographical Insights*, Federal Business Communications, Cape Town, 200-209.

Oelofse, C. (1996), 'The Integration of Three Disparate Communities: The Myths and Realities Facing Hout Bay, Cape Town', in R.J. Davies (ed), *Contemporary City Structuring: International Geographical Insights*, Federal Business Communications, Cape Town, pp. 275-287.

Ownhouse, S.J. & Nel, E.L. (1993), 'The 'Greying' of Central: A Case-Study of Racial Residential Desegregation in Port Elizabeth', *Urban Forum*, vol. 4, pp. 81-92.

Parnell, S. & Mabin, A. (1995), 'Rethinking Urban South Africa', *Journal of Southern African Studies*, vol. 21, pp. 39-61.

Petsimeris, P. (1998), 'Urban Decline and the New Social and Ethnic Divisions in the Core Cities of the Italian Industrial Triangle', *Urban Studies*, vol. 35, pp. 449-465.

Phillips, D. (1998), 'Black Minority Ethnic Concentration, Segregation and Dispersal in Britain', *Urban Studies*, vol. 35, pp. 1681-1702.

Pickard-Cambridge, C. (1988), *The Greying of Johannesburg*, South African Institute of Race Relations, Johannesburg.

Pirie, G. (1984), 'Race Zoning in South Africa: Board, Court, Parliament, Public', *Political Geography Quarterly*, vol. 3, pp. 207-221.

Pretoria News (1998), 'Finding a Way beyond the Outrages of Racism', 6 March, p. 6.

Pretoria News (1999a), 'Reality Check: Take a Look with Us into the Crystal Ball', 23 April, p. 6.

Pretoria News (1999b), 'Reality Check: Reality of Reconciliation in South Africa', 22 April, p. 6.

Prinsloo, D. (1998), 'Johannesburg CBD: Has a Turning Point Been Reached?', *Urban Development Studies Newsletter*, vol 2(4), pp. 2-4.

Prinsloo, D. (1999), 'Has the Retail Market Reached Saturation?', *Urban Development Studies Newsletter (New Series)*, vol. 10, pp. 1-3.

Prinsloo, D. & van Graan, B. (1997), 'Black Advancement into Former 'Whites Only' Suburbs', *Urban Development Studies Newsletter*, vol. 2(1), pp. 1-4.

Rapport (1986), 'Groter Stem Teen Groepsgebiede/Mening Swaai vir Gemengde Skole', 18 May, p. 6.

Retief, A. & Kelbrick, E. (1990), *Group Areas as a Form of Human Territorial Behaviour*,

André Horn 283

Report P-115, Human Sciences Research Council, Pretoria.

Rhein, C. (1998), 'Globalisation, Social Change and Minorities in Metropolitan Paris: The Emergence of New Class Patterns', *Urban Studies*, vol. 35, pp. 429-447.

Rhoodie, N.J. & Le Roux, W.L. Du P. (1983), *A Sample Survey of the Attitudes of White Residents in Randburg towards the Opening of Public/Municipal Amenties to All Races*, Report S-101, Human Sciences Research Council, Pretoria.

Robinson, J. (1997), 'The Geopolitics of South African Cities: States, Citizens, Territory', *Political Geography*, vol. 16, pp. 365-386.

Rogerson C.M. (1989), 'Urban Reform in South Africa: Policy and Practice towards Hawkers', *African Urban Quarterly*, vol. 4, pp. 293-302.

Rule, S.P. (1986), 'Suburban Demographic Change in Johannesburg: The Case of Bertrams', in R.J. Davies (ed), *Contemporary City Structuring: International Geographical Insights*, Federal Business Communications, Cape Town, pp. 210-221.

Rule, S.P. (1989), 'The Emergence of a Racially Mixed Residential Suburb in Johannesburg: Demise of the Apartheid City?', *The Geographical Journal*, vol. 155, pp. 196-203.

Saff, G. (1995), 'Residential Segregation in Postapartheid South Africa: What Can Be Learned from the United States Experience', *Urban Affairs Review*, vol. 30, pp. 782-788.

Saff, G. (1996), 'Claiming a Space in a Changing South Africa: The 'Squatters' of Marconi Beam, Cape Town', *Annals of the Association of American Geography*, vol. 86, pp. 235-255.

Schlemmer, L. & Stack, S.L. (1990a), *Black, White and Shades of Grey: A Study of Responses to Residential Segregation in the Pretoria-Witwatersrand Region*, Centre for Policy Studies, Johannesburg.

Schlemmer & Stack (1990b), 'The Illusive Ideal: International Experiences of Desegregation', in A. Bernstein, & J. Mccarthy (eds), *Opening the Cities: Comparative Perspectives on Desegregation*, The Urban Foundation/Indicator Project South Africa, Johannesburg, pp. 15-22.

Simon, D. (1989), 'Crisis and Change in South Africa: Implications for the Apartheid city', *Transactions of the Institute of British Geographers*, vol. 14, pp. 189-206.

South Africa (1905), *Report of the South African Native Affairs Commission*. Government Printer, Pretoria.

South Africa (1992a), *Presidents Council: Report of the Committee for Economic Affairs on a Revised Urbanisation Strategy for South Africa*, Government Printer, Cape Town.

South Africa (1992b), 'Population Census 1991. Selected Statistical Region Pretoria/Wonderboom/Soshanguve', *Report No. 03-01-19* (1991), Central Statistical Service, Pretoria.

South Africa (1998), *The White Paper on Local Government*, Government Printer, Cape Town.

South Africa (1999), 'Population Census 1996. Selected Statistical Region Pretoria/Wonderboom', *Digital Data* (released October 1999). Statistics South Africa, Pretoria.

Sparks, A. (1990), *The Mind of South Africa*, Heinemann, London.

Swilling, M., Cobbett, W. & Hunter, R. (1991), 'Finance, Electricity Costs, and the Rent Boycott', in M. Swilling, R. Humphries, & K. Shubane (eds), *Apartheid City in Transition*, Oxford University Press, Cape Town, pp. 174-196.

Urban Foundation (1990), 'Policy Overview: The Urban Challenge', *Urban Debate 2010: Policies for a New Urban Future*, No. 2, The Urban Foundation, Johannesburg.

Van den Berghe, P. (1965), *South Africa: A Study in Conflict*, Wesleyan University Press,

284 *Studies in Segregation and Desegregation*

Middletown.

Van Kempen, R. & Van Weesep, J. (1998), 'Ethnic Residential Patterns in Dutch Cities: Backgrounds, Shifts and Consequences', *Urban Studies*, vol. 35, pp. 1813-1833.

Van Kempen, R. & Özüekren, A.S. (1998), 'Ethnic Segregation in Cities. New Forms and Explanations in a Dynamic World', *Urban Studies*, vol. 35, pp. 1631-1656.

White, P. (1998), 'The Settlement Patterns of Developed World Migrants in London', *Urban Studies*, vol. 35, pp. 1725-1744.

12 Beijing's Socio-Spatial Structure in Transition

GU CHAOLIN AND CHRISTIAN KESTELOOT[1]

Introduction

International experiences in the 20th century show that the economic modernisation of developing countries is usually accompanied by rapid urbanisation. It is also a popular belief that socio-spatial disparities within socialist cities are lower than in their pre-socialist period as well as in cities in market economies (French and Hamilton, 1979). In China, a new stage of urban development has been reached since the implementation of economic reforms in 1978. Both rapid urbanisation and departure from a socialist urban model have generated new forms of socio-spatial differentiation. Economic reforms, boiling down to the introduction of market mechanisms in the economic system, have brought a large numbers of migrants from the countryside to the cities. At the same time, the reforms have generated a new social class of rich businessmen and well-paid managers of joint ventures and foreign companies. The former were particularly initiated by the rural reforms, the latter more by the urban reforms and the Open Door Policy. Thus, at both ends of the urban social spectrum new groups have increased social disparities. The purpose of this paper is to disentangle the complex interrelations between the economic and political transformations[2] brought about by the reforms and the

---

[1] This paper results from a fellowship form the Research Council of the Kuleuven and from the Chinese State Natural Sciences Fund research project '*Concentration and Diffusion of Economic Activities and Population in China's Urban Aggregated Regions*', 1994-96, CSNSF Grant E49331010. It also benefited from the FWO-Vlaanderen and British Council funded Academic cooperation with Dr. Terry Cannon, University of Greenwich.

[2] In a socialist planned economy, politics and economics are two faces of the same coin. Whereas there is no such thing as economic democracy in the capitalist world, in the socialist system economic decisions are taken in the political realm and the problems of economic democracy boil down to how much democracy there is in politics. Even in present-day China, with the introduction of market mechanisms, most economic

286 *Studies in Segregation and Desegregation*

changing urban social structure. Furthermore the paper explores how much this translates into a new spatial structure of the city through specific segregation processes.

In the case of Beijing, the pace and the extent of these changes have been particularly impressive. In the first part we will discuss the two layers of the city's socio-spatial organisation that make up the pre-reform structure of the city, namely traditional Chinese urbanism and socialist urban development. In the second part, the basics of the economic reforms are discussed, in order to clarify the social processes that generate the widening of the urban social structure. In the third part, the new functional structure and socio-economic composition of the population in Beijing, created by the reforms are analysed. Special attention will be paid to the new lower end of the social ladder constituted by the rural migrants and labelled the floating population. Finally we will explore how these economic and social changes translate into the socio-spatial structure of the city.

The Pre-1984 Heritage: Traditional and Socialist Elements in the Socio-Spatial Structure of Beijing

Usually, research on the traditional Chinese city emphasise its administrative function and its strong hierarchical and symbolic arrangements (e.g. Soothill, 1951; Chang, 1977; Skinner, 1977 and Hou, 1986a and b). Recent research attempts to reveal the socialist Chinese traits of the city and the shift towards a new urbanisation dynamic driven by the economic reforms (Sit, 1995 and Gaubatz, 1995). The pre-reform features of Beijing, somewhat different from other Chinese cities, due to its capital functions, can be divided into pre-socialist elements, on the one hand, and to the socialist urbanisation logic, on the other hand.

The Traditional Socio-Spatial Structure of Beijing

China's traditional urban socio-spatial structure is believed to follow the principle of the 'ideal' layout described in the book of Artificers (*Kao*

---

decision makers are in fact local political leaders of the Communist Party, the reason why something like a 'socialist' market economy could endure for a while, since these leaders found the legitimacy of their economic power in their political position (see Cannon, 2000).

Gong Ji) that was written about 2500 years ago (Hou, 1986a, 1986b). This norm defined urban space as a square, enclosed by a city wall and with a hierarchical internal arrangement. Within the city there were to be nine longitudinal and nine latitudinal thoroughfares; the centre was the palace, with the administrative centre in the front; the main market and commercial centre at the back; the memorial park of the emperor's ancestors on the left; the worship site of the gods of soil and grain on the right; and the residential area around the centre. The old Beijing city was built according to this rule and became the capital of China for the first time under the name *Da du* during the *Yuan* Dynasty (1271-1368 AD). The residential quarters were divided into 50 wards around the palace.

The social structure of the population was reflected in the spatial arrangements. The emperor's palace formed the Forbidden City, and was separated from the rest by a high wall, with only four gates linking it to the rest of the imperial city, which contained public buildings, temples, large lakes with their adjacent parks and some rich residential areas (*hutong and siheyuan*).[3] The rest of the urban population lived outside the city until the building of the outer city during the Qing Dynasty (1644-1911). The ruling Manchu conquerors evacuated all the *Han* Chinese from the inner city and moved them into the outer city where merchants and traders were confined. The outer city became a kind of 'ghetto' with poor residential areas and crowded commercial streets. As a result Beijing exhibited a north-south cleavage, with the imperial city in the north and the outer city in the south. At the founding of the People's Republic of China in 1949, Beijing still displayed the same socio-spatial structure, which was more than seven centuries old. Throughout history, the city center had remained the place of power, but under socialist rule, it was reinterpreted symbolically with the creation of the Tian'anmen square. Also, the north-south division which had persisted through history has been reproduced by the present processes of socio-spatial structuring.[4]

---

[3] The *hutong* is the traditional Beijing urban neighbourhood unit that is composed of several *siheyuan*, which are typical houses, built around a courtyard and enclosed by an external wall.

[4] Another pre-socialist layer of socio-spatial organisation of the city produced by the intrusion of western civilisation and urban culture after the first Opium War (1839-42) and the flow of foreign persons, goods and capital. But frequent conflicts, the Japanese occupation (1936-45) and the civil war hindered the processes of urban transformation. As a consequence, Beijing experienced only two relatively unimportant changes until the liberation in 1949: (1) the appearance of the foreign quarters to the east of *Tian'anmen* that accommodated the foreign embassies, banks,

288 *Studies in Segregation and Desegregation*

The Socialist Legacy

When China embarked on a socialist planned economic system, the land market and the housing market were dismantled and their impact on the socio-spatial structuring of the city was removed. They were replaced by a planned economy which determined the allocation of the labour force to the different production sectors and production units. This required the distribution of the population to correspond with the spatial structure of the production system. At the same time, this control over the population distribution allowed the planners to know where consumer goods were to be delivered and in what quantity. It is, in other words, a necessary tool for the allocation of the labour force and the distribution of consumer goods in the absence of market mechanisms (Kesteloot, 1992). This territorial control system was implemented in China through the employment system, assigning the active population to specific working units or *danwei*, the resident registration system (*hukou*) and the grain rationing system (*gongxiaoliang*). The components of this territorial control system were most important in adapting urbanisation to industrial progress. The rural communities, bound to their land since it yielded most of their resources, were simply unable to migrate to the cities because of the grain rationing system (Chan, 1994). Thus, under socialism, Chinese society had a dual character, separating urban and rural life.[5] Living in the city did not only imply access to resources through the rationing system but also access to collective goods and services provided by the State, which remained absent in the countryside. Most important, were housing, education and health services.

The socialist aim of attaining high economic development and welfare for all through a planned economic system was based on a forced speeding-up of industrialisation. Consequently, cities had to be transformed from 'consumer cities' (i.e. living on agricultural surplus) into 'producer cities' (i.e. becoming the spearheads of economic development - through expanding heavy industry). Due to the low level of industrial development of the country, the necessary investments could only be collected by 'price

---

offices, clubs, hotels and military garrisons; (2) and the construction of some churches, schools and hospitals in the city (Sit, 1995).

[5] Which is not to say that there weren't any bridges between these two worlds, the resolution of the contradictions between city and countryside, agriculture and industry, intellectuals and handworkers being a main theme of Maoism. Movements between the two worlds were, as a matter of fact, most important during the ideological periods of the Maoist era (see further).

Gu Chaolin and Christian Kesteloot 289

scissors', to the detriment of the agricultural against the industrial products and through a severe restriction of consumer, limiting the urban labour cost. 'Producing more and consuming less' was a valid slogan during nearly the whole Mao period. Investments in collective consumer goods such as urban housing,[6] schools, hospitals, roads, public facilities and seweage systems were kept low in order to favour industrialisation. Thus, in Beijing, the share of fixed capital investment in collective consumer goods declined from the inception of the planned economy from 51% (in 1952) to a minimum of 16% in 1975, of which only 6% was for housing (compared to 21% in 1952). As a result, Beijing like other Chinese cities became a production base of energy, raw materials, intermediate products and means of production. The industrial base of the city was laid during the periods covered by the first two Five-Year Plans (1953-65).[7] Later, electronics, textile, machinery and construction materials became the main industries.

Meeting the demands of such an industrialisation process, the rate of urban growth was strictly controlled by the planning regulations in order to match the needs of labour power in the urban industries. Two main channels existed for people to move to Beijing. The first one was to be assigned as a national cadre (mostly graduates, *Diao Gan*). The other was to become a permanent urban resident by living in the suburbs and shifting from the agricultural population into the non-agricultural population (*Nong zhuan Fei*). In-migration was strictly limited and checked every year by the Public Security Bureaus[8] and other administrative institutions at various levels. In the first ten years after the revolution, the urban economy was rapidly recovered and quite a large number of the rural populations moved into cities. However, two 'anti-urbanisation' campaigns occurred in the 1960s, resulting in out-migration (Sit, 1995, p. 186). The first one resulted from a large grain shortage after the Great Leap Forward and sent urban workers and cadres to do manual labour in rural areas in the early 1960s.

---

[6] Typically, housing is considered as a part of collective consumption in socialist China since it is provided by the *danwei* (the work unit to be compared with the firm in the capitalist world) and includes a lot of common facilities. Moreover the rent paid by the households is very low compared to the real costs, which are covered by the *danwei*.

[7] The second Five Year Plan was not executed but replaced by the dramatic Great Leap Forward (1958-1961), followed by a period of recovery (1962-1965). (For a short overview of the periods of development in the communist era, see Cannon & Jenkins, 1990.)

[8] The PSB are the neighbourhood police stations, usually staffed with local people and working in close connection with the neighbourhood committees.

290 *Studies in Segregation and Desegregation*

The second campaign was ideologically inspired and drove urban youths 'up to the mountains and down to the countryside' during the Cultural Revolution (1966-1976) in order to let them learn from the rural masses, from agriculture and handwork. The planned number of rural-urban migrants settling in the city was usually kept under 2% a year during the whole socialist period (Xie and Yu, 1992).

Beijing was the preferred place of residence because of a higher grain ration and the higher quality of collective consumption, linked to the management functions of the city. In a planned socialist economy, the gathering of information about the economy, on the one hand, and the implementation of the planning decisions, on the other hand, are carried out through a hierarchical urban system. Being at the top of the hierarchy, Beijing not only had greater administrative power to channel investments in its favour (nearly half of the fixed capital investment of Beijing came from the central government, while Shanghai, Jiangsu, Liaoning and Tianjin depended for nearly 80% on local government revenues),[9] it also benefited from a 'demonstration effect', namely that innovation in industries, housing and infrastructure were first tried out in Beijing by the various ministries of the central government, making it the relatively fastest growing city in China.

In search of an urban planning logic, the Chinese economic management system plagiarised the Soviet one, and thus, the socio-spatial structuring of Beijing was deeply stamped by the Soviet town planning model. The urban model implies rather monotonous building forms, corresponding to a minimisation of housing costs through economies in scale as well as intensive construction productivity. This uniformity also helped to maintain low levels of social segregation. (Considering the small range of socio-economic positions, significant differences in housing quality would have been a fundamental dimension of segregation.) The pressure on the large cities exerted by economic growth (claiming more space and more transportation and generating congestion and environmental stress) was relieved by the creation of satellite towns around the central city in a metropolitan region, while the urban open space was conceived as a green belt. These planning elements influenced the socio-spatial dynamic of Beijing until the mid 1980s.

The Soviet example was also followed in reshaping the city centre as the symbol of socialist power. *Tian'anmen* Square was enlarged and surrounded by official buildings. *Changan* Street was created as the main

---

[9] Personal communication by concerned municipal and province governors.

axis in the city, its east-west orientation contrasting intentionally with the old imperial north-south axis. However, the old road system, most imperial or noble residences with low density and gardens of the *Ming* and *Qing* dynasties were preserved. In general, the old inner city kept its traditional social and spatial features. However, the low level of investment in housing, on the one hand, and growing problems of liaison between places of residence and work, on the other hand, generated a housing shortage problem. Therefore, during the Cultural Revolution the units were permitted to build housing on available land within the city. In practice, many one-storey dwellings were built in the *siheyuan* courtyards. Thus, more than two-thirds of the total floor space in the old city was newly built. Many *siheyuan* lost their convenient traditional arrangement and became overcrowded.

In the urban fringe, a rapid spatial sprawl started in 1953. The urban built-up area increased from 109 km² in 1949 to 340 km² in 1978. In a first phase between 1953-57, new industries were concentrated at the fringe of the old city. But in 1958, in the wake of the Great Leap Forward, a master plan for Beijing was devised to ascertain that industrial development conformed to socialist ideology. Ten new industrial-residential clusters[10] were established outside the city, nowadays the suburbs.[11] They were conceived under the *danwei* principle, implying the unity of work and living but were also aimed at achieving a urban-rural unity by including rural land and bringing workers and peasants together. In addition, open space was kept between the clusters.[12] The spatial expansion of Beijing would follow this cluster pattern until the end of 1970s.

As a result, Beijing gradually displayed a dual spatial structure with a fairly well corresponding distribution of two population groups. The

---

[10] The clusters form a circle around the city (starting from north to east: Beiyuan, Jiuxianqiao, Dongba, Dingfuzhuang, Fatou, Nanyuan, Fengtai, Shijinshan, Xiyuan, Qinhe). Industrialisation also occurred in the former small towns of Shahe (northwest) and Huangchun and Liangxiang (southwest).

[11] Beijing Municipality is divided into the old city, corresponding to the pre-1949 city limits, the inner suburbs with four districts and the outer suburbs with two suburban counties and eight rural counties. Our study is confined to the city and the inner suburbs. Within this area we also consider the urban fringe, as the limit between the continuous and densely built area created in the socialist era and the open suburban area (see Figure 12.1).

[12] Stretches of fertile vegetable field, high-yield plots, orchards, forests, and clusters of wells for water resources were retained, where flowers and grass were grown, water ponds opened and trees planted on a large scale in order to realise the idea of 'the whole country becoming a garden', and 'the city becoming a garden'.

292 *Studies in Segregation and Desegregation*

traditional autochthonous population lived in the old inner city, bearing the features of the traditional Chinese urban organisation. The new Beijing population, born outside Beijing consisted of employees in state-owned enterprises, institutions and governmental departments. They tend to settle in the suburbs where their working units provide them with new housing. The same happened with the offspring of the traditional Beijing people. However, some people, who worked in the new satellite towns for various reasons prefered to live in the inner city or in the inner suburbs adjacent to the old city, thus creating traffic to and from work.

China's Economic Reforms

China's reforms, initiated by Deng at the end of the 70s, were basically aimed at speeding up economic growth through the introduction of market mechanisms and the opening of the country to foreign investment. These reforms revealed the failure of the previous economic policies (based on planning and collectivised means of production) to achieve the same efficiency (Brus & Laski, 1989; Kesteloot, 1992).[13] These reforms can be divided into three basic groups: the rural, the urban and the Open Door Policy (see for detailed accounts among others Hui, 1992, Gordon, 1993, Chai & Leung, 1987). Rural reforms were launched in 1978 and sought to increase agricultural productivity by abolishing the People's Communes and replacing the command economy (the execution of the plan) by the production responsibility system. The latter allows the peasant to market their surplus production after having delivered a fixed quota to the State (for more details, see Saith, 1987). Meanwhile, it also revealed the problem of surplus labour in the countryside and triggered rural-urban migration. The main push and pull factors for this migration were the lack of land and poverty in the rural areas, on the one hand, and economic growth and wealth in the cities, on the other.

Urban reforms stand for larger autonomy of enterprises and more responsibility and power to their managers. Such reforms were experimentally tried in 1981 within selected cities such as Shashi in Hubei

---

[13] Basically, the external character of technological progress in the planned economy (in the sense that there is no stimulation mechanism like competition in a market situation) explains the failure of socialism in its ambition to surpass capitalism in economic growth. The Open Door policy was precisely devised to capture the technology from the capitalist world (Kesteloot 1992).

province, Changshu in Jiangsu province and generalised nation-wide in 1984 (Riefler, 1991). Housing reforms (see Zhong & Hays, 1996) and changes in land development and land use allocation that mirror a land market in a situation of state land ownership (see Gar-on Yeh & Wu, 1996; Keng, 1996) can be seen as the most recent elements of the urban reforms, aiming at modifying the built environment.

Finally, the 1979 Open Door Policy opened the country to (capitalist) foreign investments, initially in the Special Economic Zones, and gradually over the whole country (Reardon, 1996). The last two sets of reforms were vital to understanding the rapid economic growth in cities and towns which formed the essential elements in the attraction to cities of the rural-urban migration.

Socio-Spatial Dynamics in Post 1984 Beijing

The Changing Economic Structure of Beijing

Since 1978, in the wake of the rural reform, local governments has gained more power to increase their own revenues in addition to funds from the central government. Thus, the revenue of the Beijing Municipal Government relies on contributions from industrial and commercial activity within its territory (both the profits from local state owned enterprises and local taxes on other activities). Naturally, Beijing tries, like other cities, to develop its manufacturing, retail and wholesale industries (Cheng, 1990). These industrial branches attract further institutions and firms, producing a further demand for more labour and, therefore, migrants and create a need for further spatial expansion of the city. This process explains why Beijing applied pressure on the iron and steel industry, petrochemicals, electronics, car manufacture and big shopping centres after the reform rather than on the service sector, science and technology as well as cultural activities.

But since the late eighties, as a result of the Open Door Policy and foreign investments, Beijing appears to have potential to be an international city. Between 1979 and 1993, China obtained about 110 billion US dollars direct from foreign investments. This amount is almost one third of the total fixed asset investment of state-owned enterprises in China in the same period. In Beijing, these investments became important from 1989 on. In 1997, the total value of investment agreements amounted to 21 billion US dollars. The actually used new investments in 1998 amounted to more than 2 billion US dollars or nearly 5% of the total investments in China. The

294 Studies in Segregation and Desegregation

contracted amounts reached nearly 8% of the country's total. Nearly 30% is invested in industrial activities and 45% in real estate.

Not only these investments themselves, but also the efforts of the city to enhance its attractiveness to investors explain the transformation from its traditional political, culture and manufacturing functional structure towards a more service and high-tech oriented economic structure. The local planning commission has developed a socio-economic strategic plan in which services and high-tech industries are seen as the most important sectors of structural adjustment of the municipal economy. According to this plan, the service sector would generate more than 50% of GDP in 2000 (Li, 1993). A new technological park was also opened in *Zhongguancun*, in the north-western part of the city in the later 1980s (Wang & Wang, 1998). Today, *Zhongguancun* Science Park includes the original park in *Haidian* and the *Changping* Scientific and Technological Park in the north-west outer suburbs, *Fengtai* Scientific and Technological Park Zone in the former south-west industrial cluster, the *Yizhuang* Zone near the Beijing-Tianjin highway and Electronics City in *Jiuxianqiao* along the airport highway. It has become the nation's largest hi-tech industrial base and a major asset for Beijing's economic development (Figure 12.2).

Industrialisation reached its ceiling in 1978, when 71% of the GDP was produced by industry. Nowadays, the city's tertiary sector is the dominant part of urban economy (54%) and for the year 2010, it should reach 63% of the GDP. Finance, culture and education, research, health services and administration have experienced rapid growth in the last decade. The construction industry displays a comparable upsurge in terms of employment. It reveals the importance of urban restructuring activities that followed the reforms and foreign investments (Figure 12.1).[14]

The Floating Population

The agricultural responsibility system greatly improved agricultural labour productivity and, thus, made a large number of peasants redundant. It has been estimated that there were some 200 millions surplus labourers in 1996, and the number may have reached 300 million in 2000. Some of this labour force reserve has been absorbed in the countryside by township and village enterprises, but most of the 'surplus' peasants are candidates for

---

[14] However, these figures do not include the floating population, since they concern only the official Beijing resident population. Employment in the construction industry, commerce and restaurants is thus strongly underestimated (see Table 11.2).

migration to the cities to find some kind of job. This rural-urban migration was also fostered through the erosion of the territorial control system of the population. As part of the reforms, and as a necessary consequence of the introduction of market mechanisms, these control systems were gradually relaxed.

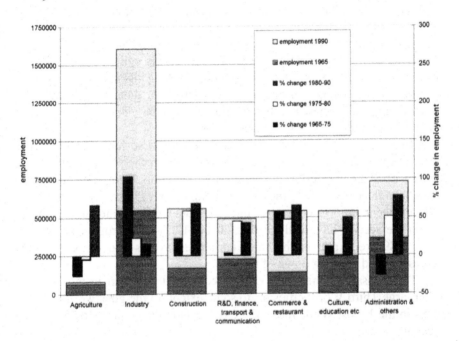

Figure 12.1 The changing economic structure of Beijing 1965-1990

This opened possibilities for rural workers to live both on a temporary and permanent basis in the city since this relaxation was matched by increasing market opportunities for generating income, obtaining food without a ration card and finding a place to live. Thus, some of the rural surplus population, estimated at more than 100 million people (Li Meng Bai, 1991; Chan, 1991), could migrate to the urban areas, forming what is called a floating population (*liudong renkou*).[15] They came to satisfy the

---

[15] Since they are not registered in the city in which they stay but in the countryside from where they come, they were classified as people found in the city for occasional reasons (like students, visitors, tourists or hospitalised persons from outside the city), and were aptly called floating population. However, many of the rural migrants permanently settle in the cities since they have no future elsewhere. This makes the

296 *Studies in Segregation and Desegregation*

increasing labour demand in construction, factories and various urban services, generated both by the urban reforms and the open door policy (Chan, 1994; Gaubatz, 1995; Gong, 1995). Although the household registration system has not yet been abolished, many farmers have broken through these restrictions, entered the cities and stayed there for a long time with temporary residence permits. The opening of the grain market in 1982 helped them to circumvent the grain rationing that had until then restricted grain distribution to the registered urban population. The re-establishment of private ownership of housing (though the land is still state or collective owned), the modification of some urban public housing and the consequent emergence of housing markets made it possible for them to rent and even purchase housing, whereas urban dwellings are otherwise only provided by the production units to their registered workers.

Rural-urban inequalities decreased in the first half of the 1980s because of positive effects of the rural reforms. In the second half of that decade, after the urban reforms were set in operation, inequalities increased again (Singh, 1993). Thus, the expected explosion of rural-urban migration did not occur immediately after the implementation of the rural reforms, but in the second half of the 1980s (Table 12.1). The drop in the figures after 1989 are explained by the Tian'anmen events and the consequent repression and slowing down of reforms.

This peasant in-migration can be compared to urban in-migration in other large Third World cities or, to some extent, to the guestworkers in the West in the 1960s. While most of the peasants in the countryside have been free of poverty and have been able to afford decent food, clothing and shelter since the 1980s as a result of successful rural economic reforms, some of the peasants who migrated to the cities face poverty. Some of them work as normal contract workers in rapidly-growing manufacturing industries, but most are casual labourers in the formal or even the informal sector. Some official Chinese channels label these rural migrants 'blindfold migrants' since they leave their situation on the countryside for an uncertain future in the city. Indeed, the massive growth of this floating population in the large cities like Beijing has resulted in growing unemployment and the spread of unstable, temporary and insecure jobs. Since the *peasant migrants* have no permanent residence permit, they have

---

term 'floating population' rather ironic, in the same sense as the term migrants is used in many West European countries to design the settled population of foreign workers, including even their descendants born in these countries.

Table 12.1 Floating population in Beijing, 1952-1994

Year	Floating Population	% of total Population
1949①	61,000	2.9
1958①	270,000	4.1
1982①	NA	1.98
1984①	200,000	2.26
1985①	312,000	3.26
1986①	600,000	6.18
1987①	800,000	8.10
1988①	900,000	8.99
1989②	1,310,000	11.9
1990②	602,131	6.02
1991②	1,200,000	10.9
1994③	3,295,000	29.9

Sources: ① Capital Planning committee, 1992. Effects of floating population in Beijing's socio-economic development. In China Urban Science Society (ed.), Study on Floating Population in Metropolitan Areas. China Society Press.
② Beijing Statistics Year-book (1989,1990,1991).
③ The census of floating population of Beijing local government, 1994.

no right to public housing, even if they work on a permanent base for official production units. This temporary status also entails the absence of access to free health and education. This exclusion from a set of public and collective consumption items generates a new urban poverty phenomenon in Beijing, which is more visible now that high-income professional and managerial jobs have appeared in joint venture companies and some new enterprises have generated conspicuous consumption.

In 1994, the Beijing Municipal Government decided to organise a survey of the floating population in the city, in order to collect the necessary information for setting up policies controlling the effects of immigration in its territory (Rocca 1995).[16] According to this survey, Beijing's floating population included 3.295 million people. The migrants from rural origin totalled 2.877 million, representing 76% of the total. The average age of the floating population was 27.7 years (28.5 for males; 26.4 for females), which is 6.6 years younger than the average permanent Beijing inhabitant. The overwhelming majority was of working age (87.9% of the floating population belongs to the 15-65 age category versus 65-70%

---

[16] Nearly all non registered inhabitants of Beijing were surveyed. The floating population, including also foreigners and temporary residents in the city, had to fill in a survey form, either at their place of residence where they are under control of the neighbourhood committee officers or in railway stations and the airport.

298 *Studies in Segregation and Desegregation*

of the Beijing population). Only 3.1% of the migrants had college education while those with middle and primary schooling accounted for 79.7%, and illiterate or almost illiterate migrants were about 5.5%. The educational level of the female migrants was lower than that of the males. Thus the proportion of over-primary schooling in the floating population was about 61% for the male, but only 31% for the female. With such education levels, these migrants were bound to work in low skilled jobs in the cities.

Although all these data concern the total floating population, i.e. including temporary visitors and foreigners,[17] the male predominance in the floating population (63.4%) reflects the demand for heavy, dirty and tiring jobs, especially in construction and heavy industry. The females are mainly engaged in the service sector and tend to stay for a shorter time (60% are aged between 15 and 29 years). Among the peasant migrants, 63% of the women were married and had an average of 1.3 children (reflecting the less stringent family planning policy and the traditional mentality of the countryside). But only a few migrant families live together. In about 10% of the cases, women live in the city with their children but without their husbands. Usually children are supported by grandparents in the area of origin and couples are separated in order to maximise their job opportunities.

The survey discloses the reasons for the presence of the floating population in Beijing. For those engaged in economic activities this refers to their occupation (Table 12.2). Nearly 20% of the floating population has a reason for staying in Beijing that is not related to employment (to which some of the 'other reasons' have to be added). For the others, mainly peasant migrants, the construction industry and work in small business are the main sources of employment.

A more detailed analysis of the economic position of the peasant migrants in the city yields a fourfold job typology.

(1) low income but formal jobs in production with high labour intensity. In most cases, migrants replace native Beijing workers in low-paid jobs under poor working conditions in manufacturing, such as spinning, casting and assembling. They work in heavily polluting chemical plants or in the construction industry. The same happens in some low-

---

[17] These figures also show that Beijing's future population growth will possibly be dominated by the floating population in the next decades. Indeed, the natural growth of urban permanent population stagnated at 0.6% in 1980s and declined to 0.3-0.5% in the 1990s.

skilled tertiary activities both in public and private business that permanent urban inhabitants do not like to take up, such as salesman, cashier, waitress, domestic worker, cleaner, or even typist.[18]

Table 12.2 Reasons for presence of floating population in Beijing (1994)

Reason/occupation	%
Academic or training activities	4.0
Business trip or stay for administrative reasons	12.5
Stay in hospital or sanatorium	1.7
Tourism	2.3
Work in agriculture	0.9
Work in factory	5.0
Work in construction industry	21.4
Work in restaurant or repairing service	5.9
Work in other small commerce or business	23.1
Family servant	1.9
Other	21.3
Total	100.0

Source: The census of floating population of Beijing Local Government, 1994.

(2) contractual but temporary jobs. These migrants are still engaged in manual labour in small private firms, mainly in the low-skilled services but also with private households. Typical temporary jobs are delivery, street cleaning, moving, housing maintenance and repair activities but also housekeeping and nursing.

(3) migrant entrepreneurship related jobs. Recently, some successful migrants have succeeded in setting up small firms, restaurants and factories themselves. However, the traditional family structure of the migrants does not yet provide sufficient conditions to allow for entrepreneurial success. The garment industry of Zhejiang migrants in Beijing is a good example. Although the clothing and fashion industry became the main occupation of

---

[18] An estimated half million native Beijing workers are laid off and paid unemployment benefits by their production units (amounting to 70% of their former salary) and keep their social insurance and housing benefits. This relatively comfortable situation of the unemployed helps to explain their replacement by migrants in unpleasant jobs.

300 *Studies in Segregation and Desegregation*

new migrants in *Zhejiang* village,[19] only a few of them are successful entrepreneurs. Most of them lack management experience for maintaining a family workshop. The same applies to restaurants, serving a regional cuisine. The *New Ajing* restaurant[20] is one of the few successful migrant-owned-enterprises, which has opened four other branch restaurants in Beijing.

(4) temporary and insecure jobs. These jobs are usually undertaken on a self-employed base, but they largely depend on access to means of production and/or production sites, which are regulated by others. Thus, in the Beijing streets, one can find peddlers, rickshaw boys, shoes menders, bicycle repairers, key adjusters, watch repairers, seal engravers, knife sharpeners and waste collectors.

In general, except perhaps for the few successful entrepreneurs of the third category, the floating population is paid less than Beijing permanent residents for similar jobs. This is easiest to compare for the two first categories. Our own fieldwork revealed that on average migrants earn half of the labour income of Beijing people (considering only wages and supplements, not housing, health insurance and other advantages). But at the same time, they have to pay more for similar services. They do not have rights to cheap dwellings allocated by the production units and, thus, pay more for housing (up to 5 times what is paid in public housing). Similarly, they do not have rights to health insurance and thus pay for health services, while these are free for permanent residents. Finally, if they have children, they pay for education, while, again, it is free for the Beijing inhabitants. These demands on their income are reinforced by their wish to save as much money as possible. Most of them see urban immigration as a way to get rich and successfully return to their place of origin or as a means to support their family remaining in their village. Single migrants try to save money for their wedding, for founding a family or for building a house. In general, they send almost one fourth of their income to their family in the rural areas.

Generally speaking, the distribution of the migrants according to their place of origin is influenced by the distance involved in the migration. On the whole, migration declines rapidly as the distance increases, but cultural

---

[19] A former rural village on the urban fringe where the farmers let their former housing to migrants from Zhejiang province (Piante & Zhu 1993) - see further Figure 11.2 and text.

[20] This is a Cantonese restaurant created by a female immigrant from *Guangdong* province.

tradition and regional variation also affect the flow of migrants to Beijing. Whereas over 21% of peasant migrants come from neighbouring *Hebei* province, 20.8% of them come from *Zhejiang* province (south of Shanghai), 12.8% of them from *Henan* province (south of the Yellow River in the Chinese plain) and 11.2% from *Anhui* province (west of Shanghai). Even large cities like Shanghai, Wuhan or Chengdu are skipped in the migration process to Beijing. Such a phenomenon points to the fierce competition for urban employment among massive numbers of jobless peasants from everywhere in China.

The Rise of Spatial Segregation in Beijing

While urban social segregation was almost eliminated under the influence of socialist transformations, the reforms have triggered strong differentiation processes in the city. The introduction of market mechanisms in China and the concomitant peasant immigration into the urban areas in the recent two decades have created strong contrasts in the Chinese urban landscape. Such a result is brought about by socio-spatial segregation processes. At the upper end of the social ladder, urban renewal and the effects of foreign direct investment, both in industrial and real estate activities, reshape the city. At the lower end of the social ladder segregation generates what can be called 'migrant villages'. The processes involved are a combination of their gravitating to areas where rental housing is available to them and of concentration tendencies among migrants from the same origin, in order to maintain and strengthen local social networks.

The housing situation of the floating population can be evaluated by the type of residence. When the migrants provide their own shelter or when their presence is not related to employment (training, travelling or health care) the type of residence is known. In other cases, one has an idea of this when their dwelling depends on the production unit that employs the floating population. Thus, the type of residence was known for about 60% of the floating population in 1994. Most of the migrants lived with their employers or in housing provided by their employers (Table 12.3). The employees of foreign institutions set up in Beijing generally lived in hotels, in training centres or housing of joint ventures with foreign companies. Academics and researchers live in academic and training centres and the personnel of Chinese institutions from other provinces live in housing

302 *Studies in Segregation and Desegregation*

Table 12.3 Housing situation of the floating population in Beijing (1994)

Type	Migrants	%
Housing provided by production unit	429.000	23.9
Hotel	208.000	11.6
Academic or training centres	93.000	5.2
Housing provided by other provinces or foreign institutions	98.000	5.4
Hospital and sanatorium	25.000	1.4
Suburban agricultural units	72.000	4.0
Construction sites	469.000	26.1
Rural families	256.000	14.2
Small commerce and restaurant service	148.000	8.2
Total	1.798.000	100.0

Source: The census of floating population of Beijing local government.

provided by their unit. Peasant migrants are sometimes housed by the production unit employing them (e.g. hotel personnel). Construction workers mainly live in temporary barracks on the construction sites (these barracks are sometimes still in use long after the completion of the works).[21] The others depend on dwelling opportunities created outside the formal economic sphere, such as living with rural families, in small business premises or even on the streets. This housing situation, sometimes in conjunction with the migration process, explains the growing segregation tendencies in Beijing.

The Spatial Concentration of the Peasant Migrants

While the overwhelming part of available housing in Beijing is allocated by the production units to their workers at a very low price (in practice even insufficient for maintenance and repair costs of dwellings built during the Mao era), the peasants who are not housed with their employers or on construction sites have to resort to the more expensive private housing market, which leaves them with two geneeral residential options (Gu, 1995b).

In the old city neighbourhoods (*hutong*), the Beijing inhabitants have ownership rights on their family dwellings, but these usually lack basic

---

[21] The 1994 survey showed that 84% of the construction workers settle on construction sites.

amenities and their quality is poor. This situation is not only explained by the age of these dwellings and the construction of additional housing in their courtyards during the Cultural Revolution but also by the severe housing shortage immediately after the Cultural revolution as a result of the return migration from youth sent to the countryside. Some of these inhabitants will let part of their dwellings to peasants in need of a location close to their workplace; others will accept better housing from their *danwei*, which in return commands the use of the old dwelling (Hou, 1986). Again, given the quality of these old dwellings, only the floating population in need of a central location is willing to live in these areas (an estimated 20% of the peasant floating population lives in such housing).

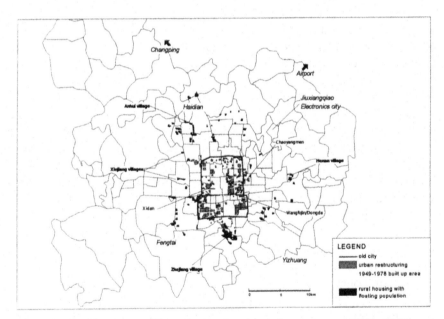

Figure 12.2 Beijing's changing socio-spatial structure 1978-1997

The other option open to migrants in the private realm is rural housing in villages close to the urban fringe (Gu, 1995a). With the expansion of the city, farmers lost their land and found new jobs and new housing, usually in the *danwei* that developed their land. However, due to the general housing shortage, their dwellings were maintained and the farmers could let them to the migrants. These villages tend to attract migrants from the same origin, actually corresponding to the former concentrated village settlement, on the

304 *Studies in Segregation and Desegregation*

one hand, and the territorial based relations between the migrants (*diyuan*), especially social networks between fellow-villagers (*laoxiang guanxi*), on the other hand. Urban observers still call these areas 'villages' in association with the province of origin of the migrants, such as *Zhejiang* village, *Henan* village, and *Anhui* village (Figure 12.2).

An estimated 60% of the peasant floating population lives in such suburban locations (Figure 12.2).[22] Within these villages, farmers or successful migrant entrepreneurs will erect some new housing, usually of a slightly better quality than the traditional farm housing and let them to the migrants who can afford it (estimated at 5% of the migrant households).

Finally, others are the victims of the general lack of housing and have to live in slums. In particular, some *Henan* migrants, specialists in garbage recycling, live near the garbage heaps.

Social networking, strengthened by chain migration and the difficulties of coping with an inhospitable environment, is also reflected in the close relation between the sources of migration and the occupations of the migrants in Beijing. According to the survey, most male migrants from *Jiangsu*, *Shandong* and *Hebei* provinces work in the construction industry as carpenters, brick-layers and plumbers. Most of the *Shandong* migrants specialise in selling vegetables from *Shangdong* in Beijing. Waste collectors, brick casters and street cleaners come from *Henan*. Most females from *Jiangsu* are spinners and assemblers or enter into small businesses, while most from *Anhui* work in families as servants, baby-sitters and housekeepers. Migrants from *Sichuan* and north-eastern China are concentrated in the catering industry. Migrants from the richer provinces are more likely to establish their own firms, which are oriented to the whole urban market. For example, *Zhejiang* migrants engage in shoemaking, locksmithing, seal engraving, and a series of repair services. Their main concentration zone, the *Zhejiang village*, south of the old city, has developed into a huge textile production and wholesale area. Some migrants from *Fujian* and *Guangdong* set up small specialised trade firms in construction materials such as wood or cement (*Fujian* people) and aluminium alloy materials (*Guangdong* people). But migrants from the poorer western provinces remain confined to local, sometimes ethnic-oriented activities like small-scale restaurants or street stalls. Thus one finds Muslim restaurants established by some migrants from *Xinjiang*

---

[22] The mapping of these areas is based on a careful analysis of a remote sensing picture of Beijing (1994). Both knowledge of the local situation and typical features of the built environment on the picture helped to delimit these areas.

(belonging to the Turkish minority of the *Uighur* - see Gu & Kesteloot, 1997) and from *Ningxia* (an autonomous region of the *Hui*, i.e. Muslims of Chinese origin). Some migrants from *Tibet* and *Qinghai* peddle local medicines and herbs. Migrant entrepreneurship particularly strengthens the concentration in the migrant villages.

Thus the housing system and the growth of an informal housing market explain the concentration of peasant migrants in the inner city and the urban fringe. Since prices are much higher for inner city private housing than for rural (ex-farmers) housing, the migrants tend to take this second opportunity if their employment does not necessitate a more central residential location (Gu, 1995b).

The Spatial Concentration of the New Elite

The better off among the floating population face the same problems of finding a residence in the city outside the *danwei* system. Most of the foreign employees live in four or five star hotels, while others settle down in good quality apartments that belong to joint venture corporations or in foreign expert housing of academic and training centres. A small part of the *danwei* housing is rented on the black market, both by individual tenants who obtain another dwelling and are able to retain their right to the former *danwei* house (usually when husband and wife work in different *danwei*) and by developers who usually rent a whole housing block to sublet it temporarily to the floating population. However, the prices are high and the tenants belong necessarily to the rich, educated floating population. In the outer suburbs, developers erect villas and better housing, in 'gated community' estates. They are the most expensive on the market and therefore only attract the same rich migrants and local successful managers. These estates tend to be concentrated in a north-eastern sector originating at the Asian Game village. Thus the survey reveals that approximately 20% of this emerging wealthy group lives in the north-eastern urban district and nearly all the others live in both the northern and eastern suburban districts of *Haidian* and *Chaoyang*.

Complete and detailed data on the spatial distribution of the floating population from the 1994 survey are not available. But a 1995 sample survey gives a broad idea of their distribution among the four urban districts and the inner suburbs. Taking the floating population on construction sites into account, which is present both in the inner city for urban restructuring and in the suburbs for urban expansion, these data broadly confirm the estimated proportion of the floating population in the

306 *Studies in Segregation and Desegregation*

inner city and in the suburbs on the basis of housing opportunities (Table 12.4). Since the wealthy floating population is nearly completely concentrated in the north and eastern districts, the peasant floating population dominates in the south.[23]

Table 12.4 Housing situation of the floating population in Beijing (1995)

	Registered population	Floating population	Share of floating population (%)	Distribution of floating population (%)
West city	783000	68000	8,7	10
East city	643000	65000	10,1	9
Shuanwu	573000	43000	7,5	6
Congwen	434000	32000	7,4	5
Inner city	2433000	208000	8,5	30
Haidian	1368000	135000	9,9	19
Chaoyang	1331000	183000	13,7	26
Fengtai	727000	131000	18,0	19
Shijinshan	302000	40000	13,2	6
Inner suburbs	3728000	489000	13,1	70
Total	6161000	697000	11,3	100

Source: Beijing Statistics Yearbook 1995.

The Effects of Market Forces in the Functional Restructuring of the City

The massive urban renewal and reconstruction in the old inner city since 1978 has two main causes. Historically, Beijing lacked a Central Business District (CBD) so that most of the administrative, financial and business buildings were dispersed in areas outside the second ring road, which delimits the old city. Pressure for having a more central and concentrated commercial and service zone has grown with the aim to develop the city as an international metropolis with an advanced service sector. The other reason also pertains to history: the dwellings in the old inner city are

---

[23] However, the sample reveals a strong underestimation of the migrants when compared to the 30% share of the floating population in Beijing's population in 1994. As a consequence these figures can only be taken as broad indicators.

generally one-storey courtyard houses of the *Ming* and *Qing* Dynasties in wood and brick, in which water tap, toilet, kitchen and heating are usually shared with several families or simply not provided. Improving the residential quality of these areas is only possible with fundamental restructuring. The implementation of the urban land-use compensation policy and the concomitant development of real estate activities speeded up the process of the urban restructuring.[24] Thus many *hutong* have been demolished and transformed into commercial and business areas (Figure 12.2).

In the inner suburbs, the most important effects of the land and housing reforms are related to the modification of public housing and the home-ownership programme. In order to obtain financial means for urban restructuring and the improvement of housing, the Chinese government encourages the selling of public housing at prices dependant on the type and quality of the dwellings. With regard to the sale of older public houses to individuals, transactions are not done through the market. In most cases, households buy the dwelling in which they are living at preferential prices. The government and the *danwei* subsidise about two-thirds of the market price. This policy is consolidating the presence of the 'new Beijing population', related to the socialist development of the city in the inner suburbs.

Foreign direct investments in new service and high-tech industries, also tend to concentrate in some inner suburban districts,[25] especially *Chaoyang* in the east and *Haidian* in the north-west (Figure 12.2). Since these investments have brought a simultaneous growth of high-skilled and well-paid jobs at the management level, they sustain the development of a new rich area in these locations.

The New Socio-Spatial Structure of Beijing

A new arrangement of social groups and activities in Beijing is rapidly emerging from these processes (Figure 12.2). An international central business district will be one of the brand new elements, with a political and cultural centre around *Tian'anmen* Square, a commercial centre in the *Wangfujin-Dongdan* and *Xidan* areas and a business and financial

---

[24] This policy introduced a quasi real estate market, where the state leases land use rights at market conditions for 40 to 70 years depending on the land use.

[25] The main sectors are assembly industries producing colour TV sets, refrigerators, washing machines, air conditioning, computers, cars and micro-electronic products.

308 *Studies in Segregation and Desegregation*

management centre situated just outside the first ring road at *Chaoyangmen* and *Jianguomen*. The growing international community and international commerce tend to develop in the area along the airport highway in the cluster of *Jiuxianqiao* (now Beijing Electronics City) and near the airport with the new Beijing Airport Industry Zone. Research and development activities and high-tech industries concentrate together with high quality residential areas in the northern outer suburbs. The new manufacturing activities are located mainly along the Beijing-Tianjin highway in the south-east (*Yizhuang* Zone or the Beijing Economic-Technological Development Area), where there is much available land and convenient transportation. Some enterprises have moved from the old city into this area. Thus two urban corridors, along the airport highway and the Beijing - Tianjin highway, will transform the classic concentric structure of the city inherited from the socialist era.

Nevertheless, this structure persists with the 'poor old Beijing people' and some new migrants concentrated in a few preserved old residential areas (*hutong*) of the inner city and the 'new Beijing people' in the inner suburbs. However, the latter concentric zone exhibits a internal sectoral pattern related to the distribution of economic activities during the socialist era. Most middle-income intellectual workers are concentrated in the north-west, associated with the cluster of cultural and educational institutions in this sector. Skilled and middle-income workers are distributed in the south-west, and the western part of the suburbs, where army, administration and the largest industrial/residential clusters were created. The remaining sectors formed the (relative) lower class area of the city.

This suburban ring is now interrupted by the concentration of highly skilled and well-paid employees and businessmen and entrepreneurs in the north-east, from where they spread into the outer suburbs along the new urban corridor. At the same time, the old spatial division between north and south is reactivated and more particularly amplified by the joint effects of the main commercial centre of *Wangfujin*, the airport, the *Zhongguancun* technology park and the upper class estates in the northern half and the predominance of the peasant migrants, concentrated in the 'migrant villages' mainly in the southern half of the urban area. Within this structure, Beijing's urban fringe is experiencing the fastest changes in the socio-spatial structure, the most urban problems and the largest disparity between the rich and the poor (Gu, 1989, 1993, 1995; Cui, 1990).

Conclusion

The main dynamics of Beijing's urban socio-spatial structure are related to the transformation of China's socio-economic system and, as a consequence, the internationalisation of Beijing's urban function and development of service and high-tech industries. These rapid transformations have led to an uncoordinated development of the urban population in which the floating population adds new social groups at both ends of a widening social spectrum. They also translate into an unbalanced spatial growth of the city. On the one hand, the core of the city is functionally reorganised through major urban renewal activities. On the other hand, the urban sprawl has become the main spatial growth pattern and the urban fringes have turned into the most problematic areas.

The arrival of migrants has changed the urban landscape, which used to be characterised by standardised housing, a relatively even social structure and social stability in the pre-reform period. The most visible result of this immigration wave is the emergence of migrant villages in former rural settlements at the fringe of Beijing's agglomeration. The living conditions in these migrant concentration areas are poor, reflecting the way the city is making a profit out of them, and sometimes leads to criminal activities. But the urban mosaic in Beijing is now much more dynamic and colourful than in the pre-reform era.

Nevertheless, the asset of urban diversification and dynamism can only be secured if the shortcomings in the state-regulated redistribution of the means of subsistance are corrected. On the one hand, individual or household rights to housing, education, health services and unemployment, pensions and illness benefits should be extended to the rural migrants. On the other hand, the central and local governments should define a policy of sustainable urban growth, which implies the easing of collective problems in these concentration areas such as water supply, sanitation, and urban transport. If one adds to this list the fact that the peasant migrants are systematically discriminated against both by private economic actors and by the state inregard to wages, housing prices, taxes and permits, three broad financial channels appear to determine poverty: wages, prices and public services. They are also the three channels through which the state can act to transform poverty into diversity and segregation into a rich variety of attractive residential environments.

310 *Studies in Segregation and Desegregation*

References

Brus W. & Laski K. (1989), *From Marx to the Market: Socialism in Search of an Economic System*, Clarendon, Oxford.

Cannon T. (2000), 'Introduction', in T. Cannon (ed), *China's Economic Growth: The Impact on Regions, Migration and the Environment*, Macmillan, Basingstoke.

Cannon T. & Jenkins A., eds. (1990), *The Geography of Contemporary China, the Impact of Deng Xiaoping's decade*, Routledge, London.

Chan, Kam Wing (1994), *Cities with Invisible Walls: Reinterpreting Urbanisation in Post-1949 China*, Oxford University Press, Hong Kong.

Chang, Sen-dou (1977), 'The Morphology of Walled Capitals', in G.W. Skinner (ed), *The City in Late Imperial China*, Stanford University Press, California.

Cheng Xuan (1990), 'Problems of Urbanisation under China's Traditional Economic System', in R. Yin-Wang Kwok, W.L. Parish, A. Gar-On-Yeh, & Xu Xueqiang (eds), *Chinese Urban Reform, What Model Now?*, M.E. Sharpe, Armonk.

Chinese Census Press (1990), *Forty Years of Beijing* (in Chinese).

Cui Gonghao et al. (1990), 'Spatial Structure and Evolution of Chinese Urban Fringe, Beijing', *Acta Geographica Sinica*, vol. 45, No. 4, pp. 399-410 (in Chinese).

French, R.A. and Hamilton, F.E.I. (1979), Is there a Socialist city, in French, R.A. and Hamilton, F.E.I. (eds.), *The Socialist City*, Wiley, Chichester, pp.1-22.

Gar-on Yeh A. & Wu F. (1996), The new land development process and urban development in Chinese cities, *International Journal of Urban and Regional Research*, vol 20, No. 2, pp.330-353.

Gaubatz, Piper (1995), Changing Beijing. *Geographical Review*, Vol. 85, No. 1, pp. 79-96.

Gong, Hongmian (1995), Spatial Patterns of Foreign Investment in China's Cities: 1980-1989. *Urban Geography*, vol. 16, No. 3, pp. 198-209.

Gu Chaolin et al. (1989), Study on Urban Fringe, Beijing: *Geographical Research*, vol. 8, No. 3, pp. 95-101 (In Chinese).

Gu Chaolin (1991), *China's Urban System*, Beijing: Commercial Press (In Chinese).

Gu Chaolin et al. (1993), The Study of the Metropolitan Fringes in China, Beijing: *Acta Geographical Sinica*, vol.45, No.4, pp. 317-28 (In Chinese).

Gu Chaolin et al. (1995a), *Study on China's Urban Fringes*, Sciences Press, Beijing (In Chinese).

Gu Chaolin (1995b), China's Urban Housing System in Transition, *Journal of Chinese Geography*, vol. 6, No. 2, pp.16-38.

Gu Chaolin & Kesteloot C. (1997), Peasant migrants and their concentration areas in Beijing, *Tijdschrift van de Belgische Vereniging voor Aardrijkskundige Studies*, vol 1, pp.107-119.

Hou Renzhi (1986), Evolution of the City Plan of Beijing, *Third World Planning Review*, vol. 8, pp.5-17.

Hou Renzhi (1986), The Transformation of the old city of Beijing, Harris, C. D. (ed.) *World Patterns of Modern Urban Change*, The University of Chicago, Chicago, pp.217-239.

Keng C.W.K. (1996), China's land disposition system, *Journal of Contemporary China*, vol. 5, No. 13, pp.325-345.

Kesteloot, C. (1992), Some spatial implications of socialist planned economies, *Acta Geographica Lovaniensia*, vol. 33, pp.277-281.

Li Rugan (1993), New period for the development of Capital Beijing, *China National Conditions Report*, No.1.

Piante C. & Zhu H. (1993), Le village de ZJ, treizième arrondissement de Pékin, *Perspective Chinoises,* No. 20, pp. 34-36.

Reardon L.C. (1996), The rise and decline of China's export processing zones, *Journal of Contemporary China,* vol. 13, pp. 281-303.

Riefler R.E. Urban industrial reform in China: problems and prospects, *International Regional Science Review,* vol. 14, No. 1, pp. 95-107.

Rocca J.L. (1995), Un mal nécessaire. Le contrôle des 'nouvelles populations' dans la municipalité de Pékin, in Henriot C. (ed.) *Les métropoles chinoises au Xxe siècle,* Editions Arguments, Paris, pp.158-169.

Saith, A. ed. (1987), *The re-emergence of the Chinese peasantry,* Croom Helm, London.

Singh A. (1993), The plan, the market and evolutionary economic reform in China, *Unctad Discussion Papers,* vol. 76, UNCTAD, Geneva.

Sit, V.F.S. (1995), *Beijing: the Nature and Planning of a Chinese Capital City,* John Wiley & Sons, Chichester.

Skinner (1977), *The city in late imperial China,* Stanford University Press, Stanford.

Solinger D.J. (1995), The floating population in the cities: chances for assimilation?, in Davis D.S, Kraus R., Naughton B. & Perry E.J. (eds.) *Urban spaces in contemporary China, the potential for autonomy and community in post-Mao China,* Cambridge University Press, Cambridge.

Soothill, W.E. (1951), *The Hall of Light: A Study of Early Chinese Kingship,* Lutterworth, London.

Wang Jici & Wang Jixian (1998), An analysis of new-tech agglomeration in Beijing: a new industrial district in the making?, *Environment and Planning A,* vol. 30, pp. 681-701.

Xie Jinyu and Yu Jing, (1992), Comparative studies on the planned rural-urban migrants and spontaneous rural-urban migrants in China, *China City Planning Review,* vol. 8, No. 6, pp.25-40.